I0014068

<u>Disclaimer</u>

Book Title: Computer Security: Bibliography Of Selected Computer Security Publications January 1980-October 1989

Book Author: Rein Turn; Lawrence E. Bassham;

Book Abstract: This bibliography cites selected books and articles on computer security published from January 1980 through October 1989. To have been selected, an article had to be substantial in content and have been published in professional or technical journals, magazines, or conference proceedings. Only very substantial articles from the popular or trade press were included. English language articles from foreign journals were included as available. The citations are listed under nine categories. A tenth category of pre- 1980 publications is also provided, as well as an appendix containing addresses of all journals and magazines referenced in the bibliography.

Citation: NIST SP - 800-1

Keyword: access controls; auditing; communications security; computer crime; computer security; confidentiality; cryptography; disaster recovery; integrity; privacy; risk management; trusted computing base.

NIST Special Publication 800-1

U.S. DEPARTMENT OF
COMMERCE
National Institute of Standards
and Technology

Bibliography of Selected Computer Security Publications January 1980– October 1989

Rein Turn

Lawrence E. Bassham III

COMPUTER SECURITY

NIST Special Publication 800-1

Bibliography of Selected Computer Security Publications January 1980– October 1989

Rein Turn, Compiler
Rein Turn Associates
Pacific Palisades, CA 90727

Lawrence E. Bassham III, Editor

COMPUTER SECURITY

National Computer Systems Laboratory

National Institute of Standards and Technology
Gaithersburg, MD 20899

December 1990

U.S. DEPARTMENT OF COMMERCE
Robert A. Mosbacher, Secretary

NATIONAL INSTITUTE OF STANDARDS
AND TECHNOLOGY
John W. Lyons, Director

Reports on Computer Systems Technology

The National Institute of Standards and Technology (NIST) has a unique responsibility for computer systems technology within the Federal Government. NIST's National Computer Systems Laboratory (NCSL) develops standards and guidelines, provides technical assistance, and conducts research for computers and related telecommunications systems to achieve more effective utilization of Federal information technology resources. NCSL's responsibilities include development of technical, management, physical, and administrative standards and guidelines for the cost-effective security and privacy of sensitive unclassified information processed in Federal computers. NCSL assists agencies in developing security plans and in improving computer security awareness training. This Special Publication 800 series reports NCSL research and guidelines to Federal agencies as well as to organizations in industry, government, and academia.

National Institute of Standards and Technology Special Publication 800-1
Natl. Inst. Stand. Technol. Spec. Publ. 800-1, 200 pages (Dec. 1990)
CODEN: NSPUE2

U.S. GOVERNMENT PRINTING OFFICE
WASHINGTON: 1990

For sale by the Superintendent of Documents, U.S. Government Printing Office, Washington, DC 20402

ABSTRACT

This bibliography cites selected books and articles on computer security published from January 1980 through October 1989. To have been selected, an article had to be substantial in content and have been published in professional or technical journals, magazines, or conference proceedings. Only very substantial articles from the popular or trade press were included. English language articles from foreign journals were included as available. The citations are listed under nine categories. A tenth category of pre-1980 publications is also provided, as well as an appendix containing addresses of all journals and magazines referenced in the bibliography.

Key Words: access controls; auditing; communications security; computer crime; computer security; confidentiality; cryptography; disaster recovery; integrity; privacy; risk management; trusted computing base.

Contents

INTRODUCTION

In recognition of the critical need for better dissemination of computer security information throughout government and industry, the National Institute of Standards and Technology (NIST) has produced this selected bibliography of key computer security literature published from January 1980 through October 1989. This bibliography was compiled by Rein Turn of Rein Turn Associates under contract to NIST.

The bibliography is organized into the following 10 sections and 2 appendices:

1. General
2. Management
3. Foundations
4. Access Control
5. Trusted Systems
6. Database Security
7. Communication and Network Security
8. Cryptography
9. Privacy
10. Pre-1980 Publications
Appendix A: Periodicals
Appendix B: List of Key Words

Citations in sections 1 through 9 are organized by subject matter; section 10 is a listing of pre-1980 publications. To have been selected, an article had to be substantial in content and have been published in professional or technical journals, magazines, or conference proceedings. Only very substantial articles from the popular or trade press were included. English language articles from foreign journals were included as available.

The individual citations have the following structure (an example is shown at the right):

Identifier	AAL-83
Author	Aalders, J.C.H.
Title	"Towards Standards in Computer Security," Proc.
Journal title (or publishing house)	IFIP/Sec. '83, Stockholm, 1983, (2: FAK-83),
Date and page (or location and year)	pp. 5-13.
Key words (two or three)	
	Key Words: guidelines, policy.

Each citation is uniquely identified by the first letters of the principal author's last name (or the publishing organization's acronym, if no author is identified or listing by organization is more meaningful) and the last two digits of the year of publication. A lowercase letter following the year serves to distinguish otherwise identical citation identifiers.

Section numbers are used to distinguish identical citations identifiers from different sections and multiple citations from the same publication [e.g. (2: NBS-81) and (7: NBS-81)].

Appendix A contains a list of the periodicals from which citations in this bibliography have been taken. The list contains publisher and editor information where appropriate in order to assist the user of this bibliography to obtain more information about documents cited.

Appendix B contains a list of all the key words used in each of the 10 sections. This list will assist the reader who would like information on a topic that spans more than one section. As an example, information on viruses can been found in each of the first three sections (General, Management, and Foundations).

1. General

This section cites general, mostly nontechnical publications on computer threats and vulnerabilities (including the hacker and computer viruses), the need for computer security, and other aspects of computer security.

AAL-83
Aalders, J.C.H.
"Towards Standards in Computer Security," Proc. IFIP/Sec. '83, Stockholm, 1983, (2: FAK-83), pp. 5-13.

Key Words: guidelines, policy.

AAL-85
Aalders, J.C.H., I.S. Herschberg, and A. Van Zanten
Handbook for Information Security, North-Holland/Elsevier Science Publishing Co., New York, 1985.

Key Words: book, general, policy, guidelines, techniques.

ABA-84
Report on Crime, American Bar Association, Section on Criminal Justice, Washington, DC, 1984.

Key Words: book, crime, laws, policy.

AGR-83
Agranoff, M.H.
"Achieving Security Awareness: Tips and Techniques," Computer Security Journal, Spring 1983, pp. 7-17.

Key Words: awareness, guidelines.

ALA-86
Alagar, V.S.
"A Human Approach to the Technological Challenges in Data Security," Computers & Security, December 1986, pp. 328-335.

Key Words: awareness, policy.

ALL-85
Allen, R.J.
"Data Security: Problems and Remedies," Today's Office, April 1985, pp. 26-27.

Key Words: crime, threats, general, techniques.

APR-81
Crime Investigation Manual, Assets Protection Publishing, Madison, WI, 1981

Key Words: book, crime.

ARD-85
Ardis, P.M., and R.M. Johnson
"Electronic and Crime Insurance in the US and UK," Computer Fraud & Security Bulletin, August 1985, pp. 1-6.

Key Words: crime, policy, international.

ARN-83
Arnell, A.
"On-Site Hazards, Off-Site Safety," Computerworld, December 12, 1983, pp. ID/13-24.

Key Words: threats, physical.

ASS-81
"An Atlas of Terrorism," Assets Protection, March/April 1981, pp. 26-36.

Key Words: crime, hackers.

ATK-85
Atkins, W.
"Jesse James at the Terminal," Harvard Business Review, July/August 1985

Key Words: crime, hackers.

BAC-83
Backwith, N.
"Unique Approach to Security Evaluation," Computers & Security, January 1982, pp. 35-40.

Key Words: guidelines, policy.

BAI-84
Bailey, D.
"Attacks on Computers: Congressional Hearings and Pending Legislation," Proc. 1984 IEEE Symp. on Sec. & Privacy (5: IEE-84), pp. 180-187.

Key Words: crime, hackers, legislation.

BAI-87
Baird, B.J., L.L. Baird, and R.P. Ranauro,
"The Moral Cracker?," Computers & Security, December 1987, pp. 471-478.

Key Words: crime, hackers.

BAI-89
> Bainbridge, D.I. "Hacking -- The Unauthorized Access of Computer Systems: The Legal Implications," Modern Law Review, March 1989, pp. 236-245.
>
> Key Words: crime, hackers, legislation.

BAK-85
> Baker, R.H. The Computer Security Handbook, TAB Books, Inc., Blue Ridge Summit, PA, 1985
>
> Key Words: book, general, policy, guidelines, techniques.

BAL-82
> Ball, L.D. "Crime," Technology Review, April 1982, pp. 21-30.
>
> Key Words: crime, policy, legislation.

BAL-88
> Ball. M. "To Catch a Thief," Security Management, March 1988, pp. 72-78.
>
> Key Words: crime, hackers, guidelines.

BAS-88
> Baskerville, R. Designing Information Systems Security, Wiley & Sons, Somerset, NJ, 1988
>
> Key Words: book, guidelines, policy, techniques, general.

BAU-84
> Bauder, D. "Electronic Funds Transfer Security," Proc. 7th Seminar, DoD Comp. Sec. Progr. (5: DOD-84), 1984, pp. 188-194.
>
> Key Words: vulnerabilities, threats, policy, guidelines.

BEA-84
> Beane, W.F., E.R. Hilton, and B. Goldstein "Computer Security: Who Is in Charge?" Security World, October 1984, pp. 42-46.
>
> Key Words: general, policy.

BEC-80
> Becker, J. "Rifkin -- A Documentary History," Computer/Laws Journal, Summer 1980, pp. 472-720.
>
> Key Words: crime.

BEC-83
> Becker, L.G. Computer Security: An Overview of National Concerns and Challenges, Report No. 83-135 SPR, Congressional Research Service, U.S. Library of Congress, Washington, DC, February 3, 1983.
>
> Key Words: crime, policy, legislation.

BEC-83a
> Becker, H.B. Information Integrity, McGraw-Hill, New York, 1983.
>
> Key Words: book, guidelines, policy, techniques.

BEC-85
> Becker, L.G. Computer Abuse and Misuse: An Assessment of State and Federal Legislative Incentives, Institute for Defense Analysis, Princeton, NJ, 1985.
>
> Key Words: crime, policy, legislation.

BEC-85a
> Becker, L.G. "Computer and Network Security Policy: A Challenge to Organizations," Proc. IFIP/Sec. '85, Dublin, 1985, (2: GRI-85), pp. 241-250.
>
> Key Words: policy, guidelines.

BEE-84
> Beebe, C.A. "Planning for Access Control," Security Management, January 1984, pp. 77+.
>
> Key Words: guidelines, policy.

BEL-87
> Belford, P., and J. Quann "The Hack Attack Increasing Computer System Awareness of Vulnerability Threats," AIAA 87-3093, Proc. 3d Aerosp. Comp. Sec. Conf. (5: IEE-87b), 1987, pp. 155-157.
>
> Key Words: awareness, hackers, threats, vulnerabilities.

BEQ-83
> Bequai, A. How to Prevent Crime, J. Wiley & Sons, New York, 1983.
>
> Key Words: book, crime, guidelines, techniques.

BEQ-83a
> Bequai, A. "What Can Be Done to Stem The Rising Electronic Crime?," The Office, November 1983, pp. 47-49.
>
> Key Words: crime, policy, guidelines.

BEQ-84
> Bequai, A. "Lack of Ethics as a Cause of Crime," Computers and People, May-June 1984, pp. 7-14.
>
> Key Words: crime, ethics.

BER-82
> Bernhard, R. "Breaching System Security," IEEE Spectrum, June 1982, pp. 24-31.
>
> Key Words: threats, crime.

BIG-81
Bigelow, R.P. (Ed.)
Computers & the Laws,
Commerce Clearing House,
Chicago, 1981.

Key Words: book, crime,
guidelines, laws.

BIG-81a
Bigelow, R.P.
"The Queen vs. McLaughlin,
or Why the Criminal
Sometimes Goes Free,"
Computer Security Journal,
Winter 1982, pp. 131-136.

Key Words: crime, laws.

BIG-81b
Bigelow, R.P.
"The Security Officer's Role
in Legal Protection of
Software," Computer Security
Journal, Winter 1982, pp. 99-
107.

Key Words: guidelines,
policy.

BLA-84
Blakney, S.
"Crime," Computerworld,
December 26, 1983, p. 57+.

Key Words: crime, threats.

BLA-88
Blatchford, C.
"A Manufacturer's Approach
to the Security of Computer
Systems," Proc. IFIP/Sec.
'88, Australia, 1989, (2:
CAE-89), pp. 187-195.

Key Words: awareness,
guidelines, policy, techniques.

BLO-80
Bloom, R.
"Catching the Computer
Crook," Infosystems, July
1980, pp. 30-35.

Key Words: crime,
guidelines.

BLO-82
BloomBecker, J.
"International Crime: Where
Terrorism and Transborder
Data Flow Meet," Computers
& Security, January 1982, pp.
41-53.

Key Words: crime, hackers,
international.

BLO-83
Blom, R., and J.-O. Bruer
"Office Information Systems
and Security," Proc. IFIP/Sec.
'83, Stockholm, 1983, (2:
FAK-83), pp. 107-110.

Key Words: guidelines,
policy.

BLO-83a
Bloom, R.
"Computers Don't Commit
Crime, People Do," Data
Management, July 1983, p.
14.

Key Words: crime.

BLO-83b
BloomBecker, J.
"Crime -- Corporate Councel's
View," Crime Digest, March
1983, pp. 7-10.

Key Words: crime, laws.

BLO-83c
BloomBecker, J.
"International Crime: A
Growing Threat,"
Transnational Data Report,
June 1983, pp. 219-230.

Key Words: crime, threats,
international.

BLO-84
Bloombecker, J.
"Introduction to Crime," Proc.
IFIP/Sec. '84, Toronto, 1984,
(2: FIN-85), pp. 423-430.

Key Words: crime, general.

BLO-85
Bloombecker, J.
"Computer Security for the
People," Transnational Data
Report, Oct./Nov. 1985, pp.
367-370.

Key Words: awareness, ethics.

BLO-85a
Bloombecker, J.
Computer-Crime Laws
Reporter, National Center for
Computer-Crime Data,
California State University,
Los Angeles, CA, 1985.

Key Words: book, crime, laws.

BLO-85b
Bloombecker, J.J.
Introduction to Crime, National
Center for Crime Data, Los
Angeles, CA, September 1985.

Key Words: book, crime, laws.

BLO-86
Bloombecker, J.J.
Crime, Computer Security,
Computer Ethics, National
Center for Crime Data, Los
Angeles, CA, February 1986.

Key Words: book, crime,
ethivcs, policy.

BLO-86a
Bloombecker, J.J.
"New Federal Laws Bolsters
Computer Security Efforts,"
Computerworld, October 27,
1986, p. 53-66.

Key Words: crime, laws.

BLO-86b
Bloombecker, J.J.
"Lobbying for Protection,"
Computerworld, August 4,
1986, pp. 55-62.

Key Words: crime, awareness.

BLO-86c
Bloombecker, J.J.
"Defense of Crime Cases,"
American Jurisprudence Trials,
Vol. 33, 1986, pp. 1-197.

Key Words: crime, laws.

BLO-88
Bloombecker, J.J.
"Captain Midnight and the Space Hackers," Security Management, July 1988, pp. 76-82.

Key Words: crime, hackers.

BLO-89
Bloombecker, J.J.
"Trends in Computer Abuse/Misuse," Proc. 12th Natl. Comp. Sec. Conf. (5: NCS-89), 1989, pp. 611-614.

Key Words: crime, threats, laws, guidelines.

BLO-89a
Bloombecker, J.J. (Ed.)
Commitment to Security, National Center for Computer Crime Data, Santa Cruz, CA, 1989.

Key Words: book, crime, policy, general.

BOL-81
Bologna, J.
"The 8-Factor Theory of White-Collar Crime Causation," Proc. Comp. Sec. & Priv. Symp., 1981 (1: HON-81), pp. 57-67.

Key Words: crime, threats, guidelines.

BOL-81a
Bologna, J.
Crime: Wave of the Future, Assets Protection Publishing, Madison, WI, 1981.

Key Words: book, crime.

BOL-81b
Bologna, J.
"MOMM's: A Taxonomy of Computer-Related Employee Theft," Assets Protection, May/June 1981, pp. 33-36.

Key Words: crime, threats.

BOL-86
Bologna, J.
"Computer Related Crime: The Who, What, Where, When, Why and How, I," Data Processing & Communications Security, Winter 1986, pp. 19-23.

Key Words: crime, general.

BOL-86a
Bologna, J.
"Computer Related Crime: The Who, What, Where, When, Why and How, II," Data Processing & Communications Security, Spring 1986, pp. 25-30.

Key Words: crime, general.

BOR-85
Borking, J.J.
Third Party Protection of Software and Firmware, North-Holland Publishing Co. Amsterdam, 1985.

Key Words: book, software privacy.

BOS-82
Bosworth, B.,
Codes, Ciphers and Computers: An Introduction to Information Security, Hayden Book Co., Rochelle Park, NJ, 1982.

Key Words: book, awareness, general.

BOT-86
Bottom, N.R., Jr., et al.
"About the Security Degree: Are We Losing It (A Discussion)," Journal of Security Administration, June 1986, pp. 7-20.

Key Words: general, policy.

BRE-86
Breton, T., and D. Beneich
Softwars, Holt, Rinehart, Winston, New York, 1986.

Key Words: book, awareness.

BRO-83
Brown, R.A.
"Crime and Computers," Criminal Laws Journal, April 1983, pp. 68-89.

Key Words: crime, laws.

BRO-83a
Browne, M.W.
"Locking Out The Hackers," Discover, November 1983, pp. 30-40.

Key Words: awareness, hackers, crime.

BUI-84
Buikema, C., et al.
"Security Regulation: A State-by-State Update," Security Management, January 1984, pp. 39-48.

Key Words: crime, laws.

BUM-84
Bump, M. Jr.
"A Primer on Software Piracy Cases in the Courts," Computers & Security, May 1984, pp. 123-134.

Key Words: awareness, laws, software piracy.

BUR-88
Burger, R.
Computer Viruses: A High-Tech Disease, Abacus, Grand Rapids, MI, 1988.

Key Words: computer viruses, threats, general.

BUS-81
"Computer-Crime -- The Spreading Danger to Business," Business Week, April 20, 1981, pp. 86-91.

Key Words: crime, threats, guidelines.

BUS-84
Buss, M.D.J., and
L.M. Salerno
"Common Sense and
Computer Security," Harvard
Business Review, March-
April 1984, pp. 112-121.

Key Words: awareness,
guidelines, policy, general.

BUS-88
"Is Your Computer Secure?,"
Business Week, August 1,
1988, pp. 64-70.

Key Words: awareness,
computer crime, policy.

BYN-85
Bynum, T.W. (Ed.)
"Computers & Ethics,"
Metaphilosophy, October
1985.

Key Words: book, ethics.

CAE-89
Caelli, W.J. (Ed.)
Computer Security in the
Age of Information,
Proceedings, IFIP/Sec '88,
Gold Coast, Queensland,
Australia, May 1988, North-
Holland/Elsevier,
Amsterdam/New York, 1989.

Key Words: proceedings,
general.

CAL-83
Calhoun, G.
"Deterring Crimes,"
Telephony, April 4, 1983, pp.
45+.

Key Words: crime, laws,
techniques.

CAM-87 Campbell, M.
"Security and Privacy: Issues
of Professional Ethics," Proc.
10th Natl. Comp. Sec. Conf.
(5: NCS-87a), 1987, pp. 326-
333.

Key Words: awareness,
ethics.

CAM-88
Campbell, D.
"Computer Sites: Targets for
Destruction," Security
Management, July 1988, pp.
56-60.

Key Words: threats, physical.

CAN-86
Canning, R.
"Information Security and
Privacy," EDP Analyzer,
February 1986, pp. 1-16.

Key Words: awareness,
general.

CAR-80
Carroll, J.M.
"Ethics for the Computer
Age," Proc. Comp. Sec. &
Priv. Symp., 1980 (1: HON-
80), pp. 17-25.

Key Words: crime, ethics.

CAR-81
Carroll, J.M.
"Decriminalization of
Computer Crime," Proc.
Comp. Sec. & Priv. Symp.
1981 (1: HON-81), pp. 61-68.

Key Words: Crime, policy.

CAT-86
Cates, H.W.
"Crime Laws: A Review of
State Statutes," Data
Processing & Communications
Security, Spring 1986, pp. 19-
21.

Key Words: crime, laws.

CHA-85
Chamoux, J.P.
"Data Security and
Confidentiality in Europe,
Computers & Security,
September 1985, pp. 207-210.

Key Words: crime, threats,
laws, international.

CHO-84
Choney, L.B.
"Software Escrow and the
Security Practioner," Computer
Security Journal, Summer
1984, pp. 65-74.

Key Words: policy, guidelines.

CJJ-88
"Crime Statutes: Are They
Bridging the Gap Between
Laws and Technology?,"
Criminal Justice Journal,
Fall/Winter 1988, pp. 203-233.

Key Words: crime, laws.

CLJ-80
"Crime, Part 1,"
Computer/Laws Journal, Spring
1980.

Key Words: crime, laws.

CLJ-80a
"Crime, Part 2,"
Computer/Laws Journal,
Summer 1980.

Key Words: crime, laws.

CLJ-83
"Misappropriation of Computer
Services: The Need to Enforce
Civil Liability,"
Computer/Laws Journal, Fall
1983, pp. 401-420.

Key Words: crime, laws.

CLY-89
Clyde, R.
"Crime Investigation
Techniques," COM-SAC:
Computer Security, Auditing
and Control, No. 1, 1989, pp.
1-7.

Key Words: crime, techniques.

COA-83
Coates, J.F.
"The Future of Data Security:
Thoughts and Proposals,"
Computer Security Journal,
Spring 1983, pp. 77-84

Key Words: awareness, policy,
general.

COL-82
Colvin, B.D.
"Training Crime
Investigators," EDPACS,
March 1982, pp. 6-11.

Key Words: crime, policy,
guidelines.

COM-83
Crime Needs International
Countermeasures: Proceedings
of London Conference, June
1983, Elsevier International
Bulletins, Oxford, England,
1983.

Key Words: proceedings,
techniques, international,
policy.

CON-80
The Government
Classification of Private
Ideas, House Report No. 96-
1540, U.S. Congress,
Washington, DC, December
22, 1980.

Key Words: Congress, policy,
government.

CON-83
Computer Security in the
Federal Government and the
Private Sector, Hearings
before Subcommittee on
Oversight of Government
Management, Senate
Committe on Government
Operations, U.S. Congesss,
Government Printing Office,
Washington, DC, 1983.

Key Words: Congress,
threats, laws, government.

CON-84
Computer and
Communications Security and
Privacy, Hearings,
Subcommittee on
Transportation, Aviation and
Materials, Committee on
Science and Technology,
House of Representatives,
Government Printing Office,
Washington, DC, 1984.

Key Words: Congress,
legislation.

CON-84a
S. 1920, Small Business
Computer Crime Act,
Hearings before the Senate
Committee on Small Business,
March 7, 1984, U.S.
Congress, Government
Printing Office, Washington,
DC, 1984.

Key Words: Congress,
legislation.

CON-84b
The Counterfeit Access
Device and Computer Security
Act of 1984, P.L. 98-473),
U.S. Congress, 1984.

Key Words: Congress,
legislation.

CON-85
Federal Government Computer
Security, Hearings before
Subcommittee on
Transportation, Aviation and
Materials of the Committee
on Science and Technology,
House of Representatives,
May 1985, U.S. Congresss,
Government Printing Office,
Washington, DC, 1985.

Key Words: Congress,
government, policy, threats.

CON-85a
Computer Security Research
and Training Act of 1985,
Hearings before Subcommittee
on Legislation and National
Security of the Committee on
Government Operations,
House of Representatives,
U.S. Congress, Government
Printing Office, Washington,
DC, 1985.

Key Words: Congress, policy.

CON-86
Computer Fraud and Abuse
Act of 1986: Report on
S.2201, Senate Committee on
the Judiciary, U.S. Congress,
Gocernment Printing Office,
Washington, DC, September
3, 1986.

Key Words: Congress,
legislation.

CON-86a
Computer Fraud and Abuse
Act of 1986, Public Laws 99-
474, U.S. Congress,
Washington, DC, October 16,
1986.

Key Words: Congress,
legislation.

CON-87
Computer Security Act of
1987, Hearings Before
Subcommittee on
Transportation, Aviation and
Materials of the Committee on
Science and Technology,
House of Representatives, U.S.
Congresss, Government
Printing Office, Washington,
DC, 1987.

Key Words: Congress,
legislation.

CON-87a
Computer Security Act of
1987, Hearings before
Subcommittee on Legislation
and National Security of the
Committee on Government
Operations, House of
Representatives, U.S.
Congresss, Government
Printing Office, Washington,
DC, 1987.

Key Words: Congress,
legislation.

CON-87b
Computer Security Act of
1987, Report No. 100-153,
Part 1, of the Committee on
Science, Space and
Technology, House of
Representatives, U.S.
Congresss, Government
Printing Office, Washington,
DC, June 11, 1987.

Key Words: Congress,
legislation.

CON-87c
Computer Security Act of 1987, Report No. 100-153, Part 2, of the Committee on Government Operations, House of Representatives, U.S. Congresss, Government Printing Office, Washington, DC, June 11, 1987.

Key Words: Congress, legislation.

CON-89
Implementation of the Computer Security Act, Hearings before Subcommittee on Transportation, Aviation and Materials of the Committee on Science and Technology, House of Representatives on September 22, 1988, U.S. Congresss, Government Printing Office, Washington, DC, 1989.

Key Words: Congress, policy, laws.

COO-84
Cooper, C.
"The Real Cost of Software Piracy," Information Age (UK), April 1984, pp. 98-102.

Key Words: software piracy.

COO-89
Cook, W.J.
"Access to the Access Codes '88-'89: A Prosecutor's Prospective," Proc. 12th National Comp. Sec.Conf. (5: NCS-89), 1989, pp. 619-623.

Key Words: hacking, policy, laws.

COR-87
Cornwall, H.
Computer Fraud, Industrial Espionage, & Information Crime, Heinemann Professional Publishing, London, 1987.

Key Words: book, crime.

COT-84
Cottrell, P., and B.D. Weiss
"Third-Party Liability Insurance: Protection in Case of Computer Error," Computerworld, April 2, 1984, pp. ID1-ID7.

Key Words: policy, laws.

COU-81
Courtney, R.H., Jr.
"The Democratization of White Collar Crime," Computer Security Journal, Spring 1981, pp. 39-44.

Key Words: crime, laws, awareness.

COU-84
Courtney, R.H., Jr.
"Computer Security Goals of the DoD--Another Opinion," Computer Security Journal, Summer 1984, pp. 60-62.

Key Words: policy, government.

COU-84a
Courtney, R.J., Jr.
"Computer Security: The Menace is Human Error," The Office, March 1984, pp. 119.

Key Words: threats, policy.

COU-87
Courtney, R.H., Jr.
"Computer Data Security: A Leadership Vacuum," Computer Security Journal, Vol. IV, No. 2, 1987, pp. 7-16.

Key Words: awareness, policy.

COU-89a
Courtney, R.H. Jr.
"Proper Assignment of Responsibility for Data Security," Security Management, March 1989, pp. 83-86.

Key Words: policy, guidelines.

CSC-88
Glossary of Computer Security Terms, NCSC-TG-004, National Computer Security Center, Ft. Meade, MD, 21 October 1988.

Key Words: guidelines, government.

CSI-83
"Making the Case for Computer Security," Special Section by Computer Security Institute, Datamation, September 1983.

Key Words: awareness, general, policy, guidelines.

CSI-84
"Computer Security: Issues and Answers," Special Section by Computer Security Institute. Datamation, September 1, 1984.

Key Words: awareness, general, policy, guidelines.

CSI-85
"Computer Security: Issues and Answers," Special Section by Computer Security Institute, Datamation, September 15, 1985.

Key Words: awareness, general, policy, guidelines.

CSI-86
"Computer Security: Issues and Responsibilities," Special Section by Computer Security Institute, Datamation, October 1, 1986.

Key Words: awareness, general, policy, guidelines.

CSI-89
"Computer Security: Issues and Trends," Special Section by Computer Security Institute, Datamation, September 15, 1989.

Key Words: awareness, general, policy, guidelines.

CWO-83

"Crime in Japan," Computerworld, November 7, 1983, pp. ID/7-20.

Key Words: crime, international.

CWO-84

"Protecting the Corporate Information Resource: Special Report," Computerworld, October 29, 1984, pp. SR/1-32.

Key Words: policy, guidelines.

CWO-85

"System Security: Protecting Corporate Information Assets," Computerworld, November 25, 1985, p. 55ff.

Key Words: policy, guidelines.

DAV-85

Davis, G.F.G. III
Software Protection: Practical and Legal Steps to Protect and Market Computer Programs, Van Nostrand Reinhold, New York, 1985.

Key Words: book, software piracy, general, laws.

DEA-83

DeAnnuntis, G.
A Bibliography of Computer Security Bibliographies, GPD Press, Wheaton, MD, February 1983.

Key Words: awareness, general.

DEL-88

Computer Viruses, Deloitte, Haskins & Sells, New York, October 1988.

Key Words: book, computer viruses, guidelines, techniques.

DEM-83

DeMaio, H.B.
"Computer Security and the End User," Proc. IFIP/Sec. '83, Stockholm, 1983, (2: FAK-83), pp. 1-4.

Key Words: awareness, policy.

DEM-88

DeMaio, H.B.
"Information Ethics -- It Doesn't Come Naturally," Computer Security Journal, Vol. V, No. 1, 1988, pp. 7-19.

Key Words: awareness, ethics.

DEM-89

DeMaio, H.B.
"Viruses -- A Management Issue," Computers & Security, August 1989, pp. 381-388.

Key Words: computer viruses, policy.

DEM-89a

DeMaio, H.B.
"Information Ethics, A Practical Approach," Proc. 12th Natl. Comp. Sec. Conf. (5: NCS-89), 1989, pp. 630-633.

Key Words: awareness, ethics, policy.

DEN-87

Denning, D.E.,
P.G. Neumann, and
D.B. Parker
"Social Aspects of Computer Security," Proc. 10th Natl. Comp. Sec. Conf. (5: NCS-87a), 1987, pp. 320-325.

Key Words: awareness, general.

DEN-88

Denning, P.J.
"Computer Viruses," American Scientist, May/June 1988, pp. 236-238.

Key Words: computer viruses, guidelines.

DEN-89

Denning, P.J.
"The Internet Worm," American Scientist, March/April 1989, pp. 126-128.

Key Words: threats, hackers, computer viruses.

DER-88

Derosier, J.
"Computer Security at Digital," Proc. IFIP/Sec. '88, Australia, 1989, (2: CAE-89), pp. 163-165.

Key Words: awareness, general.

DEW-84

Dewdney, A.K.
"A Core War Bestiary of Viruses, Worms, and Other Threats to Computer Memories," Scientific American, June 1984, pp. 14-23.

Key Words: computer viruses, general.

DEW-89

Dewdney, A.K.
"Of Worms, Viruses and Core Wars," Scientific American, March 1989, pp. 110-113.

Key Words: computer viruses.

DMA-83

"Data Security, Special Issue," Data Management, July 1983.

Key Words: general, guidelines, techniques.

DOJ-80

Crime: Legislative Resource Manual, Bureau of Justice Statistics, U.S. Department of Justice, Washington, DC, 1980.

Key Words: crime, government, guidelines, laws.

DOJ-80a
Crime: Expert Witness
Manual, Bureau of Justice
Statistics, U.S. Department of
Justice, Washington, DC,
1980.

Key Words: crime,
guidelines, government, laws.

DOJ-82
Crime: Electronic Funds
Transfer Systems and Crime,
U.S. Department of Justice,
Bureau of Justice Statistics,
Washington, DC, 1982.

Key Words: crime,
government, laws, guidelines.

DOJ-82a
Crime: Computer Security
Techniques, U.S. Department
of Justice, Bureau of Justice
Statistics, Washington, DC,
1982.

Key Words: crime, laws,
techniques.

EIS-89
Eisenberg, T., et al.
"The Cornell Commission:
On Morris and the Worm,"
Communications of the
ACM, June 1989, pp. 706-
709.

Key Words: hackers, laws,
computer viruses.

EKE-85
Ekebrink, I.
"Security of Electronic
Transactions," Proc. IFIP/Sec.
'85, Dublin, 1985, (2: GRI-
85), pp. 233-239.

Key Words: general, threats,
guidelines.

ELB-89
El-Haghdadi, M., and
M.P. Singh
"The Pivotal Role of
Computer Security," Security
Management, July 1989, pp.
63.

Key Words: awareness,
general.

ELM-88
Elmer-DeWitt, P.
"Invasion of the Data
Snatchers," Time, September
28, 1988, pp. 62-67.

Key Words: hackers, threats.

ELO-88
Eloff, J.H.P.
"Computer Security Policy:
Important Issues," Computers
& Security, December 1988,
pp. 559-562.

Key Words: awareness,
policy.

EMM-84
Emmet, A.
"Thwarting the Data Thief,"
Personal Computing, January
1984, pp. 98-105.

Key Words: hackers, threats.

EPN-85
Epner, S.A.
"Computer Security: Plenty of
Questions But No Easy
Answers," The Office, March
1985, pp. 74-76.

Key Words: awareness,
policy.

EPP-80
Epperly, E.V.
"Trends in DoD Directives:
Survey of Federal Computer
Security Policies,"
Proceedings, U.S. Army 3d
Automation Security
Conference, Williamsburg,
VA, December 1980,
International Business
Services, Inc., pp. 31-44.

Key Words: policy,
government.

ERI-83
Eriksson, A.
"Vulnerability in a
Computerized Society," Proc.
IFIP/Sec. '83, Stockholm,
1983, (2: FAK-83), pp. 27-30.

Key Words: awareness,
threats.

ERM-89
Erman, M.D., M.B. Williams,
and C. Gutierrez
Computer Ethics and Society,
Oxford University Press, New
York, 1989.

Key Words: ethics, policy.

EWI-88
Ewing, D.
"Meeting Data Security
Needs," Proc. IFIP/Sec. '88,
Australia, 1989, (2: CAE-89),
pp. 291-302.

Key Words: awareness, policy.

FAK-88
Fak, V.
"Are We Vulnerable to Virus
Attack," Computers &
Security, April 1988, pp. 151-
155.

Key Words: computer viruses,
threats.

FAU-81
Faurer, L.D.
"Keeping the Secrets Secret,"
Government Data Systems,
Nov./Dec. 1981, pp. 14-17.

Key Words: awareness, policy,
government, guidelines.

FAU-83
Faurer, L.D.
"Information Protection in
Federal and Private Sectors,"
Computer Security Journal,
Fall/Winter 1983, pp. 89-95.

Key Words: policy,
government.

FAU-84
Faurer, L.D.
"Computer Security Goals of
the Department of Defense,"
Computer Security Journal,
Summer 1984, pp. 54-59.

Key Words: policy,
government.

FEN-88
Fennelly, L.J.
Handbook of Loss Prevention and Crime Prevention
Butterworth Publishers, Stoneham, MA, 1988.

Key Words: general, guidelines, techniques.

FIF-89
Fifield, K.J.
"Smartcards Outsmart Computer Crime," Computers & Security, May 1989, pp. 247-255.

Key Words: crime, techniques.

FIT-84
Fitzgerald, K.J.
"Crime in Australia," EDPACS, August 1984, pp. 1-7.

Key Words: crime, general, international.

FIT-86
Fitzgerald, K.J.
"Security in the Automated Office," Computer Control Quarterly, Summer 1986, pp. 21-24.

Key Words: policy, guidelines.

FIT-89
Fites, P., P. Johnson and M. Kratz
The Computer Virus Crisis, Van Nostrand Reinhold Co., New York, 1989

Key Words: book, threats, computer viruses.

FOR-82
Fordyce, S.
"Computer Security: A Current Assessment," Computers & Security, January 1982, pp. 9-16.

Key Words: awareness, general.

FOR-89
Forcht, K.A.
"Ethical Use of Computers," Proc. 12th Natl. Comp. Sec. Conf. (5: NCS-89), 1989, pp. 624-626.

Key Words: awareness, ethics.

FRE-84
Freed, R.N.
"Security Interests in the Computer Age: Practical Advice to the Secured Lender," Banking Laws Journal, July/Aug. 1984, pp. 404-429.

Key Words: awareness, guidelines.

FRE-84a
Freese, J.
"What About Your Legal Parachute When Your Data Security Crashes?," Proc. IFIP/Sec. '84, Toronto, 1984, (2: FIN-85), pp. 23-28.

Key Words: awareness, laws.

FUL-84
"Computer Abuse: The Emerging Crime and Need for Legislation," Fordham Urban Laws Journal, 1983/84, pp. 73-101.

Key Words: crime, laws.

GAO-82
Federal Information Systems Remain Highly Vulnerable to Fraudulent, Wasteful, Abusive and Illegal Practices, MSAD-82-50, U.S. General Accounting Office, Washington, DC, 21 April 1982.

Key Words: crime, threats, government, general.

GAR-89
Gardner, P.E.
"The Internet Worm: What Was Said and When," Computers & Security, June 1989, pp. 291-296.

Key Words: computer viruses.

GEM-80
Gemigniani, M.
"Crime: Laws in the '80," Indiana Laws Review, April 1980, pp. 681-723.

Key Words: crime, laws.

GEM-81
Gemignani, M.C.
Laws and the Computer, CBI Publishing, Boston, 1981.

Key Words: crime, laws.

GEM-89
Gemignani, M.
"Viruses and Criminal Laws," Communications of the ACM, June 1988, pp. 669-671.

Key Words: computer viruses, threats, laws.

GLR-83
"Larceny Enters the Electronic Age: The Problem of Detecting and Preventing Crimes," Gonzaga Laws Review, 1982/83, pp. 517-538.

Key Words: crime, laws.

GOL-81 Goldstein, B.
A Pocket Guide to Computer Crime Investigation, Assets Protection Publishing, Madison, WI, 1981.

Key Words: crime, laws.

GOL-83
Goldstein, B.
"Crime and Its Prevention," Computers & Security, January 1983, pp. 63-66.

Key Words: crime, laws, guidelines, policy.

GON-83
Gonzales, P.
"Addressing Crime Legislation," Computer/Laws Journal, Summer 1983, pp. 195-206.

Key Words: crime, laws.

GOS-85
Gosler, J.R.
"Software Protection: Myth
or Reality," Proc. Crypto '85,
Santa Barbara, 1985, (9:
WIL-86), pp. 140-157.

Key Words: software piracy.

GOU-85
Goussy, A.R.
"Legal Issues in Proprietary
Security," Journal of Security
Administ., December 1985,
pp. 23-29.

Key Words: policy, laws.

GRA-84
Graham, R.L.
"The Legal Protection of
Computer Software,"
Communications of the
ACM, May 1984, pp. 422-
426.

Key Words: software piracy.

GRE-82
Greenlee, M.B.
"Financial (Banking) View of
Computer Security," Proc. 5th
Seminar, DoD Comp. Sec.
Progr. (5: DOD-82), 1982,
pp. 167-176.

Key Words: awareness,
policy.

GRE-84
Greguras, F.M.
"Technical and Other
Practical Software Protection
Measures," TeleSystems
Journal, March/April 1984,
pp. 28-32.

Key Words: policy,
techniques.

GRE-84a
Greguras, F.M.
"Software Protection: Beyond
Copyright," Computerworld,
Dec. 12, 1983, pp. ID25-
ID32.

Key Words: software piracy.

GUY-81
Guynes, S.
"Software Security: Legal
Aspects and Traditional
Considerations," Journal of
Systems Management, April
1981, pp. 34-38.

Key Words: awarenss, laws.

GUY-83
Guynes. V.
"EFTS Impact on Computer
Security," Computers &
Security, January 1983, pp.
73-77.

Key Words: awareness,
policy.

HAF-88
Hafner, K.M., et al.
"Is Your Computer Secure,"
Business Week, August 1,
1988, pp. 64-72.

Key Words: awareness,
general.

HAM-84
Hammond, R.G.
"Theft of Information," The
Laws Quarterly Review, April
1984, pp. 252-264.

Key Words: crime, laws,
threats.

HAN-89
Hankinson, A.L.
"Computer Assurance:
Security, Safety and
Economics," Proc. COMPASS
'89: Comp. Assurance (2:
IEE-89), 1989, pp. 1-7.

Key Words: general,
guidelines.

HAR-82
Harris, B.
"Data Security: Plan for the
Worst," Infosystems, June
1982, pp. 52-58.

Key Words: awareness,
general, policy.

HAR-83
Hartson, D.R.
"Teaching Protection in
Computing: A Research-
Oriented Graduate Course,"
Computers & Security,
November 1983, pp. 248-255.

Key Words: awareness,
general.

HAR-83a
Harari, A.
"Education and Training of
Computer Security Staff:
Methodology and Course
Topics," Proc. IFIP/Sec. '83,
Stockholm, 1983, (2: FAK-83),
pp. 287-292.

Key Words: awareness,
general.

HAR-85
Harry, M.
The Computer Undeground,
Loompanics Unlimited, Port
Townsend, WA, 1985.

Key Words: book, hackers,
threats.

HEL-88
Helfant, R., and
G.J. McLoughlin
Computer Viruses: Technical
Overview and Policy
Considerations, CRS Report to
the Congress, No. 88-556 SPR,
Congressional Research
Service, Washington, DC,
December 15, 1988.

Key Words: computer viruses,
policy.

HEL-89
Helsing, C., M. Swanson, and
M.A. Todd
Executive Guide to the
Protection of Information
Resources, SP 500-169,
National Institute of Standards
and Technology, Gaithersburg,
MD, October 1989.

Key Words: guidelines, policy,
government.

HEL-89a
Helsing, C., M. Swanson, and M.A. Todd
Management Guide to the Protection of Information Resources, SP 500-170, National Institute of Standards and Technology, Gaithersburg, MD, October 1989.

Key Words: guidelines, policy.

HEL-89b
Helsing, C., M. Swanson, and M.A. Todd
Computer User's Guide to the Protection of Information Resources, SP 500-171, National Institute of Standards and Technology, Gaithersburg, MD, October 1989.

Key Words: guidelines, techniques.

HER-84
Herschberg, I.S., and R. Paans
"The Programmer's Threat: Cases and Causes," Proc. IFIP/Sec. '84, Toronto, 1984, (2: FIN-85), pp. 409-422.

Key Words: threats, crime.

HER-87
Herschberg, I.S.
"Hackers' Comfort," Computers & Security, April 1987, pp. 133-138.

Key Words: crime, hackers.

HER-88
Herschberg, I.S.
"Make the Tigers Hunt for You," Computers & Security, April 1988, pp. 197-203.

Key Words: crime, hackers.

HHS-83
Computer Related Fraud and Abuse in Government Agencies, Office of the Inspector General, U.S. Dept. of Health and Human Services, Washington, DC, 1983.

Key Words: crime, government, threats.

HIG-89
Higgins, J.C.
"Information Security as a Topic for Undergraduate Education for Computer Scientists," Proc. 12th Natl. Comp. Sec. Conf. (5: NCS-89), 1989, pp. 553-557.

Key Words: awareness, guidelines.

HIG-89a
Highland, H.J.
"What If a Computer Virus Strikes," EDPACS, July 1989, pp. 11-17.

Key Words: computer viruses, threats.

HJL-84
"Legislative Issues in Crime," Harvard Journal on Legislation, Winter 1984, pp. 239-254.

Key Words: crime, legislation.

HOF-82
Hoffman, L.J.
"Impacts of Information System Vulnerabilities on Society," Proceedings, 1982 National Computer Conference, AFIPS Press, Reston, VA, 1982, pp. 461-467.

Key Words: awareness, threats.

HOF-86
Hoffman, K.J., and L.M. Moran
"Societal Vulnerability to Computer System Failures," Computers & Security, September 1986, pp. 211-217.

Key Words: awareness, threats, vulnerabilities

HOL-80
Holman, W.D.
"Remedies Available to Victims of Crimes," Proc. Comp. Sec. & Priv. Symp., 1980 (1: HON-80), pp. 77-86.

Key Words: crime, policy.

HON-80
Computer Security and Privacy Symposium Proceedings, Honeywell Information Systems, Phoenix, AZ, April 1980.

Key Words: proceedings, general.

HON-81
Computer Security and Privacy Symposium Proceedings, Honeywell Information Systems, Phoenix, AZ, April 1981

Key Words: proceedings, general.

HOR-85
Horgan, J.
"Thwarting the Information Thieves," IEEE Spectrum, July 1985, pp. 30-41.

Key Words: crime, threats, laws.

HOW-82
Howe, C.L.
"Coping with Computer Criminals," Datamation, January 1982, pp. 118-126.

Key Words: crime, laws, guidelines.

HUB-86
Huband, F.L., and
R.D. Shelton
Protection of Computer
Systems and Software, Laws
& Business, Inc., Clifton, NJ,
1986.

Key Words: book, general,
policy, guidelines, techniques.

HUN-87
Hunt, D.B., and
F.G. Tompkins
"Protecting Sensitive Systems
and Data in an Open
Agency," AIAA 97-3092,
Proc. 3d Aerospace Comp.
Sec. Conf. (5: IEE-87b),
1987, pp. 158ff.

Key Words: policy,
guidelines.

IBM-83
Report on the Data Security
Leaders' Conference, San
Jose, CA, April 1982, IBM
Corp., White Plains, NY,
1983.

Key Words: proceedings,
general. guidelines,
techniques.

IBM-86
Security, Auditability,
Systems Control Publications
Bibliography, G320-9279-1,
IBM Corp., White Plains,
NY, May 1986.

Key Words: awareness,
general.

ING-80
Ingraham, D.G.
"On Charging Crime,"
Computer/Laws Journal,
Spring 1980, pp. 429-456.

Key Words: crime, laws,
guidelines.

IRM-84
"Information Security and
Data Integrity. Special Issue,"
Information Resource
Management, (UK), March
1984.

Key Words: awareness,
general.

ISR-87
Israel, H.
"Computer Viruses: Myth or
Reality?, Proc. 10th Natl.
Comp. Sec. Conf. (5: NCS-
87a), 1987, pp. 226-230.

Key Words: computer viruses,
threats, awareness, guidelines.

JAC-80
Jacks, E.L.
"Computer Security Interest in
the Private Sector," Proc. 2nd
Seminar, DoD Comp. Sec.
Progr. (5: DOD-80a), 1980,
pp. E1-E10.

Key Words: awareness,
policy.

JAS-83
Jaslow, M.D.
"How to Fight Computer
Fraud," EDPACS, July 1983,
pp. 6-9.

Key Words: crime, policy,
guidelines.

JOH-85
Johnson, D.G.
Computer Ethics, Prentice-
Hall, Englewood Cliffs, NJ,
1985

Key Words: awareness, ethics.

JON-88
Jones, L.G.
"Computer Viruses: Threat or
Media Hype?," The EDP
Auditor Journal, Vol. 3, 1988.

Key Words: computer viruses,
awareness, threats.

KAN-89
Kane, P.
V.I.R.U.S.: Vital Information
Resources Under Siege,
Bantam Books, New York,
1989.

Key Words: virus, threats,
awareness, guidelines.

KAP-84
Kaperonis, I.
"Industrial Espionage,"
Computers & Security, May
1984, pp. 117-122.

Key Words: awareness, threats,
guidelines, techniques.

KAY-86
Kay, R.
"Computer Security
Information Sources,"
Computer Security Journal,
Vol. 4, No. 1, 1986, pp. 29-
40.

Key Words: awareness,
general.

KAY-86a
Kay, R. (Ed.)
"Data Security Scoreboard,"
Computer Security Journal,
Vol. 4, No. 1, 1986, pp. 41-
54.

Key Words: awareness,
general.

KEL-88
Kelley, D.W.
"A Guide to Cost-Effective PC
Security," Security
Management, October 1988,
pp. 55-58.

Key Words: guidelines, policy,
PC.

KEN-85
Kenny, J.J.P.
Data Privacy and Security,
Pergamon Infotech, Oxford,
1985.

Key Words: book, general,
policy, guidelines, techniques.

KIR-81
Kirchner, J.
"Vulnerability: Will the U.S.
Confront Its Systems'
Flaws?," Computerworld,
December 28, 1981, pp. 36-
32.

Key Words: vulnerabilities,
awareness, threats.

KIR-83
Kirby, M.D.
"Computer Crime and Law
Reform in Australia,"
Information Age (UK),
October 1983, pp. 241-247.

Key Words: crime, laws,
policy, international.

KLI-80
Kling, R.
"Computer Abuse and
Computer Crime as
Organizational Activities,"
Computer/Law Journal,
Spring 1980, pp. 403-427.

Key Words: crime, threats,
policy.

KNA-83
Knapp, T.J.
"Selling Data Security to
Upper Management," Data
Management, July 1983, pp.
22-25.

Key Words: policy,
guidelines.

KRA-88
Kratz, M.
"Computer Crime Legislation
in Canada" Proc. IFIP/Sec.
'88, Australia, 1989, (2:
CAE-89), pp. 101-118.

Key Words: crime,
international, legislation.

KRA-88a
Kratz, M.
"Industrial Espionage and
Theft of Information," Proc.
IFIP/Sec. '88, Australia, 1989,
(2: CAE-89), pp. 279-289.

Key Words: crime, threats,
laws.

KRI-80
Krieger, M.M.
"Current and Proposed
Computer Crime Legislation,"
Computer/Law Journal,
Summer 1980, pp. 721-771.

Key Words: crime, threats,
laws.

KRU-86
Krull, A.
"Ten Losing Strategies for
Data Security," Computer
Security Journal, Vol. 4, No.
1, 1986, pp. 21-28.

Key Words: awareness,
general, policy, guidelines.

KUO-87
Kuong, J.F.
"Computer Disasters and
Corporate Amnesia and
Corporate Paralysis," CPR-J:
Contingency Planning &
Recovery Journal, No. 4,
1987, pp. 1-4.

Key Words: Awareness,
threats, vulnerabilities, policy.

KUO-88
Kuong, J.F.
"Computer Viruses -- Are
They a Threat to Business
Continuity?," CPR-J:
Contingency Planning &
Recovery Journal, No 2, 1988,
pp. 5-7.

Key Words: viruses, threats,
awareness, policy.

KUR-82
Kurzban, S.A.
"A Selective, Slightly
Annotated Bibliography on
Works on Data Security and
Privacy," Computers &
Security, January 1982, pp. 57-
64.

Key Words: awareness,
general.

KUR-86
Kurzban, S.A.
"Careers in Computer Misuse -
- Not So Appealing After All,"
Computers & Society, Winter
1986, pp. 7-9.

Key Words: general, crime,
threats.

LAN-85
Landreth, B.
(with H. Rheingold)
Out of the Inner Circle,
Microsoft Press, Bellevue,
WA, 1985

Key Words: book, hackers,
general, vulnerabilities.

LAS-81
Lasden, M.
"Computer Crime," Computer
Decisions, June 1981, pp. 104-
124.

Key Words: awareness, crime,
threats, general.

LAU-88
Laureson, A.
"Keeping Your PCs Where
They Belong," Security
Management, July, 1988, pp.
53-55.

Key Words: guidelines, PC,
policy.

LEE-86
Lee, J.A.N., G. Segal, and
R. Steier
"Positive Alternatives: A
Report on an ACM Panel on
Hacking," Communications of
the ACM, April 1986, pp.
297-299.

Key Words: hackers, general,
policy.

LEH-82
Lehman, R.L.
"Tracking Potential Security Violations," Security Audit & Control Review, Winter 1981/82, pp. 26-39.

Key Words: policy, guidelines.

LOB-81
Lobel, J.
"The Foreign Corrupt Practices Act Applied to Information Systems," Proc. Comp. Sec. & Priv. Symposium, Phoenix, AZ, 1981 (1: HON-81), pp. 69-78.

Key Words: legislation, policy.

LOB-83
Lobel, J.
"The State-of-the-Art In Computer Security," Computers & Security, November 1983, pp. 218-222.

Key Words: awareness, techniques.

LOB-86
Lobel, J.
"Impact of Technology on Computer Security," Information Age, (U.K.) April 1986, pp. 77-80.

Key Words: general, techniques.

LON-87
Longley, D., and M. Shain Data & Computer Security: Dictionary of Standards and Terms, Stockton Press, New York, 1987

Key Words: book, guidelines, laws, general, policy.

LOU-84
Louwerse, C.P., and J.M.L. Kouwenberg·
"Data Protection Aspects in an Integrated Hospital Information System," Computers & Security, November 1984, pp. 286-294.

Key Words: general, guidelines, policy, techniques.

LYN-83
Lyndon, K.
"A New Policy in Protection - - Computer Crime Insured," Security World, January 1983, pp. 38-40.

Key Words: general, policy.

MAD-88
Madsen, C.
"The World Meganetwork and Terrorism," Proc. IFIP/Sec. '88, Australia, 1989, (2: CAE-89), pp. 343-349.

Key Words: awareness, policy, threats, international.

MAN-84
Mantle, R.A.
"Trade Secret and Copyright Protection of Computer Software," Computer/Law Journal, Spring 1984, pp. 669-694.

Key Words: software piracy, laws.

MAR-83
Marbach, W.D., et al.
"Beware: Hackers at Play," Newsweek, Sept. 5, 1983, p. 5+.

Key Words: awareness, hackers, crime, threats.

MAR-84
Martin, W.P.
"Arresting Computer Crime," Interface Age, (U.K.) February 1984, pp. 71-75

Key Words: crime, laws, threats, guidelines.

MAR-88
Marx, P.
"The Legal Risks of Using Information as a Competetive Weapon," Software Law Journal, Spring 1988, pp. 185-201.

Key Words: awareness, general, policy, laws.

MAX-85
Maxfield, J.F.
"Computer Bulletin Boards and the Hacker Problem," EDPACS, October 1985, pp. 1-11.

Key Words: hackers, threats.

MAY-85
Mayo, K.
"Business Battles In-House Pirates," Business Computer Systems, February 1985, pp. 60-65.

Key Words: software piracy.

MCA-89
McAfee, J., and C. Haynes Computer Viruses, Worms, Data Diddlers, Killer Programs, and Other Threats to Your System, St. Martin's Press, New York, 1989.

Key Words: book, viruses, threats, vulnerabilities.

MCA-89a
McAfee, J.D.
"Managing the Virus Threat," Computerworld, February 13, 1989, pp. 89-96.

Key Words: viruses, threats.

MCI-81
McIsaac, D.
"Introduction to Computers: Security Problems and Considerations," Assets Protection, November/December 1981, pp. 13-22.

Key Words: awareness, general, threats, policy.

1-15

MCL-88
McLeod, K.
"Computer Insecurity,"
Information Age, (U.K.),
April 1988, pp. 89-93.

Key Words: awareness,
general, crime, threats.

MIL-85
Millard, C.J.
Legal Protection of Computer
Programs and Data, Carswell
Co., Ltd, Toronto, 1985.

Key Words: software piracy,
laws.

MIS-85
Miskiewicz, J.
"DP Security: A Delicate
Balance," Computer
Decisions, April 23, 1985,
pp. 104ff.

Key Words: awareness,
general, policy.

MOS-88
Mosaccio, J.
"Computer Sites: Assessing
the Threat," Security
Management, July 1988, pp.
40-51.

Key Words: vulnerabilities,
threats, general.

MOU-81
Moulton, R.T.
"System Security Standards,"
Computer Security Journal,
Spring 1981, pp. 73-82.

Key Words: general,
guidelines.

MOU-81a
Moulton, R.T.
"Prevention: Better Than
Protection," Government Data
Systems, Nov./Dec. 1981, pp.
20-23.

Key Words: awareness,
general, guidelines, policy.

MOU-82
Moulton, R.T.
"A Strategy for Dealing with
Computer Fraud and Abuse,"
Computer Security Journal,
Winter 1982, pp. 31-40.

Key Words: crime, threats,
policy, guidelines.

MUR-86
Murphy, I.
"Aspects of Hacker Crime:
High-Technology Tomfoolery
or Theft?," Information Age,
(U.K.) April 1986, pp. 69-73.

Key Words: crime, policy,
laws, hackers, threats.

MUR-86a
Murray, W.H.
"Security Concepts and the
New Computer Economics,"
Computer Security Journal,
Vol. 4, No. 1, 1986, pp. 7-14.

Key Words: general, policy.

MYE-83
Myers, J.
"Fraud and Computers," New
Law Journal, January 21,
1983, pp. 71-72.

Key Words: crime, threats,
laws.

NAF-80
Naftalis, G.P.
White Collar Crimes,
American Law Institute and
American Bar Association,
Philadelphia, PA, 1980.

Key Words: book, crime,
general.

NBS-80
Guidelines for Security of
Computer Applications, FIPS
PUB 73, National Bureau of
Standards, Gaithersburg, MD,
June 1980.

Key Words: general,
guidelines, techniques, policy.

NEU-86
Neugent, W.
"Preposterous Opinions About
Computer Security," Security,
Audit & Control Review,
Summer 1986, pp. 1-8.

Key Words: awareness,
general.

NOR-83
Norman, A.R.D.
Computer Insecurity, Chapman
and Hall, London, 1983.

Key Words: book, awareness,
general, threats.

NOR-84
Norman, A.
"Crime by Computer,"
Information Resources
Management (UK), March
1984, pp. 18-21.

Key Words: crime, threats,
general, policy.

NYE-81
Nye, J.M.
"A Primer on Security, Part
1," Mini-Micro Systems, June
1981, pp. 139-148.

Key Words: awareness,
general.

NYE-81a
Nye, J.M.
"A Primer on Security, Part
2," Mini-Micro Systems, July
1981, pp. 166-174.

Key Words: awareness,
general.

OLI-85
Oliver, C.R.
"A Psychological Approach to
Preventing Computer Abuse --
A Case History," Computer
Security Journal, Winter 1985,
pp. 51-56.

Key Words: crime, threats,
laws, guidelines, policy.

OMB-85
Management of Federal Information Resources, OMB Circular No. A-130, Office of Management and Budget, Washington, DC, December 1985.

Key Words: government, policy.

OTA-81
Computer-Based National Information Systems: Technology and Public Policy Issues, Office of Technology Assessment, Washington, DC, September 1981.

Key Words: government, policy, guidelines, laws.

OTA-86
Intellectual Property Rights in an Age of Electronics and Information, OTA-CIT-302, U.S. Congress, Office of Technology Assessment, Washington, DC, April 1986

Key Words: government, policy, legislation.

PAR-80
Parker, D.B.
"Computer Abuse Research Update," Computer/Law Journal, Spring 1980, pp. 329-352.

Key Words: crime, threats, policy, awareness, laws.

PAR-81
Parker, D.B.
Ethical Conflicts in Computer Science and Technology, AFIPS Press, Reston, VA, 1981.

Key Words: general, policy, ethics.

PAR-83
Parker, D.B.
Fighting Computer Crime, Charles Scribner's Sons, New York, 1983.

Key Words: crime, general, policy, guidelines, laws.

PAR-83a
Parker, D.B.
"How Much Computer Abuse Is There?" Computer Security Journal, Spring 1983, pp. 85-89.

Key Words: crime, general, threats, awareness.

PAR-84
Parker, D.B.
"A Strategy for Preventing Program Theft and System Hacking," Computer Security Journal, Summer 1984, pp. 21-32.

Key Words: hackers, crime, threats, policy, guidelines.

PAR-84a
Parker, D.B., and S.H. Nycum
"Computer Crime," Communications of the ACM, April 1984, pp. 313-315.

Key Words: crime, threats, general, awareness, guidelines.

PER-84
Perry, T., and P. Wallich
"Can Computer Crime Be Stopped?," IEEE Spectrum, May 1984, pp. 34-49.

Key Words: crime, policy, laws.

POD-86
Podell, H.G., and M.W. Abrams
"Computer Security Glossary for the Advanced Practitioner," Computer Security Journal, Vol. 4, No. 1, 1986, pp. 69-88

Key Words: guidelines, general.

REB-86
Reber, J.
"The Essence of Industrial Espionage," Data Processing & Communications Security, Winter 1986, pp. 24-25.

Key Words: awareness, general, threats, laws.

RIC-84
Richards, T.C.
"A Computer Fraud Survey," ACM Security Audit & Control Review, Spring-Sum. 1984, pp. 17-23.

Key Words: awareness, computer crime, general, threats.

RIC-86
Richards, R.M., and J.L. Guynes
"A Strategic Plan for Reducing Consumer Anxiety About EFTS Security," Security, Audit & Control Review, Spring 1986, pp. 4-8.

Key Words: awareness, policy.

RIC-86a
Richards, R.M.
"Insuring Computer Risks," Computers & Security, September 1986, pp. 207-210.

Key Words: policy, guidelines.

RIC-86b
Richards, T.C.
"A Historical Perspective of Computer Related Fraud," Security, Audit & Control Review, Summer 1986, pp. 15-25.

Key Words: crime, threats, awareness, general.

ROB-88
Roberts, R.
Computer Viruses, Compute! Books, Greensboro, NC, 1988

Key Words: book, viruses, threats.

ROB-88a
Roberts, W.
"Remember to Lock the Door: MMI and the Hacker," Information Age, (U.K.), July 1988, pp. 146-150.

Key Words: hackers, awareness, threats, guidelines.

ROS-85
Ross, S.J. (Ed.)
"Computer Security Issues: A
Roundtable," Computer
Security Journal, Winter
1985, pp. 39-50

Key Words: awareness,
policy.

SAM-85
Samociuk, M.
"Hacking or the Art of
Armchair Espionage,"
Computer Fraud and Security
Bulletin, July 1985.

Key Words: hacking, crime,

SAT-89
Sato, O.
"Controlling End-User
Computing: An Analytical
Framework," ACM Security,
Audit and Control Review,
Fall 1989, pp. 6-12.

Key Words: policy,
guidelines.

SCH-80
Schulte, L.A.
"Computer Crime
Bibliography," Computer/Law
Journal, Summer 1980, pp.
787-803.

Key Words: awareness,
general, crime, guidelines.

SCH-83
Schwartz, M.B.
"Safeguarding EFTS,"
Datamation, February 1983,
pp. 148-160.

Key Words: policy,
guidelines, techniques.

SCH-84
Schmucker K.J.
"Computer Crime: Fiction
and Science Fact," Abacus,
Spring 1984, pp. 8-21.

Key Words: awareness,
crime.

SCH-84a
Scherer, M.E.
"Unsafe Software -- The
Missing Security Perspective,"
Computer Security Journal,
Summer 1984, pp. 43-52.

Key Words: awareness,
threats.

SCH-85
Schweitzer, J.A.
"A Management View:
Computer Security as a
Discretionary Decision,"
Computers & Security, March
1985, pp. 13-22.

Key Words: policy,
guidelines.

SCH-86
Schweitzer, J.A.
"Who Owns Information
Security?" Security, Audit &
Control Review, Spring 1986,
pp. 1-3.

Key Words: awareness,
general.

SCH-86a
Schweitzer, J.A.
Computer Crime and Business
Information, Elsevier, New
York, 1986

Key Words: crime, threats.

SEC-86
"How Business Battles Crime
by Computer," Security
World, October 1986, pp. 54-
60.

Key Words: crime, policy.

SEC-89
"10 Top Security
Trends,"Security, February
1989, pp. 47-51.

Key Words: policy,
techniques.

SEI-84
Seif, R.A.
"Contingency Planning in the
Banking Community,"
Computers & Security,
February 1984, pp. 29-34.

Key Words: awareness, policy.

SER-83
"Industrial Espionage,"
Security World, April 1983,
pp. 33-39.

Key Words: crime, threats.

SEW-84
Sewell, C.
"Screening Out The People
Problem," Security World,
October 1984, pp. 50-52.

Key Words: policy, guidelines.

SEY-85
Seymour, J.
"Locking Up Your Information
Assets," Today's Office, April
1985, p. 23ff.

Key Words: policy, guidelines.

SIE-87
Sieber, U.
The International Handbook on
Computer Crime: Computer-
Related Economic Crime and
the Infringements of Privacy,
J. Wiley & Sons, Somerset,
NJ, 1987

Key Words: crime, threats,
general, international.

SIL-83
Silverman, M.E.
"Selling Security to Senior
Management, DP Personnel
and Users," Computer Security
Journal, Fall/Winter 1983, pp.
7-18.

Key Words: awareness,
general, policy, guidelines.

SIL-85
Silverman, M.E.
"Strategic Planning -- The
Missing Link in Computer
Security" Computer Security
Journal, Winter 1985, pp. 31-
38.

Key Words: policy,
guidelines.

SIM-81
Simkin, M.C.
"Computer Crime: Lessons
and Directions," The CPA
Journal, December 1981, pp.
10-14.

Key Words: crime, threats,
policy.

SMA-84
"Controlling Computer
Crime," Security Managment,
January 1984, pp. 19-34.

Key Words: crime, policy,
techniques.

SMI-83
Smith, T.H.
"Computers and the Law of
Evidence," Transnational Data
Report, December 1983, pp.
451-454.

Key Words: crime, policy,
laws.

SOK-90
Sokolik, S.L.
"Computer Crime -- The
Need for Deterrent
Legislation," Computer/Law
Journal, Spring 1980, pp.
333-383.

Key Words: crime,
legislation.

STA-84
Staikos, N.
"Designs for Computer
Security," Security World,
March 1984, pp. 52-55.

Key Words: policy,
guidelines, techniques.

STA-85
Stanley, P.M.
"Educating Computer Crime
Investigators," Proc. IFIP/Sec.
'85, Dublin, 1985, (2: GRI-
85), pp. 313-322.

Key Words: crime, guidelines.

STA-86
Straub, D.W.
"Computer Abuse and
Security: Update of an
Empirical Pilot Study,"
Security, Audit & Control
Review, Spring 1986, pp. 21-
31.

Key Words: crime, guidelines,
techniques.

STR-88
Straub, D.W., and
W.D. Nance
"Uncovering and Disciplining
Computer Abuse:
Organizational Responses and
Options," Information Age,
(U.K.), July 1988, pp. 151-
156.

Key Words: crime, policy,
threats, guidelines.

TUR-82
Turn, R.
"Private Sector Needs for
Trusted/Secure Computer
Systems," Proceedings, 1982
National Computer
Conference, AFIPS Press,
Reston, VA, 1982, pp. 449-
460.

Key Words: policy,
guidelines.

TUR-85
Turner, B.M.
"Terrorist Attacks Upon
Technological Systems,"
Journal of Security
Administration, December
1984, pp. 25-32.

Key Words: crime, threats.

TUR-86
Turn, R.
"Security and Privacy
Requirements in Computing,"
Proc., ACM/IEEE Fall Joint
Computer Conference,
November 1986, pp. 1106-
1113.

Key Words: policy, guidelines.

TUR-86a
Turn, R.
"Security, Privacy, Safety
andResiliency in Computing,"
in J. Skwirzynski (Ed.),
Software Design Methods,
NATO ASDI Series Volume
F22, Springer-Verlag, New
York, 1986, pp. 653-679.

Key Words: policy, guidelines,
techniques.

VAN-84
Van Hoboken, W.R.C.
"The Burglar's Viewpoint,"
Computers & Security,
November 1984, pp. 295-302.

Key Words: crime, threats.

VAN-85
van Tongeren, H.
"Information Security in the
Framework of the International
Information Flow Debate: A
Business View," Proc.
IFIP/Sec'85 (2: GRI-85), pp.
323-328.

Key Words: policy, guidelines,
international.

VOL-80
Volgyes, M.R.
"The Investigation, Prosecution
and Prevention of Computer
Crime: A State of the Art
Review," Computer/Law
Journal, Spring 1980, pp. 385-
402.

Key Words: crime, guidelines,
policy, laws.

VOL-83
Volkman, T.C.
"Computers -- America's
Achilles' Heel," <u>Air
University Review</u>, May-June
1983, pp. 43-47.

Key Words: vulnerabilities,
threats.

WAR-83
Ware, W.H.
"Computer Security Standards
for Government and Industry:
Where Will They Come
From?," <u>Computer Security
Journal</u>, Spring 1983, pp. 71-
76.

Key Words: policy,
guidelines, government.

WAR-84
Ware, W.H.
"Information Systems
Security and Privacy,"
<u>Communications of the
ACM</u>, April 1984, pp. 315-
312.

Key Words: awareness,
general.

WAR-88
Ware, W.H.
"Perspectives on Trusted
Computer Systems," <u>Proc.
IFIP/Sec. '88</u>, Australia,
1989, (2: CAE-89), pp. 309-
330.

Key Words: awareness,
general, techniques.

WEB-85
Webster, W.H.
"Technology Transfer,
Industrial Espionage and
Computer Crime: The
Problems We Are Facing,"
<u>Computer Crime Digest</u>,
January 1985, pp. 1-5.

Key Words: crime,
guidelines, policy, techniques.

WEB-85a
Webster, W.H.
"Technology Transfer,
Industrial Espionage, &
Computer Crime: The FBI's
Activities," <u>Computer Security
Journal</u>, Winter 1985, pp. 7-
12.

Key Words: crime,
government, guidelines,
policy.

WEI-82
Weiss, E.A.
"Self-Assessment Procedure
Dealing With Ethics in
Computing," <u>Communications
of the ACM</u>, March 1982, pp.
181-195.

Key Words: awareness, ethics.

WEI-84
Weinberger, F.
"Computer Security: Plan for
Action," <u>TeleSystems Journal</u>,
March/April 1984, pp. 11-21.

Key Words: awareness,
policy, guidelines.

WEL-86
Weller, R., and S. Wall
"Source Code Under Lock
and Key," <u>Computerworld</u>,
June 2, 1986, p. 69.

Key Words: guidelines,
techniques.

WON-83
Wong, K.
"Computer-Related Fraud,"
<u>Information Age (UK)</u>,
January 1983, pp. 16+

Key Words: awareness,
general, crime, threats,

WON-83a
Wong, K.
"Computer-Related Fraud in
the U.K.," <u>Information Age,
(U.K.)</u>, October 1983, pp.
238-240.

Key Words: awareness, crime,
international.

WON-84
Wong, K.
"Computer-Related Fraud in
the U.K.," <u>EDPACS</u>, June
1984, pp. 5-9.

Key Words: awareness, crime,
international.

WON-85
Wong, K.K.
"Computer Disaster in the
United Kingdom," <u>EDPACS</u>,
January 1985, pp. 1-7.

Key Words: awareness, crime,
international.

WOO-82
Wood, M.
<u>Introducing Computer Security</u>,
NCC Publications, Manchester,
England, 1982.

Keyword: awareness, general.

YNG-88
Yngstrom, L.
"Experiences from a One-Year
Academic Programme in
Security Informatics," <u>Proc.
IFIP/Sec. '88</u>, Australia, 1989,
(2: CAE-89), pp. 83-86.

Keyword: awareness, general.

YOS-85
Yost, G.
<u>Spy-Tech</u>, Fact On File Pub.,
New York, 1985.

Key Words: awareness,
general.

YOU-82
Yourdan, E.
<u>Silent Witness</u>, Yourdan Press,
New York, 1982.

Key Words: awareness,
general.

YOV-89
Yovel. S.
"On Viruses and Top
Managers," <u>Information Age,
(U.K.)</u>, September 1989, pp.
202-210.

Key Words: awareness,
viruses, guidelines.

ZAJ-85
   Zajac, B.P., Jr.
   "Police Response to
   Computer Crime in the
   United States," The Computer
   Law and Security Report,
   July-August 1985, pp. 16-17.

   Key Words: crime,
   legislation.

ZAJ-86
   Zajac, B.P., Jr.
   "What to Do When You
   Have Reason to Believe Your
   Computer Has Been
   Compromised". Computers &
   Security, March. 1986, pp.
   11-16.

   Key Words: hackers, viruses,
   threats, guidelines.

ZAL-83
   Zalud, B.
   "Computer Criminals Will Be
   Prosecuted: Adoping A
   'Prevention First' Approach,"
   Data Management, April
   1983, pp. 30+.

   Key Words: crime, policy,
   guidelines.

ZIM-84
   Zimmerman, J.S.
   "The Human Side of
   Computer Security," Computer
   Security Journal, Summer
   1984, pp. 7-20.

   Key Words: awareness,
   general, threats, guidelines.

ZIM-85
   Zimmerman, J.S.
   "PC Security: So What's
   New?" Datamation, November
   1, 1985, pp. 86-92

   Key Words: awareness,
   general, PC.

2. Management

The section cites publications on various management issues, including: the need for security in mainframe, minicomputer and personal computer systems (risk management, risk analysis); administrative and personnel policies and controls; physical security in computing facilities; and operational (disaster) recovery. Also included are publications containing technical discussions of threats and vulnerabilities (e.g., viruses).

ADD-87
Addison, K., et al. "Computer Security at SUN Microsystems, Inc.," Proc. 10th Natl. Comp. Sec. Conf., (5: NCS-87a), 1987, pp. 216-219.

Key Words: company, general, policy, management, techniques

AFC-85
Proceedings, Symposium on Physical/Electronic Security, AFCEA, 1986.

Key Words: proceedings, physical.

AFC-86
Proceedings, 2nd Annual Symposium on Physical/Electronic Security, AFCEA, Philadelphia, PA, August 1986.

Key Words: proceedings, physical.

AFC-87
Proceedings, 3d Annual Symposium on Physical/Electronic Security, AFCEA, 1987.

Key Words: proceedings, physical.

AIM-81
AIM/SAFE: A Data Processing Contingency Planning Methodology, Advanced Information Management, Inc., Woodbridge, VA, 1981.

Key Words: guidelines, recovery, techniques.

ALD-88
Aldridge, B.T. "Preliminary Formulation of a Policy Based on Risk (PBR) Asessment Methodology," Proc. Comp. Sec. Risk Manag. Model Builders Workshop, 1988 (2: NBS-88), pp. 225-242.

Key Words: risk, policy, methods.

ALK-89
Alkemi
Computer Risk Manager, Elsevier Advanced Technology New York, NY, 1989.

Key Words: risk, management, methods.

ALL-81
Allen, B.R. "Threat Teams: A Technique for the Detection and Prevention of Fraud in Automated and Manual Systems," Computer Security Journal, Spring 1981, pp. 1-13.

Key Words: guidelines, techniques.

ALS-86
Al-Saffar, H. "Using SMF Data for Audit Purposes," EDPACS, February 1986, pp. 1-14.

Key Words: auditing, methods.

ANC-83
Ancker, A. "Facilities for Computers and Office: Security Conscious Planning," Proc. IFIP/Sec. '83, Stockholm, 1983, (2: FAK-83), pp. 143-146.

Key Words: guidelines, physical.

AUS-81
Austin, B.B. "Controlling Physical Access from a Central Locations," Computer Security Journal, Spring 1981, pp. 83-98.

Key Words: physical, control, techniques.

BAD-89
Badenhorst, K.P., and J. Eloff "Framework of a Methodology for the Life Cycle of Computer Security in an Organization," Computers & Security, August 1989, pp. 433-442.

Key Words: general, methods.

BAK-85
Baker, R.H.
The Computer Security
Handbook, TAB Professional
and Reference Books, Blue
Ridge Summit, PA, 1985.

Key Words: book, geberal,
techniques.

BAL-87
Baldwin, R.W.
"Rule Based Analysis of
Computer Security,"
Proceedings, IEEE Compcon
1987, pp. 227-233.

Key Words: general,
methods.

BAR-80
Barbarino, P.
"Multi-Tiered Approach to
System Security," Proc. 1980
IEEE Symp. on Security &
Privacy, (5: IEE-80), pp.
114-120.

Key Words: general, method,
techniques.

BEA-84
Beatman, L.
"Microcomputer in the Audit
Function," EDPACS,
September 1984, pp. 4-6.

Key Words: auditing,
methods.

BEA-85
Beatson, J.G.
"Development and
Organization of the Audit
and Security Function," Proc.
IFIP/Sec. '85, Dublin, 1985,
(2: GRI-85), pp. 251-259.

Key Words: audit,
management.

BEA-86
Beatson, J.G.
"Managing the EDP Audit
and Security Function,"
Computers & Security,
September 1986, pp. 201-206.

Key Words: audit,
management.

BEC-83
Becker, H.B.
Information Integrity: A
Structure for Its Definition
and Management, McGraw-
Hill, New York, 1983

Key Words: book, integrity,
general, methods, guidelines.

BEC-84
Becker, H.B.
"Security Considerations in
the Small Systems
Environment," Proc. IFIP/Sec.
'84, Toronto, 1984, (2: FIN-
85), pp. 501-516.

Key Words: general,
guidelines.

BEI-84
Beitman, L.
"An Audit Software Program
Base," EDPACS, March 1984,
pp. 6-8.

Key Words: auditing,
software.

BEN-89
Benzel, T.C.V.
"Integrating Security
Requirements and Software
Development Standards," Proc.
12th Natl. Comp. Sec.Conf.
(5: NCS-89), 1989, pp. 435-
458.

Key Words: methods,
software

BER-83
Bermhed, L.
"A Method for Testing
Vulnerability," Proc. IFIP/Sec.
'83, Stockholm, 1983, (2:
FAK-83), pp. 161-166.

Key Words: vulnerability,
methods.

BER-83a
Bernhard, R.
"Foiling the Spoofers, Trap-
Doors, Trojan Horses...,"
Systems and Software, April
1983, pp. 67-68.

Key Words: hackers, threats,
methods.

BER-83b
Bernstein, R.A.
"Contingency Planning -- A
Case Study," EDPACS,
October 1983, pp. 9-12.

Key Words: contingency,
methods.

BER-84
Berg, R.
"Risk Management for
Computer Centers,"
Informormation Resource
Management (U.K), March
1984, pp. 16-17.

Key Words: risk, management,
methods.

BES-88
Bessenhoffer, R.
"Designing Security Into a
Modern Data Processing
Center," Computer Security
Journal, Volume V, No. 1,
1988, pp. 53-66.

Key Words: methods,
techniques.

BIC-89
Bickner, L.
"Security Engineering of
Secure Ground Stations," Proc.
Aerospace Comp. Sec. Conf.
(5: IEE-85a), 1985, pp. 49-54.

Key Words: physical,
techniques.

BIS-86
Bishop, M.
"Analyzing the Security of An
Existing Computer System,"
Proceedings, ACM/IEEE Fall
Joint Computer Conference,
Nov. 1986, pp. 1115-1119.

Key Words: risk, methods.

BLA-81
Blanding, S.F.
"Computer Fraud Auditing --
A Case Study," EDPACS,
Aug./Sept. 1981, pp. 4-24.

Key Words: crime, auditing,
company.

BOL-84
Bologna, J.
"Disaster/Recovery Planning:
A Qualitative Approach,"
Data Processing &
Communications Security,
March/April 1984, pp. 11-15.

Key Words: contingency,
recovery, management.

BOL-88
Bologna, G.J., and
R.J. Linquist
Fraud Auditing and Forensic
Accounting, J. Wiley &
Sons, New York, 1988.

Key Words: book, auditing,
control.

BOL-88a
Bologna, J.
"Selection Risks in Hiring
Information Systems
Personnel," Computers &
Security, August 1988, pp.
353-355.

Key Words: risk, personnel.

BOL-89
Bologna, J.
"The One Minute Fraud
Auditor," Computers &
Security, February 1989, pp.
29-31.

Key Words: crime, auditing.

BON-81
Bonyun, D.
"The Role of a Well Defined
Auditing Process in the
Enforcement of Privacy
Policy and Data Security,"
Proc. 1981 IEEE Symp. on
Sec. & Privacy, (5: IEE-81),
pp. 19-25.

Key Words: policy, auditing,
methods.

BON-81a
Bonyun, D.A.
"Towards A Standard All-
Purpose Activity Log,"
Proceedings, Honeywell
Computer Security and
Privacy Symposium, April
1981, pp. 133-145.

Key Words: auditing,
guidelines.

BON-88
Bonyun, D.A., and J. Graeme
"An Expert Systems Approach
to the Modelling of Risks in
Dynamic Environment," Proc.
Comp. Sec. Risk Manag.
Model Builders Workshop,
1988 (2: NBS-88), pp. 203-
223.

Key Words: risk, methods,
management.

BOU-83
Bound, W.A.J., and D.R. Ruth
"Risk Mangement -- How It
Can Become a Useful Tool,"
Proc. IFIP/Sec. '83,
Stockholm, 1983, (2: FAK-
83), pp. 147-160.

Key Words: risk, methods,
management.

BOU-83a
Bound, W.A.J., and D.R. Ruth
"Making Risk Analysis A
Useful Management Tool with
Microcomputer Electronic
Worksheet Packages,"
Computers & Security, June
1983, pp. 102-115.

Key Words: risk, methods,
management.

BOY-82
Boyer, T.J.
"Contingency Planning: An
Opportunity for DP
Management," Computer
Security Journal, Winter 1982,
pp. 41-49.

Key Words: contingency,
recovery, methods.

BRA-81
Brafman, M.J.
"Evaluating Computer Controls
Using the Matrix Approach,"
EDPACS, December 1981, pp.
1-10.

Key Words: risk, control,
methods.

BRI-83
Brill, A.E.
Building Controls into
Structured Systems, Yourdon
Press, New York, 1983.

Key Words: controls, methods.

BRO-84
Browne, P.S.
"The Automated Risk Profile
(RiskPac), Proc. 7th Seminar,
DoD Comp. Sec. Progr. (5:
DOD-84), 1984, pp. 402-404.

Key Words: risk, methods,
management.

BRO-86
Brown, R.V.
"Managing Diffuse Risks from
Adversarial Sources (DR/AS)
with Special Refernce to
Computer Security," Proc. 9th
Natl. Comp. Sec. Conf. (5:
NCS-86), 1986, pp. 162-167.

Key Words: risk, management,
methods.

BRO-87
Brown, R.L.
"Specification for a
CanonicalConfiguration
Management Tool," Proc. 10th
Natl. Comp. Sec. Conf. (5:
NCS-87a), 1987, pp. 84-90.

Key Words: management,
methods.

BRO-88

Browne, P.S., and J.E. Laverty "Using Decision Analysis to Estimate Computer Security Risk," Proc. Comp. Sec. Risk Manag. Model Builders Workshop, 1988 (2: NBS-88), pp. 117-134.

Key Words: risk, management, methods.

BRO-89

Brothers, M.H. "A 'How To' Guide for Computer Virus Protection in MS-DOS," Proc. 12th Natl. Comp. Sec. Conf. (5: NCS-89), 1989, pp. 349-358.

Key Words: virus, guidelines, methods.

BRU-85

Bruske, S.Z., R.E. Wright, and W.D. Geaslen "Potential Uses of Probabilistic Risk Assessment Techniques for Space Station Development," Proc. Aerospace Comp. Sec. Conf. (5: IEE-85a), 1985, pp. 21-29.

Key Words: risk, methods.

BUC-87

Buck, E.R. An Introduction to Data Security and Controls, Q.E.D. Information Sciences, Inc., Wellesley, MA, 1987.

Key Words: book, control, methods.

BUI-87

Bui, T., and T.R. Sivasankaran "Cost-Effectiveness Modeling for a Decision Support System in Computer Security," Computers & Security, April 1987, pp. 139-151.

Key Words: methods, management.

BUR-85

Burns, R.W. "Security Implications of the Space Station Information System," Proc. Aerospace Comp. Sec. Conf. (5: IEE-85a), 1985, pp. 3-10.

Key Words: requirements, government.

BUR-88

Burger, R.H. Computer Viruses: A High-Tech Disease, Abacus, Grand Rapids, MI, 1988.

Key Words: book, general, virus, risk, techniques.

BUU-84

Buurmeijer, F. "IBM's Data Security Strategy: Some Implementation Aspects," Computers & Security, November 1984, pp. 273-277.

Key Words: methods, company.

CAE-89

Caelli, W.J. (Ed.) Computer Security in the Age of Information, Proc. IFIP/Sec. '88, Gold Coast, Australia, May 1988, North-Holland, Amsterdam 1989.

Key Words: proccedings, general, international.

CAM-83

Campbell, R.P. "Locking Up the Mainframe, Part 1," Computerworld, October 10, 1983, pp. ID1-ID15.

Key Words: threats, policy, methods.

CAM-83a

Campbell, R.P. "Locking Up the Mainframe, Part 2," Computerworld, October 17, 1983, pp. ID1-ID14.

Key Words: threats, policy, methods.

CAR-82

Carroll, J.M. Controlling White Collar Crime: Design and Audit for Systems Security, Butterworths, Woburn, MA, 1982.

Key Words: book, crime, auditing.

CAR-83

Carroll, J.M., and O. Wu "Methodology for Security Analysis of Data Processing Systems," Computers & Security, January 1983, pp. 24-34.

Key Words: risk, threats, methods, managements.

CAR-83a

Carroll, J.M. "Descision Support for Risk Analysis," Computers & Security, November 1983, pp. 230-236.

Key Words: risk, threats, methods, management.

CAR-84

Carrroll, J.M. Managing Risk: A Computer-Aided Strategy, Butterworth, Stoneham, MA 1984.

Key Words: book, risk, methods. management.

CAR-84a

Carroll, J.M., and W.R. MacIver "Towards an Expert System for Computer-Facility Certification," Proc. IFIP/Sec. '84, Toronto, 1984, (2: FIN-85),'84, pp. 293-306.

Key Words: physical, methods, risk.

CAR-85

Carroll, J.M., and W.W. Mac Iver "COSSAC: A Framework for Analyzing and Configuring Secure Computer Facilities," Computers & Security, March 1985, pp. 5-12.

Key Words: physical, methods.

CAR-87
Carroll, J.M.
Computer Security, Second
Edition, Butterworths, Boston,
MA, 1987

Key Words: book, general,
methods, guidelines,
techniques.

CER-85
Cerullo, M.J.
"General Controls in
Computer Systems,"
Computers & Security, March
1985, pp. 33-45.

Key Words: controls,
methods.

CHA-82
Chambers, A.D.
Computer Auditing,
Commerce Clearing House,
Inc., Chicago, 1982.

Key Words: auditing,
methods.

CHA-85
Chalmers, L.S.
"A Low-Cost Approach to
Disaster Recovery Planning,"
Computer Security Journal,
Winter 1985, pp. 57-61.

Key Words: contingency,
recovery, methods,
maangement.

CHA-86
Chalmers, L.S.
"An Analysis of the
Differences Between
Computer Security Practices
in the Military and Private
Sectors," Proc. 1986 IEEE
Symp. on Security & Privacy
(5: IEE-86), pp. 71-77.

Key Words: policy, methods,
management.

CHA-88
Chantino
Disaster Recovery, Elsevier,
New York, NY, 1988.

Key Words: book, recovery,
methods.

CHO-89
Chokhani, S.
"Protection of Call Detail
Records Data in Federal
Telecommunications," Proc.
5th Sec. Applicat. Conf. (4:
IEE-89c), 1989, pp. 70-77.

Key Words: government,
threats, policy, methods,
techniques.

CLA-86
Clark, R.
"Risk Mangement -- A New
Approach," Proc. IFIP/Sec.
'86, Monte Carlo, 1986, (2:
GRI-89).

Key Words: risk, methods,
management.

CLY-87
Clyde, A.R.
"Insider Threat Identification
System," Proc. 10th Natl.
Comp. Sec. Conf. (5: NCS-
87a), 1987, pp. 343-356.

Key Words: threats, risk,
methods.

COC-84
Cochrane, J.S.
"Automated Data Processing
Security Accreditation
Program (A Composite
Guideline)," Proc. 7th
Seminar, DoD Comp. Sec.
Progr. (5: DOD-84), 1984, pp.
351-363.

Key Words: guidelines,
accreditation.

COH-84
Cohen, F.
"Computer Viruses: Theory
and Experiments," Proc. 7th
Seminar, DoD Comp. Sec.
Progr. (5: DOD-84), 1984, pp.
240-263.

Key Words: virus, techniques,
theory.

COH-84a
Cohen, F.
"Computer Viruses: Theory
and Experience," Proc.
IFIP/Sec. '84, Toronto, 1984,
(2: FIN-85), pp. 143-158.

Key Words: virus, theory,
techniques.

COH-87
Cohen, F.
"Computer Viruses: Theory
and Experiments," Computers
& Security, February 1987, pp.
22-25.

Key Words: virus, techniques,
theory.

COH-88
Cohen, F.
"On the Implications of
Computer Viruses and
Methods of Defense,"
Computers & Security, April
1988, pp. 167-184.

Key Words: virus, threats,
methods.

COH-88a
Cohen, F.
"Maintaining a Poor Person's
Information Integrity,"
Computers & Security, October
1988, pp. 489-494.

Key Words: integrity, methods.

COH-88b
Cohen, F.
"Terminal Viruses," The
Sciences, Nov.-Dec. 1988, pp.
24-30.

Key Words: virus, techniques.

COH-89
Cohen, F.
"Computational Aspects of
Computer Viruses," Computers
& Security, June 1989, pp.
325-344.

Key Words: virus, techniques.

COO-89
Cooper, J.A.
Computer and
Communications Security:
Strategies for the 1990s,
McGraw-Hill, New York,
1989.

Key Words: book, general,
networks.

COP-88
Copigneaux, F., and
S. Martin
"Software Security Evaluation
Based on Top-Down McCall-
Like Approach," Proc. 4th
Aerosp. Comp. Sec. Conf. (4:
IEE-88b), 1988, pp. 414-418.

Key Words: risk, methods.

COR-82
Coryen, G.C.
A Methodology for Assessing
Security Risks Associated
with Computer Sites and
Networks, UCRL-53292,
Lawrence Livermore National
Laboratory, Livermore, CA,
June 23, 1982.

Key Words: risk, methods,
networks.

COR-87
Corelis, J.
"Source Code Security: A
Checklist for Managers,"
ACM Sec. Audit & Control
Review, Spring 1987, pp. 12-
16.

Key Words: software,
guidelines.

COU-84
Courtney, R.H., and
M.A. Todd
"Problem Definition: An
Essential Prerequisite to the
Implementation of Security
Measures," Proc. IFIP/Sec.
'84, Toronto, 1984, (2: FIN-
85), pp. 97-106.

Key Words: methods,
techniques.

COU-85
Courtney, R.H., and
M.A. Todd
"Problem Quantification:
Importance of Cost-Effective
Security," Proc. IFIP/Sec. '85,
Dublin, 1985, (2: GRI-85),
pp. 55-63.

Key Words: methods,
techniques.

COU-86
Courtney, R.H.
"Security Measures Are
Inherently Undesirable,"
EDPACS, March 1986, pp. 9-
12.

Key Words: methods,
management.

COU-86a
Courtney, R.H.
"An Economically Feasible
Approach to Contingency
Planning," Proc. 9th Natl.
Comp. Sec. Conf. (5: NCS-
86), 1986, pp. 237-244.

Key Words: contingency,
recovery, methods.

COU-88
Courtney, R.H.
"Another Perspective on
Sensitive But Unclassified
Data," Computers & Security,
February 1988, pp. 19-23.

Key Words: policy,
requirements.

COU-89
Courtney, R.H.
"Proper Assignment of
Responsibility for Data
Security," Information Age,
(U.K.) April 1989, pp. 83-87.

Key Words: policy,
management.

CRO-82
Crow, W.
"Making the ATM More
Secure," The Bankers
Magazine, Jan./Feb. 1982, pp.
70-74.

Key Words: policy,
techniques.

CRO-84
Croft, R.B.
"A Flow Charting Technique
for Designing On-Line Data
Security," TeleSystems Journal,
March/April 1984, pp. 22-27.

Key Words: risk, techniques.

CRO-85
Cronhjort, B.T., and
A. Mustonen
"Computer Assisted Reduction
of Vulnerability of Data
Centers," Proc. IFIP/Sec. '84,
Toronto, 1984, (2: FIN-85),
pp. 397-425.

Key Words: risk,
vulnerabilities, methods,
techniques.

CRO-86
Cronin, D.
Microcomputer Data Security:
Issues & Strategies, Brady
Communicat./Prentice-Hall,
Englewood Cliffs, NJ, 1986.

Key Words: book,
management, PC, techniques.

CRO-89
Crocker, S., and M. Pozzo
"A Proposal for Verification-
Based Virus Filter," Proc. 1989
IEEE Symp. on Sec. &
Privacy (5: IEE-89b), pp. 319-
324.

Key Words: virus, techniques.

CSC-85
PC Security Considerations,
NSSC-TG-002-85, National
Computer Security Center, Ft.
Meade, MD, 1985.

Key Words: guidelines, PC,
techniques.

CSI-83
Computer Security Handbook,
Computer Security Institute,
Northboro, MA, 1983.

Key Words: book, guidelines,
general, techniques,
management.

CSI-87
"A Guide to Commercial Disaster Recovery Services," Computer Security Journal, Volume IV, No. 2, 1987, pp. 49-64.

Key Words: contingency, recovery.

CWO-86
"Disaster Recovery Hot Sites," Computerworld, May 12, 1986, p. 62ff.

Key Words: contingency, recovery.

DAV-87
Davis, F.G.F., and R.E. Gantenbein "Recovering from a Computer Virus Attack," Journal of Systems and Software, December 1987, pp. 253-258.

Key Words: virus, recovery, methods.

DAV-89
Davida, G.I., Y.G. Desmet, and B.J. Matt "Defending Systems Against Viruses through Cryptographic Authentication," Proc. 1989 IEEE Symp. on Sec. & Privacy (5: IEE-89b), pp. 312-318.

Key Words: virus, techniques, cryptography.

DEL-89
Computer Viruses: Proceedings, Invitational Symposium, October 10-11, 1988, Deloite Haskings & Sells, New York, 1989.

Key Words: proceedings, virus, methods, management.

DEM-85
DeMaio, H.B. "Controlling Advanced Information System Technology," Computer Security Journal, Winter 1985, pp. 63-67.

Key Words: management, control.

DEN-81
de Boef, A. "Audit Monitoring of Production Data Files," EDPACS, February 1981, pp. 1-16.

Key Words: auditing, methods.

DEN-87
Denning, D.E. "An Intrusion-Detection Model," IEEE Trans. on Software Engr., February 1987, pp. 222-232.

Key Words: threats, methods.

DES-88
Desman, M.B. "Recovery Palnning -- Pay Attention to Your People," Computer Security Journal, Volume V, No. 1, 1988, pp. 49-51.

Key Words: policy, personnel, management.

DEV-83
DeVries, D. "A Baker's Dozen: Security Suggestions for Moving a Data Center," Computer Security Journal, Spring 1983, pp. 91-95.

Key Words: guidelines, physical.

DOD-88
Security Requirements for Automated Information Systems (AIS), U.S. Department of Defense, Washington, DC, March 1988.

Key Words: policy, requirements, government.

DON-84
Donovan, J.F. "Industrial Relations and Contingency Planning," Proc. IFIP/Sec. '84, Toronto, 1984, (2: FIN-85), pp. 401-406.

Key Words: contingency, management.

DOS-85
Doswell, R.T. "The Audit, Control and Security of the Project Life Cycle -- Pre-Implementation Stage," Proc. IFIP/Sec. '85, Dublin, 1985, (2: GRI-85), '85, pp. 277-281.

Key Words: auditing, management.

DPC-84
"Computer Security Administration and Staffing," Data Processing & Communications Security, May/June 1984.

Key Words: management, personnel.

DPC-84a
"Physical Security for Data Processing Facilities," Data Processing & Communications Security, Sept./Oct. 1984.

Key Words: physical, techniques.

DUG-86
Dugan, E. "Disaster Recovery Planning: Crisis Doesn't Equal Catastrophe," Computerworld, January 27, 1986, pp. 67-74.

Key Words: contingency, recovery, management.

DUN-84
Dunmore, D. "An EDP Risk Analysis Model," EDPACS, October 1984, pp. 6-11.

Key Words: risk, management, methods.

EAS-82

Eason, T.S., and D.A. Webb
Nine Steps to Effective EDP
Loss Control, Digital Press,
Bedford, MA, 1982.

Key Words: book, control,
policy, guidelines.

EIC-89

Eichin, M.Q.W., and
J.A. Rochlis
"With Microscope and
Tweezers: An Analysis of the
Internet Virus of November
1988," Proc. 1989 IEEE
Symp. on Sec. & Privacy (5:
IEE-89b), pp. 326-343.

Key Words: virus, methods.

ENG-80

Enger, N.L., and
P.W. Hoverton
Computer Security: A
Management Audit Approach,
Anacom, New York, 1980.

Key Words: book, auditing,
methods,

EPP-80

Epperly, E.V.
"The Department of Defense
Computer Security Initiative
Program and Current and
Future Security Policies,"
Proc. 2nd Seminar, DoD
Comp. Sec. Prog. (5: DOD-
80a), 1980, pp. J1-J34.

Key Words: policy,
government.

EPP-82

Epperly, E.V.
"Computer Security Policies -
Challenges and Prospects,"
Proc. 5th Seminar, DoD
Comp. Sec. Prog. (5: DOD-
82), 1982, pp. 99-137.

Key Words: policy,
government.

ESS-85

Essen, J., and B. Lindberg
"The Bofors-Model for
Working ADP Security," Proc.
IFIP/Sec. '85, Dublin, 1985,
(2: GRI-85), pp. 47-53.

Key Words: risk, threats,
methods.

FAK-83

Fak, V.A. (Ed.)
Security, Proc. of IFIP/Sec'83,
Stockholm, Sweden, May 16-
19, 1983, North-Holland
Publishing Co., Amsterdam,
1983.

Key Words: proceedings,
general, international.

FAS-89

Fastiggi, M.V.
"Detection of Surreptitious
Insertion of Trojan Horse or
Viral Code in Computer
Application Programs,"
Information Age, (U.K.),
January 1989, pp. 3-10.

Key Words:

FED-85

Proceedings, Federal
Information System Risk
Analysis Workshop, U.S. Air
Force Computer Security
Program Office, San Antonio,
TX, January 1985.

Key Words: proceedings, risk.

FER-87

Ferris, M., and A. Cerulli
"Certification: A Risky
Business," Proc. 10th Natl.
Comp. Sec. Conf. (5: NCS-
87a), 1987, pp. 266-272.

Key Words: cerification,
policy.

FEU-88

Feuerlicht, J., and P. Grattan
"The Role of Classification of
Information in Controlling
Data Proliferation in End-User
PC Environment," Proc.
IFIP/Sec. '88, Australia, 1989,
(2: CAE-89), pp. 167-176.

Key Words: control, methods
management.

FEU-89

Feuerlicht, J., and P. Grattan
"The Role of Classification of
Information in Controlling
Data Proliferation in End-User
Personal Computer
Environment," Computers &
Security, February 1989, pp.
59-66.

Key Words: control, methods,
management.

FIE-82

Fierello, M.
"Cost-Benefit Impact Analysis
of Computer Security
Standards & Guidelines," Proc.
5th Seminar, DoD Comp. Sec.
Prog. (5: DOD-82), 1982, pp.
177-201.

Key Words: guidelines,
methods, management.

FIN-85

Finch, J.H., and
E.G. Dougall (Eds.)
Computer Security: A Global
Challenge. Proc., IFIP/SEC
'84, Toronto, Canada, 12-12
Sept., 1984, North-Holland
Publishing Company,
Amsterdam, 1985.

Key Words: proceedings,
general, international.

FIS-89

Fish, T. and S. Meglathery
"Professional Certification for
Computer Security
Practitioners," Proc. 12th Natl.
Comp. Sec. Conf. (5: NCS-
89), 1989, pp. 433-434.

Key Words: personnel,
management.

FIT-81
Fitzgerald, J.
"EDP Risk Analysis Using Matrices," EDPACS, November 1981, pp. 1-7.

Key Words: risk, methods, management.

FIT-89
Fites, P.E.
Control and Security of Computer Information Systems, Computer Science Press, Rockville, MD, 1989.

Key Words: book, control, methods.

FLA-86
Flach, J.
"Disaster Planning -- Beyond a Prayer," Computer Security Products Report, Spring 1986, pp. 9-11.

Key Words: contingency, recovery.

FRA-83
Francella, K.
"Multiple Controls Combat Computer Crime," Data Management, July 1983, pp. 21+.

Key Words: crime, controls, methods, management.

FRI-82
Friedman, S.D.
"Contingency and Disaster Planning," Computers and Security, January 1982, pp. 34-40.

Key Words: contingency, recovery, management.

FRI-84
Friedman, S.D.
"Contingency and Disaster Planning in EDP," EDPACS, January 1984, pp. 4-9.

Key Words: contingency, recovery, management.

FRY-83
Fry, B.G.P, and W.F. Main
"A Conceptual Methodology for Evaluating Security Requirements for Data Assets," Computers & Security, November 1983, pp. 237-241.

Key Words: requirements, methods.

FUG-84
Fugini, M., and C. Martella
"Security Mangement in Office Information Systems," Proc. IFIP/Sec. '84, Toronto, 1984, (2: FIN-85), pp. 487-498.

Key Words: management, policy.

GAG-85
Gage, D.W.
"Security Considerations for Autonomous Robots," Proc. 1986 IEEE Symp. on Sec. & Privacy (5: IEE-86), pp. 224-228.

Key Words: requirements.

GAL-85
Gallery, S.M.
Computer Security: Readings from Security Management Magazine, Butterworths, Boston, 1987.

Key Words: book, general, methods.

GAO-80
Most Federal Agencies Have Done Little Planning for ADP Disasters, AFMD-81-16, U.S. General Accounting Office, Washington, DC, 18 December 1980.

Key Words: contingency, recovery, government, management.

GAO-81
Federal Agencies Still Need to Develop Greater Computer Audit Capabilities, AFMD-82-7. U.S. General Accounting Office, Washington, DC, 16 October 1981.

Key Words: auditing, management, government.

GAO-81a
Evaluating Internal Controls in Computer-Based Systems, AFMD-81-76, U.S. General Accounting Office, Washington, DC, June 1981.

Key Words: control, government.

GAR-87
Garcia, A.A. (Ed.)
Computer Security: A Comprehensive Controls Checklist, J. Wiley & Sons, Somerset, NJ, 1987.

Key Words: guidelines, methods.

GAR-88
Garnett, P.D.
"Selective Disassembly: A First Step Towards Developing Virus Filter," Proc. 4th Aerospace Comp. Sec. Conf. (4: IEE-88b), 1988, pp. 2-6.

Key Words: virus, techniques.

GAR-89
Gardner, P.E.
"Analysis of Five Risk Assessment Programs," Computers & Security, October 1989, pp. 479-485.

Key Words: risk, management, techniques.

GAS-86
Gascoyne, R.J.N.
"Basic Protection for Microcomputers," EDPACS, June 1986, pp. 5-6.

Key Words: PC, techniques, management.

GIL-81
Gilhooley, I.A.
"Controlling the EDP
Auditor," EDPACS, January
1981, pp. 1-7.

Key Words: auditing, control,
management.

GIL-84
Gilhooley, I.A.
"Auditing System
Development Methodology,"
EDPACS, July 1984, pp. 1-8.

Key Words: auditing,
methods.

GIL-84a
Gillin, P.
"Tightening Controls on
MicroBased Software,"
Computerworld, December 5,
1984, pp. 41-44.

Key Words: control, PC,
software.

GIL-85
Gilhooley, I.A.
"The Impact of Current EDP
Development on Separation
of Duties," COM-SAC,
Computer Security, Auditing
& Controls, No. 2, 1985, pp.
A7-A14.

Key Words: management,
methods.

GIL-86
Gilhooley, I.A.
"Productivity and Control in
System Development,"
EDPACS, July 1986, pp. 1-6.

Key Words: control,
management.

GIL-86a
Gilhooley, I.A.
"Controlling End-User
Computing," EDPACS,
October 1986, pp. 1-9.

Key Words: control,
management.

GIL-89
Gilbert, I.E.
Guide for Selecting
Automated Risk Analysis
Tools, SP 500-174, National
Institute of Standards and
Technology, Gaithersburg,
MD, October 1989.

Key Words: risk,
management, methods,
guidelines.

GIN-89
Ginn, R.
Continuity Planning:
Preventing, Surviving and
Recovering from Disaster,
Elsevier Advanced
Technology New York, NY,
1989.

Key Words: book,
contingency, recovery,
management.

GLE-89
Gleissner, W.
"A Mathematical Theory for
the Spread of Computer
Viruses," Computers &
Security, February 1989, pp.
35-41.

Key Words: virus, theory.

GOT-81
Gottlieb, M.
"Audit Concerns About
Minicomputers," EDPACS,
Oct. 1981, pp. 12-15.

Key Words: auditing,
methods.

GRE-81
Greguras, F.M.
"DP Contingency Planning:
The Legal Considerations,"
Assets Protection, May/June
1981, pp. 26-29.

Key Words: contingency,
laws.

GRE-81a
Green, G., and R.G. Farber
Introduction to Security
Principles & Practices, Security
World Publishing, Los
Angeles, 1981.

Key Words: general, methods,
policy, techniques.

GRE-89
Green, J.L., and P. L. Sisson
"The 'Father Christmas
Worm'," Proc. 12th Natl.
Comp. Sec. Conf. (5: NCS-
89), 1989, pp. 359-368.

Key Words: virus, techniques.

GRI-85
Grimson, J.B.,
H.J. Kugler (Eds.)
Computer Security: The
Practical Issues in a Troubled
World, Proc. IFIP/Sec '85,
Dublin, Ireland, 12-15 August,
1985, North-Holland Elsevier
Publishing Company,
Amsterdam/New York, 1985

Key Words: proceedings,
general, international.

GRI-89
Grissonnanche,A. (Ed.)
Security Protection in
Information Systems,
Proceedings IFIP/Sec '86,
Monte Carlo, December 1986,
North Holland/Elsevier,
Amsterdam, 1989.

Key Words: proceedings,
general, international.

GUA-87
Guarro, S.B.
"Principles and Procedures of
the LRAM Approach to
Information Systems Risk
Analysis and Management,"
Computers & Security,
December 1987, pp. 493-504.

Key Words: risk, methods.

GUA-88
Guarro, S.B.
"Analytical and Decision
Models of the Livermore
Risk Analysis Methodology,"
Proc. Comp. Sec. Risk
Manag. Model Builders
Workshop, 1988 (2: NBS-
88), pp. 49-71.

Key Words: risk, methods.

GUI-89
Guinier, D.
"Biological Versus Computer
Viruses," ACM Sec., Audit
& Control Rev., Summer
1989, pp. 1-15.

Key Words: virus, general.

GUS-88
Gustoff, M.E.
"Personal Computer
Security," Information Age,
(U.K.), October 1988, pp.
195-202.

Key Words: PC, techniques.

HAE-84
Haeckel, D.A., and
B.B. Johnson
"Complete the Cycle of
Information Security
Planning," Security
Management, May 1984, pp.
54-59.

Key Words: management,
methods.

HAH-88
Hahn, M.
"Auditing Changes to MVS,"
Proc. IFIP/Sec. '88, Australia,
1989, (2: CAE-89), pp. 407-
424.

Key Words: auditing,
methods.

HAL-86
Halme, L.R., and
J. Van Horne
"Automated Analysis of
Computer System Audit
Trails for Security Purposes,"
Proc. 9th Natl. Comp. Sec.
Conf. (5: NCS-86), 1986, pp.
71-74.

Key Words: auditing,
methods.

HAL-88
Halme, L.R., and B.L. Kahn
"Building a Security Monitor
with Adaptive User Work
Profiles," Proc. 11th Natl.
Comp. Sec. Conf. (5: NCS-
88), 1988, pp. 374-383.

Key Words: auditing,
techniques.

HAM-82
Hammer, C.
"Managing Computer
Security," Computer Security
Journal, Winter 1982, pp. 17-
21.

Key Words: management,
methods.

HAN-83
Hansen, J.V. and
W.F. Messier
"Scheduling the Monitoring of
EDP Controls in Online
Systems," Internatl. Journal of
Computer and Information
Sciences, February 1983, pp.
35-46.

Key Words: control, methods.

HAN-83a
Hansen, J.V.
"Audit Considerations in
Distributed Processing
Systems," Communications of
the ACM, August 1983, pp.
562-569.

Key Words: auditing,
methods.

HAR-80
Hardenburg, K.L.
"Controlling Systems
Programming Activities,"
EDPACS, January 1980, pp.
1-24.

Key Words: control,
management.

HAR-80a
Hardenburg, K.L.
"Auditing the MVS Operating
Systems," EDPACS, June
1980, pp. 1-10.

Key Words: auditing,
techniques.

HEA-83
Healy, R.J
Design for Security, 2nd Ed.,
John Wiley & Sons, New
York, 1983.

Key Words: book, physical,
methods, techniques.

HEA-86
Heaton, Y.
"The Human Risks -- An
Auditor's Point of View," The
Computer Law and Security
Report, Sept.-Oct. 1986, pp.
21-23.

Key Words: risk, personnel.

HEA-87
Hearden, K.
A Handbook of Computer
Security, Kogan Page, London,
1987.

Key Words: book, general,
methods, guidelines,
management.

HEB-80
Hebbard, B., et al.
"A Penetration Analysis of the
Michigan Terminal System,"
ACM Operating Systems
Review, January 1980, pp. 7-
20.

Key Words: vulneabilities,
threats.

HEN-85
Henrion, M., and
M. G. Morgan,
"A Computer Aid for Risk and
Other Policy Analysis," Risk
Analysis, September 1985, pp.
195-208.

Key Words: risk, management,
policy, methods.

HER-84
Herschberg, I.S. and R. Paans
"The Programmer's Threat:
Cases and Causes,"
Computers & Security,
November 1984, pp. 263-272.

Key Words: threats,
personnel, management.

HIG-83
Highland, H.J.
"Impact of Microcomputers
on Total Computer Security,"
Proc. IFIP/Sec. '83,
Stockholm, 1983, (2: FAK-
83), pp. 119-129.

Key Words: PC, techniques,
management.

HIG-83a
Highland, H.J.
"Impact of Microcomputers
on Total Computer Security,"
Computers & Security, June
1983, pp. 171-183.

Key Words: PC, techniques,
management.

HIG-83b
Highland, H.J.
"Operational Security for
Microcomputers,"
Proceedings, 1983
COMPCON Fall, IEEE
Computer Society, 1983.

Key Words: PC, techniques.

HIG-84
Highland, H.J.
"Data Protection in a
Microcomputer Environment,"
Proc. IFIP/Sec. '84, Toronto,
1984, (2: FIN-85), pp. 517-
531.

Key Words: PC, techniques.

HIG-84a
Highland, H.J.
Protecting Your
Microcomputer System, J.
Wiley & Sons, New York,
1984.

Key Words: book, PC,
techniques.

HIG-85
Highland, H.J.
"Microcomputer Security:
Data Protection Techniques,"
Computers & Security, June
1985, pp. 123-134.

Key Words: PC, techniques.

HIG-87
Highland, H.J.
"Data Physician -- A Virus
Protection Program,"
Computers & Security,
February 1987, pp. 73-79.

Key Words: virus, techniques.

HIG-87a
Highland, H.J.
"How to Evaluate
Microcomputer Encryption
Software and Hardware,"
Computers & Security, June
1987, pp. 229-244.

Key Words: PC, cryptography.

HIG-88
Highland, H.J.
"Computer Viruses: A Post
Mortem," Computers &
Security, April 1988, pp. 117-
122.

Key Words: virus, techniques.

HIG-88a
Highland, H.J.
"The Anatomy of a Virus
Attack," Computers &
Security, April 1988, pp. 145-
150.

Key Words: virus, techniques.

HIG-88b
Highland, H.J.
"An Overview of 18 Virus
Protection Programs,"
Computers & Security, April
1988, pp. 157-163.

Key Words: virus, techniques.

HIG-88c
Highland, H.J.
"The Brain Virus: Fact and
Fantasy," Computers &
Security, August 1988, pp.
367-370.

Key Words: virus, techniques.

HIG-89
Highland, H.J.
"The Milnet/Arpanet Attack,"
Computers & Security,
February 1989, pp. 3-10.

Key Words: virus, techniques.

HIG-89a
Highland, H.J.
"A Macro Virus" Computers &
Security, May 1989, pp. 178-
182.

Key Words: virus, techniques.

HIG-89b
Highland, H.J.
"The Marijuana Virus
Revisited," Computers &
Security, August 1989, pp.
369-373.

Key Words: virus, techniques.

HIG-89c
Highland, H.J.
"The Italian or Ping-Pong
Virus," Computers & Security,
April 1989, pp. 91-94.

Key Words: virus, techniques.

HIG-89d
Highland, H.J.
"Anatomy of Three Computer
Virus Attacks," Computers &
Security, October 1989, pp.
461-466.

Key Words: virus, techniques.

HIG-89e
Highland, H.J.
"Secure File Storage and
Transfer," Computers &
Security, October 1989, pp.
466-474.

Key Words: database,
techniques.

HIG-89f
Highland, H.J.
"Secret Disk II --
Administrator," Computers &
Security, November 1989, pp.
563-568.

Key Words: virus,
techniques.

HIG-89g
Highland, H.J.. (Ed.)
The Computer Virus
Handbook, Elsevier Advanced
Technology, New York, NY,
1989.

Key Words: book, virus,
methods, techniques,
guidelines.

HIG-89h
Highland, H.J.
"Datacrime Virus and New
Anti-Virus Products,"
Computers & Security,
December 1989, pp. 659-661.

Key Words: virus,
techniques.

HIG-89i
Highland, H.J.
"VCHECKER -- A Virus
Search Program," Computers
& Security, December 1989,
pp. 669-674.

Key Words: virus,
techniques.

HIL-83
Hildebrand, J.
"Records Retention:
Management's Involvement is
Critical," Data Management,
July 1983, pp. 18+.

Key Words: contingency,
recovery.

HIL-84
Hiller, E.
"Up from Disaster,"
Computerworld, March 26,
1984, pp. ID/9-16.

Key Words: contingency,
recovery.

HIR-89
Hirst, J.
"Rotten to the Core: Bombs,
Trojans, Worms, and Viruses,"
New Scientist, March 4, 1989,
pp. 40-41.

Key Words: virus, threats.

HOA-82
Hoar, T.
"Controls and Risk in Data
Processing," The Bankers
Magazine, May/June 1982, pp.
49-52.

Key Words: risk,
management.

HOE-86
Hoebeke, L.
"Computer Security --
Prevention: Lessons from the
Operation of a Nuclear Power
Plant," Computers & Security,
June 1986, pp. 122-127.

Key Words: methods,
management.

HOF-81
Hoffman, L.J., and
L.A. Neitzel
"Inexact Analysis of Risk,"
Computer Security Journal,
Spring 1981, pp. 61-72.

Key Words: risk, techniques.

HOF-85
Hoffman, L.J., and
A.F. Westin
"A Survey: Office Automation
Security and Private
Practices," Computer Security
Journal, Winter 1985, pp. 69-
76.

Key Words: methods,
management.

HOF-86
Hoffman, L.J.
Computer Security Risk
Analysis: Problems and
Issues, GWU-IIST-86-04, The
George Washington
University, Washington, DC,
March 1986.

Key Words: risk,
management.

HOF-86a
Hoffman, L.J.
"Risk Analysis and Computer
Security: Bridging the Cultural
Gap," Proc. 9th Natl. Comp.
Sec. Conf. (5: NCS-86), 1986,
pp. 156-161.

Key Words: risk, management.

HOF-88
Hoffman, L.J.
"A Prototype Implementation
of a General Risk Model,"
Proc. Comp. Sec. Risk Manag.
Model Builders Workshop,
1988 (2: NBS-88), pp. 135-
144.

Key Words: risk, techniques.

HOF-89
Hoffman, L.J.
"Smoking Out the Bad Actors:
Risk Analysis in the Age of
Microcomputer," Computers &
Security, June 1989, pp. 299-
302.

Key Words: risk, PC,
management, techniques,
methods.

HRU-88
Hruska, J., and K. Jackson
The PC Security Guide 88/89,
Elsevier Advanced Technology,
New York, NY, 1988.

Key Words: PC, guidelines.

HUT-88
Hutt, A.E., et al., (Eds.),
Computer Security Handbook,
McMillan Publishing Co., New
York, 1988.

Key Words: book, general,
methods, techniques,
guidelines.

IBM-84
Good Security Practices for
Dial-Up Systems, G320-0690-
0, IBM Corporation, White
Plains, NY, March 1984.

Key Words: techniques,
methods.

IBM-84a
Good Security Practices for Personal Computers, G320-9280-0, IBM Corporation, White Plains, NY, March 1984.

Key Words: PC, techniques.

IBM-85
Information Systems Security: Executive Checklist, GX20-2430, IBM Corporation, White Plains, NY, 1985.

Key Words: guidelines, methods.

IBM-86
Control Planning for Catastrophic Events in Data Processing Centers, G320-6729, IBM Corporation, White Plains, NY, 1986.

Key Words: contingency, recovery, management.

IEE-87
Proceedings, COMPASS '87: Computer Assurance, Washington, DC, June 1987, IEEE Publishing Service, New York, 1987.

Key Words: proccedings, general.

IEE-88
Proceedings, COMPASS '88: Computer Assurance, Gaithersburg, MD, June 1988, IEEE Publishing Service, New York, 1988.

Key Words: proceedings, general.

IEE-89
Proceedings, COMPASS '89: 4th Annual Conference on Computer Assurance, Gaithersburg, MD, June 1989, IEEE Publishing Service, New York, 1989.

Key Words: proceedings, general.

ISA-83
Isaacson, G.I. "A Guide to Commercial BackupServices," Computer Security Journal, Spring 1983, pp. 51-69.

Key Words: contingency, recovery.

JAC-81
Jacobson, R.V. "Analyzing the Limits of Risk," Government Data Systems, Nov.-Dec., 1981, pp. 28-29.

Key Words: risk, management.

JAC-81a
Jacobson, R.V. "Optimizing Disaster Recovery Planning," Proceedings, Honeywell Computer Security and Privacy Symposium, April 1981, pp. 95-100.

Key Words: contingency, recovery.

JAC-86
Jackson, C.B. "Making Time for DP Risk Analysis," Security World, March 1986, pp. 68-70.

Key Words: risk, management.

JAC-86a
Jackson, C.B. "Data Processing Risk Analysis: Beneficial or Unnecessary?" ISSA Newsletter, July/August/September 1986, pp. 6-8.

Key Words: risk, management.

JAC-88
Jacobson, R.V. "IST/RAMP and CRITI-CALC: Risk Managemnt Tools," Proc. Comp. Sec. Risk Manag. Model Builders Workshop, 1988 (2: NBS-88), pp. 73-87.

Key Words: risk, techniques, methods.

JAE-84
Jaehne, E.M. "Security and Productivity," Proc. IFIP/Sec. '84, Toronto, 1984, (2: FIN-85), pp. 107-111.

Key Words: management, methods.

JAN-81
Jancura, E.G., and R. Boos Establishing Controls and Auditing the Computerized Accounting System, Van Nostrand, New York, 1981.

Key Words: book, auditing, methods, management.

JAR-83
Jarvis, M. "Designing Security into the Computer Environment," Assets Protection, March/April 1983, pp. 9-12.

Key Words: management, methods.

JOH-80
Johnson, K.P. and R.H. Jaenicke Evaluating Internal Control: Concepts, Guidelines, Documentation, J. Wiley & Sons, New York, 1980.

Key Words: book, control, methods.

JOH-83a
Johnson, T.W. "Auditing DOS/VSE System Software," EDPACS, January 1983, pp. 1-14.

Key Words:

JOH-88
Johnson, H.L., and J.D. Layne "Modeling Security Risk in Networks," Proc. 11th Natl. Comp. Sec. Conf. (5: NCS-88), 1988, pp. 59-64.

Key Words:

JOH-88a
Johnson, H.L.
"Security Protection Based on Mission Criticality," Proc. 4th Aerospace Comp. Sec. Conf. (4: IEE-88b), 1988, pp. 228-232.

Key Words: risk, requirements.

JOS-88
Joseph, M.K., and A.A. Avizienis
"A Fault-Tolerance Approach to Computer Viruses," Proc. 1988 IEEE Symp. on Sec. & Privacy, (5: IEE-88a), pp. 52-58.

Key Words: virus, techniques.

JUD-87
Judd, T.C., and H.W. Ward, Jr.
"Return to Normalcy: Issues in Contingency Planning," Proc. 10th Natl. Comp. Sec. Conf., (5: NCS-87a), 1987, pp. 379-383.

Key Words: contingency, recovery, management.

JUI-89
Juitt, D.
"Security Assurance Through System Management," Proc. 12th Natl. Comp. Sec. Conf., (5: NCS089), 1989, pp. 418-422.

Key Words: methods, management.

KAR-85
Karabin, S.J.
"Data Classification for Security and Control," EDPACS, December 1985, pp. 1-20.

Key Words: guidelines, management.

KAR-88
Karrent, D.T.
"Typical System Access Control Problems and Solutions," Information Age (U.K.), January 1989, pp. 41045.

Key Words: guidelines, methods.

KEA-86
Kearby, D.B.
"Personnel Policies Procedures and Practices: Key to Computer Security," Computer Security Journal, Vol. 4, No. 1, pp. 63-68, 1986.

Key Words: policy, personnel, management, methods.

KEE-88
Keenan, T.
"Emerging Vulnerabilities in Office Automation Security," Proc. IFIP/Sec. '83, Stockholm, 1983, (2: FAK-83), pp. 139-145.

Key Words: vulnerabilities.

KIN-86
Kinnon, A., and R.H. Davis
"Audit and Security Implications of Electronic Funds Transfer," Computers & Security, March 1986, pp. 17-23.

Key Words: auditing, requirements.

KNE-83
Kneeer, D.C., and J.C. Lampe
"Distributed Data Processing: Internal Control Issues and Safeguards," EDPACS, June 1983, pp. 1-14.

Key Words: control, methods.

KOB-89
Kobus, P. Jr., and G.H. Rovin
"C-Guard Computer Security Systems," Information Age, (U.K.), January 1989, pp. 41-45.

Key Words: policy, techniques.

KOC-84
Koch, H.S.
"Auditing On-Line Systems: An Evaluation of Parallell vs. Continuous and Intermittent Simulation," Computers & Security, February 1984, pp. 9-20,

Key Words: auditing, methods.

KRA-80
Krauss, L.I.
SAFE: Security Audit and Field Evaluation for Computer Facilities and Information Systems, Amacom, New York, 1980.

Key Words: book, auditing, methods.

KUH-86
Kuhn, J.
"Research Toward Intrusion Detection Through Automated Abstraction of Audit Data," Proc. 9th Natl. Comp. Sec. Conf. (5: NCS-86), 1986, pp. 204-208

Key Words: auditing, methods.

KUO-82
Kuong, J.F.
Audit and Control of Computerized Systems, Management Advisory Publications, Wellesley Hills, MA, 1983.

Key Words: book, auditing, control

KUO-83
Kuong, J.F.
Controls for Advanced/On-Line/Database Systems, Management Advisory Publications, Wellesley Hills, MA, 1983.

Key Words: book, control, general.

KUO-85

Kuong, J.F.
"What to Look for When Auditing Your Company's EDP Contingency and Recovery Plan for Business Continuity," COM-AND, Computer Audit News & Developments, September-October, 1985.

Key Words: auditing, guidelines, contingency, recovery.

KUO-85a

Kuong, J.F.
"Evolution of Information Processing Technology, and Deficiencies in the Present Internal Control Methodologies," COM-AND, Computer Audit News & Developments, November-December, 1985.

Key Words: control, methods.

KUO-86

Kuong, J.F.
"Reducing Your Audit Risk Level and Improving Audit Option Reliability when Auditing Computer Based Systems," COM-AND, Computer Audit News & Developments, January-February, 1986.

Key Words: auditing, risk, methods.

KUO-86a

Kuong, J.F.
"Towards a Unified View to the Building and Assessing of Internal Control in Computerized Systems," COM-AND, Computer Audit News & Developments, March-April, 1986.

Key Words: control, policy.

KUO-86b

Kuong, J.F.
"What Are EDP Audit Test Objectives, and How to Develop Them," COM-AND, Computer Audit News & Developments, July-August, 1986.

Key Words: auditing, policy, methods, management.

KUO-86c

Kuong, J.F.
"Pinpointing Areas of High Exposure for Effective Safeguards," COM-SAC, Computer Security, Auditing & Controls, Volume 13, No. 1, 1986, pp. A1-A4.

Key Words: risk, vulnerabilities, methods, management.

KUO-88

Kuong, J.F.
"Computer Viruses: Should the Audit and Security Professional Be Concerned?," COM-AND, Computer Audit News and Developments, No. 3, 1988, pp. 1-4.

Key Words: virus, auditing, threats.

KUO-89

Kuong, J.F.
"Test Approaches and Techniques for Testing EDP Disaster Recovery Provisions," COM-AND, Computer Audit News and Developments, No. 2, 1989, pp. 1-7.

Key Words: contingency, recovery, management.

KUR-86

Kurzban, S.A.
"Computer System Defenses" ACM Security, Audit & Control Rev., Winter 1986, pp. 1-27.

Key Words: methods, techniques.

LAN-85

Lane, V., and J. Step
"The Formidable - If Not Insurmountable - Organizational Problems in Disaster Recovery Planning," Proc. IFIP/Sec. '84, Toronto, 1984, (2: FIN-85), pp. 361-369.

Key Words: contingency, recovery, management.

LAP-86

Lapid, Y., N. Ahituv, and S. Neumann
"Approaches to Handling 'Trojan Horse' Threats," Computers & Security, September 1986, pp. 251-256.

Key Words: threats, techniques.

LEC-83

Lechter, M.A.
"Protecting Software and Firmware Development," IEEE Computer, September 1983, pp. 73-82.

Key Words: methods, management.

LEE-88

Lee, W.
"Automation of Internal Control Evaluation," Proc. IFIP/Sec. '88, Australia, 1989, (2: CAE-89), pp. 391-406.

Key Words: control, management.

LIT-81

Litecky, C.R., and L.E. Rittenberg
"The External Auditor's Review of Computer Controls," Communications of the ACM, May 1981, pp. 289-295.

Key Words: auditing, controls.

LOB-80
  Lobel, J.
  "Risk Analysis in the 1980s,"
  Proceedings, 1980 National
  Computer Conference, AFIPS
  Press, Reston, VA, 1980, pp.
  831-836.

  Key Words: risk,
  management.

LOB-89
  Lobel, J.
  "Managing Information
  Security in the Space Age,"
  Information Age (U.K.),
  September 1989, pp. 195-198.

  Key Words: management,
  policy.

LOT-80
  Lott, R.W.
  Auditing the Data Processing
  Functions, Amacom, New
  York, 1980.

  Key Words: auditing,
  methods.

LUN-89
  Lunt, T.F.
  "Real Time Intrusion
  Detection," Proceedings,
  IEEE Compcon Spring, 1989,
  pp. 348-353.

  Key Words: methods,
  techniques.

MAL-83
  Malvik, C.
  "Security and the Home
  Computer," Information Age
  (UK), April 1983, pp. 87-90.

  Key Words: requirements,
  PC.

MAR-83
  Mar, S.
  "Long Range Planning for
  EDP Audits," COM-SAC:
  Computer Security, Auditing,
  and Control, January 1983,
  pp. A1-A8.

  Key Words: auditing,
  management.

MAR-84
  Mar, S.
  "EDP Security & EDP Audit
  Team Work," COM-SAC,
  Computer Security, Auditing
  and Control, January 1984,
  pp. A1-A4.

  Key Words: auditing,
  methods.

MAU-84
  Maude, T., and D. Maude
  "Hardware Protection Against
  Software Piracy,"
  Communications of the ACM,
  September 1984, pp. 950-959.

  Key Words: software piracy.

MAY-87
  Mayerfield, H.N., et al.
  "M2 RX: Model Based Risk
  Assessment Expert," AIAA
  No. 87-3080, Proc. 3d
  Aerosp. Comp. Sec. Conf. (5:
  IEE-87b), 1987, pp. 87-92.

  Key Words: risk,
  management.

MCA-89
  McAfee, J.D.
  "Managing the Virus Threat,"
  Computerworld, February 13,
  1989, pp. 89-96.

  Key Words: virus, threats,
  management.

MCC-85
  McCormack, W.G., III
  "The Audit of EDP Backup,"
  EDPACS, November 1985,
  pp. 1-5.

  Key Words: auditing,
  contingency.

MEN-85
  Menkus, B.
  "The EDP Auditor's Role in
  Computer Security,"
  Computers & Security, June
  1985, pp. 135-138.

  Key Words: auditing,
  methods.

MEN-85a
  Menkus, B.
  "The Impacts of the Bell
  System Breakup on DP
  Disaster Recovery Planning,"
  Computers & Security,
  September 1985, pp. 219-222.

  Key Words: contingency,
  recovery, management.

MEY-83
  Meyer, M.M.
  "Checking References: It's
  Worth the Investment,"
  Security Management, March
  1983, pp. 10+.

  Key Words: personnel,
  methods. management.

MIC-83
  "Microcomputers: A Checklist
  of Security and Recovery
  Considerations," Assets
  Protection, May/June 1983, pp.
  15-16.

  Key Words: guidelines, PC,

MIG-87
  Migues, S.
  "A Guide to Effective Risk
  Management," AIAA No. 87-
  3078, Proc. 3d Aerospace
  Comp. Sec. Conf. (5: IEE-
  87b), 1987, pp. 66-86.

  Key Words: risk, guidelines.

MIL-85
  Miller, J.E.
  "Transaction Controls: Steps to
  Take After the Equipment Has
  Been Secured," Computers &
  Security, June 1985, pp. 139-
  141.

  Key Words: control,
  guidelines.

MOE-88
  Moeller, R.
  "Considering Security when
  Auditing Applications Under
  Development," Proc. IFIP/Sec.
  '88, Australia, 1989, (2: CAE-
  89), pp. 245-262.

  Key Words: auditing, methods.

MOL-84
Molnar, L.
"Disaster Recovery Testing,"
EDPACS, November 1984,
pp. 1-6.

Key Words: contingency,
recovery.

MOR-81
Morrison, R.M.
"Advanced Audit Concepts
for A Distributed System,"
Proceedings, Honeywell
Security and Privacy
Symposium, April 1981, pp.
119-127.

Key Words: auditing,
methods.

MOU-84
Moulton, R.T.
"Data Security Is A
Management Responsibility,"
Computers & Security,
February 1984, pp. 3-8.

Key Words: management,
policy.

MOU-84a
Moulton, R.T.
"A Practical Approach to
System Security Devices,"
Computers & Security, May
1984, pp. 93-100.

Key Words: techniques,
methods.

MOU-86
Moulton, R.T.
Computer Security Handbook:
Strategies and Techniques for
Preventing Data Loss or
Theft, Prentice-Hall, Inc.
Englewood Cliffs, NJ, 1985

Key Words: book, guidelines,
techniques, methods.

MUR-80
Murray, W.H.
"Good Security Practices,"
EDPACS, October 1980, pp.
1-6.

Key Words: methods,
techniques.

MUR-81
Murray, J.P.
"Protecting Corporate Data
with Off-Site Vault Storage,"
Computerworld, March 16,
1981, pp. ID/1-ID/24.

Key Words: contingency,
recovery.

MUR-82
Murray, J.P.
"Contingency Planning,"
Computerworld, May 10,
1982, pp. ID/36-ID/44.

Key Words: contingency,
recovery.

MUR-83
Murray, W.H.
"Good Computer Security
Practices for Two Areas of
Current Concern: Personal
Computers and Dial-Up
Systems," Computer Security
Journal, Fall/Winter 1983, pp.
77-88.

Key Words: techniques,
methods, PC.

MUR-83a
Murray, W.H.
"Computer Security:
Observations on the State of
the Technology," Computers
& Security, January 1983, pp.
16-23.

Key Words: techniques,
methods.

MUR-84
Murray, J.P.
"Surviving (and Profiting
from) the Audit: Manager's
View," Computerworld,
September 24, 1984, pp.
ID/13-23.

Key Words: auditing,
management.

MUR-84a
Murray, W.H.
"Security Considerations for
Personal Computers," IBM
Systems Journal, Vol. 23, No.
3, 1983, pp. 297-304.

Key Words: requirements, PC.

NAN-86
Nancekivell, B.D.
"Auditing IBM System/38
Security," EDPACS, January
1986, pp. 1-10.

Key Words: auditing, methods.

NBS-81
Guidelines for ADP
Contingency Planning, FIPS
PUB 87, National Bureau of
Standards, Gaithersburg, MD,
27 March 1981.

Key Words: contingency,
recovery, guidelines.

NBS-83
Guidelines for Life Cycle
Validation, Verification and
Testing of Computer Software,
FIPS PUB 101, National
Bureau of Standards,
Gaithersburg, MD, 1983.

Key Words: guidelines,
software.

NBS-83a
Guidelines for Computer
Security Certification and
Accreditation, FIPS PUB 102,
National Bureau of Standards,
Gaithersburg, MD, September
27, 1983.

Key Words: guidelines,
methods, certification.

NBS-88
Proceedings, 1988 Computer
Security Risk Management
Model Builders Workshop,
National Bureau of Standards
et al., Denver, CO, May 24-
26, 1988

Key Words: proceedings, risk.

NES-85
Nesbit, I.S.
"On Thin Ice: Micros and
Data Integrity," Datamation,
November 1, 1985, pp. 80-84.

Key Words: integrity, PC.

NEU-82
> Neugent, W.
> "Acceptance Criteria for
> Computer Security,"
> Proceedings, 1982 National
> Computer Conference, AFIPS
> Press, Reston, VA, 1982, pp.
> 441-448.
>
> Key Words: guidelines,
> methods.

NOL-85
> Nolan, M.
> "Disaster Recovery for
> Online Systems," Proc.
> IFIP/Sec. '84, Toronto, 1984,
> (2: FIN-85), pp. 163-174.
>
> Key Words: contingency,
> revovery.

ORL-88
> Orlandi, E.
> "Computer Security:
> Operational or Investment
> Cost," Proc. IFIP/Sec. '88,
> Australia, 1989, (2: CAE-89),
> pp. 381-390.
>
> Key Words: management,
> methods.

OTW-89
> Otwell, K., and B. Aldridge
> "The Role of Vulnerability in
> Risk Management," Proc. 5th
> Security Applicat. Conf., (4:
> IEE-89c), 1989, pp. 32-38.
>
> Key Words: vulnerabilities,
> risk.

PAR-81
> Parker, D.B.
> Computer Security
> Management, Reston
> Publishing Co., Reston, VA,
> 1981.
>
> Key Words: book, risk,
> management.

PAR-84
> Parker, D.B.
> "Safeguard Selection
> Principles," Computers &
> Security, May 1984, pp. 81-
> 92.
>
> Key Words: guidelines,
> methods.

PAS-86
> Passori, A.
> "Contingency Planning
> Options Protect Corporate
> Data Assets," Computerworld,
> January 27, 1986, pp. 73-74.
>
> Key Words: contingency,
> recovery, management,
> methods.

PED-86
> Pedigo, J.
> "Disaster Recovery: Making
> Plans That Could Save Your
> Company," Computerworld,
> May 12, 1986, pp. 49-60.
>
> Key Words: contingency,
> recovery, management.

PER-80
> Perry, W.E.
> Controls in Data Base
> Environment, Q.E.D.
> Information Systems,
> Wellesley Hills, MA, 1980.
>
> Key Words: book, control,
> database.

PER-80a
> Perry, W.E.
> How to Test Internal Control
> and Integrity in Computerized
> Systems, Management
> Advisory Publications,
> Wellesley Hills, MA, 1980.
>
> Key Words: book, control,
> integrity.

PER-80b
> Perry, W.E.
> Selecting ADP Audit Areas,
> EDP Auditors Foundation,
> Altamonte Springs, FL, 1980.
>
> Key Words: auditing,
> guidelines.

PER-80c
> Management Guide to
> Computer Security, J. Wiley
> & Sons, New York, 1980.
>
> Key Words: book, guidelines,
> methods.

PER-81
> Perley, E.H.
> "Optimizing the EDP Security
> Function," EDPACS, April
> 1981, pp. 1-11.
>
> Key Words: management,
> policy.

PER-81a
> Perry, W.E.
> Computer Control and
> Security, J. Wiley & Sons,
> New York, 1981.
>
> Key Words: book, control,
> methods.

PER-82
> Perry, W.E.
> "Developing Computer
> Security and Control Strategy,"
> Computers & Security, January
> 1982, pp. 17-26.
>
> Key Words: control,
> management.

PER-82a
> Perry, W.E. and J.F. Kuong
> EDP Risk Analysis and
> Controls, Management
> Advisory Publications,
> Wellesley Hills, MA, 1982.
>
> Key Words: book, risk,
> controls.

PER-82b
> Perry, W.E., and J.F. Kuong
> Effective Computer Audit
> Practices -- ECAP MAnual,
> Management Advisory
> Publications, Wellesley Hills,
> MA, 1982.
>
> Key Words: book, auditing,
> methods.

PER-82c
Perry, W.E., and J.F. Kuong
Generalized Computer Audit
Software: Selection and
Application, Management
Advisory Publications,
Wellesley Hills, MA, 1982.

Key Words: book, auditing,
software, guidelines, methods.

PER-82d
Perry, W.E. and J.F. Kuong
How to Test Internal Control
and Integrity in Computerized
Systems, Management
Advisory Publications,
Wellesley Hills, MA, 1982.

Key Words: book, control,
guidelines.

PER-83
Perry, W.E.
Ensuring Data Base Integrity,
J. Wiley & Sons, New York,
1983.

Key Words: book, integrity,
methods.

PHE-86
Phelps, N.L.
"Top Management's Role in
Disaster Recovery," Data
Processing &
Communications Security,
Summer 1986, pp. 16-19.

Key Words: contingency,
recovery, policy,
management.

PIC-84
Pickard, W.V.
"EDP Benefits Control -- A
Management Function,"
EDPACS, February 1984, pp.
1-5.

Key Words: control,
management, policy.

POR-81
Porter, W.T., and W.E. Perry
EDP Controls and Auditing,
3d Ed., Kent Publishing,
Boston, MA, 1981.

Key Words: book, auditing,
methods, control, techniques.

PRA-85
Prause, P.N., and
G.I. Isaacson
"Protecting Personal
Computers: A Checklist
Approach," Computer Security
Journal, Winter 1985, pp. 13-
24.

Key Words: guidelines, PC.

PRE-89
Preston, C.M.
"Artificial intelligence Applied
to Information System
Security," Information Age
(U.K.), September 1989, pp.
217-221.

Key Words: methods,
techniques.

PRI-80
Prichard, J.
"Computer Security and
Unionization," Information
Privacy (UK), March 1980,
pp. 69-74.

Key Words: personnel,
management.

PRI-84
Prigge, E.
"Security and Integrity Issues
in End-User Computing,"
Computer Security, Auditing
& Controls, October 1984, pp.
A7+.

Key Words: awareness,
requirements, integrity.

PRU-86
Pryijm, R.A.M.
"The Audit of Software
Maintenance," EDPACS,
August 1986, pp. 1-5.

Key Words: auditing,
software.

PWA-84
Managing Computer Risks: A
Guide for the Policymaker,
Price Waterhouse, Inc., 1984.

Key Words: book, risk,
threats, magagement,
guidelines.

QUA-89
Quant, H.
"Virus vs. Vaccine,"
Information Age, April 1989,
pp. 138-143.

Key Words: virus, techniques.

RAO-89
Rao, K.N.
"Security Audit for Embedded
Avionics Systems," Proc. 5th
Security Applicat. Conf., (4:
IEE-89c), 1989, pp. 78-84.

Key Words: auditing, methods.

RAT-84
Rattner, J.
"Security Controls in a
Manufacturing Applications
System," TeleSystems Journal,
March/April 1984, pp. 33-37.

Key Words: controls, methods.

RCM-82
EDP Threat Assessment
Concepts and Planning Guide,
SIP No.2, Royal Canadian
Mounted Police, Ottawa,
January 1982.

Key Words: book, guidelines,
threats, risk.

RIC-86
Richards, R.M., and
J. Yestingsmeier
"Risk Management -- A Key
to Security in Electronic Funds
Transfer Systems," Computers
& Security, June 1986, pp.
135-140.

Key Words: risk, management,
methods.

RID-86
Riddle, C., and J. Austin
"Updating Security, Auditing
and Quality Assurance -- The
Dedicated On-Line Computer
Security Monitor," COM-SAC,
Computer Security, Auditing &
Controls, Volume 13, No. 1,
1986, pp. A5-A6.

Key Words: auditing, methods.

ROB-83
Roberts, M.B.
EDP Controls: A Guide for EDP Auditors and Accountants, J. Wiley & Sons, New York, 1983.

Key Words: book, auditing.

ROD-81
Rodgers, G.L.
"Auditor's Watchdog Role in Computer Fraud," Commercial Law Journal, May 1981, pp. 172-178.

Key Words: auditing, crime.

RUB-85
Rubin, H.
"Patient Auditing with Potent Results," Security Audit & Control Review, Winter 1985, pp. 4-9.

Key Words: auditing, methods.

RUL-80
Rullo, T.A. (Ed.)
Advances in Computer Security Management, Vol. 1, Heyden & Son, Philadelphia, 1980.

Key Words: book, management.

RUT-80
Ruthberg, Z.G. (Ed.)
Audit and Evaluation of Computer Security II: System Vulnerabilities and Controls Workshop Report, SP 500-57, National Bureau of Standards, Gaithersburg, MD, April 1980.

Key Words: proceedings, auditing.

RUT-84
Ruthberg, Z.G., and W. Neugent
Overview of Computer Security Certification and Accreditation, SP 500-109, National Bureau of Standards, Gaithersburg, MD, April 1984.

Key Words: certification, methods.

RUT-86
Ruthberg, Z., and B. Fisher (Eds.)
Work Priority Scheme for EDP Audit and Computer Security NBSIR 86-3386, National Bureau of Standards, Gaithersburg, MD, March 1986.

Key Words:

SAA-89
Saari, J., and D.B. Parker
"New Baseline Methodology Applied to Reviewing Security Experiences from USA and Finland," Information Age (U.K.), September 1989, pp. 195-198.

Key Words: awareness, methods, international.

SAR-81
Sardinas, J.L., Jr., et al.
EDP Auditing Primer, J. Wiley & Sons, New York, 1981.

Key Words: book, auditing.

SAR-82
Sardinas, J.L., and R.J. Asebrook
"Bridging the Gap Between DP Professionals and Auditors," Computer Security Journal, Winter 1982, pp. 91-97.

Key Words: auditing, personnel.

SCH-80
Schweitzer, J.A.
"Policy Structure Gives the Basis for An Effective Security Program," Security Management, December 1980, pp. 18-25.

Key Words: policy, management.

SCH-80a
Schweitzer, J.A.
"Personal Computing and Data Security," Security World, June 1980, pp. 30-35.

Key Words: guidelines, PC.

SCH-81
Schweitzer, J.A.
"Computing Security Risk Analysis -- Is It Worth It?," Security Management, August 1981, pp. 104-106.

Key Words: risk, management.

SCH-82
Schweitzer, J.A.
Managing Information Security -- A Program for the Electronic Information Age, Butterworth, Woburn, MA, 1982.

Key Words: book, policy, management, methods.

SCH-82a
Schmitt, W.R.
"Data Security Program Development: An Overview," Computer Security Journal, Winter 1982, pp. 23-29.

Key Words: policy, management.

SCH-83
Schweitzer, J.A.
Protecting Information in the Electronic Workplace: A Guide to the Managers, Reston Publish., Reston, VA, 1983.

Key Words: book, guidelines, methods, management.

SCH-83a
Schmidt, P.
"Evaluating Backup
Services," Data Mangement,
July 1983, pp. 30+.

Key Words: contingency,
recovery.

SCH-84
Schweitzer, J.A.
"Personal Workstation
Automation Security
Vulnerabilities," Computers &
Security, February 1984, pp.
21-28.

Key Words: vulnerabilities,
PC.

SHA-82
Shaw, J.K., and S.W. Katzke
Executive Guide to ADP
Contingency Planning, SP
500-85, National Bureau of
Standards, Gaithersburg, MD,
January 1982.

Key Words: contingency,
guidelines, recovery,
management.

SIL-83
Silverman, M.E.
"Contingency Planning: The
Backup Site Decision,"
Computer Security Journal,
Spring 1983, pp. 43-50.

Key Words: contingency,
recovery, management,
methods.

SIZ-89
Sizer, R.
"Computer Security -- A
Pragmatic Approach for
Managers," Information Age
(U.K.), January 1989, pp. 88-
97.

Key Words: policy,
management guidelines.

SKU-84
Skundra, V.J., and
F.J. Lackner
"The Implementation of
Concurrent Audit Techniques
in Advanced EDP Systems,"
EDPACS, April 1984, pp. 1-
10.

Key Words: auditing,
techniques.

SMI-80
Smith, J.E.
"Risk Management for Small
Computer Installations," in
Rullo, T.A. (Ed.), Advances
in Computer Security
Management, Vol. 1, Heyden,
Philadelphia, 1980, pp. 3-32.

Key Words: risk,
management, methods.

SNO-84
Snow, M.
"The First-Time EDP Audit,"
EDPACS, February 1984, pp.
6-8.

Key Words: auditing,
guidelines.

SNO-87
Snow, D., and R.J. Aguilar
"A Mission Driven Process
for the Risk Management of
ADP Systems," AIAA No.
87-3077, Proc. 3d Aerospace
Comp. Sec. Conf., (5: IEE-
87b), 1987, pp. 184-154.

Key Words: risk,
management, techniques,
methods.

SOB-84
Sobol, M.I.
"Data Communications Primer
for Auditors," EDPACS,
March 1984, pp. 1-5.

Key Words: auditing,
networks, methods.

SOC-83
Socha, W.J.
"The Auditor's Own
Microcomputer," EDPACS,
December 1983, pp. 5-15.

Key Words: auditing, methods,
PC.

SRI-81
Srinivasan, C.A., and
P.E. Dascher
"Computer Security and
Integrity: Problems and
Prospects," Infosystems, May
1981, pp. 116-123.

Key Words: awareness,
integrity, requirements,
methods.

STC-83
St.Clair, L.
"Security for Small Computer
Systems," EDPACS, November
1983, pp. 1-10.

Key Words: awareness,
methods, PC.

STE-84
Steinauer, D.D.
"Security of Personal
Computers: A Growing
Concern," Computer Security
Journal, Summer 1984, pp. 33-
42.

Key Words: awareness, PC,
methods, requirements, policy.

STO-80
Stokel, K.J.
"How to Audit Library Control
Software," EDPACS, May
1980, pp. 1-10.

Key Words: auditing,
guidelines.

STR-82
Streeter, B.
"People, More than the
Technology Are Still Key to
EFT Security," ABA Banking
Journal, July 1982, pp. 32-37.

Key Words: personnel, threats.

TAL-81
Talbot, J.R.
<u>Management Guide to</u>
<u>Computer Security</u>, Halsted
Press/J. Wiley & Sons, New
York, 1981.

Key Words: book,
management, guidelines.

TEA-84
Teas, H.
"Self-Audit of Microcomputer
Controls," <u>EDPACS</u>,
December 1984, pp. 1-6.

Key Words: auditing, PC,
methods.

TIN-89
Ting, T.C.
"Application of Information
Security Semantics: A Case
of Mental Health Delivery,"
<u>Proc. IFIP WG 11.3 (Data</u>
<u>base) Workshop</u> (6: IFI-89),
1989.

Key Words: methods,
database.

TOD-89
Todd, M.A., and C. Guitian
<u>Computer Security Training</u>
<u>Guidelines</u>, SP 500-172,
National Institute of
Standards and Technology,
Gaithersburg, MD, November
1989.

Key Words: awareness,
guidelines.

TOI-87
Toigo, J.W.
<u>Disaster Recovery Planning:</u>
<u>Managing Risk and</u>
<u>Catastrophe in Information</u>
<u>Systems</u>, Yourdan Press,
Englewood Cliffs, NJ, 1987

Key Words: risk, recovery.

TOM-86
Tomkins, F.G., and R.Rice
"Integrating Security Activities
into the Software
Development Life Cycle and
the Software Quality
Assurance Process,"
<u>Computers & Security</u>,
September 1986, pp. 218-242.

Key Words: management,
software.

TOP-84
Toppen, R.
"Infinite Confidence: The
Audit of Communication
Networks" <u>Computers &</u>
<u>Security</u>, November 1984, pp.
303-313.

Key Words: auditing,
networks.

TRO-84
Troy, G.
"Thwarting the Hackers,"
<u>Datamation</u>, July 1, 1984.

Key Words: hackers,
techniques.

TRO-86
Troy, E.F.
<u>Security for Dial-Up Lines</u>,
SP 500-137, National Bureau
of Standards, Gaithersburg,
MD, 1986.

Key Words: techniques,
network.

VAN-85
van Eck, W.
"Electromagnetic Radiation
from Video Display Units: An
Eavesdropping Risk?,"
<u>Computers & Security</u>,
December 1985, pp. 269-286

Key Words: threats,
vulnerabilities.

VAN-87
Van Meter, S.D., and
J.D. Veatch
"Space Station Program Threat
and Vulnerability Analysis,"
AIAA No. 87-3082, <u>Proc. 3d</u>
<u>Aerospace Comp. Sec. Conf.</u>,
(5: IEE-87b), 1987, pp. 104-
107.

Key Words: threats,
vulnerabilities.

VDB-84
vd Berg, B., and H. Leenaars
"Advanced Topics on
Computer Center Auditing,"
<u>Computers & Security</u>, October
1984, pp. 171-185.

Key Words: auditing, methods.

VOU-88
Vouitilainen, R.
"Experience in the Use of the
SBA Vulnerability Analysis for
Improving Computer Security
in Finland," <u>Proc. IFIP/Sec.</u>
<u>'88</u>, Australia, 1988, (2: CAE-
89), pp. 263-271.

Key Words: risk, international.

WAC-89
Wack, J.P., and L.J. Carnahan
<u>Computer Viruses and Related</u>
<u>Threats: A Management Guide</u>,
SP 500-166, National Institute
of Standards and Technology,
Gaithersburg, MD, August
1989.

Key Words: viruses,
guidelines.

WAD-82
Wade, J.R.
"The Basics of EDP Risk
Assessment," <u>Security</u>
<u>Management</u>, March 1982, pp.
56-70.

Key Words: risk, management.

WAI-84
Wainwright, O.O.
"Security Management of the
Future," <u>Security Management</u>,
March 1984, pp. 47-51.

Key Words: management,
policy.

WAR-81
Wardlaw, J.
"Pattern Matching for EDP Auditors," EDPACS, March 1981, pp. 1-12.

Key Words: auditing, techniques.

WAR-83
Warren, A.D.
"Evaluating Risks of Computer Fraud and Error," Computers & Security, June 1983, pp. 231-143.

Key Words: risks, techniques.

WAR-83a
Ward, G.
"Micros Pose Mainframe Size Security Problems," Data Mangement, July 1983, pp. 38+

Key Words: vulnerabilities, PC.

WAR-84
Ward, G.M, and R.D. Paterson
"Surviving (and Profiting from) the Audit: Auditors View," Computerworld, September 24, 1984, pp. ID/13-18.

Key Words: auditing, management.

WAR-84a
Warren, A.
"Auditing Computer Systems," Information Resource Management, (UK), March 1984, pp. 36-39.

Key Words: auditing, methods.

WAR-86
Ward, G.M., and J.D. Harris
Managing Computer Risk: A Guide for the Policymaker, J. Wiley & Sons, Inc., 1986.

Key Words: book, risk, methods, guidelines, management.

WEB-81
Weber, R.
EDP Auditing: Conceptual Foundations and Practice, McGraw-Hill, Highstown, NJ, 1981.

Key Words: book, auditing, methods, techniques, management.

WHI-89
White, S.R. and D.M. Chess
Coping with Computer Viruses and Related Problems, RC 14405, IBM Thomas J. Watson Research Center, Yorktown, NY, January 30, 1989

Key Words: viruses, guidelines.

WIE-86
Wiesand, C.G.
"An Audit Approach to Microcomputers," EDPACS, May 1986, pp. 1-18.

Key Words: auditing, methods, PC.

WIL-84
Wilkes, M.V.
"Security Management and Protection: A Personal Approach," The Computer Journal (UK), February 1984, pp. 3-7.

Key Words: management, policy, methods, guidelines.

WIN-83
Winters, C.M.
"Auditing Data Communications Networks," EDPACS, August 1983, pp. 1-9.

Key Words: auditing, networks.

WIN-89
Winkler, J.R., and W.J. Page
"Intrusion and Anomaly Detection in Trusted Systems," Proc. 5th Security Applicat. Conf., (4: IEE-89c), 1989, pp. 39-45.

Key Words: auditing, threats, methods, techniques.

WOD-88
Woda, A.
"Ensuring Reliability and Integrity of Data in EDP Application Systems," COM-SAC, Computer Sec. Auditing & Control, No. 2, 1988, pp. A1-A6.

Key Words: integrity, methods.

WOF-83
Wofsey, M.M. (Ed.)
Advances in Computer Security Management, Vol. 2, J. Wiley & Sons, New York, 1983.

Key Words: book, general, methods, management, techniques.

WON-85
Wong, K.
"Computer Crime -- Risk Management and Computer Security," Computers & Security, December 1985, pp. 287-295.

Key Words: crime, risk, methods, management.

WON-86
Wong, K.
"The Risks Involved in Computerization," The Computer Law and Sec. Report, March-April 1986, pp. 15-18.

Key Words: threats, risks, laws.

WON-86a
Wong, K.
"Effective Computer Security Management," EDPACS, July 1986, pp. 7-10.

Key Words: management, methods.

WOO-83
Wood, C.C.
"Enhancing Information Security with the Information Resource Management Approach," Computers & Security, November 1983, pp. 223-229.

Key Words: management, methods.

WOO-84
Wood, M., and T. Elbra
System Design for Data Protection, National Computer Centre (UK), J. Wiley & Sons, Chichester, 1984.

Key Words: book, techniques.

WOO-85
Wood, C.C.
"Floppy Diskette Security Measures," Computers & Security, September 1985, pp. 223-228.

Key Words: techniques, PC.

WOO-86
Wood, C.C.
"Establishing Internal Technical System Security Standards," Computers & Security, June 1986, pp. 193-200.

Key Words: policy, guidelines, management.

WOO-86a
Wood, C.C.
"Quantitative Risk Analysis and Information System Security," Data Processing & Communications Security, Winter 1986, pp. 8-11.

Key Words: risk, techniques.

WOO-87
Wood, C.C., et al.
Computer Security: A Comprehensive Controls Checklist, J. Wiley & Sons, Somerset, NJ, 1987

Key Words: book, controls, methods, guidelines.

WYS-84
Wysong, E.M., and I. DeLotto
Information Systems Auditing. Proceedings, International Conference, Milan, 1983, North-Holland, Amsterdam, 1984.

Key Words: proceedings, auditing, methods, management.

YAR-84
Yarberry, W.A.
"Managing the EDP Audit Function - A Practical Approach," EDPACS, May 1984, pp. 6-8.

Key Words: auditing, management, personnel.

YAR-84a
Yarberry, W.A.
"Auditing the Change Control System," EDPACS, June 1984, pp. 1-5.

Key Words: auditing, methods, techniques.

YAR-84b
Yarberry, W.A.
"Audit Software: Eliminating the Middle Man," EDPACS, September 1984, pp. 1-4.

Key Words: auditing, software, methods.

3. Foundations

This section cites publications that emphasize fundamental principles, concepts, and models of computer security.

ADK-89
Adkins, M.M., et al.
"The Argus Security Model,"
Proc. 12th Natl. Comp. Sec.
Conf., (5: NCS-89), 1989,
pp. 123-134.

Key Words: models,
description.

BAD-89
Badger, L.
"A Model for Specifying
Multi-Granularity in Integrity
Policies," Proc. 1989 IEEE
Symp. on Sec. & Privacy, (5:
IEE-89b), pp. 269-277.

Key Words: models,
integrity, policy.

BEL-88
Bell, D.E.
"Concerning 'Modeling' of
Computer Security," Proc.
1988 IEEE Symp. on Sec. &
Privacy, (5: IEE-88a), pp. 8-
13.

Key Words: modeling,
theory, policy.

BEL-88a
Bell, D.E.
"Security Policy Modeling for
the Next-Generation Packet
Switch," Proc. 1988 IEEE
Symp. on Sec. & Privacy, (5:
IEE-88a), pp. 212-216.

Key Words: models, policy,
network.

BEN-89
Benson, G., W. Appelbe, and
I. Akyildiz
"The Hierarchical Model of
Distributed Systems Security,"
Proc. 1989 IEEE Symp. on
Sec. & Privacy, (5: IEE-89b),
pp. 194-203.

Key Words: model,
hierarchical, network.

BER-87
Berry, D.M.
"Towards a Formal Basis for
the Formal Development
Method and the InaJo
Specification Language," IEEE
Trans. on Software Engr.,
February 1987, pp. 184-200.

Key Words: formal,
specification.

BIS-81
Bishop, M.
"Hierarchical Take-Grant
Systems," Proceedings, 8th
ACM Symposium on
Operating System Principles,
December 1981, pp. 109-122.

Key Words: models, take-
grant.

BIS-88
Bishop, M.
"Theft of Information in the
Take-Grant Protection Model,"
Proc. Comp. Sec. Foundat.
Workshop, 1988, (3: CSF-88),
pp. 194-218.

Key Words: models, take-
grant.

BIS-89
Bishop, M.
"A Model of Security
Modeling," Proc. 5th Security
Applicat. Conf., (4: IEE-89c),
1989, pp. 46-52

Key Words: models, theory.

BOE-84
Boebert, W.E.
"On the Inability of an
Unmodified Capability
Machine to Enforce the -
Property," Proc. 7th Seminar,
DoD Comp. Sec. Progr., (5:
DOD-84), 1984, pp. 291-293.

Key Words: models, capability,
MLS

BOE-85
Boebert, W.E., and R.Y. Kain
"A Practical Alternative to
Hierarchical Integrity Policies,"
Proc. 8th National Comp. Sec.
Conf., (5: NCS-85), 1985, pp.
18-27.

Key Words: policy, integrity,
methods.

BOE-85a
Boebert, W.E., and
C.T. Ferguson
"A Partial Solution to the
Discretionary Trojan Horse
Problem," Proc. 8th Natl.
Comp. Sec. Conf., (5: NCS-
85), 1985, pp. 141-144.

Key Words: discretionary,
method.

BOE-86
Boebert, W.E., R.Y. Kain, and
W.D. Young
"The Extended Matrix Model
of Computer Security," ACM
Software Engr. Notes, August
1985, pp. 119-125.

Key Words: models, technique.

BOS-89
    Boshoff, W.H., and
    S.H. von Solms
    "A Path Context Model for
    Addressing Security in
    Potentially Non-Secure
    Environments," Computers &
    Security, August 1989, pp.
    417-425.

    Key Words: models, policy,
    methods.

BOT-83
    Bottom, N.R. Jr.
    "An Informational Theory of
    Security," Computers &
    Security, November 1983, pp.
    275-280.

    Key Words: models, theory.

BRE-89
    Brewer, D.F.C., and
    M.J. Nash
    "The Chinese Wall Security
    Policy," Proc. 1989 IEEE
    Symp. on Sec. & Privacy, (5:
    IEE-89b), pp. 206-214.

    Key Words: models, policy,
    theory.

BUD-83
    Budd, T.A.
    "Safety in Grammatical
    Protection Systems,"
    International Journal of
    Computer and Information
    Sciences, Vol. 12, No. 6,
    1987, pp. 413-431.

    Key Words: models, policy,
    safety.

BUR-88
    Burrows, M., R. Needham,
    and M. Abadi
    "Authentication: A Practical
    Study in Belief and Action,"
    Proceedings, 2nd Conference
    on Theoretical Aspects of
    Reasoning About Knowledge,
    Morgan Kaufmann
    Publishers, Los Altos, CA,
    1988, pp. 325-342.

    Key Words: proceedings,
    theory, authentication,
    methods.

BUR-89
    Burrows, M., M. Abadi, and
    R. Needham
    "A Logic of Authentication,"
    ACM Operating Systems
    Review, December 1989, pp.
    1-13.

    Key Words: authentication,
    theory.

CAR-84
    Carroll, J.M.
    "Intractable Problems in
    Computer Security,"
    Transnational Data Report,
    December 1984, pp. 472- 474.

    Key Words: theory, models,
    policy.

CHE-88
    Cheng, P.-C. and V.D.Cligor
    "A Model for Secure
    Distributed Computation in
    Heterogenous Environment,"
    Proc. 4th Aerospace Comp.
    Sec. Conf., (4: IEE-88b),
    1988, pp. 233-241.

    Key Words: model, networks.

CLA-87
    Clark, D.D., and D.R. Wilson
    "A Comparison of
    Commercial and Military
    Computer Security Policies,"
    Proc. 1987 IEEE Symp. on
    Sec. & Privacy, (5: IEE-87a),
    pp. 184-194.

    Key Words: models, policy,
    integrity.

CLA-88
    Clark, D.D. and D.R. Wilson
    "Evolution of a Model for
    Computer Integrity,"
    Postscript, 11th Natl. Comp.
    Sec. Conf., (5: NCS-88a),
    1988, pp. 14-27.

    Key Words: models, integrity.

COH-89
    Cohen, F.
    "Models of Practical Defenses
    Against Computer Viruses,"
    Computers & Security, April
    1989, pp. 149-160.

    Key Words: models, virus,
    methods.

CSF-88
    Proceedings, The Computer
    Security Foundations
    Workshop, Franconia, NH,
    June 1988, Report M88-37,
    The Mitre Corporation,
    October 1988.

    Key Words: proceedings,
    models, theory, methods.

DAS-89
    Dasher, D.N.
    "Modular Presentation of
    Hardware: Bounding the
    Reference Monitor Concept,"
    Proc. 12th Natl. Comp. Sec.
    Conf., (5: NCS-89), 1989, pp.
    591-600.

    Key Words: models, methods,
    MLS.

DIO-81
    Dion, L.C.
    "A Complete Protection
    Model," Proc. 1981 IEEE
    Symp. on Sec. & Privacy, (5:
    IEE-81), pp. 49-55.

    Key Words: models, theory.

DIV-88
    DiVito, B.L.
    "Derived Information
    Sensitivity as a Modeling
    Technique," Proc. Comp. Sec.
    Foundat. Workshop, 1988, (3:
    CSF-88).

    Key Words: models,
    techniques.

DOB-89
Dobson, J.E., and
J.A. McDermid
"A Framework for Expressing
Models of Security Policy,"
Proc. 1989 IEEE Symp. on
Sec. & Privacy, (5: IEE-89b),
pp. 229-239.

Key Words: models,
methods, general.

DOB-89a
Dobson, J.
"Conversational Structures as
a Means of Specifying
Security Policy," Proc. IFIP
WG 11.3 (Data Base)
Workshop, (6: IFI-89), 1989.

Key Words: specification,
methods.

ELO-85
Eloff, J.H.P.
"The Development of a
Specification Language for a
Computer Security System,"
Computers & Security, June
1985, pp. 143-147.

Key Words: specification,
methods.

FIN-89
Fine, T., et al.
"Noninterference and
Unwinding in LOCK," Proc.
Comp. Sec. Foundat.
Workshop II, 1989, (3: IEE-
89a), pp. 22-28.

Key Words: models,
inference, methods.

FOL-87
Foley, S.N.
"A Universal Theory of
Information Flow," Proc.
1987 IEEE Symp. on Sec. &
Privacy, (5: IEE-87a), pp.
116-121.

Key Words: models, theory,
flow.

FOL-89
Foley, S.N.
"A Model of Secure
Information Flow," Proc. 1989
IEEE Symp. on Sec. &
Privacy, (5: IEE-89b), pp.
248-258.

Key Words: models, theory,
flow.

FRE-88
Freeman, J., R. Neely, and
G. Dinolt
"An Internet System Security
Policy and Formal Model,"
Proc. 11th Natl. Comp.
Sec.Conf., (5: NCS-88), 1988,
pp. 10-19.

Key Words: model, formal,
network.

FUG-84
Fugini, M., and G. Martella
"ACTEN: A Conceptual
Model for Security Systems
Design," Computers &
Security, October 1984, pp.
196-214.

Key Words: model, theory.

FUG-87
Fugini, M.G., and G. Martella
"A Petri Net Model of Access
Control Mechanisms,"
Information Systems, Vol. 13,
No. 1, 1988.

Key Words: model, control.

GAS-89
Gasser, M.
"An Optimization for
Automated Information Flow
Analysis," IEEE Cipher, Jan.
1989, pp. 32-36.

Key Words: flow, techniques.

GLA-85
Glasgow, J.I., and
G.H. MacEwen
"A Two-Level Security Model
for a Secure Network," Proc.
8th Natl. Comp. Sec. Conf.,
(5: NCS-85), 1985, pp. 56-63.

Key Words: models, network.

GLA-87
Glasgow, J.J., and
G.H. McEwen
"The Development and Proof
of a Formal Specification for a
Multi-Level Secure System,"
ACM Trans. on Computing
Systems, Vol. 5, No.2, 1987,
pp. 151-184.

Key Words: formal,
specifications.

GLA-88
Glasgow, J.J., and
G.H. MacEwen
"Reasoning About Knowledge
in Multi-level Secure
Distributed Systems," Proc.
1988 IEEE Symp. on Sec. &
Privacy, (5: IEE-88a), pp. 122-
128.

Key Words: models, theory,
MLS.

GLA-88a
Glasgow, J., G.H. MacEwen,
and P. Panangaden
"Reasoning about Knowledge
and Permission in Secure
Distributed Systems," Proc.
Comp. Sec. Foundat.
Workshop, 1988, (3: CSF-88),
pp. 139-146.

Key Words: models, theory,
MLS.

GLA-89
Glasgow, J.I., and
G.H. MacEwen
"Obligation as the Basis of
Integrity Specification," Proc.
Comp. Sec. Foundat.
Workshop II, 1989, (3: IEE-
89a), pp. 64-70.

Key Words: specification,
methods.

GOG-82
Goguen, J.A., and J. Meseguer,
"Security Policies & Security
Models," Proc. 1982 IEEE
Symp. on Sec. & Privacy, (5:
IEE-82), pp. 11-20.

Key Words: models, policy,
theory.

GOU-84
Gougen, J.A., and J. Mesgeur "Unwinding and Inference Control," Proc. 1984 IEEE Symp. on Sec. & Privacy, (5: IEE-84), pp. 75-86.

Key Words: model, inference, theory.

GOV-85
Gove, R.A. "Modeling of Computer Networks," Proc. 8th Natl. Comp. Sec. Conf., (5: NCS-85), 1985, pp. 47-55.

Key Words: models, methods, netowrks.

GRO-84
Grove, R.A. "Extending the Bell & LaPadula Security Model," Proc. 7th Seminar, DoD Comp. Sec. Program, (5: DOD-84), 1984, pp. 112-119.

Key Words: models, theory, MLS.

GUT-87
Guttman, J. "Information Flow and Invariance," Proc. 1987 IEEE Symp. on Sec. & Privacy, (5: IEE-87a), pp. 67-73.

Key Words: models, flow, theory.

GUT-88
Guttman, J., and M. Nadel "What Needs Securing," Proc. Comp. Sec. Foundat. Workshop, 1988, (3: CSF-88), pp. 34-57.

Key Words: models, theory.

GUT-89
Guttman, J.D. "The Second Computer Security Foundations Workshop," IEEE Cipher, Fall 1989, pp. 15-26.

Key Words: awareness, models.

HAI-84
Haigh, J.T. "Comparison of Formal Security Policy Models," Proc. 7th Seminar, DoD Comp. Sec. Progr., (5: DOD-84), 1984, pp. 88-111.

Key Words: models, theory, general.

HAI-86
Haigh, J. and W.D. Young "Extending the Noninterference Version of MLS for SAT," Proc. 1986 IEEE Symp. on Sec. & Privacy, (5: IEE-86), pp. 232-239.

Key Words: models, MLS, methods.

HAI-87
Haigh, J. and W.D. Young "Extending the Noninterference Version of MLS for SAT," IEEE Trans. on Software Engr., February 1987, pp. 141-150.

Key Words: models, MLS, methods.

HAR-85
Harrison, M.A. "Theoretical Issues Concerning Protection in Operating Systems," in M.C. Yovits, Ed., Advances in Computers, Vol. 24, Academic Press, New York, 1985.

Key Words: models, theory, general.

HAR-88
Hartman, B.A. "A General Approach to Tranquility in Information Flow Analysis," Proc. Comp. Sec. Foundat. Workshop, 1988, (3: CSF-88).

Key Words: models, flow, methods.

HAR-88a
Harkness, W., adn P. Pittelli "Command Authorization as a Component of Information Integrity," Proc. Comp. Sec. Foundat. Workshop, 1988, (3: CSF-88), pp. 201-226.

Key Words: integrity, techniques.

HEA-89
Heany, J., et al. "Security Model Development Environment," Proc. 5th Security Applicat. Conf., (4: IEE-89c), 1989, pp. 299-307.

Key Words: models, techniques.

HER-89
Herlihy, M.P., and J.M. Wing "Specifying Security Constraints with Relaxation Lattices," Proc. Comp. Sec. Foundat. Workshop II, 1989, (3: IEE-89a), pp. 47-53.

Key Words: specification, methods.

IEE-89
Proceedings, The Computer Security Foundations Workshop II, Franconia, NH, June 11-14, 1989, IEEE Computer Society Press, Washington, DC, June 1989.

Key Words: proceedings, models, theory, methods.

JAC-88
Jacob, J. "Security Specifications," Proc. 1988 IEEE Symp. on Sec. & Privacy, (5: IEE-88a), pp. 14-23.

Key Words: specification, methods.

JAC-88a
Jacob, J.L. "A Security Framework," Proc. Comp. Sec. Foundat. Workshop, 1988, (3: CSF-88), pp. 98-111.

Key Words: models, theory, general.

JAC-89
Jacob, J.
"On the Derivation of Secure Components," Proc. 1989 IEEE Symp. on Sec. & Privacy, (5: IEE-89b), pp. 242-247.

Key Words: models, theory, methods.

JAC-89a
Jacob, J.
"A Note on the Use of Separability for Detection of Covert Channels," IEEE Cipher, Summer 1989, pp. 25-33.

Key Words: covert channel, methods.

JOH-88
Johnson, D.M., and F.J. Thayer
"Stating Security Requirements with Tolerable Sets," ACM Trans. on Computer Systems, Vol. 6, No. 3, 1988.

Key Words: requirements, methods.

JOH-88a
Johnson, D.M., and F.J. Thayer
"Security and Composition of Machines," Proc. Comp. Sec. Foundat. Workshop, 1988, (3: CSF-88), pp. 72-89.

Key Words: models, theory.

JOH-89
Johnson, D.M., and F.J. Thayer
"Security Properties Consistent with Testing Semantics for Communicating Processes," Proc. Comp. Sec. Foundat. Workshop, 1988, (3: CSF-88), pp. 9-21.

Key Words: models, theory, methods.

KAT-89
Katzke, S.W., and Z. G. Ruthberg (Eds)
Report of the 1987 Invitational Workshop on Integrity Policy in Computer Information System, SP 500-160, National Institute of Standards and Technology, Gaithersburg, MD, 1989.

Key Words: integrity, policy.

KEE-88
Keefe, T.F., W.T. Tsai, and M.B. Thuraisingham
"A Multilevel Security Model for Object-Oriented Systems," Proc. 11th Natl. Comp. Sec. Conf., (5: NCS-88), 1988, pp. 1-9.

Key Words: models, MLS, methods.

KEE-89
Keefe, T., and W. Tsai
"Security Model Consistency in Secure Object-Oriented Systems" Proc. 5th Security Applicat. Conf., (4: IEE-89c), 1989, pp. 290-298.

Key Words: models, theory, MLS.

KOH-89
Ko, H.-P.
"Security Properties of Ring Brackets," Proc. Comp. Sec. Foundat. Workshop II, 1989, (3: IEE-89a), pp. 41-46.

Key Words: models, techniques.

KOR-88
Korelsky, T., et al.
"ULYSSES: A Computer-Security Modeling Environment," Proc. 11th Natl. Comp. Sec. Conf., (5: NCS-88), 1988, pp. 20-28

Key Words: modeling, techniques.

KOR-88a
Korelsky, T., et al.
"Security Modeling in the Ulysses Environment," Proc. 4th Aerosp. Comp. Sec. Conf., (4: IEE-88b), 1988, pp. 386-392.

Key Words: modeling, techniques.

KRE-80
Kreissig, G.
"A Model to Describe Protection Problems," Proc. 1980 IEEE Symp. on Sec. & Privacy, (5: IEE-80), pp. 9-17.

Key Words: models, methods.

LAN-81
Landwehr, C.E.
"Formal Models for Computer Security," ACM Computing Surveys, September 1981, pp. 247-278.

Key Words: models, formal, general.

LAN-82
Landauer, C., and S. Crocker
"Precise Information Flow Analysis by Program Verification," Proc. 1982 IEEE Symp. on Sec. & Privacy, (5: IEE-82), pp. 74-80.

Key Words: verification, methods.

LAN-84
Landwehr, C.E., C.L. Heitmeyer, and J. McLean
"A Security Model for Military Message Systems," ACM Trans. on Computer Systems, August 1984, pp. 198-222.

Key Words: models, techniques.

LAN-89
Landauer, J., T. Redmond, and T. Benzel "Formal Policies for Trusted Processes," Proc. Comp. Sec. Foundat. Workshop II, 1989, (3: IEE-89a), pp. 31-40.

Key Words: policy, formal, models.

LAP-89
La Padula, L.J. "The 'Basic Security Theorem' of Bell and La Padula Revisited," IEEE Cipher, January 1989, pp. 26-31.

Key Words: awareness, models, theory, formal.

LEI-83
Leiss, E.L. "On Authorization Systems With Grant-or-Controlled Propagation of Privileges," Proceedings, 1983 COMPCON Spring, 1983, pp. 499-502.

Key Words: models, authorization, techniques.

LIN-88
Lin, T.Y. "A Generalized Information Flow Model and the Role of the Security Officer," Proc. IFIP WG 11.3 Meeting, (6: LAN-88), 1987, pp. 85-103.

Key Words: models, flow, methods.

LIN-89
Lin, T.Y. "Chinese Wall Security Policy -- An Aggressive Model," Proc. 5th Security Applicat. Conf., (4: IEE-89c), 1989, pp. 282-289.

Key Words: models, policy, theory.

LIN-89a
Lin, T.Y., L. Kershberg, and R.P. Trueblood "Security Algebras and Formal Models -- Using Petri Net Theory," Proc. IFIP WG 11.3 (Data Base) Workshop, (6: IFI-89), 1989.

Key Words: models, theory, methods

LIU-80
Liu, L. "On Security Flow Analysis in Computer Systems," Proc. 1980 IEEE Symp. on Sec. & Privacy, (5: IEE-80), pp. 22-33.

Key Words: models, flow, methods, techniques.

LOC-82
Lockman, A., and N. Minsky, "Unidirectional Transport of Rights and Take-Grant Control," IEEE Trans. on Software Engr., December 1982, pp. 597-604.

Key Words: models, take-grant, techniques, methods.

LUB-89
Lubarsky, R.S. "Hook-Up Security and Generalized Restrictiveness," Proc. 12th Natl. Comp. Sec. Conf., (5: NCS-89), 1989, pp. 112-122.

Key Words: models, theory.

LUN-88
Lunt, T.F. "Access Control Policies: Some Unanswered Questions," Proc. Comp. Sec. Foundat. Workshop, 1988, (3: CSF-88), pp. 227-245.

Key Words: policy, control.

MAC-87
MacEwen, G.H., V.Q.W. Poon, and J.I. Glasgow "A Model for Multilevel Security Based on Operator Nets," Proc. 1987 IEEE Symp. on Sec. & Privacy, (5: IEE-87a), pp. 130-160.

Key Words: models, MLS, methods.

MAR-86
Marcus, L., and T. Redmond "Semantics of Read," Proc. 9th Natl. Comp. Sec. Conf., (5: NCS-86), 1986, pp. 184-193.

Key Words: models, theory.

MAR-88
Marcus, L., and T. Redmond "A Model-Theoretic Approach to Specifying, Verifying, and Hooking Up Security Policies," Proc. Comp. Sec. Foundat. Workshop, 1988, (3: CSF-88), pp. 127-138.

Key Words: models, theory, policy.

MAR-89
Marcus, L., and T. Menas "Safety via State Transition Language Plus Invariants," Proc. Comp. Sec. Foundat. Workshop II, 1989, (3: IEE-89a), pp. 71-77.

Key Words: theory, methods, safety.

MAR-89a
Marcus, L. "The Search for a Unifying Framework for Computer Security," IEEE Cipher, Fall 1989, pp. 55-63.

Key Words: models, theory, general.

MCC-87
McCullough, D.M.
"Specifications for Multilevel
Security and a Hook-Up
Property," Proc. 1987 IEEE
Symp. on Sec. & Privacy, (5:
IEE-87a), pp. 161-166.

Key Words: specification,
MLS.

MCC-88
McCullough, D.M.
"Noninterference and the
Composability of Security
Properties," Proc. 1988 IEEE
Symp. on Sec. & Privacy, (5:
IEE-88a), pp. 177-186.

Key Words: inference,
theory.

MCC-88a
McCullough, D.M.
"Covert Channels and
Degrees of Insecurity," Proc.
Comp. Sec. Foundat.
Workshop, 1988, (3: CSF-
88), pp. 1-33.

Key Words: covert channel,
theory.

MCC-88b
McCullough, D.M.
Foundations of Ulysses: The
Theory of Security, RADC-
TR-87-222, U.S. Air Force
Rome Air Development
Center, Rome, NY, July
1988.

Key Words: verification,
theory, MLS.

MCD-89
McDermid, J., and
E. Hocking
"Security Policies for
Integrated Project Support
Environments," Proc. IFIP
WG 11.3 (Data Base)
Workshop, (6: IFI-89), 1989.

Key Words: policy,
techniques.

MCH-86
McHugh, J., and A.P. Moore
"A Security Policy and
Formal Top Level
Specification for a Multi-
Level Secure Local Area
Network," Proc. 1986 IEEE
Symp. on Sec. & Privacy, (5:
IEE-86), pp. 34-39

Key Words: specification,
MLS, LAN.

MCH-87
McHugh, J.
"Active vs. Passive Security
Models: The Key to Real
Systems," Proc. 3d Aerospace
Comp. Sec. Conf., (5: IEE-
87b), 1987, pp. 15-20.

Key Words: models, theory,
general.

MCH-88
McHugh, J.
"A Formal Definition for
Information Flow Analysis,"
Proc. Comp. Sec. Foundat.
Workshop, 1988, (3: CSF-88),
pp. 147.

Key Words: formal, models,
flow.

MCL-84
McLean, J., C.E. Landwehr,
and C.L. Heitmyer
"A Formal Statement of the
MMS Security Model," Proc.
1984 IEEE Symp. on Sec. &
Privacy, (5: IEE-84), pp. 188-
194.

Key Words: formal, models,
network.

MCL-85
McLean, J.
"A Comment on the Basic
Security Theorem of Bell and
LaPadula," Information
Processing Letters, February
1985, pp. 67-70.

Key Words: models, formal,
theory.

MCL-87
McLean, J.
"Reasoning About Security
Models," Proc. 1987 IEEE
Symp. on Sec. & Privacy, (5:
IEE-87a), pp. 123-131

Key Words: models, theory,
general.

MCL-88
McLean, J.
"The Algebra of Security,"
Proc. 1988 IEEE Symp. on
Sec. & Privacy, (5: IEE-88a),
pp. 2-7.

Key Words: models, theory.

MCL-89
McLean, J., and C. Meadows
"Composable Security
Properties," IEEE Cipher, Fall
1989, pp. 27-36.

Key Words: models, theory.

MEN-81
Mennie, A.L., and
G.H. MacEwen
"Information Flow Certification
Using an Intermediate Code
Program Representation," IEEE
Trans. on Software Engr.,
November 1981, pp. 594-607.

Key Words: flow, techniques,
verification.

MIL-81
Millen, J.K.
"Information Flow Analysis of
Formal Specifications," Proc.
1981 IEEE Symp. on Sec. &
Privacy, (5: IEE-81), pp. 3-8.

Key Words: specification,
formal, flow, methods.

MIL-84
Millen, J.K.
"A1 Policy Modelling," Proc.
7th Seminar, DoD Comp. Sec.
Progr., (5: DOD-84), 1984, pp.
137-145.

Key Words: models, MLS,
methods.

MIL-87
Millen, J.K.
"Covert Channel Capacity,"
Proc. 1987 IEEE Symp. on
Sec. & Privacy, (5: IEE-87a),
pp. 60-66

Key Words: covert channel,
models.

MIL-87a
Millen, J.K.
"Interconnection of
Accredited Systems," AIAA
No. 87-3075, Proc. 3d
Aerosp. Comp. Sec. Conf.,
(5: IEE-87b), 1987, pp. 60-
65.

Key Words: models,
techniques.

MIL-89
Millen, J.K.
"Finite-State Noiseless Covert
Channels," Proc. Comp. Sec.
Foundat. Workshop II, 1989,
(3: IEE-89a), pp. 81-86.

Key Words: covert channel,
models.

MIL-89a
Millen, J.K.
"Models of Multilevel
Computer Security," in M.
Yovits, (Ed), Advances in
Computers, Academic Press,
New York, 1989, pp. 1-40.

Key Words: models, MLS.
general.

MIN-83
Minsky, N.H.
"On the Transportation of
Privileges," Proc. 1983 IEEE
Symp. on Sec. & Privacy, (5:
IEE-83a), pp. 41-48.

Key Words: models, take-
grant, methods.

MIN-84
Minsky, N.,
"Selective and Logically
Controlled Transport of
Privileges," ACM Trans. on
Programming Languages and
Systems, Vol. 6, No. 4, 1984,
pp. 573-602.

Key Words: models, take-
grant, methods.

MOR-88
Morgenstern, M.
"Spiral Classification for
Multilevel Data and Rules,"
Proc. 11th Natl. Comp. Sec.
Conf., (5: NCS-88), 1988, pp.
270-273.

Key Words: models,
techniques, MLS.

MOS-87
Moser, L.E.
"Graph Homomorphisms and
the Design of Secure
Computer Systems," Proc.
1987 IEEE Symp. on Sec. &
Privacy, (5: IEE-87a), pp. 88-
96

Key Words: models, theory,
methods.

MOS-89
Moser, L.E.
"A Logic of Knowledge and
Belief for Reasoning about
Computer Security," Proc.
Comp. Sec. Foundat.
Workshop II, 1989, (3: IEE-
89a), pp. 57-63.

Key Words: theory, methods,
general.

NEU-83
Neumann, P.G.
"Experiences with Formality
in Software Development," in
D. Ferrari et al (Eds.), Theory
and Practice of Software
Technology, North-Holland,
Amsterdam, 1983.

Key Words: formal, software,
methods.

PAG-89
Page, J. et al.
"Evaluation Security Model
Rule Base," Proc. 12th Natl.
Comp. Sec. Conf., (5: NCS-
89), 1989, pp. 98-111.

Key Words: models, theory,
methods.

PIT-87
Pittelli, P.A.
"The Bell-LaPadula Computer
Security Model Represented as
a Special Case of the
Harrison-Ruzzo-Ullman
Model," Proc. 10th Natl.
Comp. Sec. Conf., (5: NCS-
87a), 1987, pp. 118-121.

Key Words: models, theory,
methods.

PIT-88
Pittelli, P.A.
"Formalizing Integrity Using
Non-Interference," Proc. 11th
National Comp. Sec. Conf., (5:
NCS-88), 1988, pp. 38-42.

Key Words: formal, integrity,
theory.

RAN-88
Rangan, P.V.
"An Axiomatic Basis of Trust
in Distributed Systems," Proc.
1988 IEEE Symp. on Sec. &
Privacy, (5: IEE-88a), pp. 204-
211.

Key Words: models, theory,
network.

ROS-88
Rosenthal, D.
"An Approach to Increasing
Automation of Verification of
Security," Proc. Comp. Sec.
Foundat. Workshop, 1988, (3:
CSF-88), pp. 90-97.

Key Words: verification,
techniques.

ROS-88a
Roskos, J.E.
"Minix Security Policy
Model," Proc. 4th Aerospace
Comp. Sec. Conf., (4: IEE-
88b), 1988, pp. 393-399.

Key Words: models, policy,
decription.

RUS-84
Rushby, J.
"The Security Model of
Enhanced HDM," Proc. 7th
Seminar, DoD Comp. Sec.
Progr., (5: DOD-84), 1984,
pp. 120-136.

Key Words: models,
description.

SAN-85
Sandhu, R.S.
"Analysis of Acyclic
Attenuating Systems for the
SSR Protection Model," Proc.
1986 IEEE Symp. on Sec. &
Privacy, (5: IEE-86), pp.
197-206.

Key Words: models,
description.

SAN-86
Sandhu, R.S., and M.E. Share
"Some Owner Based
Schemes With Dynamic
Groups in the Schematic
Protection Model," Proc.
1986 IEEE Symp. on Sec. &
Privacy, (5: IEE-86), pp. 61-
70

Key Words: models,
methods.

SAN-88
Sandhu, R.S.
"The Schematic Protection
Model: Its Definition and
Analysis of Acyclic
Attenuation Schemes,"
Journal of the ACM, No. 2,
1988, pp. 404-432.

Key Words: models,
description.

SAN-88a
Sandhu, R.S.
"Expressive Power of the
Schematic Protection Model,"
Proc. Comp. Sec. Foundat.
Workshop, 1988, (3: CSF-88),
pp. 188-193.

Key Words: models,
description.

SAN-89
Sandhu, R.S.
"Transformation of Access
Rights," Proc. 1989 IEEE
Symp. on Sec. & Privacy, (5:
IEE-89b), pp. 259-268.

Key Words: control,
techniques.

SAN-89a
Sandhu, R.
"Currrent State of the Safety
Problem in Access Control,"
IEEE Cipher, Fall 1989, pp.
37-46.

Key Words: control, safety,
general.

SAY-86
Saydjari, O.S., and
T. Kremann
"A Standard Notation in
Computer Security Models,"
Proc. 9th Natl. Comp. Sec.
Conf., (5: NCS-86), 1986, pp.
194-203.

Key Words: models, methods,
general.

SIL-83
Silverman, J.M.
"Reflections on the
Verification of the Security of
an Operating System,"
Proceedings, 9th ACM
Symposium on Operating
Systems Principles, October
1983, pp. 143-154.

Key Words: verification,
description.

SNY-81
Snyder, L.
"Formal Models of Capability-
Based Protection Systems,"
IEEE Trans. on Computers,
March 1981, pp. 172-181

Key Words: formal, models,
capability.

SNY-81b
Snyder, L.
"Theft and Conspiracy in the
Take-Grant Model," Journal
Comp. and System Sciences,
December 1981, pp. 333-347.

Key Words: models, take-
grant, threats.

SOR-83
Sorkin, A., and C.J. Buchanan
"Measurement of
Cryptographic Capability
Protection Algorithms,"
Computers & Security,
November 1983, pp. 101-116.

Key Words: capability,
techniques.

STO-81
Stoughton, A.
"Access Flow: A Protection
Model which Integrates Access
Control and Information
Flow," Proc. 1981 IEEE Symp.
on Sec. & Privacy, (5: IEE-
81), pp. 9-18.

Key Words: models, flow,
control.

SUT-86
Sutherland, D.
"A Model of Information,"
Proc. 9th National Computer
Sec. Conf., (5: NCS-86), 1986,
pp. 175-183.

Key Words: models, theory,
general.

SUT-89
Sutherland, I., S. Perlo, and R. Varadarajaan "Deducibility Security with Dynamic Level Assignments," Proc. Comp. Sec. Foundat. Workshop II, 1989, (3: IEE-89a), pp. 3-8.

Key Words: models, theory, general.

TAY-84
Taylor, T. "Comparison Paper Between the Bell-La Padula Model and the SRI Model," Proc. 1984 IEEE Symp. on Sec. & Privacy, (5: IEE-84), pp. 195-202.

Key Words: models, theory, general.

TAY-87
Taylor, T., and B. Hartman "Formal Models, Bell-LaPadula, and Gypsy," Proc. 10th Natl. Comp. Sec. Conf., (5: NSC-10), 1987, pp. 193-200.

Key Words: models, formal, general.

TER-89
Terry, P., and S. Wiseman "A 'New' Security Policy Model," Proc. 1989 IEEE Symp. on Sec. & Privacy, (5: IEE-89b), pp. 215-228.

Key Words: models, theory.

TRU-86
Trueblood, R.P., and A. Sengupta "Dynamic Analysis of the Effects Access Rule Modifications Have Upon Security," IEEE Trans. on Software Engr., August 1986, pp. 866-870.

Key Words: models, techniques.

TSA-87
Tsai, C.-R, V.D. Gligor, and C.S. Chandersekaran "A Formal Method For the Identification of Covert Storage Channels in Source Code," Proc. 1987 IEEE Symp. on Sec. & Privacy, (5: IEE-87a), pp. 74-86

Key Words: covert channel, formal, methods, techniques.

TSA-88
Tsai, C.-R., and V.D. Gligor "A Bandwidth Computation Model for Covert Storage Channels and Its Applications," Proc. 1988 IEEE Symp. on Sec. & Privacy, (5: IEE-88a), pp. 108-121.

Key Words: covert channel, models, techniques.

WEB-89
Weber, D.G., and R. Lubarsky "The SDOS Project -- Verifying Hook-Up Security," Proc. 3d Aerospace Comp. Sec. Conf., (5: IEE-87b), 1987, pp. 7-14.

Key Words: verification, description.

WIL-87
Williams, J.C. and G.W. Dinolt "A Graph-Theoretic Formulation of Multilevel Secure Distributed Systems: An Overview" Proc. 1987 IEEE Symp. on Sec. & Privacy, (5: IEE-87a), pp. 97-103.

Key Words: theory, models, general.

WIL-88
Williams, J.C. and M.L.Day "Security Labels and Security Profiles," Proc. 11th Natl. Comp. Sec. Conf., (5: NCS-88), 1988, pp. 257-266.

Key Words: models, methods, MLS.

WIT-89
Wittbold, J.T., "Controlled Signalling Systems and Covert Channels," Proc. Comp. Sec. Foundat. Workshop II, 1989, (3: IEE-89a), pp. 87-104.

Key Words: covert channel, methods, techniques.

WRA-89
Wray, J.C. "An Optimization for Information Flow Analysis," Proc. Comp. Sec. Foundat. Workshop II, 1989, (3: IEE-89a), pp. 105-110.

Key Words: models, flow, methods.

WUM-81
Wu, M.S. "Hierarchical Protection Systems," Proc. 1981 IEEE Symp. on Sec. & Privacy, (5: IEE-81), pp. 113-123.

Key Words: models, hierarchical.

YOU-89
Young, W.D. "Toward Foundations of Security," IEEE Cipher, Fall 1989, pp. 47-54.

Key Words: models, theory, general.

4. Access Control

This section cites publications on identification and authentication methods (e.g., passwords, biometrical identifiers), traditional access control methods (such as memory and file protection), the use of capabilities and access control lists, and add-on software packages for discretionary access control.

AHI-87
Ahituv, N., Y.Lapid, and S. Neumann "Verifying Authentication of an Information System User," Computers & Security, April 1987, pp. 152-157.

Key Words: authentication, techniques.

ALV-88
Alvare, A., and E. Schultz "A Framework for Password Selection," Proceedings, USENIX UNIX Security Workshop, August 1988.

Key Words: authentication, methods, passwords.

AND-88
Anderson, L. "UNIX Password Security," Proceedings, USENIX UNIX Security Workshop, August 1988.

Key Words: authentication, methods, passwords.

ANC-83a
Ancilotti, P., N.Lijtmaer, and M. Boari "Language Features for Access Control," IEEE Trans. on Software Engr., January 1983, pp. 16-24.

Key Words: control, techniques.

BAC-89
Bacic, E. "Process Execution Controls as a Mechanism to Ensure Consistency," Proc. 5th Security Applicat. Conf. (4: IEE-89c), 1989, pp. 114-120.

Key Words: controls, OS, techniques.

BAN-84
Banton, B.F. and M.S. Barton "User-Friendly Password Methods for Computer-Mediated Information Systems," Computers & Security, October 1984, pp. 186-195.

Key Words: authentication, methods, passwords.

BEK-88
Beker, H. "Secure Access Control and MAC-Based Signatures," Information Age, (U.K.) January 1988, pp. 20-22.

Key Words: control, mandatory.

BON-83
Bonyun, D.A. "The Use of Architectural Principles in the Design of Certifiably Secure Systems," Proc. IFIP/Sec. '83, Stockholm, 1983, (2: FAK-83), pp. 81-94.

Key Words: architecture, design.

BOU-83
Bound, W.A.J. "Securing the Automated Office," Computer Security Journal, Fall/Winter 1983, pp. 97-103.

Key Words: control, techniques.

BOW-88
Bowers, D.M. Access Control and Personal Identification Systems, Butterworths, Boston, 1988.

Key Words: book, control, general.

BRA-84
Brand, S.L., and M.E. Flaherty "Password Management in Practice," Proc. 7th Seminar, DOD Comp. Sec. Progr., (5: DOD-84), 1984, pp. 264-269.

Key Words: authetication, methods, passwords, management.

BRO-84
Brown, R.L. "Computer System Access Control Using Passwords," Proc. IFIP/Sec. '84, Toronto, 1984, (2: FIN-85), pp. 129-142.

Key Words: control, passwords.

BUN-87
Bunch, S.
"The Setuid Feature in UNIX and Security," Proc. 10th Natl. Comp. Sec. Conf., (5: NCS-87a), 1987, pp. 245-253.

Key Words: authentication, methods.

BUR-89
Burk, H., and A. Pfitzmann
"Digital Payment Systems Enabling Security and Unobservability," Computers & Security, August 1989, pp. 399-416.

Key Words: control, methods.

CAR-83
Carlsson, A.
"The Active Card and its Contribution to EDP Security," Proc. IFIP/Sec. '83, Stockholm, 1983, (2: FAK-83), pp. 69-72.

Key Words: control, techniques.

CAR-87
Carroll, J.M.
Computer Security, 2nd Edition, Butterworths, Boston, 1987.

Key Words: book, general, methods, techniques.

CAR-88
Carroll, J.M., et al.
"The Password Predictor -- A Training Aid for Raising Security Awareness," Computers & Security, October 1988, pp. 475-481.

Key Words: authentication, passwords, awareness, techniques.

CAR-88a
Carlton, S.F., J.W. Taylor, and J.L. Wyszynski
"Alternate Authentication Mechanisms," Proc. 11th Natl. Comp. Sec. Conf., (5: NCS-88), 1988, pp. 333-338.

Key Words: authentication, techniques.

CHA-85
Chaum, D.
"Security Without Identification: Transaction Systems to Make Big Brother Obsolete," Communications of the ACM, October 1985, pp. 1030-1044.

Key Words: general, methods.

CHA-86
Chang, C.C.
"On the Design of a Key-Lock-Pair Mechanism in Information Protection Systems," BIT, July 1986, pp. 410-417.

Key Words: control, techniques.

CLE-87
Clements, P.C.
"Engineering More Secure Software Systems," Proc. COMPASS '87: Comp. Assurance, (2: IEE-87), 1987, pp. 79-81.

Key Words: architecture, design.

COH-88
Cohen, F.
"Designing Provably Correct Information Networks with Digital Diodes," Computers & Security, June 1988, pp. 279-286.

Key Words: design, network, hardware.

COM-84
Comer, M. (Ed.)
"How Passwords are Cracked," Computer Fraud and Security Bulletin (U.K.), November 1984, pp. 1-10.

Key Words: threats, passwords.

CON-83
Connolly, W.
"Bypassing the Passwords," Computer Fraud and Security Bulletin, July 1983, pp. 1-7.

Key Words: threats, passwords.

COO-84
Cooper, J.A.
Computer Security Technology, Lexington Books, Lexington, MA, 1984.

Key Words: book, general, methods.

CSC-85
Department of Defense Password Management Guideline, CSC-STD-002-85, National Computer Security Center, Ft. Meade, MD, 12 April 1985.

Key Words: guidelines, passwords.

CSC-88
Trusted Unix Working Group (TRUSIX) Rationale for Selecting Access Control Features for the Unix System, NCSC-TG-020-A, National Computer Security Center, Ft. Meade, MD, 18 August 1988.

Key Words: control, guidelines.

CUS-80
Cushing, S.
"Software Security and How to Handle It," in Rullo, T.A. (Ed.), Advances in Computer Security Management, Vol. 1, Heyden & Son, Philadelphia, 1980, pp. 79-105.

Key Words: software, guidelines.

DAV-81
Davida, G.I., and J. Livesey
"The Design of Secure CPU-Multiplexed Computer Systems: The Master/Slave Approach," Proc. 1981 IEEE Symp. on Security & Privacy (5: IEE-81), pp. 133-139.

Key Words: design, control, methods.

DAV-85
Davida, G.I. and B.J. Matt
"Crypto-Secure Operating Systems," Proceedings, 1985 National Computer Conference, AFIPS Press, Reston, VA, 1985, pp. 575-581.

Key Words: control, OS, techniques.

DAV-88
Davida, G.I., and B.J. Matt
"UNIX Guardians: Active User Intervention in Data Protection," Proc. 4th Aerosp. Comp. Sec. Conf., (4: IEE-88b), 1988, pp. 199-204.

Key Words: control, techniques.

DEB-85
de Bruyne, P.
"Signature Verification Using Holistic Measures," Computers & Security, December 1985, pp. 309-315.

Key Words: authentication, methods, techniques.

DEC-89
Security for VAX Systems, Digital Equipment Corporation, Maynard, MA, 1989.

Key Words: book, control, general.

DEH-89
Dehnad, K.
"A Simple Way of Improving the Login Security," Computers & Security, November 1989, pp. 607-611.

Key Words: authentication, methods.

DEN-86
Denning, D.E.
"An Intrusion Detection Model," Proc. 1986 IEEE Symp. on Security & Privacy, (5: IEE-86), pp. 118-131.

Key Words: auditing, techniques.

DES-86
Deswarte, Y., et al.
"A Saturation Network to Tolerate Faults and Intrusions," Proceedings, 5th IEEE Symposium on Reliability in Distributed Software and Database Systems, January 1986, pp. 74-81.

Key Words: architecture, design.

DOB-86
Dobson, J.E., and B. Randell
"Building Reliable Secure Computing Systems out of Unreliable, Insecure Components," Proc. 1986 IEEE Symp. on Sec. & Privacy, (5: IEE-86), pp. 187-193

Key Words: architecture, design.

DOW-84
Downs, D.D.
"Operating Systems Key Security with Basic Software Mechanisms," Electronics, March 8, 1984, pp. 122-127.

Key Words: OS, techniques.

DPC-83
"Special Issue on Access Control," Data Processing & Comm. Security, Sept/Oct. 1983, pp. 8-29.

Key Words: control, methods, general.

DUC-85
du Croix, A.J.
"Data Sharing and Access Protection in Business System 12," Computers & Security, December 1985, pp. 317-323.

Key Words: control, techniques.

DUP-86
Dupy, M., et al.
"About Software Security with CP8 Card," Proc. IFIP/Sec. '86, Monte Carlo, 1986, (2: GRI-89).

Key Words: software, techniques.

DUV-88
Duval, S., et al.
"Use of Fingerprints as Identity Verification," Proc. IFIP/Sec. '88, Australia, 1989, (2: CAE-89), pp. 479-481.

Key Words: authentication, methods.

ELO-83
Eloff, J.H.P.
"Selection Process for Security Packages," Computers & Security, November 1983, p. 256.

Key Words: software, guidelines.

ELS-88
Elsbury, J.
"Personal Authentication Devices: Data Security Applications," Proc. IFIP/Sec. '88, Australia, 1989, (2: CAE-89), pp. 471-478.

Key Words: authentication, methods, techniques.

ENG-87
Engelman, P.D.
"The Application of 'Orange Book' Standards to Secure a Telephone Switching System," Proc. 10th Natl. Comp. Sec. Conf., (5: NCS-87a), 1987, pp. 282-287.

Key Words: control, techniques.

EST-89
Estrin, D., and G. Tsudik
"Security Issues in Policy Routing," Proc. 1989 IEEE Symp. on Sec. & Privacy, (5: IEE-89b), pp. 183-193.

Key Words: control, requirements.

EVA-83
"Evaluating Security Software," Assets Protection, July/August 1983, pp. 9-13.

Key Words: guidelines, software.

FAK-84
Fak, V.
"Characteristics of Good One-Way Encryption Functions for Passwords -- Some Rules for Creators and Evaluators," Proc. IFIP/Sec. '84, Toronto, 1984, (2: FIN-85), pp. 189-191.

Key Words: passwords, techniques.

FAR-86
Farrow, R.
"Security for Superusers, Or How to Break the UNIX System," UNIX/World, May 1986, pp. 65-70.

Key Words: OS, vulnerabilities.

FAY-86
Fray, J.-M., and J.-C. Fraga
"Fragmented Data Processing: An Approach to Secure and Reliable Processing in Distributed Computing Systems," Preprints, International Working Conference on Dependable Computing for Critical Applications, Santa Barbara, CA, August 1989, pp. 131-137.

Key Words: architecture, design.

FEI-86
Feinstein, H.
"Security in Unclassified Sensitive Computer Systems," Proc. 9th Natl. Comp. Sec. Conf., (5: NCS-86), 1986, pp. 81-90.

Key Words: control, techniques.

FIL-86
Filipski, A., and J. Hanko
"Making UNIX Secure," Byte, April 1986, pp. 113-128.

Key Words: control, OS, design.

FIS-84
Fisher, R.P.
Information Systems Security, Prentice-Hall, New York, 1984.

Key Words: book, general, methods, techniques.

FIS-88
Fish, T.
"A Model for Mainframe Access Control Software Selection," EDPACS, May 1988, pp. 1-5.

Key Words: control, model, methods.

FIT-88
Fitzgerald, K.
"Choosing a Logical Access Control Strategy," Proc. IFIP/Sec. '88, Australia, 1989, (2: CAE-89), 1988, pp. 235-244.

Key Words: control, guidelines.

FRA-86
Fray, J.M., Y. Deswarte, and D. Powell
"Intrusion-Tolerance Using Fine-Grain Fragmentation Scattering," Proc. 1986 IEEE Symp. on Sec. & Privacy, (5: IEE-86), pp. 194-201.

Key Words: architecture, design.

FRI-88
Friedman, M.
"Access-Control Software, Information Age, (U.K.), July 1988, pp. 157-161.

Key Words: control, software.

FUG-88
Fugini, M., and R. Zicari
"Authorization and Access Control in the Office-Net Systems," Proc. IFIP/Sec. '88, Australia, 1989, (2: CAE-89), pp. 147-162.

Key Words: control, techniques.

GON-89
Gong, L.
"A Secure Identity-Based Capability System," Proc. 1989 IEEE Symp. on Sec. & Privacy, (5: IEE-89b), pp. 56-63.

Key Words: architecture, capability.

GON-89a
Gong, L.
"On Security of Capability-Based Systems', ACM Operating Systems Review, April 1989, pp. 56-60.

Key Words: control, capability.

GRA-84
Grampp, F.T., and R.H. Morris
"UNIX Operating System Security," Bell System Technical Journal, August 1984, pp. 1651-1971.

Key Words: control, OS, design.

GRA-89
Graubart, R.
"On the Need for a Third Form of Access Control," Proc. 12th Natl. Comp. Sec. Conf., (5: NCS-89), 1989, pp. 296-303.

Key Words: control, requirements.

GRE-81
Green, G., and R.G. Farber
Introduction to Security Principles & Practices, Security World Publishing, Los Angeles, CA, 1981.

Key Words: book, general, methods, techniques.

GRO-84
Grossman, G.
"Gould Software Division's Security Program," Proc. 7th Seminar, DoD Comp. Sec. Progr., (5: DOD-84), 1984, pp. 180-187.

Key Words: control, techniques.

GUY-85
Guynes, S.
"Security of Computer Software," Security Audit & Control Review, Winter 1985, pp. 31-35.

Key Words: control, software, design.

HAG-86
Hagopian, G.
"Planning and Implementing a Security Package, Part I," Computer Security Products Report, Winter 1986, pp. 18-22.

Key Words: control, software, design.

HAG-86a
Hagopian, G.
"Planning and Implementing a Security Package, Part II," Computer Security Products Report, Spring 1986, pp. 18-20.

Key Words: control, software, design.

HAS-84
Haskett, J.A.
"Pass-Algorithms: A User Validation Scheme Based on Knowledge of Secret Algorithms," Communications of the ACM, August 1984, pp. 777-781.

Key Words: control, techniques.

HAY-88
Haykin, M.E., and R.B.J. Warner
Smart Card Technology: New Methods for Computer Access Control, SP 500-157, National Institute of Standards and Technology, Gaithersburg, MD, 1988.

Key Words: control, methods.

HEB-80
Hebbard, B., et al.
"A Penetration of the Michigan Terminal System," ACM Operating Systems Review, January 1980, pp. 7-20.

Key Words: vulnerabilities, OS.

HEN-87
Henning, R.R., and S. A. Walker
"Data Integrity vs. Data Security: A Workable Compromise," Proc. 10th Natl. Comp. Sec. Conf., (5: NCS-87a), 1987, pp. 334-339.

Key Words: control, integrity, design.

HEN-87a
Henderson, S.C.
"A Comparison of Data Access Control Packages: Part I," Computer Security Journal, Vol. IV, No. 2, 1987, pp. 75-111.

Key Words: control, software.

HEN-88
Henderson, S.C.
"A Comparison of Data Access Control Packages: Part II," Computer Security Journal, Vol. V, No. 1, 1988, pp. 67-104.

Key Words: control, software.

HER-89
Herlihy, M.P., and J.D. Tygar
"Implementing Distributed Capabilities Without a Trusted Kernel," International Working Conf. on Dependable Comp. for Critical Applic., Santa Barbara, CA, Aug. 1989, pp. 113-120.

Key Words: OS, capabilities, design.

HIG-85
Highland, H.J.
"Microcomputer Security: Data Protection Techniques," Computers & Security, June 1985, pp. 123-134.

Key Words: control, PC, general.

HIG-86
Highland, H.J.
"How to Modify a
Microcomputer Operating
System for Added Security,"
Computers & Security,
December 1986, pp. 340-343.

Key Words: OS, PC,
guidelines.

HIG-88
Highland, H.J.
"Program Aids for Office
Automation Security,"
Computers & Security,
February 1988, pp. 37-43.

Key Words: control,
software.

HOG-88
Hogan, C.B.
"Protection Imperfect: The
Security of Some Computing
Environments," ACM
Operating Systems Review,
July 1988.

Key Words: control, general,
design.

HOS-88
Hosmer, H.H. and
M. Merriman
"Using CASE Tools to
Improve the Security of
Application Systems," Proc.
4th Aerosp. Comp. Sec.
Conf., (4: IEE-88b), 1988,
pp. 205-208.

Key Words: control,
techniques, methods, design.

HOV-83
Hovig, P.L.
"To Install an Access Control
System: Activities and
Checklists," Proc. IFIP/Sec.
'83, Stockholm, 1983, (2:
FAK-83), pp. 57-67.

Key Words: control,
guidelines.

IBM-83
System Security Guide, IBM
System 36, FSC 219042, IBM
Corporation, White Plains,
NY, 1983.

Key Words: control,
guidelines.

IBM-88
AS/400 Programming:
Security Concepts and
Planning, SC21-8083, IBM
Corporation, White Plains,
NY, June 1988.

Key Words: control,
guidelines.

ISR-83
Israel, J.E. and T.A. Linden
"Authentication in Office
System Internetworks," ACM
Trans. on Office Infor. Syst.,
July 1983, pp. 192-210.

Key Words:

JOB-89
Jobush, D.L., and
A.E. Oldenhoeft
"A Survey of Password
Mechanisms: Weaknesses and
Potential Improvements, Part
1," Computers & Security,
November 1989, pp. 587-604.

Key Words: control,
passwords.

JOB-89a
Jobush, D.L., and
A.E. Oldenhoeft
"A Survey of Password
Mechanisms: Weaknesses and
Potential Improvements. Part
2," Computers & Security,
December 1989, pp. 675-689.

Key Words: control,
passwords.

JOH-81
Johnston, R.E.
"Security Software Packages,"
Computer Security Journal,
Spring 1981, pp. 15-38.

Key Words: control, software.

JOH-83
Johnston, R.E.
"Comparison of Access
Control Software Packages,"
Computer Security Journal,
Fall/Winter, 1983, pp. 19-58.

Key Words: control, software.

JOH-83a
Johnston, R.E.
"Security Software Packages
for CICS," Computer Security
Journal, Spring 1983, pp. 19-
41.

Key Words: control, software.

JOH-83b
Johnston, R.E.
"Comparison of Access
Control Software for IBM
Operating Systems: ACF2,
RACF, SAC, SECURE, TOP
SECRET," Computer Security
Journal, Fall/Winter 1983, pp.
19-58.

Key Words: control, software.

JOH-89
Johnson, H.L., and C. Arvin
"Security for Embedded
Tactical Systems," Proc. 12th
Natl. Comp. Sec. Conf., (5:
NCS-89), 1989, pp. 339-348.

Key Words: control,
requirements.

JON-80
Jonekait, J.
"Gnosis: A Secure Capability
Based 370 Operating System,"
Proc., 3d Seminar, DoD Comp.
Sec. Progr., (5: DOD-80a),
1980, pp. G1-G16.

Key Words: control, OS,
capability.

JON-86
Jones, R.W.
"The Design of Distributed
Secure Logical Machines," ICL
Technical Journal (UK),
November 1986, pp. 291-308.

Key Words: control, design,
network.

JON-89
    Jones, R.W.
    "Security Classes and Access
    Rights in a Distributed
    System," Report, Invitat.
    Workshop on Data Integrity,
    NIST, (4: RUT-89), 1989,
    pp. A.6.1-27.

    Key Words: control, network,
    design.

JOS-89
    Joseph, M.K.
    "Integration Problems in
    Fault-Tolerant Secure
    Computer Design," Preprints,
    International Working
    Conference on Dependable
    Computing for Critical
    Applications, Santa Barbara,
    CA, Aug. 1989, pp. 141-147.

    Key Words: architecture,
    design.

JUE-88
    Juenemann, R.R.
    "Integrity Controls for
    Military and Commercial
    Applications," Proc. 4th
    Aerosp. Comp. Sec. Conf.,
    (4: IEE-88b), 1988, pp. 298-
    322.

    Key Words: control, integrity.

JUE-89
    Jueneman, R.R.
    "Integrity Controls for
    Military and Commercial
    Applications, II," Report,
    Invitat. Workshop on Data
    Integrity, NIST, (4: RUT-89),
    1989, pp. A.5.1-61.

    Key Words: control, integrity.

KAH-88
    Kahane, Y., S.Neumann, and
    C.S. Tapiero
    "Computer Backup Pools,
    Disaster Recovery, and
    Default Risks,"
    Communications of the
    ACM, January 1988, pp. 78-
    83.

    Key Words: contingency,
    risks.

KAI-86
    Kain, R.Y., and
    C.E. Landwehr
    "On Access Checking in
    Capability-Based Systems,"
    Proc. 1986 IEEE Symp. on
    Sec. & Privacy, (5: IEE-86),
    pp. 95-101

    Key Words: control,
    capability.

KAI-87
    Kain, R.Y., and
    C.E. Landwehr
    "On Access Checking in
    Capability-Based Systems,"
    IEEE Trans. on Software
    Engr., February 1987, pp.
    202-207.

    Key Words:

KAR-88
    Karger, P.A.
    "Implementing Commercial
    Data Integrity with Secure
    Capabilities," Proc. 1988
    IEEE Symp. on Sec. &
    Privacy, (5: IEE-88a), pp.
    130-139.

    Key Words: integrity,
    capability.

KAR-88a
    Karren, D.T.
    "Typical System Access
    Control Problems and
    Solutions," Information Age
    (U.K.), January 1988, pp. 23-
    32.

    Key Words: control,
    techniques.

KAR-89
    Karger, P.A.
    "New Methods for Immediate
    Revocation," Proc. 1989 IEEE
    Symp. on Sec. & Privacy, (5:
    IEE-89b), pp. 48-55.

    Key Words: capability,
    methods.

KIE-88
    Kielsky, M.
    "Security and Access Control
    Features of the VAX/VMS
    Operating System," Information
    Age (U.K.), October 1988, pp.
    203-210.

    Key Words: control, OS,
    methods.

KNO-87
    Knowles, F., and S. Bunch
    "A Least Privilege Mechanism
    for Unix," Proc. 10th Natl.
    Comp. Sec. Conf., (5: NCS-
    87a), 1987, pp. 257-262.

    Key Words: control, technique.

KNO-88
    Knox, M.J., and E.D. Bowden
    "Unix System Security Issues,"
    Information Age (U.K.), April
    1988, pp. 67-72.

    Key Words: OS, techniques,
    methods.

KOE-84
    Koehring, J.
    "Automatic Identity
    Verification," Information Age,
    (UK), April 1984, pp. 103-110.

    Key Words: authentication,
    methods.

KON-81
    Konigsford, w.L.
    "Developing Standards for
    Operating System Security,"
    Computer Security Journal,
    Spring 1981, pp. 45-60.

    Key Words: control, OS,
    methods.

KRA-88
    Krayem, R.
    "Smart Cards: A New Tool for
    Identification and Access
    Protection," Information Age,
    (U.K.), April 1988, pp. 85-88.

    Key Words: control,
    techniques, authentication.

KUR-85
Kurth, H.
"Paper Output Labeling in a
Dedicated System Running
Under MVS," Proc. 8th Natl.
Comp. Sec. Conf., (5: NCS-
85), 1985, pp. 86-90.

Key Words: techniques,
methods.

KUR-85a
Kurzban, S.A.
"Easily Remembered
Passphrases -- A Better
Approach," ACM Sec., Audit
& Control Review, Fall-
Winter 1985, pp. 10-21.

Key Words: control,
passwords.

KUR-89
Kurzban, S.
"Toward a Model for
Commercial Access Control,"
Report, Invitat. Workshop on
Data Integrity, NIST, (4:
RUT-89), 1989, pp. A.9.1-6.

Key Words: control, models.

LAI-89
Laih, C.S., L. Harn, and
J.Y. Lee
"On the Design of a Single-
Key-Lock Mechanism Based
on Newton's Interpolating
Polynomial," IEEE Trans. on
Software Engr., September
1989, pp. 1135-1137.

Key Words: control,
techniques.

LAM-81
Lamport, L.
"Passwords Authentication
With Insecure
Communication,"
Communications of the
ACM, November 1981, pp.
770-772.

Key Words: authentication,
methods, passwords, network.

LAN-89
Landau, C.R.
"Security in a Secure
Capability-Based System,"
ACM Operating Systems
Review, October 1988, pp. 2-
4.

Key Words: control,
capability, techniques.

LAR-86
Larson, J.A.
"Granting and Revoking
Discretionary Authority,"
Information Systems (U.K.),
Vol. 13, No. 1, 1988.

Key Words: control,
discretionary, methods,
techniques.

LEE-84
Lee, T.M.P.
"Future Directions of Security
for Sperry Series 1100
Computers," Proc. 7th
Seminar, DoD Comp. Sec.
Progr., (5: DOD-84), 1984,
pp. 161-168.

Key Words: control, design,
methods.

LEE-88
Lee, T.M.P.
"Using Mandatory Integrity to
Enforce 'Commercial'
Security," Proc. 1988 IEEE
Symp. on Sec. & Privacy, (5:
IEE-88a), pp. 140-146.

Key Words: control, integrity,
methods.

LEG-83
Legrand, S.
"Access Control for a Safety
Critical Distributed System
Interface Set," AIAA No. 87-
3083, Proc. 3d Aerosp. Comp.
Sec. Conf., (5: IEE-87b),
1987, pp. 108-113.

Key Words: control,
techniques.

LEG-88
Legge, J.
"Rendering a Commercial
Operating System Security,"
Proc. IFIP/Sec. '88, Australia,
1989, (2: CAE-89), pp. 273-
289.

Key Words: control, OS,
methods.

LEV-83
Leveson, N.G., and
P.R. Harvey
"Analyzing Software Safety,"
IEEE Trans. on Software
Engr., September, 1983, pp.
569-579.

Key Words: software, safety.

LIP-82
Lipner, S.B.
"Nondiscretionary Controls for
Commercial Applications,"
Proc. 1982 IEEE Symp. on
Sec. & Privacy, (5: IEE-82),
pp. 2-10.

Key Words: controls, methods,
techniques.

LIP-85
Lipner, S.B.
"Secure System Development
at Digital Equipment:
Targetting the Needs of a
Commercial and Government
Customer Base," Proc. 9th
Natl. Comp. Sec. Conf., (5:
NCS-85), 1985, pp. 120-123.

Key Words: developemnt,
description.

LIP-85a
Lipton, D.L. and H.K.T. Wong
"Modern Trends in
Authentication," ACM Security
Audit & Control Review,
Winter 1985, pp. 35-42.

Key Words: authentication,
general.

LIP-86
Lipton, D.L.
"Logical Authentication
Study," ACM Sec., Audit &
Control Review, Spring 1986,
pp. 9-20.

Key Words: authentication,
methods.

LOP-84
Lopriore, L.
"Capability Based Tagged
Architectures," IEEE Trans.
on Computers, September
1984, pp. 786-803.

Key Words: architecture,
capability.

LUK-84
Luke, L.R.
"Password Security Systems,"
EDPACS, October 1984, pp.
1-6.

Key Words: control,
passwords.

LUN-89
Lunt, T.F.
"Access Control Policies:
Some Unanswered
Questions," Computers &
Security, February 1989, pp.
43-54.

Key Words: control, policy.

MAR-87
Maria, A.
"RACF Implementation at
Pudget Power," Proc. 10th
Natl. Comp. Sec. Conf., (5:
NCS-87a), 1987, pp. 91-97.

Key Words: control,
software,

MAR-88
Martin, D.F., and J.V. Cook
"Adding ADA Program
Verification Capability to the
State Delta Verification
System (SDVS)," Proc. 11th
Natl. Comp. Sec. Conf., (5:
NCS-88), 1988, pp. 139-146.

Key Words: verification,
methods.

MEN-88
Menkus, B.
"Understanding the Use of
Passwords," Computers &
Security, April 1988, pp. 132-
136.

Key Words: awareness,
passwords.

MEN-88a
Menkus, B.
"Understanding Password
Compromise," Computers &
Security, December 1988, pp.
549-552.

Key Words: awareness,
passwords.

MIL-89
Miller, D.V., and
R.W. Baldwin
"Access Control by Boolean
Expression Evaluation," Proc.
5th Security Applic. Conf., (4:
IEE-89c), 1989, pp. 131-139.

Key Words: control,
techniques.

MIN-84
Minsky, N.H.
"Selective and Locally
Controlled Transport of
Privileges," ACM Trans. on
Programming Languages and
Systems, October 1984.

Key Words: control,
techniques.

MOF-88
Moffett, J.D. and
M.S. Sloman
"The Source of Authority for
Commercial Access Control,"
IEEE Computer, February
1988, pp. 59-69.

Key Words: control,
management.

MOL-84
Molloy, C.
"Improving Security Controls
within CICS," TeleSystems
Journal, March/April 1984,
pp. 3-11.

Key Words: control, methods.

MON-84
Montini, G., and F. Sirovich
"Access Control Models and
Office Structures," Proc.
IFIP/Sec. '84, Toronto, 1984,
(2: FIN-85), pp. 473-485.

Key Words: control, models.

MOR-86
Morshedian, D.
"How to Fight Passwords
Pirates and Win," IEEE
Computer, January 1986, pp.
104-105.

Key Words: control,
passwords.

MUR-84
Murray, W.H.
"Security Considerations for
Personal Computers," IBM
Systems Journal, No. 3, 1984,
pp. 297-304.

Key Words: control, PC,
methods.

NBS-85
Password Usage. FIPS-PUB
112, National Bureau of
Standards, Gaithersburg, MD,
May 1985.

Key Words: passwords,
guidelines, techniques,
management.

NBS-85a
Standard on Computer Data
Authentication, FIPS-PUB 113,
National Bureau of Standards,
Gaithersburg, MD, May 1985.

Key Words: authentication,
methods, guidelines,
techniques.

NES-83
Nessett, D.M.
"Security Mechanisms in
LINCS," Proc. 6th Seminar,
DoD Comp. Sec. Progr., (5:
DOD-83a), 1983, pp. 60-64.

Key Words: control,
description.

NEW-86
Newsome, R.M.
"Access Controls Within an IBM System/34 Environment," EDPACS, December 1986, pp. 1-6.

Key Words: control, description.

NEW-88
Newberry, M., and J. Seberry
"Experience in Using a Type Signature Password for User Authentication in a Heavily Used Computing Environment," Proc. IFIP/Sec. '88, Australia, (2: CAE-89), 1989, pp. 303-307.

Key Words: control, passwords.

OPA-86
Opaska, W.P.
"Access Control Systems for Personal Computers," EDPACS, August 1986, pp. 6-8.

Key Words: control, PC, methods.

OPA-86a
Opaska, W.P.
"Closing the VAX Default Password 'Backdoor'," EDPACS, September 1986, pp. 6-9.

Key Words: control, passwords, vulnerabilities.

PAA-83
Paans, R., and G. Bonnes
"Surreptitious Security Violation in the MVS Operating System," Computers & Security, June 1983, pp. 144-152.

Key Words: threats, OS, methods.

PAA-86
Paans, R.
A Close Look at MVS Systems: Mechanisms, Performance and Security, North-Holland Elsevier, New York, 1986.

Key Words: book, control, methods.

PAA-86a
Paans, R.
"Performance Aspects of MVS Access Control," Proc. IFIP/Sec. '86, Monte Carlo, 1986, (2: GRI-89).

Key Words: control, description.

PAA-86b
Paans, R., and I.S. Herschberg
"How to Control MVS User SuperVisor Calls," Computers & Security, March 1986, pp. 46-54.

Key Words: control, description.

POS-87
Post, G.V.
"Improving Operating System Security," Computers & Security, October 1987, pp. 417-425.

Key Words: control, OS, methods.

POW-87
Power, J.M., and S.R. White
"Authentication in a Heterogenous Environment," Computers & Security, February 1987, pp. 41-48.

Key Words: authentication, methods.

POZ-86
Pozzo, M.M., and T.E. Gray
"Managing Exposure to Potentially Malicious Programs," Proc. 9th Natl. Comp. Sec. Conf., (5: NCS-86), 1986, pp. 75-80.

Key Words: threats, management.

POZ-89
Pozzo,M., and S. Crocker
"Work-In Progress: Transformation Procedure (TP) Certification," Report, Invitat. Workshop on Data Integrity, NIST, (4: RUT-89), 1989, pp. A.8.1-15.

Key Words: certification, methods.

RAB-89
Rabin, M.O.
"Efficient Dispersal of Information for Security, Load Balancing, and Fault Tolerance," Journal of the ACM, April 1989, pp. 335-348.

Key Words: control, design, methods.

RAJ-82
Rajunas, S.A.
"Meeting Policy Requirements Using Object-Oriented Systems," Proc. 5th Seminar, DoD Comp. Sec. Progr., (5: DOD-82), 1982, pp. 227-232.

Key Words: requirements, policy.

RAL-88
Raleigh, T., and R. Underwood
"CRACK: A Distributed Password Adviser," Proceedings, USENIX UNIX Security Workshop, August 1988.

Key Words: control, passwords.

RAN-86
Randell, B., and J.E. Dobson
"Reliability and Security Issues in Distributed Computing Systems," Proceedings, 5th IEEE Symposium on Reliability in Distributed Software and Database Systems, January 1986, pp. 113-118.

Key Words: control, design, methods.

REE-84
Reeds, J., and P. Weinburger
"File Security and the UNIX System Crypt Command," AT&T Bell Lab. Technical Journal, October 1984, pp. 1673-1684.

Key Words: control, techniques.

REI-86
Reid, B.
"Lessons from the UNIX Breakin at Stanford," ACM Software Engineering Notes, October 1986, pp. 29-35.

Key Words: OS, vulnerabilities.

REI-88
Reisinger, D.A.
"Access Control Methods of VAX/VMA," Information Age, (U.K.), July 1988, pp. 162-168.

Key Words: control, descriptions.

RID-89
Riddle, B.L., M.S. Miron, and J.A. Semo
"Passwords in Use in a University Timesharing Environment," Computers & Security, November 1989, pp. 569-579.

Key Words: control, passwords.

ROW-87
Rowe, K.E., and C.O. Ferguson, Jr.
"ADA Technology/Compusec Insertion Status Report," Proc. 10th Natl. Comp. Sec. Conf., (5: NCS-87a), 1987, pp. 357-360.

Key Words: control, requirements.

RUT-89
Ruthberg, Z.G., and W.T. Polk
Report of the Invitational Workshop on Data Integrity, SP 500-168, National Institute of Standards and Technology, Gaithersburg, MD, Sept. 1989.

Key Words: proceedings, integrity.

SAN-88
Sandhu, R.
"Transaction Control Expressions for Separation of Duties," Proc. 4th Aerosp. Comp. Sec. Conf., (4: IEE-88b), 1988, pp. 282-286.

Key Words: integrity, techniques.

SAN-88a
Sandhu, R.S.
"The N-Tree: A Two Dimensional Partial Order for Protection," ACM Trans. on Computer Systems, May 1988, pp. 197-222.

Key Words: control, methods.

SAN-88b
Sandhu, R.S.
"Nested Categories for Access Control," Computers & Security, December 1988, pp. 599-605.

Key Words: control, methods.

SAN-89
Sandhu, R.
"Terminology, Criteria and System Architectures for Data Integrity," Report, Invitat. Workshop on Data Integrity, NIST, (4: RUT-89), 1989, pp. A.4.1-14.

Key Words: control, general, methods, guidelines.

SAT-88
Satyanarayanan, M.
"Integrating Security in a Large Distributed System," Postscript, 11th Natl. Comp. Sec. Conf., (5: NCS-88a), 1988, pp. 91-108.

Key Words: control, design, network.

SCH-83
Schweitzer, J.A.
"Computer Security: Make Your Passwords More Effective," EDPACS, February 1983, pp. 6-11.

Key Words: control, passwords, methods.

SCH-88
Schokley, W.R.
"Implementing the Clark/Wilson Integrity Policy Using Current Technology," Postscript, 11th Natl. Comp. Sec. Conf., (5: NCS-88a), 1988, pp. 29-37.

Key Words: intgerity, policy, methods.

SHA-87
Shannon, T.C.
"An Introduction to VAX/VMS Security Mechanisms and Techniques," Computer Security Journal, Vol. IV, No. 2, 1987, pp. 39-47.

Key Words: control, description.

SHE-89
Sherizen, S., and F. Engel
"Striving for Unix Security," Computerworld, March 20, 1989, pp. 85-93.

Key Words: control, description.

SIM-81
Simmons, G.J.
"Half a Loaf Is Better than None: Some Novel Integrity Problems," Proc. 1981 IEEE Symp. on Sec. & Privacy, (5: IEE-81), pp. 65-69.

Key Words: integrity, design, methods, requirements.

SIN-85
Singh, K.
"On Improvements to Password Security," ACM Operating Systems Review, January 1985, pp. 53-60.

Key Words: control, passwords.

SMI-87
Smith, S.L.
"Authenticating Users by Word Association," Computers & Security, December 1987, pp. 464-470.

Key Words: authentication, methods.

SOL-88
Sollins, K.R.
"Cascaded Authentication," Proc. 1988 IEEE Symp. on Sec. & Privacy, (5: IEE-88a), pp. 156-163.

Key Words: authentication, methods.

SPE-87
Spender, J.-C.
"Identifying Computer Users with Authentication Devices (Tokens)," Computers & Security, October 1987, pp. 385-395.

Key Words: authentication, methods.

STE-83
Steinauer, D.D.
"Technical Security Issues in Small Computer Systems," Proceedings, 1983 COMPCON Fall, September 1983.

Key Words: control, PC, methods.

STO-89
Stotts, P.S., and R. Furuta
"Access Control and Verification in Petri-Net-Based Hyperdocuments," Proc. COMPASS '89: Comp. Assurance, (2: IEE-89), 1989, pp. 49-55.

Key Words: control, verification, methods.

SUM-84
Summers, R.C.
"An Overview of Computer Security," IBM Systems Journal, Vol. 23, No. 4, 1984, pp. 309-325.

Key Words: control, awareness, general.

SYM-84
Symons, C.R., and J.A. Schweitzer
"A Proposal for an Automated Logical Access Control Standard," Proc. IFIP/Sec. '84, Toronto, 1984, (2: FIN-85), pp. 115-127.

Key Words: control, guidelines.

TAN-82
Tangney, J.D., and P.S. Tasker
"Safeguarding Today's Interactive Computer Systems," Computer Security Journal, Winter 1982, pp. 57-70.

Key Words: control, techniques.

TEN-87
Tensa, D.
"Typical Weaknesses in Operating Systems Software," Information Age, (U.K.), April 1987, pp. 74-78.

Key Words: OS, vulnerabilities.

TEN-88
Tener, W.
"AI and 4GL: Automated Detection and Investigation Tools," Proc. IFIP/Sec. '88, Australia, 1989, (2: CAE-89), pp. 23-29.

Key Words: methods, techniques.

THO-82
Thom, A.B.
"Hardware Security," Computer Security Journal, Winter 1982, pp. 105-107.

Key Words: control, methods, architecture.

THO-88
Thomas, T.
"A Mandatory Access Control Mechanism for the UNIX File System," Proc. 4th Aerosp. Comp. Sec. Conf., (4: IEE-88b), 1988, pp. 173-177,

Key Words: control, mandatory, description.

TUR-86
Turn, R., and J. Habibi
"On the Interactions of Security and Fault-Tolerance," Proc. 9th Natl. Comp. Sec. Conf., (5: NCS-86), 1986, pp. 138-142.

Key Words: control, design, methods.

USA-80
Proceedings, Third Automation Security Workshop, U.S. Army Computer Systems Command, December 1989.

Key Words: proceedings, control.

VAC-89
Vaccaro, H.S., and G.E. Liepins
"Detection of Anomalous Computer Session Activity," Proc. 1989 IEEE Symp. on Sec. & Privacy, (5: IEE-89b), pp. 289-289.

Key Words: control, techniques.

VAN-83
Van de Riet, R.R., and
M.L. Kersten
"Privacy and Security in
Information Systems Using
Language Features,"
Information Systems, (U.K.),
Vol. 8, No. 2, 1983, pp. 95-
103.

Key Words: control, methods.

VAN-84
Van de Goor, A.J.
"Effects of Technical
Developments on System
Security," Computers &
Security, November 1984, pp.
315-322.

Key Words: control, design,
methods.

VAS-83
Vasak, J.M.
"Issues in Secure System
Acquisition," AIAA No. 87-
3089, Proc. 3d Aerosp.
Comp. Sec. Conf., (5: IEE-
87b), 1987, pp. 114-117.

Key Words: control, design,
methods.

VET-80
Vetter, L.L.
"Computer Access Control
Software," EDPACS,
February 1980, pp. 1-12.

Key Words: control,
software.

VIN-88
Vinter, S.T.
"Extended Discretionary
Access Controls," Proc. 1988
IEEE Symp. on Sec. &
Privacy, (5: IEE-88a), pp. 39-
49.

Key Words: control,
discretionary.

WAG-88
Wagner, D.A.
"System Security in Space
Flight Operations Center,"
Proc. 4th Aerosp. Comp. Sec.
Conf., (4: IEE-88b), 1988, pp.
426-430.

Key Words: control,
description.

WAL-81
Walsh, M.E.
"Software Security," Journal
of Systems Management,
October 1981, pp. 6-13.

Key Words: control, software.

WAT-81
Wattam, K.W.
"Virtual Machine Environment
-- Security Aspects,"
Information Privacy, (U.K.),
March 1981, pp. 68-74.

Key Words: control,
architecture.

WEI-88
Weiss, J.D., and
E.G. Amoroso
"Ensuring Software Integrity,"
Proc. 4th Aerosp. Comp. Sec.
Conf., (4: IEE-88b), 1988, pp.
323-330.

Key Words: integrity,
software,

WEL-84
Wells, P.
"On-Chip Hardware Supports
Computer Security Features,"
Electronics, March 8, 1984,
pp. 128-130.

Key Words: control,
architecture.

WEL-88
Wells, C.
"A Note on 'Protection
Imperfect'," ACM Operating
Systems Review, October
1988.

Key Words: control, methods.

WIL-81
Wilkinson, A.L., et al.
"Penetration, Analysis of the
Burroughs Large Systems,"
ACM Operating Systems
Review, January 1981, pp. 14-
25.

Key Words: vulnerabilities,
threats, description.

WON-85
Wong, R.
"One-Time Passwords Fortify
System Security,"
Computerworld, December 23,
1985, pp. 31-32.

Key Words: control,
passwords.

WON-89
Wong, R.M. and Y.E. Ding
"Providing Software Integrity
Using Type Managers," Proc.
4th Aerosp. Comp. Sec. Conf.,
(4: IEE-88b), 1988, pp. 287-
298.

Key Words: integrity, software,
techniques, methods.

WOO-80
Wood, H.M.
"A Survey of Computer-Based
Password Techniques," in
Rullo, T.A., (Ed.), Advances in
Computer Security
Management, Vol. 1, Heyden
& Son, Inc. Philadelphia, PA,
1980, pp. 140-167.

Key Words: control,
passwords, general.

WOO-83
Wood, C.C.
"Effective Information Systems
Security With Password
Controls," Computers &
Security, January 1983, pp. 5-
10.

Key Words: control passwords.

WOO-84
Wood, M., and T. Elbra
System Design for Data
Protection, National
Computer Centre (UK), J.
Wiley & Sons, Chichester,
1984.

Key Words: book, general,
control, design, methods.

WOO-85
Wood, C.C.
"Floppy Diskette Security
Measures," Computers &
Security, September 1985, pp.
223-228.

Key Words: control, PC,
methods.

WOO-85a
Wood, P.H., and S.G.
Kochan
UNIX System Security,
Hayden Publishing Co.,
Hasbrouck Heights, NJ, 1985.

Key Words: book, control,
methods, description.

WOO-86
Wood, C.C., and
H.M. Zeidler
"Security Modules: Potent
Information Security System
Components," Computers &
Security, June 1986, pp. 114-
121.

Key Words: control,
techniques.

WOO-87
Woodcock, M.E.
"The Use of ADA in Secure
and Reliable Software," Proc.
10th Natl. Comp. Sec. Conf.,
(5: NCS-87a), 1987, pp. 362-
365.

Key Words: control, software,
methods.

WOO-88
Wood, C.C.
"Extended User
Authentication: The Next
Major Enhancement to Access
Packages," Proc. IFIP/Sec.
'88, Australia, (2: CAE-89),
1989, pp. 223-234.

Key Words: authentication,
methods.

WOR-85
Worthington, T.K., et al.
"IBM Dynamic Signature
Verification," Proc. IFIP/Sec.
'84, Toronto, 1984, (2: FIN-
85), pp. 129-154.

Key Words: authentication,
methods.

WUM-84
Wu, M.L., and T.Y. Hwang
"Access Control with Single
Key-Lock," IEEE Trans. on
Software Engr., May 1984, pp.
185-191.

Key Words: control, technique.

YEO-85
Yeo, G.K.
"Incorporating Access Control
in Forms Systems," Computers
& Security, June 1985, pp.
109-122.

Key Words: control, methods.

ZAJ-88
Zajac, B.P., Jr.
"Dial-Up Communication
Lines: Can They Be Secured,"
Computers & Security,
February 1988, pp. 35-36.

Key Words: control, network.

5. Trusted Systems

This section cites publications on trusted operating systems and trusted systems architecture research and development, formal evaluation criteria, implementation of the reference monitor concept, design of trusted operating systems, descriptions of specific systems, correctness proof methods and techniques for trusted systems, and certification criteria.

ABR-86
Abrams, M.D.,
H.J. Podell (Eds.),
Computer and Network
Security Tutorial, IEEE
Computer Society Press,
Washington, DC, 1986.

Key Words: book, general,
methods.

AKL-82
Akl, S.G., and P.D. Taylor
"Cryptographic Solution to a
Multilevel Security Problem,"
Proc. Crypto '82, Santa
Barbara, (9: CHA-83b), 1982,
pp. 237-249.

Key Words: MLS,
cryptography.

ALB-87
Albert, S.B.
"Criteria Extension for
Distributed Systems," AIAA
No. 87-3095, Proc. 3d
Aerosp. Comp. Sec. Conf.,
(5: IEE-87b), 1987, pp. 122-
127.

Key Words: criteria,
networks.

AME-80
Ames, S.R., and
J.G. Keeton-Williams
"Demonstrating Security for
Trusted Applications on a
Security Kernel," Proc. 1980
IEEE Symp. on Sec. &
Privacy, (5: IEE-80), 145-
156.

Key Words: tusted, kernel,
methods.

AME-81
Ames, S.R., Jr.
"Security Kernels: A Solution
or a Problem," Proc. 1981
IEEE Symp. on Sec. &
Privacy, (5: IEE-81), pp. 141-
150.

Key Words: kernels, general,
methods.

AME-83
Ames, S.R. Jr., M. Gasser,
and R.R. Schell
"Security Kernel Design and
Implementation: An
Introduction," IEEE Computer,
July 1983, pp. 14-22.

Key Words: kernel, design,
general.

AND-82
Anderson, J.P.
"Accelerating Computer
Security Innovations," Proc.
1982 IEEE Symp. on Sec. &
Privacy, (5: IEE-82), pp. 91-
97.

Key Words: trusted, methods,
general.

AND-83
Anderson, J.P.
"An Approach to
Identification of Minimum
TCB requirements for Various
Threat/Risk Environments,"
Proc. 1983 IEEE Symp. on
Sec. & Privacy, (5: IEE-83a),
pp. 102-104.

Key Words: TCB,
requirements, risk.

AND-85
Anderson, E.R.
"ADA's Suitability for Trusted
Computer Systems," Proc.
1985 IEEE Symp. on Sec. &
Privacy, (5: IEE-85), pp. 184-
189.

Key Words: trusted,
requirements.

ARN-84
Arnold, T.S.
"The Practical Aspects of
Multi-level Security," Proc. 7th
Seminar, DoD Comp. Sec.
Progr., (5: DOD-84), 1984, pp.
30-37.

Key Words: MLS, design,
methods.

ARN-85
Arnold, T.S.
"Multilevel Security from a
Practical Point of View," Proc.
8th Natl. Comp. Sec. Conf.,
(5: NCS-85), 1985, pp. 43-46.

Key Words: MLS, design,
methods.

ASH-89
Asby, V.A., T. Gregg,
and A. Lee
"Security Approach for Rapid
Prototyping in Mutlilevel
Secure Systems," Proc. 5th
Security Applicat. Conf., (4:
IEE-89c), 1989, pp. 328-334.

Key Words: MLS, design,
methods.

BAR-84

Barnes, D.
"Secure Communications Processor Research," Proc. 7th Seminar, DoD Comp. Sec. Progr., (5: DOD-84), 1984, pp. 312-318.

Key Words: MLS, design, network.

BAR-88

Barker, W.C., P. Cochrane, and M. Branstad "Embedding Cryptography into a Trusted Mach System," Proc. 4th Aerosp. Comp. Sec. Conf., (4: IEE-88b), 1988, pp. 379-383.

Key Words: OS, design, cryptography.

BAR-89

Barker, W.C.
"Use of Privacy-Enhanced Mail for Software Distribution," Proc. 5th Security Applicat. Conf., (4: IEE-89c), 1989, pp. 344-347.

Key Words: methods, software.

BAX-86

Baxter, M.S.J.
"A Layered Architecture for Multilevel Security," Proc. IFIP/Sec. '86, Monte Carlo, 1986, (2: GRI-89).

Key Words: MLS, architecture.

BEL-84

Bell, D.E.
"Working Toward A1," Proc. 7th Seminar, DoD Comp. Sec. Progr., (5: DOD-84), 1984, pp. 24-29.

Key Words: MLS, trusted, design.

BEN-84

Benzel, T.V.
"Analysis of a Kernel Verification," Proc. 1984 IEEE Symp. on Sec. & Privacy, (5: IEE-84), pp. 125-131.

Key Words: verification, kernel.

BEN-85

Benzel, T.C.V. and D.A. Travilla,
"Trusted Software Verification: A Case Study," Proc. 1985 IEEE Symp. on Sec. & Privacy, (5: IEE-85), pp. 14-31.

Key Words: verification, software.

BEN-89

Benzel, T.C.V.
"Developing Trusted Systems Using DOD-STD-2167A," Proc. 5th Sec. Applicat. Conf., (4: IEE-89c), 1989, pp. 166-176.

Key Words: trused, design, methods.

BER-80

Berstis, V.
"Security and Protection of Data in the IBM System/38," Proceedings, 7th IEEE Conference on Computer Architectures, 1980, pp. 245-252.

Key Words: design, methods, case.

BER-88

Berch, R., et al.
"Use of Automated Verification Tools in a Secure Software Development Methodology," Proc. 11th Natl. Comp. Sec. Conf., (5: NCS-88), 1988, pp. 284-289.

Key Words: verification, software.

BEV-89

Bevier, W.R.
"Kit: A Study in Operating System Verification," IEEE Trans. on Software Engr., November 1989, pp. 1382-1396.

Key Words: verification, OS, case.

BIR-86

Birrell, A.D., et al.
"A Global Authentication Service Without Global Trust," Proc. 1986 IEEE Symp. on Sec. & Privacy, (5: IEE-86), pp. 223-230.

Key Words: authentication, methods.

BLA-81

Blakely, G.R., G. Ma, and L. Swanson
"Security Proofs for Information Protection Systems," Proc. 1981 IEEE Symp. on Sec. & Privacy, (5: IEE-81), pp. 75-88.

Key Words: verification, methods.

BLO-86

Blotcky, S., K. Lynch, and S. Lipner
"SE/VMS: Implementing Mandatory Security in VAX/VMS," Proc. 9th Natl. Comp. Sec. Conf., (5: NCS-86), 1986, pp. 47-54.

Key Words: MLS, design, case.

BOE-85

Boebert, W.E., R.Y. Kain, and W.D. Young
"Secure Computing: The Secure Ada Target Approach," Scientific Honeyweller, July 1985, pp. 1-17.

Key Words: MLS, design, methods.

BOE-85a
Boebert, W.E., et al.
"Secure Ada Target: Issues,
System Design, and
Verification," Proc. 1986
IEEE Symp. on Sec. &
Privacy, (5: IEE-86), pp.
176-183.

Key Words: MLS,
verification, design.

BOE-88
Boebert, W.E.
"The LOCK Demonstration,"
Postscript, 11th Natl. Comp.
Sec. Conf., (5: NCS-88a),
1988, pp. 73-88.

Key Words: TCB,
architecture, design.

BOE-88a
Boebert, W.E.
"Constructing an Infosec
System Using the LOCK
Technology," Postscript, 11th
Natl. Comp. Sec. Conf., (5:
NCS-88a), 1988, pp. 89-95.

Key Words: TCB, design,
techniques.

BON-83
Bonyun, D.A.
"The Use of Architectural
Principles in the Design of
Certifiably Secure Systems,"
Computers & Security, June
1983, pp. 153-162.

Key Words: architecture,
TCB, design.

BON-84
Bonyun, D.A.
"Formal Verification: Its
Purpose and Practice," Proc.
IFIP/Sec. '84, Toronto, 1984,
(2: FIN-85), pp. 217-223.

Key Words: verification,
general.

BON-89
Bondi, J.O., and
M.A. Branstad
"Architectural Support of
Fine-Grained Secure
Computing," Proc. 5th
Security Applicat. Conf., (4:
IEE-89c), 1989, pp. 121-130.

Key Words: architecture,
design.

BRA-84
Brand, S.L.
"Environmental Guidelines for
Using the DoD Trusted
Computer Systems Evaluation
Criteria," Proc. 7th Seminar,
DoD Comp. Sec. Progr., (5:
DOD-84), 1984, pp. 17-23.

Key Words: criteria,
guidelines.

BRA-86
Branstad, M.A., et al.
"Trust Issues of MACH-1,"
Proc. 9th Natl. Comp. Sec.
Conf., (5: NCS-86), 1986, pp.
209-212.

Key Words: trusted, OS,
policy, case.

BRA-87
Branstad, M., et al.
"Trusted Mach Design," Proc.
3d Aerosp. Comp. Sec. Conf.,
(5: IEE-87b), 1987, pp. 24-29.

Key Words: OS, design, case.

BRA-88
Branstad, M., and F.L. Mayer
"Access Mediation in Server-
Oriented Systems: An
Examination of Two
Systems," Proc. 11th Natl.
Comp. Sec. Conf., (5: NCS-
88), 1988, pp. 309-318.

Key Words: control, design,
methods.

BRA-88a
Branstad, M., H. Tajalli,
and F. Mayer
"Security Issues of the Trusted
Mach System," Proc. 4th
Aerosp. Comp. Sec. Conf., (4:
IEE-88b), 1988, pp. 362-367.

Key Words: trusted, OS,
policy, case.

BRA-89
Branstad, M., et al.
"Access Mediation in a
Message Passing Kernel,"
Proc. 1989 IEEE Symp. on
Sec. & Privacy, (5: IEE-89b),
pp. 66-72.

Key Words: control, kernel,
design.

BRA-89a
Branstad., M., and J. Landauer
"Assurance for the Trusted
Mach Operating System," Proc.
COMPASS-89, Comp.
Assurance, (4: IEE-89), pp.
103-108.

Key Words: verification, OS,
case.

BRI-85
Britton, D.E.
"Verlangen: A Verification
Language for Designs of
Secure Systems," Proc. 8th
Natl. Comp. Sec. Conf., (5:
NCS-85), 1985, pp. 70-81.

Key Words: verification,
methods.

BRO-88
Brown, G.L.
"Interdependence of Evaluated
Subsystems," Proc. 11th Natl.
Comp. Sec. Conf., (5: NCS-
88), 1988, pp. 330-332.

Key Words: trusted, design,
general.

BUS-83
Bussolati, U. and G. Martella
"The Design of Secure
Distributed Systems,"
Proceedings, 1983 IEEE
Compcon Spring Conf., 1983,
pp. 492-498.

Key Words: trusted, design,
general.

CAR-86
Carlson, R.A., and T.F. Lunt,
"The Trusted Domain
Machine: A Secure
Communications Device for
Security Guard Applications,"
Proc. 1986 IEEE Symp. on
Sec. & Privacy, (5: IEE-86),
pp. 182-186.

Key Words: trusted, network,
design.

CAR-87
Carson, M.E., et al.
"From B2 to CMU: Building
a Compartmental Mode
Workstation on a Secure
Xenix Base," Proc. 3d
Aerosp. Comp. Sec. Conf.,
(5: IEE-87b), 1987, pp. 35-
43.

Key Words: MLS, design,
case.

CAR-88
Carroll, J.M.
"Implementing Multilevel
Security by Violation
Privilege," Computers &
Security, December 1988, pp.
563-573.

Key Words: MLS, design,
methods.

CAS-88
Casey, T.A., et al.
"A Secure Distributed
Operating System," Proc.
1988 IEEE Symp. on Sec. &
Privacy, (5: IEE-88a), pp. 27-
38.

Key Words: MLS, OS,
network, design.

CAS-89
Casey, T., et al.
"Secure Automated Document
Delivery," Proc. 5th Security
Applicat. Conf., (4: IEE-89c),
1989, pp. 348-355.

Key Words: trusted, methods.

CHE-81
Cheheyl, M.H., et al.
"Verifying Security," ACM
Computing Surveys,
September 1981, pp. 279-339.

Key Words: verification,
general.

COO-88
Cook, J., and D.F. Martin
"Adding Ada Program
Verification Capability to the
State Delta Verification
System (SDVS)," Proc. 11th
Natl. Comp. Sec. Conf., (5:
NCS-88), 1988, pp. 139-146.

Key Words: verification,
methods.

COR-84
Cornwell, M.R. and
R.J.K. Jacob
"Structure of a Rapid
Prototype Secure Military
Message System," Proc. 7th
Seminar, DoD Comp. Sec.
Program, (5: DOD-84), 1984,
pp. 48-57.

Key Words: MLS, design,
case, network.

COR-89
Cornwell, M.R.
"A Software Engineering
Approach to Designing
Trustworthy Software," Proc.
1989 IEEE Symp. on Sec. &
Privacy, (5: IEE-89b), pp.
148-156

Key Words: trusted, software,
design.

COX-81
Cox, L.A., and R.R. Schell
"The Structure of a Security
Kernel for a Z8000
Multiprocessor," Proc. 1981
IEEE Symp. on Sec. &
Privacy, (5: IEE-81), pp. 124-
129.

Key Words: kernel, design,
case, architecture.

CRA-84
Craigen, D.,
"Ottawa Euclid and EVES: A
Status Report," Proc. 1984
IEEE Symp. on Sec. &
Privacy, (5: IEE-84), pp. 114-
124.

Key Words: verification,
design, case.

CRA-87
Craigen, D.
"m-EVES," Proc. 10th Natl.
Comp. Sec. Conf., (5: NCS-
87a), 1987, pp. 109-117.

Key Words: verification,
design, case, methods.

CRO-88
Crocker, S.D., et al.
"Reverification of a
Microprocessor," Proc. 1989
IEEE Symp. on Sec. &
Privacy, (5: IEE-89b), pp. 166-
176.

Key Words: verification,
architecture, techniques,
methods, case.

CRO-88a
Crow, J.S., et al.
"EHDM Verification
Environment -- An Overview,"
Proc. 11th Natl. Comp. Sec.
Conf., (5: NCS-88), 1988, pp.
147-155.

Key Words: verification,
design, case.

CRO-89
Crocker, S.D., and
E.J. Siarkiewics
"Software Methodology for
Development of a Trusted
MBS," Proc. 5th Security
Applicat. Conf., (4: IEE-89c),
1989, pp. 148-165.

Key Words: trusted, software,
methods.

CSC-85
Computer Security
Requirements -- Guidance for
Applying the Department of
Defense Trusted Computer
System Evaluation Criteria,
CSC-STD-003-85, National
Computer Security Center, Ft.
Meade, MD, 25 June 1985.

Key Words: guidelines,
criteria.

CSC-85a
Technical Rationale Behind
CSC-STD-003-85: Computer
Security Requirements, CSC-
STD-004-85, National
Computer Security Center, Ft.
Meade, MD, 25 June 1985.

Key Words: criteria,
guidelines.

CSC-87
A Guide to Understanding
Discretionary Access Control
in Trusted Systems, NCSC-
TG-003, National Computer
Security Center, Ft. Meade,
MD, 1 June 1988.

Key Words: guidelines,
control.

CSC-88
A Guide to Understanding
Configuration Management in
Trusted Systems, NCSC-TG-
006, National Computer
Security Center, Ft. Meade,
MD, 28 March 1988.

Key Words: guidelines,
design.

CSC-88a
A Guide to Understanding
Audit inTrusted Systems,
NCSC-TG-001, National
Computer Security Center, Ft.
Meade, MD, 1 June 1988.

Key Words: guidelines,
auditing.

CSC-88b
Computer Security Subsystem
Interpretation of the Trusted
Computer System Evaluation
Criteria, NCSC-TG-009,
National Computer Security
Center, Ft. Meade, MD, 16
September 1988.

Key Words: guidelines, TCB,
criteria.

CSC-88c
A Guide to Understanding
Design Documentation in
Trusted Systems, NCSC-TG-
007, National Computer
Security Center, Ft. Meade,
MD, 2 October 1988.

Key Words: guidelines,
design.

CSC-88d
A Guide to Understanding
Trusted Distribution in
Trusted Systems, NCSC-TG-
008, National Computer
Security Center, Ft. Meade,
MD, 15 December 1988.

Key Words: guidelines,
design.

CSC-89
Guidelines for Formal
Verification Systems, NCSC-
TG-014, National Computer
Security Center, Ft. Meade,
MD, 1 April 1989.

Key Words: guidelines,
verification.

CSC-89a
Rating Maintenance Phase
Program Document, NCSC-
TG-013, National Computer
Security Center, Ft. Meade,
MD, 23 June 1989.

Key Words: guidelines, design.

CUM-87
Cummings, P.T., et al.
"Compartmented Mode
Workstation: Results Through
Prototyping," Proc. 1987 IEEE
Symp. on Sec. & Privacy, (5:
IEE-87a), pp. 2-12.

Key Words: MLS, design,
case, methods.

CUT-88
Cutler, M.
"Verifying Implementation
Correctness Using the State
Delta Verification System
(SDVS)," Proc. 11th Natl.
Comp. Sec. Conf., (5: NCS-
88), 1988, pp. 156-161.

Key Words: verification,
design, case.

DAN-82
Dannenberg, R.B., and
G.W. Ernst
"Formal Program Verification
Using Symbolic Execution,"
IEEE Trans. on Software
Engr., January 1982, pp. 43-
52.

Key Words: verification,
methods.

DAV-80
Davida, G.I., et al.
"A System Architecture to
Support a Verifiably Secure
Multi-Level Security System,"
Proc. 1980 IEEE Symp. on
Sec. & Privacy, (5: IEE-80),
pp. 137-144.

Key Words: MLS, architecture,
design.

DIT-82
>   Dittrich, K.R., et al.
>   "Protection in the OSKAR
>   Operating System: Goals,
>   Concepts, Consequences,"
>   Proc. 1982 IEEE Symp. on
>   Sec. & Privacy, (5: IEE-82),
>   pp. 46-56.
>
>   Key Words: OS, policy,
>   methods, case.

DIV-87
>   Di Vito, B.L., and
>   L.A. Johnson
>   "A Gypsy Verifier Assistant,"
>   Proc. 10th Natl. Comp. Sec.
>   Conf., (5: NCS-87a), 1987,
>   pp. 183-192.
>
>   Key Words: verification,
>   methods.

DOD-80
>   Proceedings, Second Seminar
>   onthe DoD Computer
>   Security Initiative Program,
>   Department of Defense,
>   Washington, DC, January
>   1980.
>
>   Key Words: proceedings,
>   MLS, design.

DOD-80a
>   Proceedings, Third Seminar
>   on the DoD Computer
>   Security Initiative Program,
>   Department of Defense,
>   Washington, DC, November
>   1980.
>
>   Key Words: proceedings,
>   MLS, design.

DOD-81
>   Proceedings, Fourth Seminar
>   on the DoD Computer
>   Security Initiative Program,
>   Department of Defense,
>   Washington, DC, August
>   1981.
>
>   Key Words: proceedings,
>   MLS, design.

DOD-82
>   Proceedings, Fifth Seminar on
>   the DoD Computer Security
>   Initiative Program, Department
>   of Defense, Washington, DC,
>   May 1982.
>
>   Key Words: proceedings,
>   MLS, design.

DOD-83
>   Proceedings, Sixth Seminar on
>   the DoD Computer Security
>   Initiative, National Bureau of
>   Standards, November 1983.
>
>   Key Words: proceedings,
>   MLS, design.

DOD-83a
>   Department of Defense
>   Trusted Computer System
>   Evaluation Criteria, CSC-STD-
>   001-83, DoD Computer
>   Security Center, Ft. George G.
>   Meade MD, 15 August 1983.
>
>   Key Words: MLS, criteria,
>   policy, verification, TCB,
>   design.

DOD-84
>   Proceedings, Seventh Seminar
>   onthe DoD Computer Security
>   Initiative, DoD Computer
>   Security Center, Ft. Meade,
>   MD, September 1984.
>
>   Key Words: proceedings,
>   MLS, design.

DOD-85
>   Department of Defense
>   Trusted Computer System
>   Evaluation Criteria, DoD
>   5200.28-STD, U.S.
>   Department of Defense,
>   Washington, DC, December
>   1985.
>
>   Key Words: MLS, TCB,
>   criteria.

DOW-85
>   Downs, D.D. et al.
>   "Issues in Discretionary
>   Access Control," Proc. 1985
>   IEEE Symp. on Sec. &
>   Privacy, (5: IEE-85), pp. 208-
>   218.
>
>   Key Words: discretionary,
>   control.

ECK-87
>   Eckman, S.T.
>   "InaFlo: The FDM Flow
>   Tool," Proc. 10th Natl. Comp.
>   Sec. Conf., (5: NCS-87a),
>   1987, pp. 175-182.
>
>   Key Words: verification,
>   methods.

ELO-85
>   Eloff, J.H.P.
>   "The Development of a
>   Specification Language for a
>   Computer Security System,"
>   Computers & Security, June
>   1985, pp. 143-147.
>
>   Key Words: specification,
>   methods.

FAR-86
>   Farmer, W.M., D.M. Johnson,
>   and F.J. Thayer
>   "Towards A Discipline for
>   Developing Verified Software,"
>   Proc. 9th Natl. Comp. Sec.
>   Conf., (5: NCS-86), 1986, pp.
>   91-98.
>
>   Key Words: verification,
>   software.

FEL-87
>   Fellows, J., et al.
>   "The Architecture of a
>   Distributed Trusted Computing
>   Base," Proc. 10th Natl. Comp.
>   Sec. Conf., (5: NCS-87a),
>   1987, pp. 68-77.
>
>   Key Words: architecture, TCB,
>   network.

FET-88
>   Fetzer, J.H.
>   "Program Verification: The
>   Very Idea," Communications
>   of the ACM, September 1988.
>
>   Key Words: verification,
>   general.

FRA-83
　　Fraim, L.J.
　　"SCOMP: A Solution to the
　　MLS Problem," Proc.
　　IFIP/Sec. '83, Stockholm,
　　1983, (2: FAK-83), pp. 275-
　　286.

　　Key Words: MLS, design,
　　network, case.

FRA-86
　　Fraim, L.J.
　　"The Challenge After A1 --
　　A View of the Security
　　Market," Proc. 9th Natl.
　　Comp. Sec. Conf., (5: NCS-
　　86), 1986, pp. 41-46.

　　Key Words: trusted, design,
　　general.

FRE-88
　　Freeman, J., R. Neely, and
　　L. Megalo
　　"Developing Secure Systems:
　　Issues and Solutions," Proc.
　　4th Aerosp. Comp. Sec.
　　Conf., (4: IEE-88b), 1988,
　　pp. 183-190.

　　Key Words: MLS, design,
　　general.

GAB-86
　　Gabriele, M.
　　"Smart Terminals for Trusted
　　Computer Systems," Proc. 9th
　　Natl. Comp. Sec. Conf., (5:
　　NCS-86), 1986, pp. 16-20.

　　Key Words: trusted, MLS,
　　design, network.

GAM-88
　　Gambel, D., and S. Walter
　　"Retrofitting and Developing
　　Applications for a Trusted
　　Computing Base," Proc. 11th
　　Natl. Comp. Sec. Conf., (5:
　　NCS-88), 1988, pp. 344-346.

　　Key Words: TCB, design,
　　techniques.

GAS-88
　　Gasser, M.
　　Building a Secure Computer
　　System, Van Nostrand
　　Reinhold, New York, 1988

　　Key Words: book, general,
　　MLS, design.

GAS-89
　　Gasser, M., et al.
　　"The Digital Distributed
　　System Security Architecture,"
　　Proc. 12th Natl. Comp. Sec.
　　Conf., (5: NCS-89), 1989, pp.
　　305-319.

　　Key Words: architecture,
　　design, case.

GLA-84
　　Glasgow, J.I., et al.
　　"Specifying Multilevel
　　Security in a Distributed
　　System," Proc. 7th Seminar,
　　DoD Comp. Sec. Program, (5:
　　DOD-84), 1984, pp. 319-340.

　　Key Words: MLS,
　　specification, design.

GLI-83
　　Gligor, V.D.
　　"A Note on the Denial of
　　Service Problem," Proc. IEEE
　　Symposium on Security and
　　Privacy, April 1983, pp. 139-
　　149.

　　Key Words: denial, threats,
　　design.

GLI-83a
　　Gligor, V.D.
　　"The Verification of
　　Protection Mechanisms of
　　High-Level Language
　　Machines," International
　　Journal of Computer and
　　Information Sciences, August
　　1983, pp. 211-246.

　　Key Words: verification,
　　methods.

GLI-84
　　Gligor, V.D.
　　"A Note on Denial-of-Service
　　Problem in Operating
　　Systems," IEEE Trans. on
　　Software Engr., May 1984, pp.
　　320-324.

　　Key Words: denial, threats,
　　design.

GLI-85
　　Gligor, V.D.,
　　"Analysis of the Hardware
　　Verification of the Honeywell
　　SCOMP," Proc. 1985 IEEE
　　Symp. on Sec. & Privacy, (5:
　　IEE-85), pp. 32-44.

　　Key Words: verification, case.

GLI-86
　　Gligor, V.D., et al.
　　"On the Design and the
　　Implementation of Secure
　　Xenix Workstations," Proc.
　　1986 IEEE Symp. on Sec. &
　　Privacy, (5: IEE-86), pp. 102-
　　117.

　　Key Words: MLS, policy,
　　design, case.

GLI-86a
　　Gligor, V.D., and
　　C.S. Chandersekaran
　　"Toward the Development of
　　Secure Distributed Systems,"
　　Proc. IFIP/Sec. '86, Monte
　　Carlo, 1986, (2: GRI-89).

　　Key Words: MLS, network,
　　design.

GLI-86b
　　Gligor, V.D., et al.
　　"A New Security Testing
　　Method and Its Application to
　　the Secure Xenix Kernel,"
　　Proc. 9th Natl. Comp. Sec.
　　Conf., (5: NCS-86), 1986, pp.
　　40-59

　　Key Words: verification,
　　design, case.

GLI-87
Gligor, V.D., et al.
"Design and Implementation
of Secure Xenix," IEEE
Trans. on Software Engr.,
February 1987, pp. 208-221.

Key Words: MLS, policy,
design, case.

GLI-87a
Gligor, V.D., et al.
"A New Security Testing
Method and Its Application
to Secure Xenix Kernel,"
IEEE Trans. on Software
Engr., February 1987, pp.
169-183.

Key Words: verification,
caase.

GOL-81
Golberg, D.L.
"The SDC Communications
Kernel," Proc. 4th Seminar,
DoD Comp. Sec. Progr., (5:
DOD-81), 1981, pp. P1-P33.

Key Words: kernel, network,
case.

GOL-84
Gold, B.D., R.R. Linde, and
P.F. Cudney
"KVM/370 in Retrospect,"
Proc. 1984 IEEE Symp. on
Sec. & Privacy, (5: IEE-84),
pp. 13-23.

Key Words: kernel, design,
case.

GOO-88
Good, D.I.
"Producing Secure Digital
Information Systems," Proc.
4th Aerosp. Comp. Sec.
Conf., (4: IEE-88b), 1988,
pp. 180-182.

Key Words: MLS, design,
techniques.

GRA-88
Graubart., R.D.
"Dual Labels Revisited," Proc.
4th Aerosp. Comp. Sec.
Conf., (4: IEE-88b), 1988, pp.
167-172.

Key Words: MLS, design,
techniques.

GRE-89
Grenier, G.-L., R.C. Holt, and
M. Funkenhauser
"Policy vs. Mechanism in
Secure TUNIS Operating
System," Proc. 1989 IEEE
Symp. on Sec. & Privacy, (5:
IEE-89b), pp. 84-93.

Key Words: policy, design,
case.

GUS-87
Guspari, D., C.D. Harper,
and N. Ramsey
"An ADA Verification
Environment," Proc. 10th
Natl. Comp. Sec. Conf., (5:
NCS-87a), 1987, pp. 366-371.

Key Words: verification, case.

HAD-88
Hadley, S., et al.
"A Secure SDS Software
Library," Proc. 11th Natl.
Comp. Sec. Conf., (5: NCS-
88), 1988, pp. 246-249.

Key Words: trusted, software,
case.

HAI-86
Haigh, J.T., et al.,
"An Experience Using Two
Covert Channel Analysis
Techniques on a Real System
Design," Proc. 1986 IEEE
Symp. on Sec. & Privacy, (5:
IEE-86), pp. 14-24.

Key Words: covert channel,
case.

HAI-87
Haigh, J.T, et al.
"An Experience Using Two
Covert Channel Analysis
Techniques on a Real System
Design," IEEE Trans. on
Software Engr., February 1987,
pp. 157-168.

Key Words: covert channel,
case.

HAI-87a
Haigh, J.T. and W.D. Young
"Extending the Noninterference
Version of MLS for SAT,"
IEEE Trans. on Software
Engr., February 1987, pp. 141-
150.

Key Words: MLS, model,
case.

HAL-85
Haley, C.J., and F.L. Mayer
"Issues on the Development of
Security Related Functional
Tests," Proc. 8th Natl. Comp.
Sec. Conf., (5: NCS-85), 1985,
pp. 82-85.

Key Words: verification,
design.

HAL-86
Halpern, J.D., et al.
"MUSE -- A Computer-
Assisted Verification System,"
Proc. 1986 IEEE Symp. on
Sec. & Privacy, (5: IEE-86),
pp. 25-32

Key Words: verification, case.

HAL-87
Halpern, J.D., et al.
"MUSE -- A Computer-
Assisted Verification System,"
IEEE Trans. on Software
Engr., February 1987, pp. 151-
156.

Key Words: verification, case.

HAL-87a
Halpern, J.D., and S. Owre
"Specification and
Verification Tools for Secure
Distributed Systems," Proc.
10th Natl. Comp. Sec. Conf.,
(5: NCS-87a), 1987, pp. 78-
83.

Key Words: verification,
general.

HAL-87b
Hale, M.W.
"Using the Computer Security
Subsystem Interpretation,"
AIAA No. 87-3097, Proc. 3d
Aerosp. Comp. Sec. Conf.,
(5: IEE-87b), 1987, pp. 128-
130.

Key Words: TCB, criteria,
general.

HAR-84
Hartman, B.A.
"A Gypsy-Based Kernel,"
Proc. 1984 IEEE Symp. on
Sec. & Privacy, (5: IEE-84),
pp. 219-226.

Key Words: verification,
kernel, case.

HAR-85
Hardy, N.
"KeyKOS Architecture,"
ACM Operating Systems
Review, October, 1985.

Key Words: architecture,
kernel, case.

HAR-89
Harrold, C.L.
"An Introduction to the
SMITE Approach to Secure
Computing," Computers &
Security, October 1989, pp.
495-505.

Key Words: MLS, methods,
design, case.

HAR-89a
Harrison, L.J.
"Security Issues and Ada
Runtime Support," Proc. 5th
Security Applicat. Conf., (4:
IEE-89c), 1989, pp. 177-183.

Key Words: MLS, methods,
case.

HEN-85
Henning, R.R.
"Multilevel Application
Development," Proc. 8th Natl.
Comp. Sec. Conf., (5: NCS-
85), 1985, pp. 137-140.

Key Words: MLS, design,
methods.

HEN-88
Henning, M., and A. Rhode
"On the Suitability of Z for
the Specification of Verifiably
Secure Systems," Proc.
IFIP/Sec. '88, Australia, 1989,
(2: CAE-89), pp. 197-221.

Key Words: specification,
case.

HIN-89
Hinke, T.H.
"The Trusted Server Approach
to Multilevel Security," Proc.
5th Security Applicat. Conf.,
(4: IEE-89c), 1989, pp. 335-
341.

Key Words: MLS, methods,
design.

IEE-80
Proceedings, 1980 IEEE
Symposium on Security and
Privacy, Oakland, CA, April
14-16, 1980, IEEE Computer
Society Press, Washington,
DC, 1980.

Key Words: proceedings,
research.

IEE-81
Proceedings, 1981 IEEE
Symposiumon Security and
Privacy, Oakland, CA, April
27-29, 1981, IEEE Computer
Society Press, Washington,
DC, 1981.

Key Words: proceedings,
research.

IEE-82
Proceedings, 1982 IEEE
Symposium on Security and
Privacy, Oakland, CA, April
1982, IEEE Computer Society
Press, Washington, DC, 1982.

Key Words: proceedings,
research.

IEE-83
"Data Security in Computer
Networks, Special Issue," IEEE
Computer, February 1983.

Key Words: MLS, networks,
methods, design, cryptography.

IEE-83a
Proceedings, 1983 IEEE
Symposium on Security and
Privacy, Oakland, CA, April
25-27, 1983, IEEE Computer
Society Press, Washington,
DC, 1983.

Key Words: proceedings,
research.

IEE-83b
"Computer Security
Technology, Special Issue,"
IEEE Computer, July 1983.

Key Words: MLS, methods,
design, kernel, research.

IEE-84
Proceedings, 1984 IEEE
Symposium on Security and
Privacy, Oakland, CA, April
29-May 2, 1984, IEEE
Computer Society Press,
Washington, DC, 1984.

Key Words: proceedings,
research.

IEE-85

Proceedings, 1985 IEEE Symposiumon Security and Privacy, Oakland, CA, April 22-24, 1985, IEEE Computer Society Press, Washington, DC, 1985.

Keywords; proceedings, research.

IEE-85a

Proceedings, 1985 IEEE Aerospace Computer Security Conference, IEEE Computer Society Press, Washington DC, March 1985.

Key Words: proceedings, design, methods, case.

IEE-86

Proceedings, 1986 IEEE Symposium on Security and Privacy, Oakland, CA, April 7-9, 1986, IEEE Computer Society Press, Washington, DC, 1986.

Key Words: proceedings, research.

IEE-86a

Proceedings, Second Aerospace Computer Security Conference, IEEE Computer Society Press, Washington, DC, 1986.

Key Words: proceedings, design, methods, case.

IEE-87

Proceedings, 1987 IEEE Symposium on Security and Privacy, Oakland, CA, April 27-29, 1987, IEEE Computer Society Press, Washington, DC, 1987.

Key Words: proceedings, research.

IEE-87a

Proceedings, Third Aerospace Computer Security Conference, IEEE Computer Society Press, Washington, DC, 1987.

Key Words: proceedings, design, methods, case.

IEE-88

Proceedings, 1988 IEEE Symposiumon Security and Privacy, Oakland, CA, April 18-21, 1988, IEEE Computer Society Press, Washington, DC, 1988.

Key Words: proceedings, research.

IEE-88a

Proceedings, Fourth Aerospace Computer Security Conference, IEEE Computer Society Press, Washington, DC, December 1988.

Key Words: proceedings, design, methods, case.

IEE-89

Proceedings, 1989 IEEE Symposium on Security and Privacy, Oakland, CA, May 1-3, 1989, IEEE Computer Society Press, Washington, DC, 1989.

Key Words: proceedings, research.

IEE-89a

Proceedings, Fifth Security Applications Conference, IEEE Computer Society Press, Washington, DC, December 1989.

Key Words: proceedings, design, case.

IRV-88

Irvine, C.E., et al. "Genesis of a Secure Application: A Multilevel Secure Message Preparation Workstation Development," Proc. 4th Aerosp. Comp. Sec. Conf., (4: IEE-88b), 1988, pp. 16-29.

Key Words: MLS, policy, design, case.

JAN-89

Janieri, J.V.A., J.S. Barlas, and L.L. Chang "Adding CASE Technologies to Formal Verification"' Proc. 12th Natl. Comp. Sec. Conf., (5: NCS-89), 1989, pp. 52-64.

Key Words: verification, methods.

JOH-89

Johnson, L.A. "Formal Specification & Verification: Fundamental Concerns," IEEE Cipher, April 1989, pp. 25-33.

Key Words: verification, general.

JOS-87

Joseph, M.K. "Toward the Elimination of the Effects of Malicious Logic: Fault Tolerance Approaches," Proc. 10th Natl. Comp. Sec. Conf., (5: NCS-87a), 1987, pp. 238-244.

Key Words: denial, design, methods.

KAR-84

Karger, P.A., and A.J. Herbert "An Augmented Capability Architecture to Support Lattice Security and Traceability of Access," Proc. 1984 IEEE Symp. on Sec. & Privacy, (5: IEE-84), pp. 2-12.

Key Words: architecture, capability.

KAR-87

Karger, P.A. "Limiting the Damage Potential of Discretionary Trojan Horses," Proc. 1987 IEEE Symp. on Sec. & Privacy, (5: IEE-87a), pp. 32-37.

Key Words: threats, vulnerabilities, methods, discretionary.

KAU-87
Kaufmann, M., and
W.D. Young
"Comparing Specification
Paradigms for Secure
Systems: Gypsy and the
Boyer-Moore Model," Proc.
10th Natl. Comp. Sec. Conf.,
(5: NCS-87a), 1987, pp. 122-
128.

Key Words: specification,
methods, design, case.

KEM-80
Kemmerer, R.
"FDM: A Formal
Methodology for Software
Development," Proc. 3d
Seminar, DoD Comp. Sec.
Progr., (5: DOD-80b), 1980,
pp. L1-19.

Key Words: specification,
methods, case.

KEM-82
Kemmerer, R.A.
"A Practical Approach to
Identifying Storage and
Timing Channels," Proc.
1982 IEEE Symp. on Sec. &
Privacy (5: IEE-82), pp. 66-
73.

Key Words: covert channel,
methods.

KEM-86
Kemmerer, R.A.
Verification Assessment
Study Final Report, C3-
CR01-86, National Computer
Security Center, Ft. Meade,
MD, 1986.

Key Words: verification,
general.

KET-88
Ketcham, L.R.
"Program Containment in a
Software-Based Security
Architecture," Proc. 11th
Natl. Comp. Sec. Conf., (5:
NCS-88), 1988, pp. 299-308.

Key Words: design, methods,
software.

KIN-88
King, G., and B. Smith
"INFOSEC IRAD at
Magnavox: The Trusted
Military Message Processor
(TRUMMP) & the Military
Message Embedded Executive
(ME2)," Proc. 11th Natl.
Comp. Sec. Conf., (5: NCS-
88), 1988, pp. 250-256.

Key Words: design, network,
case.

KIN-88a
King, G., and W. Smith
"An Alternative
Implementation of the
Reference Monitor Concept,"
Proc. 4th Aerosp. Comp. Sec.
Conf., (4: IEE-88b), 1988, pp.
159-166.

Key Words: MLS, model,
design.

KOR-84
Korelskiy, T., and
D. Sutherland
"Formal Specification of a
Multi-Level Secure Operating
System," Proc. 1984 IEEE
Symp. on Sec. & Privacy, (5:
IEE-84), pp. 209-218.

Key Words: MLS,
specification, case.

KRA-83
Kramer, S.M., and D.P. Sidhi
"Security Information Flow in
Multidimensional Arrays,"
IEEE Trans. on Computers,
December 1983, pp. 1188-
1190.

Key Words: MLS, models,
flow.

KRA-84
Kramer, S.
"Linus IV--An Experiment in
Computer Security," Proc.
1984 IEEE Symp. on Sec. &
Privacy, (5: IEE-84), pp. 24-
32.

Key Words: MLS, OS,
design, case.

KUH-88
Kuhn, D.R.
"Static Analysis Tools for
Software Security
Certification," Proc. 11th Natl.
Comp. Sec. Conf., (5: NCS-
88), 1988, pp. 290-298.

Key Words: certification,
software.

LAM-85
Lampson, B.W.
"Protection," ACM Operating
Systems Review, December
1985, pp. 13-24.

Key Words: policy, models,
general.

LAN-81
Landwehr, C.E.
"Assertions for Verification of
Multi-Level Secure Military
Message Systems," ACM
Software Engineering Notes,
Vol. 5, No.3, July 1980.

Key Words: verification,
methods.

LAN-82
Landauer, C., and S. Crocker
"Precise Information Flow
Analysis by Program
Verification," Proc. 1982 IEEE
Symp. on Sec. & Privacy, (5:
IEE-82), pp. 74-80.

Key Words: verification,
methods, flow.

LAN-83
Landwehr, C.E.
"The Best Available
Technologies for Computer
Security," IEEE Computer,
July 1983, pp. 89-100.

Key Words: design, methods,
general.

LAN-83a
Landwehr, C.E.
"Requirements for Class A1 Systems and Major Differences between Division A and Division B Systems," Proc. 6th Seminar, DoD Comp. Sec. Program, (5: DOD-83a), 1983, pp. 27-32

Key Words: MLS, criteria, general.

LAN-84
Landwehr, C.E., and J.M. Carroll
"Hardware Requirements for Secure Computer Systems: A Framework," Proc. IEEE Sympos. on Security and Privacy, April 1984, pp. 34-40.

Key Words: architecture, general.

LAN-85
Landwehr, C.E., and H.O. Lubbes
"Determining Security Requirements for Complex Systems with the Orange Book," Proc. 8th Natl. Comp. Sec. Conf., (5: NCS-85), 1985, pp. 156-162.

Key Words: requirements, criteria.

LEE-89
Lee, T.M.P.
"Statistical Models of Trust: TCBs vs. People," Proc. 1989 IEEE Symp. on Sec. & Privacy, (5: IEE-89b), pp. 10-19.

Key Words: trusted, models, general.

LEV-80
Levitt, K.N., P.G. Neumann, and L. Robinson
The SRI Hierarchical Development Methodology and Its Application to Development of Secure Systems, SP 500-67, NBS, Gaithersburg, MD, 1980.

Key Words: MLS, methods, design, case.

LEV-89
Levin, T, S.J. Padilla, and C.E. Irvine
"A Formal Model for UNIX Setuid," Proc. 1989 IEEE Symp. on Sec. & Privacy, (5: IEE-89b), pp. 73-83.

Key Words: models, OS, case.

LEV-89a
Levin, T.E., S.J.Padilla, and R.R. Schell
"Engineering Results from the A1 Formal Verification Process," Proc. 12th Natl. Comp. Sec. Conf., (5: NCS-89), 1989, pp. 65-74.

Key Words: verification, design, case.

LOE-85
Loeper, K.
"Resolving Covert Channels Within a B2 Class Secure System," ACM Operating Systems Review, July 1985.

Key Words: covert channel, case.

LOE-89
Loepere, K.
"The Covert Channel Limiter Revisted," ACM Operating Systems Review, April 1989, pp. 39-44.

Key Words: covert channel, case.

LUC-86
Luckenbaugh, G.L., et al.
"Interpretation of the Bell-LaPadula Model in Secure Xenix," Proc. 9th Natl. Comp. Sec. Conf., (5: NCS-86), 1986, pp. 113-125.

Key Words: model, methods, case.

LUM-89
Lu, M.M.
"Guidelines for Formal Verification Systems: Overview and Rationale," Proc. 12th Natl. Comp. Sec. Conf., (5: NCS-89), 1989, pp. 75-82.

Key Words: verification, guidelines.

MAC-83
MacEwen, G.H.
"The Design for A Secure System Based on Program Analysis," IEEE Trans. on Software Engr., May 1983, pp. 289-298.

Key Words: MLS, design, case.

MAC-84
MacEwen, G.H., and D.T. Barnard
"The Euclid Family and Its Relation to Secure Systems," Proc. 7th Seminar, DoD Comp. Sec. Program, (5: DOD-84), 1984, pp. 79-87.

Key Words: specification, case.

MAC-84a
MacEwen, G.H., B. Burwell, and Z.J. Lu,
"Multi-Level Security Based on Physical Distribution," Proc. 1984 IEEE Symp. on Sec. & Privacy, (5: IEE-84), pp. 167-177.

Key Words: MLS, nethods, design.

MAR-83
Marick, B.
"The VERUS Design Verification System," Proc. 1983 IEEE Symp. on Sec. & Privacy, (5: IEE-83a), pp. 150-160.

Key Words: verification, case.

MAR-84
Margulis, B.I.
"An Overview of Multics Security," Proc. IFIP/Sec. '84, Toronto, (2: FIN-85), 1984, pp. 225-235.

Key Words: architecture, design, case.

MAR-88
Marmor-Squires, A.B., and P.A. Rougeau
"Issues in Process Models and Integrated Environments for Trusted Systems Development," Proc. 11th Natl. Comp. Sec. Conf., (5: NCS-88), 1988, pp. 109-113.

Key Words: trusted, models, design, general.

MAR-89
Marceau, C., and C.D. Harper
"An Interactive Approach to ADA Verification," Proc. 12th Natl. Comp. Sec. Conf., (5: NCS-89), 1989, pp. 28-51.

Key Words: verification, methods, case.

MAR-89a
Marmor-Squires, A., et al.
"A Risk Driven Process Model for the Development of Trusted Systems," Proc. 5th Security Applicat. Conf., (4: IEE-89c), 1989, pp. 184-192.

Key Words: trusted, model, risk, methods, design.

MAY-88
Mayer, F.L.
"An Interpretation of a Refined Bell-LaPadula Model for the T-Mach Kernel," Proc. 4th Aerosp. Comp. Sec. Conf., (4: IEE-88b), 1988, pp. 368-378.

Key Words: MLS, model, kernel, case, methods, design.

MAY-89
Mayer, F.L., and J.N. McAuliffe
"The Design of the Trusted Workstation: A True 'INFOSEC' Product," Proc. 12th Natl. Comp. Sec. Conf., (5: NCS-89), 1989, pp. 135-145.

Key Words: trusted, design, case, network.

MCD-88
McDermott, J.
"A Technique for Removing an Important Class of Trojan Horses from Higher Order Languages," Proc. 11th Natl. Comp. Sec. Conf., (5: NCS-88), 1988, pp. 114-117.

Key Words: threats, techniques.

MCH-85
McHugh, J.
"An EMACS Based Downgrader for the SAT," Proc. 8th Natl. Comp. Sec. Conf., (5: NCS-85), 1985, pp. 133-136.

Key Words: MLS, techniques, case.

MCH-85a
McHugh, J. and D.I. Good
"An Information Flow Tool for Gypsy," Proc. 1985 IEEE Symp. on Sec. & Privacy, (5: IEE-85), pp. 46-48.

Key Words: verification, methods, case.

MCM-85
McMahon, E.M.
"Restricted Access Processor -- An Application of Computer Security Technology," Proc. Aerospace Computer Sec. Conf., (5: IEE-85a), 1985, pp. 71-73.

Key Words: MLS, methods, design, case.

MEA-87
Meadows, C.
"The Integrity Lock Architecture and Its Application to Message Systems: Reducing Covert Channels," Proc. 1987 IEEE Symp. on Sec. & Privacy, (5: IEE-87a), pp. 212-218.

Key Words: covert channel, methods, architecture, case.

MIG-87
Migues, S.
"The Need for Rigorous Informal Verification of Specifications-to-Code Correspondence," Proc. COMPASS '87: Comp. Assurance, (2: IEE-87), 1987, pp. 13-25.

Key Words: verification, methods specification.

MIL-81
Miller, J.S.
"Military Message Systems: Applying a Security Model," Proc. 1981 IEEE Symp. on Sec. & Privacy, (5: IEE-81), 101-111.

Key Words: models, methods, case.

MIL-82
Millen, J.K.
"Kernel Isolation for the PDP 11/70," Proc. 1982 IEEE Symp. on Sec. & Privacy, (5: IEE-82), pp. 57-65.

Key Words: kernel, technique, case.

MIZ-87
Mizuno, M., and A.E. Oldenhoeft
"Information Flow Control in a Distributed Object-Oriented System with Statistically Bound Object Variables," Proc. 10th Natl. Comp. Sec. Conf., (5: NCS-87a), 1987, pp. 56-67.

Key Words: control, slow, techniques.

MUR-88
Murray, M., R. Berch, and S. Caperton "Use of Automated Verification Tools in a Secure Software Development Methodology," Proc. 11th Natl. Comp. Sec. Conf., (5: NCS-88), 1988, pp. 284-289.

Key Words: verification, software, methods, design, case.

NCS-85
Proceedings, 8th National Computer Security Conference, National Bureau of Standards/National Computer Security Center, September 1985.

Key Words: proceedings, general.

NCS-86
Computer Security - For Today... and for Tomorrow, Proceedings, 9th National Computer Security Conference, National Bureau of Standards/National Computer Security Center, September 1986.

Key Words: proceedings, general.

NCS-87
Computer Security... From Principles to Practice, Proceedings, 10th National Computer Security Conference, National Bureau of Standards/ National Computer Security Center, September 1987.

Key Words: proceedings, general.

NCS-88
Computer Security ... Into the Future, Proceedings, 11th National Computer Security Conference, National Institute of Standards and Technology/ National Computer Security Center, October, 1988.

Key Words: proceedings, general.

NCS-88a
Computer Security ... Into the Future, A Postscript, 11th National Computer Security Conference, National Institute of Standards and Technology/ National Computer Security Center, October 1988.

Key Words: proceedings, general.

NCS-89
Information Systems Security: Solutions for Today -- Concepts for Tomorrow, Proceedings, 12th National Computer Security Conference, National Institute of Standards and Technology/ National Computer Security Center, October 1989.

Key Words: proceedings, general.

NEE-85
Neely, R.B. and J.W. Freeman, "Structuring Systems for Formal Verification," Proc. 1985 IEEE Symp. on Sec. & Privacy, (5: IEE-85), pp. 2-13.

Key Words: verification, design.

NEE-89
Neely, R.B., J.W. Freeman, and M.D. Krenzin "Achieving Understandable Results in a Formal Design Verification," Proc. Comp. Sec. Foundat. Workshop II, (3: IEE-89a), 1989, pp. 115-124.

Key Words: verification, methods.

NEI-84
Neilson, J.O., and F.E. Wuebker "Design Experiences from the Multilevel Secure MCF," Proc. 1984 IEEE Symp. on Sec. & Privacy, (5: IEE-84), pp. 204-208.

Key Words: MLS, design, case.

NEU-86
Neumann, P.G. "On Hierarchical Design of Computer Systems for Critical Applications," IEEE Trans. on Software Engr., September 1986, pp. 905-920.

Key Words: models, methods, design.

NEU-88
Neugent, W., "Security Guards: Issues and Approaches," IEEE Communications Magazine, August 1988, pp. 25-29.

Key Words: MLS, methods, design.

NEU-89
Neugent, W. "Guidelines for Specifying Security Guards," Proc. 12th Natl. Comp. Sec. Conf., (5: NCS-89), 1989, pp. 320-338.

Key Words: MLS, methods, design.

ONE-86
O'Neil-Dunne, J. "The Access Path," Proc. 9th Natl. Comp. Sec. Conf., (5: NCS-86), 1986, pp. 149-155.

Key Words: TCB, control, design.

PAR-88
Parker, T.A. "Structuring Trust in a Large General Purpose Operating System," Proc. 4th Aerosp. Comp. Sec. Conf., (4: IEE-88b), 1988, pp. 152-158.

Key Words: trusted, OS, design, case.

PAR-89
Partney, T.J. "The Incorporation of Multi-Level IPC into UNIX," Proc. 1989 IEEE Symp. on Sec. & Privacy, (5: IEE-89b), pp. 94-99.

Key Words: MLS, methods, design, case.

PER-84
Perrine, T., J. Codd, and B. Hardy
"An Overview of the Kernelized Secure Operating System (KSOS)," Proc. 7th Seminar, DoD Comp. Sec. Progr., (5: DOD-84), 1984, pp. 146-160.

Key Words: OS, kernel, design, case.

PFL-88
Pfleeger, C.P., and S.L. Pfleeger
"A Transaction Flow Approach to Software Security Certification for Document Handling Systems," Computers & Security, October 1988, pp. 495-502.

Key Words: certification, case.

PFL-89
Pfleeger, C.P., S.L. Pfleeger, and M.F. Theofanos
"A Methodology for Penetration Testing," Computers & Security, November 1989, pp. 613-620.

Key Words: vulnerabilities, methods.

PFL-89a
Pfleeger, C.P.
Security in Computing, Prentice Hall, Englewood Cliffs, NJ, 1989

Key Words: book, MLS, cryptography general.

PLA-81
Platek, R.A.
"The Evaluation of Three Specification and Verification Methodologies," Proc. 4th Seminar, DoD Comp. Sec. Progr., (5: DOD-81), 1981, pp. X1-X17.

Key Words: verification, methods, specification, case.

POZ-84
Pozzo, M.M.
"Life Cycle Assurance for Trusted Computer Systems: A Configuration Mangement Strategy for Multics," Proc. 7th Seminar, DoD Comp. Sec. Progr., (5: DOD-84), 1984, pp. 169-179.

Key Words: trusted, methods, design, case.

PRO-85
Proctor, N.
"The Restricted Access Processor, an Example of Formal Verification," Proc. 1985 IEEE Symp. on Sec. & Privacy, (5: IEE-85), pp. 49-53.

Key Words: verification, case.

PRO-89
Proctor, N., and R. Wong
"The Security Policy of Secure Distributed Operating System Prototype," Proc. 5th Security Applicat. Conf., (4: IEE-89c), 1989, pp. 95-102.

Key Words: OS, policy, design, case.

RAJ-86
Rajunas, S.A., et al.
"Security in KeyKOS," Proc. 1986 IEEE Symp. on Sec. & Privacy, (5: IEE-86), pp. 78-85

Key Words: methods, design, case.

ROS-89
Rosenthal, D.
"Implementing a Verification Methodology for McCullough Security," Proc. Comp. Sec. Foundat. Workshop II, 1989 (3: IEE-89a), pp. 133-140.

Key Words: verification, design, case.

ROU-87
Rougeau, P.A.
"Integrating Security into a Total Systems Architecture," Proc. 3d Aerosp. Comp. Sec. Conf., (5: IEE-87b), 1987, pp. 118-121.

Key Words: TCB, architecture, design.

RUS-81
Rushby, J.M.
"The Design and Verification of Secure Systems," ACM Operating Systems Review, Vol. 15, 5, 1982, pp. 12-21.

Key Words: verification, design.

RUS-82
Rushby, J.M.
"Proof of Separability, A Verification Technique for A Class of Security Kernels," in Proceedings, International Symposium on Programming, Springer, Berlin, 1982, pp. 352-367.

Key Words: verification, techniques.

RUS-83
Rushby, J.M., and B. Randell
"A Distributed Secure System," Proc. 1983 IEEE Symp. on Sec. & Privacy, (5: IEE-83a), pp. 127-135.

Key Words: architecture, design, case.

RUS-84
Rushby, J.M.
"A Trusted Computing Base for Embedded Systems," Proc. 7th Seminar, DoD Comp. Sec. Progr., (5: DOD-84), 1984, pp. 294-311.

Key Words: TCB, design, case.

RUS-89
Russell, T.T., and M.Schaefer
"Toward a High B Level
Security Architecture for the
IBM ES/3090 Processor
Resource/System Manger,"
Proc. 12th Natl. Comp. Sec.
Conf., (5: NCS-89), 1989,
pp. 184-196.

Key Words: architecture,
design, case.

SAY-87
Saydjari, O.S.,
J.M. Beckman, and
J.R. Leaman
"Locking Computers
Securely," Proc. 10th Natl.
Comp. Sec. Conf., (5: NCS-
87a), 1987, pp. 129-141.

Key Words: TCB,
architecture, case.

SAY-89
Saydjari, O.S., J.M.
Beckman,
and J.R. Leaman
"LOCK Track: Navigating
Uncharted Space," Proc. 1989
IEEE Symp. on Sec. &
Privacy, (5: IEE-89b), pp.
167-175.

Key Words: TCB,
artchitecture, case.

SCH-83
Schell, R.R.
"Evaluating Security
Properties of Computer
Systems," Proc. 1983 IEEE
Symp. on Sec. & Privacy, (5:
IEE-83a), pp. 89-95.

Key Words: methods, design,
general.

SCH-83a
Schell, R.R.
"A Security Kernel for A
Multi-Processing Micro-
Computer," IEEE Computer,
July 1983, pp. 47-53.

Key Words: kernel, design,
case.

SCH-84
Schaefer, M., and R.R. Schell
"Toward an Understanding of
Extensible Architectures for
Evaluated Trusted Computer
System Products," Proc. 1984
IEEE Symp. on Sec. &
Privacy, (5: IEE-84), pp. 41-
51.

Key Words: architecture,
general.

SCH-84a
Schell, R.R., and T.F. Tao
"Microprocessor-Based
Trusted Systems for
Communication and
Workstation Application,"
Proc. 7th Seminar, DoD
Comp. Sec. Progr., (5: DOD-
84), 1984, pp. 277-290.

Key Words: architecture,
design,

SCH-84b
Schell, R.R.
"Future of Trusted Computer
Systems," Proc. IFIP/Sec. '84,
Toronto, 1984, (2: FIN-85),
pp. 55-67.

Key Words: trusted, general.

SCH-85
Schell, R.R., T.F. Tao, and
M. Heckman
"Designing the GEMSOS
Security Kernel for Security
and Performance," Proc. 8th
Natl. Comp. Sec. Conf., (5:
NCS-85), 1985, pp. 108-120.

Key Words: kernel, design,
case.

SCH-86
Schultz, A.C.
"Using Software Tools to
Analyze the Security
Characteristics of HOL
Programs," Proc. 9th Natl.
Comp. Sec. Conf., (5: NCS-
86), 1986, pp. 108-112.

Key Words: methods,
techniques, design.

SCH-87
Schockley, W.R., and
R.R. Schell
"TCB Subsets for Incremental
Evaluation," Proc. 3d Aerosp.
Comp. Sec. Conf., (5: IEE-
87b), 1987, pp. 131-139.

Key Words: TCB, methods,
design.

SCH-88
Schaffer, M.A., and G. Walsh
"LOCK/ix: On Implementing
Unix on the LOCK TCB,"
Proc. 11th Natl. Comp. Sec.
Conf., (5: NCS-88), 1988, pp.
319-329.

Key Words: OS, architecture,
design, case.

SCH-88a
Schockley, W.R., T.F. Tao,
and M.F. Thompson
"An Overview of the
GEMSOS A1 Technology and
Applications Experience," Proc.
11th Natl. Comp. Sec. Conf.,
(5: NCS-88), 1988, pp. 238-
245.

Key Words: MLS, OS, kernel,
methods, design, case.

SCH-89
Schaefer, M.
"Symbol Security Condition
Considered Harmful," Proc.
1989 IEEE Symp. on Sec. &
Privacy, (5: IEE-89b), pp. 20-
46.

Key Words: model,
requirement, case.

SCH-89a
Schallenmuller, E., et al.
"Development of a Multilevel
Data Generation Application
for GEMSOS," Proc. 5th
Security Applicat. Conf., (4:
IEE-89c), 1989, pp. 86-90.

Key Words: MLS, design,
case.

SHI-81
Shirley, L.J., and R.R. Schell
"Mechanism Sufficiency
Validation by Assignment,"
Proc. 1981 IEEE Symp. on
Sec. & Privacy, (5: IEE-81),
pp. 26-32.

Key Words: requirements,
methods.

SID-84
Sidhu, D.P.
"Executable Logic
Specifications: A New
Approach to Computer
Security," Proc. 1984 IEEE
Symp. on Sec. & Privacy, (5:
IEE-84), pp. 142-153.

Key Words: specification,
methods.

SIE-87
Siebert, W.O., et al.
"Unix and B2: Are They
Compatible?," Proc. 10th
Natl. Comp. Sec. Conf., (5:
NCS-87a), 1987, pp. 142-
149.

Key Words: MLS, criteria,
case.

SIL-83
Silverman, J.
"Reflections on the
Verification of the Security
of an Operating System
Kernel," Proc., 9th ACM
Symp. on Operating Syst.
Principles, 1983, pp. 143-154.

Key Words: OS, verification,
case.

SMI-86
Smith, T.A.
"User-Definable Domains as
a Mechanism for
Implementing the Least
Privilege Principle," Proc. 9th
Natl. Comp. Sec. Conf., (5:
NCS-86), 1986, pp. 143-155.

Key Words: design,
techniques.

SOL-81
Solomon, D.J.
"Processing Multilevel Secure
Objects," Proc. 1981 IEEE
Symp. on Sec. & Privacy, (5:
IEE-81), pp. 56-61.

Key Words: MLS, methods,
design.

STA-86
Stauffer, B.C., and R.U. Fujii
"Informal Verification
Analysis," Proc. 9th Natl.
Comp. Sec. Conf., (5: NCS-
86), 1986, pp. 126-129.

Key Words: verification,
methods.

SWA-85
Swaminathan, K.
"Negotiated Access Control,"
Proc. 1986 IEEE Symp. on
Sec. & Privacy, (5: IEE-86),
pp. 190-196.

Key Words: control, methods.

TAY-89
Taylor, T.
"FTLS-Based Security Testing
for LOCK," Proc. 12th Natl.
Comp. Sec. Conf., (5: NCS-
89), 1989, pp. 136-145.

Key Words: verification, case.

TUR-81
Turn, R. (Ed.)
Advances in Computer System
Security, Artech House,
Dedham, MA, 1981.

Key Words: book, general.

TUR-84
Turn, R. (Ed.)
Advances in Computer System
Security, Vol. 2, Artech
House, Dedham, MA, 1984.

Key Words: book, general.

TUR-88
Turn, R. (Ed.)
Advances in Computer System
Security, Vol. 3, Artech
House, Norwood, MA, 1988.

Key Words: book, general.

VAR-89
Varadharajan, V., and
S. Black
"Formal Specifiaction of a
Secure Distributed Messaging
System," Proc. 12th Natl.
Comp. Sec. Conf., (5: NCS-
89), 1989, pp. 146-171.

Key Words: specification, case.

VON-88
von Henke, F.W., et all.
"EHDM Verification
Environment: An Overview,"
Proc. 11th Natl. Comp. Sec.
Conf., (5: NCS-88), 1988, pp.
147-155.

Key Words: verification, case.

WAL-80
Walker, S.T.
"The Advent of Trusted
Systems," Proceedings, 1980
Natl. Comp. Conference,
AFIPS Press, Reston, VA,
1980, pp. 655-666.

Key Words: trusted, plicy,
methods.

WAL-80a
Walker, B.J., R.A. Kemmerer,
and G.J. Popek
"Specification and Verification
of the UCLA Unix Security
Kernel," Communications of
the ACM, February 1980, pp.
118-131.

Key Words: specification,
methods, verification, case.

WEI-82
Weissman, C.
"Bizarre Bazaar: An Approach
to Security Technology
Transfer," Proc. 5th Seminar,
DoD Comp. Sec. Progr., (5:
DOD-82), 1982, pp. 233-240.

Key Words: MLS, methods,
techniques.

WHI-87
White, S.R.
"ABYSS: A Trusted
Architecture for Software
Protection," Proc. 1987 IEEE
Symp. on Sec. & Privacy, (5:
IEE-87a), pp. 38-51.

Key Words: TCB,
architecture, case.

WIL-89
Williams, J.C., and
G.W. Dinolt
"Formal Model of a Trusted
File Server," Proc. 1989
IEEE Symp. on Sec. &
Privacy, (5: IEE-89b), pp.
157-166.

Key Words: model, truatsed,
case.

WIN-86
Wing, J.M., and M.R. Nixon
"Extending Ina-Jo with
Temporal Logic," Proc. 1986
IEEE Symp. on Sec. &
Privacy, (5: IEE-86), pp. 2-
13.

Key Words: specification,
methods, techniques, case.

WIN-89
Wing, J.M., and M.R. Nixon
"Extending InaJo with
Temporal Logic," IEEE
Trans. on Software Engr.,
February 1989, pp. 181-197.

Key Words: specification,
methods, techniques, case.

WIS-86
Wiseman, S.
"A Secure Capability
Computer System," Proc.
1986 IEEE Symp. on Sec. &
Privacy, (5: IEE-86), pp. 86-
94

Key Words: architecture,
capability.

WIS-88
Wiseman, S., et al.
"The Trusted Path Between
SMITE and the User," Proc.
1988 IEEE Symp. on Sec. &
Privacy, (5: IEE-88a), pp.
147-155.

Key Words: TCB, technique,
case.

WIT-80
Withington, P.T.
"The Trusted Function in
Secure Decentralized
Processing," Proc. 1980 IEEE
Symp. on Sec. & Privacy, (5:
IEE-80), pp. 67-79.

Key Words: trusted, methods,
design.

WON-89
Wong, R., et al.
"The SDOS System: A Secure
Distributed Operating System
Prototype," Proc. 12th Natl.
Comp. Sec. Conf., (5: NCS-
89), 1989, pp. 172-183.

Key Words: OS, trusted, case.

WOO-83
Woodie, P.E.
"Security Enhancement
Through Product Evaluation,"
Proc. 1983 IEEE Symp. on
Sec. & Privacy, (5: IEE-83a),
pp. 96-101.

Key Words: methods,
techniques.

WOO-86
Woodie, P.
"Distributed Processing
System Security:
Communications, Computer or
Both," Proc. IEEE Internat.
Conf. on Data Engr., 1986,
pp. 630-636.

Key Words: requirements,
design.

WOO-87
Woodward, J.P.L
"Exploiting the Dual Nature of
Sensitivity Labels," Proc. 1987
IEEE Symp. on Sec. &
Privacy, (5: IEE-87a), pp. 23-
30

Key Words: MLS, methods,
techniques.

YOU-85
Young, W.D., W.E. Boebert,
and R.Y. Kain
"Proving a Computer System
Secure," Scientific
Honeyweller, July 1985, pp.
18-27.

Key Words: verification,
general.

YOU-86
Young, W.D., P.A. Telga, and
W.E. Boebert
"A Verified Labeler for the
Secure Ada Target," Proc. 9th
Natl. Comp. Sec. Conf., (5:
NCS-86), 1986, pp. 55-61.

Key Words: MLS, techniques,
case.

YOU-87
Young, W.D.
"Coding For A Believable
Specification to
Implementation Mapping,"
Proc. 1987 IEEE Symp. on
Sec. & Privacy, (5: IEE-87a),
pp. 140-148.

Key Words: specification,
methods.

YOU-89
Young, W.D.
"Comparing Specification
Paradigms," Proc. 12th Natl.
Comp. Sec. Conf., (5: NCS-
89), 1989, pp. 83-97.

Key Words: specification,
general.

YUC-88

Yu, C.-F, and V.D. Gligor "A Formal Specification and Verification Method for the Prevention of Denial of Service," Proc. 1988 IEEE Symp. on Sec. & Privacy, (5: IEE-88a), pp. 187-202.

Key Words: specification, methods, verification, denial.

6. Database Security

The section cites publications on models of database security, specific implementations, statistical database inference problem, and general aspects of database security.

ADA-89
    Adam, B.R., and
    J.C. Wortmann
    "Security Control Methods
    for Statistical Databases: A
    Comparative Survey," ACM
    Computing Surveys,
    December 1989, pp. 515-556.

    Key Words: database,
    control.

AHI-88
    Ahituv, N., Y. Lapid,
    and S. Neumann
    "Protecting Statistical
    Databases Against Retrieval
    of Private Information,"
    Computers & Security,
    February 1988, pp. 59-63.

    Key Words: statistical,
    inference.

AKL-87
    Akl, S.G., and D.E. Denning
    "Checking Classification
    Constraints for Consistency
    and Completeness," Proc.
    1987 IEEE Symp. Sec. &
    Privacy, (5: IEE-87a), pp.
    196-201.

    Key Words: database,
    methods.

BAX-86
    Baxter, V.,
    "Improving the Security
    Posture in Existing
    Installations," Proc. NCSC
    Workshop on Database
    Security, (6:COA-86), 1986,
    pp. H1-H11.

    Key Words: database,
    methods.

BEC-80
    Beck, L.L.
    "A Security Mechanism for
    Statistical Databases," ACM
    Trans. on Database Systems,
    September 1980, pp. 316-338.

    Key Words: statistical,
    inference.

BER-87
    Berson, T.A., and T.F. Lunt
    "Multilevel Security for
    Knowledge-Based Systems,"
    Proc. 1987 IEEE Symp. on
    Sec. & Privacy, (5: IEE-87a),
    pp. 235-242.

    Key Words: database, policy,
    methods.

BIS-87
    Biskup, J.
    "Privacy Respecting
    Permissions and Rights," Proc.
    IFIP WG 11.3 Meeting, (6:
    LAN-88), 1987, pp. 173-185.

    Key Words: database, policy,
    methods.

BIS-88
    Biskup, J., and H. Graf
    "Analysis of the Privacy
    Model for the Information
    System DORIS," Proc. IFIP
    WG 11.3 Workshop, (6:
    LAN-89b), 1988, pp. 123-140.

    Key Words: models, methods,
    case.

BLA-85
    Blakley, G.R., and
    C. Meadows
    "A Database Encryption
    Scheme which Allows the
    Computation of Statistics
    Using Encrypted Data," Proc.
    1985 IEEE Symp. on Sec. &
    Privacy, (5: IEE-85), pp. 116-
    122.

    Key Words: statistical,
    encryption

BOE-86
    Boebert, W.E., B.B. Dillaway,
    and J.T. Haigh
    "Mandatory Security and
    Database Management
    Systems," Proc. NCSC
    Workshop on Database
    Security, (6: COA-86), 1986,
    pp. A1-A21.

    Key Words: DBMS, policy,
    requirements.

BON-80
    Bonyun, D.A.
    "The Secure Relational
    Database Management System
    Kernel -- Three Years Alter,"
    Proc. 1980 IEEE Symp. on
    Sec. & Privacy, (5: IEE-80),
    pp. 34-37.

    Key Words: DBMS, relational,
    kernel.

BON-84
    Bonyun, D.A.
    "Rules as the Basis of Accesss
    Control in Database
    Mangement Systems," Proc.
    7th Seminar, DoD Comp. Sec.
    Progr., (5: DOD-84), 1984, pp.
    38-47.

    Key Words: DBMS, control,
    methods.

BON-86
Bonyun, D.
"A New Look at Integrity Policy for Database Management Systems," Proc. NCSC Workshop on Database Security, (6: COA-86), 1986, pp. B1-B18.

Key Words: DBMS, polcy, integrity.

BON-87
Bonyun, D.A.
"Logging and Accountability in Database Mangement Systems," Proc. IFIP WG 11.3 Meeting, (6: LAN-88), 1987, pp. 223-227.

Key Words: DBMS, auditing, methods.

BON-89
Bonyun, D.A.
"Using MAPLESS as a Framework for Secure Database Mangement," Proc. IFIP WG 11.3 (Data Base) Workshop, (6: IFI-89), 1989.

Key Words: DBMS, methods, case.

BOU-84
Boukaert, A.
"Security of Transportable Computerized Files," Proc. Eurocrypt '84, Paris, 1984, (9: BET-85), pp. 416-425.

Key Words: database, techniques.

BUC-89
Buczkowski, L.J.
"Database Inference Controller," Proc. IFIP WG 11.3 (Data Base) Workshop, (6: IFI-89), 1989.

Key Words: control, inference.

BUR-86
Burns, R.K.
"Towards Practical MLS Database Management Systems Using the Integrity Lock Technology," Proc. 9th Natl. Comp. Sec. Conf., (5: NCS-86), 1986, pp. 25-29.

Key Words: MLS, DBMS, techniques.

BUR-87
Burns, R.K.
"Operational Assurances for a Trusted DBMS," Proc. IFIP WG 11.3 Meeting, (6: LAN-88), 1987, pp. 241-251.

Key Words: DBMS, trusted, nethods.

BUR-89
Burns, R.K.
"The Homework Problem," in Lunt, T.F., Research Directions in Database Security, (6: LUN-90), May 1989, pp. 84-86.

Key Words: MLS, database, design.

BUS-83
Bussollati, U., and G. Martella
"Toward A New Approach to Secure Data Base Design," Computers & Security, January 1983, pp. 49-62.

Key Words: database, methods.

CAR-85
Carroll, J.M., and H. Jurgensen
"Design of a Secure Relational Data Base," Proc. IFIP/Sec. '85, Dublin, 1985, (2: GRI-85), pp. 1-16.

Key Words: database, design, methods, relational.

CAR-87
Carson, et al.
"Toward a Multilevel Document System," No. 87-3064, Proc. 3d Aerospace Comp. Sec. Conf., (5: IEE-87b), 1987, pp. 1-6.

Key Words: MLS, database.

CHI-80
Chin, F.Y., and G. Ozsoyoglu
"Security of Statistical Data Bases," in Rullo, T.A. (Ed.), Advances in Computer Security Management, Vol. 1, Heyden & Son, Philadelphia, PA, 1980, pp. 57-76.

Key Words: statistical, methods.

CHI-81
Chin, F.Y., and G. Ozsoyoglu
"Statistical Data Base Design," ACM Trans. on Database Systems, March 1981, pp. 113-139.

Key Words: statistical, design.

CHI-82
Chin, F.Y., and G. Ozsoyoglu
"Auditing and Inference Control in Statistical Databases," IEEE Trans. on Software Engr., November 1982, pp. 574-582

Key Words: statistical, auditing.

CHI-86
Chin, F.Y.
"Security Problems on Inference Control for SUM, MAX and MIN Queries," Journal of the ACM, July 1986, pp. 451-464.

Key Words: statistical, inference.

CLA-83
Claybrook, B.G.
"An Approach to Developing Multilevel Secure Data Base Management Systems," Proc. 1983 IEEE Symp. on Sec. & Privacy, (5: IEE-83a), pp. 4-17.

Key Words: DBMS, design, methods.

COA-86
Coates, C. and M. Hale (Eds.)
Proceedings of the NCSC Invitational Workshop on Database Security, National Computer Security Center, Ft. Meade, MD, June 1986.

Key Words: proceedings, database.

COX-80
Cox, L.H.
"Suppression Methodology and Statistical Disclosure Control," Journal of American Statistical Association, June 1980, pp. 377-385.

Key Words: statistical, methods.

COX-86
Cox, L.H.
"Inference Control for Frequency Count Tables," IEEE Cipher, June 1986, pp. 4-14.

Key Words: statistical, inference.

COX-87
Cox, L.H.
"Modelling and Controlling User Inference," Proc. IFIP WG 11.3 Meeting, (6: LAN-88), 1987, pp. 167-171.

Key Words: database, inference.

COX-88
Cox, L.H.
"Inference Controls for Frequency Count Tables: An Update," Proc. 4th Aerospace Comp. Sec. Conf., (4: IEE-88b), 1988, pp. 112-117.

Key Words: statistical, inference.

CRO-89
Crocker, S., and E. Siarkiewicz
"Software Methodology for Development of a Trusted DBMS: Identification of Critical Problems," Proc. 5th Security Applicat. Conf., (4: IEE-89c), 1989, pp. 148-165.

Key Words: DBMS, methods, software.

DAV-81
Davida, G.I., D.L. Wells, and J.B. Kam
"A Database System with Subkeys," ACM Trans. on Database Systems, June 1981, pp. 312-328.

Key Words: database, encryption.

DAV-88
Davidson, J.W.
"Implementation Design for a Kernelized Trusted DBMS," Proc. 4th Aerosp. Comp. Sec. Conf., (4: IEE-88b), 1988, pp. 91-98.

Key Words: DBMS, kernel, design.

DEJ-83
DeJonge, W.
"Compromising Statistical Data Bases Responding to Queries About Means," ACM Trans. on Database Systems, March 1983, pp. 60-80.

Key Words: statistical, inference.

DEN-80
Denning, D.E., and J. Schlorer
"A Fast Procedure for Finding a Tracker in a Statistical Database," ACM Trans. on Database Systems, March 1980, pp. 88-102.

Key Words: statistical, inference.

DEN-80a
Denning, D.E.
"Secure Statistical Databases Under Random Sample Queries," ACM Trans. on Database Systems, September 1980, pp. 291-315.

Key Words: statistical, techniques.

DEN-81
Denning, D.E.
"Restricting Queries that Might Lead to Compromise," Proc. 1981 IEEE Symp. on Sec. & Privacy, (5: IEE-81), pp. 33-40.

Key Words: statistical, inference, techniques.

DEN-82
Denning, D.E., J. Schlorer, and E. Wehrle
"Memoryless Inference Controls for Statistical Databases," Proc. 1982 IEEE Symp. on Sec. & Privacy, (5: IEE-82), pp. 38-43.

Key Words: statistical, inference.

DEN-83
Denning, D.E.
"The Many-Time Pad: Theme and Variations," Proc. 1983 IEEE Symp. on Sec. & Privacy, (5: IEE-83a), pp. 23-30.

Key Words: database, encryption.

DEN-83a
   Denning, D.E., and
   J. Schlorer
   "Inference Controls for
   Statistical Data Bases," IEEE
   Computer, July 1983, pp. 69-
   82.

   Key Words: statistical,
   inference.

DEN-83b
   Denning, D.E.
   "Field Encryption and
   Authentication," Proc.
   Crypto-83, Santa Barbara,
   1983, (9: CHA-84b), pp.
   231-247.

   Key Words: statistical,
   encryption.

DEN-84
   Denning, D.E.
   "Cryptographic Checksums
   for Multilevel Database
   Security," Proc. 1984 IEEE
   Symp. on Sec. & Privacy,
   (5: IEE-84), pp. 52-61.

   Key Words: MLS, database,
   encryption.

DEN-85
   Denning, D.E.
   "Commutative Filters for
   Reducing Inference Threats
   in Multilevel Database
   Systems," Proc. 1985 IEEE
   Symp. on Sec. & Privacy,
   (5: IEE-85), pp. 134-146.

   Key Words: MLS, database,
   inference.

DEN-86
   Denning, D.E., et al.
   "Views for Multilevel
   Database Security," Proc.
   1986 IEEE Symp. on Sec. &
   Privacy, (5: IEE-86), pp.
   156-172.

   Key Words: MLS, database,
   views.

DEN-86a
   Denning, D.E.
   "A Preliminary Note on the
   Inference Problem in
   Multilevel Database Systems,"
   Proc. NCSC Workshop on
   Database Security, (6: COA-
   86), 1986, pp. I1-I14.

   Key Words: MLS, database,
   inference.

DEN-87
   Denning, D.E., et al.
   "Views for Multilevel
   Database Security," IEEE
   Trans. on Software Engr.,
   February 1987, pp. 129-140.

   Key Words: MLS, database,
   views.

DEN-87a
   Denning, D.E., et al.
   "A Multilevel Relational Data
   Model," Proc. 1987 IEEE
   Symp. on Sec. & Privacy,
   (5: IEE-87a), pp. 220-234.

   Key Words: MLS, database,
   models.

DEN-87b
   Denning, D.E.
   "Database System Lessons
   Learned from Modeling a
   Secure Multilevel Relational
   Database System," Proc. IFIP
   WG 11.3 Meeting, (6: LAN-
   88), 1987, pp. 35-43.

   Key Words: MLS, database,
   models, relational, case.

DEN-88
   Denning, D.E., et al.
   "The SeaView Security
   Model," Proc. 1988 IEEE
   Symp. on Sec. & Privacy,
   (5: IEE-88a), pp. 218-233.

   Key Words: stabase, model,
   views.

DEN-88a
   Denning, D.E.
   "Database Security," in Traub,
   J.F., et al., (Eds.), Annual
   Review of Computer Science,
   Volume 3, Annual Reviews,
   Inc., Palo Alto, CA, 1988, pp.
   1-22.

   Key Words: database, general.

DEN-88b
   Denning, D.E.
   "An Evolution of Views,"
   Proc. RADC Data Base
   Security Invitational Workshop,
   Menlo Park, CA, May 1988
   (6: LUN-90), pp. 74-77.

   Key Words: MLS, database,
   views.

DEN-89
   Denning, D.E.
   "Toward a General Multi-Level
   Data Model," IEEE Cipher,
   April 1989, pp. 34-40.

   Key Words: MLS, database,
   models.

DIL-86
   Dillaway, B.B., and
   J.T. Haigh
   "A Practical Design for Multi-
   Level Security in Secure
   Database Management
   Systems," Proc. 2nd Aerosp.
   Comp. Sec. Conf., (5: IEE-
   86a), 1986.

   Key Words: MLS, database,
   design, case.

DIT-88
   Dittrich, K.R., et al.
   "Analysis of the Privacy
   Model for the Information
   System DORIS," Proc. IFIP
   WG 11.3 Workshop, (6: LAN-
   89b), 1988, pp. 105-121.

   Key Words: database, model,
   case.

DOB-87
    Dobson, J.
    "Sec. & Databases: A
    Personal View," Proc. IFIP
    WG 11.3 Meeting, (6: LAN-
    88), 1987, pp. 11-22.

    Key Words: database,
    general.

DOB-88
    Dobson, J.E., and
    J.A. McDermid
    "Security Models and
    Enterprise Models," Proc.
    IFIP WG 11.3 Workshop, (6:
    LAN-89b), 1988, pp. 1-39.

    Key Words: databse, models,
    general.

DOW-86
    Downs, D.D.
    "Applicability of the TCSEC
    to DBMS," Proc. NCSC
    Workshop on Database Sec.,
    (6: COA-86), 1986, pp. J1-
    J11.

    Key Words: MLS, DBMS,
    criteria.

DOW-86a
    Downs, D.D.
    "Discretionary Security in
    Database Management
    Systems," Proc. NCSC
    Workshop on Database Sec.,
    (6: COA-86), 1986, pp. K1-
    K10.

    Key Words: DBMS, policy,
    discretionary.

DOW-89
    Downing, A.R., I.B.
    Greenburg, and T.F. Lunt
    "Issues in Distributed
    Database Security," Proc. 5th
    Security Applicat. Conf., (4:
    IEE-89c), 1989, pp. 196-203.

    Key Words: database,
    network, general.

DUC-85
    du Croix, A.J.
    "Data Sharing and Access
    Protection in Business System
    12," Computers & Security,
    December 1985, pp. 317-323.

    Key Words: database, control,
    case.

DUN-86
    Duncan, G., and D. Lambert
    "Disclosure-Limited Data
    Dissemination," Journal of the
    American Statistics
    Association, Vol. 81, No. 393,
    pp. 10-18.

    Key Words: statistical,
    methods.

DWY-87
    Dwyer, P.A., G.D. Jelatis, and
    B.M. Thuraisingham
    "Multi-Level Security in
    Database Management
    Systems," Computers &
    Security, June 1987, pp. 252-
    260.

    Key Words: MLS, DBMS,
    methods.

DWY-88
    Dwyer, P., et al.
    "Query Processing in LDV: A
    Secure Database System,"
    Proc. 4th Aerosp. Comp. Sec.
    Conf., (4: IEE-88b), 1988, pp.
    118-124.

    Key Words: database,
    techniques.

ERI-83
    Eriksson, R., and K. Beckman
    "Protecting of Data Bases
    Using File Encryption," Proc.
    IFIP/Sec. '83, Stockholm,
    1983, (2: FAK-83), pp. 217-
    221.

    Key Words: database,
    encryption.

FEE-86
    Feeney, T.
    "Security Issues and Features
    of Database Management
    Systems," Information Age,
    (U.K.), April 1986, pp. 85-94.

    Key Words: DBMS, policy,
    methods.

FER-81
    Fernandez, E.B., R.C.
    Summers, and C. Wood
    Database Sec. & Integrity,
    Addison-Wesley, Reading,
    MA, 1981.

    Key Words: book, database,
    general.

FER-89
    Fernandez, E.B., E.Gudes,
    and H.Song
    "A Security Model of Object-
    Oriented Databases," Proc.
    1989 IEEE Symp. on Sec. &
    Privacy, (5: IEE-89b), pp. 110-
    115.

    Key Words: database, models.

FRA-85
    Fraga, J., and D. Powell
    "A Fault and Intrusion-Tolerant
    File System," Proc. IFIP/Sec.,
    Dublin, 1985, (2: GRI-85), pp.
    203-218.

    Key Words: database, methods,
    case.

FRI-80
    Friedman, A.D., and
    L.J. Hoffman
    "Towards a Fail-Safe Approach
    to Secure Databases," Proc.
    1980 IEEE Symp. on Sec. &
    Privacy, (5: IEE-80), pp. 18-
    21.

    Key Words: statistical,
    methods.

FRO-88
> Froscher, J.N., and
> C. Meadows
> "Achieving a Trusted
> Database Mangement System
> Using Prallelism," Proc. IFIP
> WG 11.3 Workshop, (6:
> LAN-89b), 1988, pp. 151-
> 160.
>
> Key Words: DBMS, trusted,
> methods.

FUG-85
> Fugini, M.
> "Design of a Relational
> Schema for Database
> Dynamic Authorization
> Management," Proc. IFIP/Sec.
> '85, Dublin, 1985, (2: GRI-
> 85), pp. 17-25.
>
> Key Words: database,
> control, methods.

FUG-88
> Fugini, M.G.
> "Secure Database
> Development Methodologies,"
> Proc. IFIP WG 11.3 Meeting,
> (6: LAN-88), 1987, pp. 103-
> 129.
>
> Key Words: database,
> methods.

GAJ-88
> Gajnak, G.E.
> "Some Results from Entity-
> Relationship Multilevel
> Secure DBMS Project," Proc.
> 4th Aerosp. Comp. Sec.
> Conf., (4: IEE-88b), 1988,
> pp. 66-71.
>
> Key Words: MLS, DBMS,
> case.

GAJ-88a
> Gajnak, G.E.
> "Some Results from
> Entity/Relationship Multilevel
> Secure DBMS Project," Proc.
> RADC Data Base Security
> Invitational Workshop, Menlo
> Park, CA, May 1988, (6:
> LUN-90), pp. 144-156.
>
> Key Words: MLS, DBMS,
> case.

GAL-85
> Gal, G., and W.E. McCarthy
> "Specification of Internal
> Accounting Controls in a
> Database Environment,"
> Computers & Security, March
> 1985, pp. 23-32.
>
> Key Words: database,
> auditing.

GAR-86
> Garvey, C.
> "Architecture Issues in Secure
> Database Mangement
> Systems," Proc. NCSC
> Workshop on Database Sec.,
> (6: COA-86), 1986, pp. D1-
> D19.
>
> Key Words: DBMS, design,
> methods.

GAR-88
> Garvey, C., and A. Wu
> "ASD-Views," Proc. 1988
> IEEE Symp. on Sec. &
> Privacy, (5: IEE-88a), pp. 85-
> 95.
>
> Key Words: MLS, DBMS,
> views.

GAR-88a
> Garvey, C., N. Jensen,
> and J. Wilson
> "The Advanced Secure
> DBMS: Making Secure
> DBMSs Usable," Proc. IFIP
> WG 11.3 Workshop, (6:
> LAN-89b), 1988, pp. 187-195.
>
> Key Words: MLS, DBMS,
> case.

GAR-88b
> Garvey, C.E., and
> P.N. Papaccio
> "Multilevel Data Store
> Design," Proc. 2nd Aerosp.
> Comp. Sec. Conf., (5: IEE-
> 86a), 1986, pp. 58-64.
>
> Key Words: MLS, database,
> design.

GAR-89
> Garvey, C., et al.
> "A Layered TCB
> Implementation Versus the
> Hinke-Schaefer Approach,"
> Proc. IFIP WG 11.3 (Data
> Base) Workshop, (6: IFI-89),
> 1989.
>
> Key Words: DBMS, design,
> case.

GIL-80
> Gilhooley, I.A.
> "Data Security, in Rullo, T.A.
> (Ed.), Advances in Computer
> Security Management, Vol. 1,
> Heyden & Son, Philadelphia,
> PA, 1980, pp. 33-56.
>
> Key Words: database, methods,
> general.

GLA-88
> Glasgow, J., G. MacEwen,
> and P. Panangaden
> "Security by Permission in
> Databases," Proc. IFIP WG
> 11.3 Workshop, (6: LAN-89b),
> 1988, pp. 197-205.
>
> Key Words: database, control,
> methods.

GRA-82
> Graubart, R., and
> J.P.L. Woodward
> "A Preliminary Naval
> Surveillance DBMS Security
> Model," Proc. 1982 IEEE
> Symp. on Sec. & Privacy,
> (5: IEE-82), pp. 21-37.
>
> Key Words: DBMS, models,
> case.

GRA-84
> Graubart, R.
> "The Integrity Lock Approach
> to Secure Database
> Management," Proc. 1984
> IEEE Symp. on Security
> Privacy, (5: IEE-84), pp. 62-
> 74.
>
> Key Words: DBMS, design,
> methods.

GRA-84a
Graubart, R.D., and
S. Kramer
"The Integrity Lock Support
Environment," Proc. IFIP/Sec.
'84, Toronto, 1984, (2: FIN-
85), pp. 249-268.

Key Words: database, design,
methods.

GRA-89
Graubart, R.
"Comparing DBMS and
Operating System Security
Requirements -- The Need
for Separate DBMS Security
Criteria," Proc. IFIP WG
11.3 (Data Base) Workshop,
(6: IFI-89), 1989.

Key Words: DBMS,
requirements, criteria.

GRA-89a
Graubart, R.
"A Comparison of Three
Secure DBMS Architectures,"
Proc. IFIP WG 11.3 (Data
Base) Workshop, (6: IFI-89),
1989.

Key Words: DBMS, design,
case.

GUD-80
Gudes, E.
"The Design of a
Cryptography Based Secure
File System," IEEE Trans. on
Software Engr., September
1980, pp. 411-420.

Key Words: database,
cryptography.

GUY-89
Guynes, C.S.
"Protecting Statistical
Databases: A Matter of
Privacy," Computers &
Society, March 1989, pp. 15-
20.

Key Words: statistical,
requirements.

HAI-87
Haigh, J.T.
"Modeling Database Security
Requirements," Proc. IFIP
WG 11.3 Meeting, (6: LAN-
88), 1987, pp. 45-56.

Key Words: database,
requirements.

HAI-89
Haigh, J.T., et al.
"The LDV Approach to
Database Security," Proc. IFIP
WG 11.3 (Data Base)
Workshop, (6: IFI-89), 1989.

Key Words: MLS, database,
methods.

HAL-87
Hale, M.W.
"Status of Trusted Database
System Interpretations," Proc.
IFIP WG 11.3 Meeting, (6:
LAN-88), 1987, pp. 263-268.

Key Words: database, criteria.

HAR-81
Hartson, H.R.
"Data Base Security System
Architectures," Information
Systems, Vol. 6, No. 1, 1981,
pp. 1-22.

Key Words: database, design.

HEN-86
Henning, R.R., and
S.A. Walker
"Computer Architectures and
Database Security," Proc. 9th
Natl. Comp. Sec. Conf., (5:
NCS-86), 1986, pp. 216-230.

Key Words: database, design.

HEN-87
Henning, R.R.
"The Allocation of Database
Management System Security
Responsibilities," Proc. IFIP
WG 11.3 Meeting, (6: LAN-
88), 1987, pp. 131-148.

Key Words: database,
management.

HEN-88
Henning, R.R., R.P. Simonian
"Security Analysis of Database
Schema Information," Proc.
IFIP WG 11.3 Workshop, (6:
LAN-89b), 1988, pp. 233-245.

Key Words: database, methods.

HEN-88a
Henning, R.R.
"Industry and Government
DBMS Security & Privacy
Needs--A Comparison," Proc.
4th Aerosp. Comp. Sec. Conf.,
(4: IEE-88b), 1988, pp. 99-
105.

Key Words: DBMS,
requirements.

HEN-89
Henning, R.R.
"DAC Mechanisms in Trusted
Database Management
Systems," Proc. 2nd RADC
Data Base Security Workshop,
(6:RAD-90), May 1989.

Key Words: DBMS,
discretionary.

HIN-86
Hinke, T.H.
"Secure Database Management
System Architectural Analysis,"
Proc. NCSC Workshop on
Database Sec., (6: COA-86),
1986, pp. E1-E15.

Key Words: DBMS, design,
methods.

HIN-87
Hinke, T.H.
"DBMS Technology vs.
Threats," Proc. IFIP WG 11.3
Meeting, (6: LAN-88), 1987,
pp. 57-87.

Key Words: DBMS, threats,
general.

HIN-88
Hinke, T.H.
"Inference Aggregation
Detection in Database
Management Systems," Proc.
1988 IEEE Symp. on Sec. &
Privacy, (5: IEE-88a), pp. 96-
106.

Key Words: database,
inference.

HIN-88a
Hinke, T.H.
"Database Inference Engine
Design Approach," Proc. IFIP
WG 11.3 Workshop, (6:
LAN-89b), Oct. 1988, pp.
247-262.

Key Words: database,
inference, design.

HIN-88b
Hinke, T.H., et al.
"A Secure DBMS Design,"
Postscript, 11th Natl. Comp.
Sec. Conf., (5: NCS-88a),
1988, pp. 1-13.

Key Words: database, design,
methods.

HIN-89
Hinke, T.H.
"DBMS Trusted Computing
Data Taxonony," Proc. IFIP
WG 11.3 (Data Base)
Workshop, (6: IFI-89), 1989.

Key Words: DBMS, methods,
design.

HIN-89a
Hinke, T.H.
"Database Design with Row
Level MAC and Table Level
DAC," Proc. 2nd RADC
Data Base Security
Workshop, (6: RAD-90),
May 1989.

Key Words: MLS, database,
design.

HON-82
Hong, Y.-C., and S.Y.W. Su
"A Mechanism for Database
Protection in Cellular-Logic
Devices," IEEE Trans. on
Software Engr., November
1982, pp. 583-596.

Key Words: database,
techniques.

HOP-88
Hoppenstand, G.S., and
D.K. Hsiao
"Secure Access Control with
High Access Precision: An
Efficient Approach to
Multilevel Security," Proc.
IFIP WG 11.3 Workshop, (6:
LAN-89b), 1988, pp. 167-176.

Key Words: MLS, database,
control.

HOS-88
Hosmer, H.H., and
B.K. Burns
"Designing Multilevel Secure
Distributed Databases," Proc.
IFIP WG 11.3 Workshop, (6:
LAN-89b), 1988, pp. 161-165.

Key Words: MLS, database,
design.

HOS-89
Hosmer, H.H.
"Handling Integrity Lock
Violations," Proc. IFIP WG
11.3 (Data Base) Workshop,
(6: IFI-89), 1989.

Key Words: database,
techniques.

HSI-87
Hsiao, D.K.
"Database Security Course
Module," Proc. IFIP WG 11.3
Meeting, (6: LAN-88), 1987,
pp. 269-301.

Key Words: database,
awareness, general.

HUB-86
Hubbard, B.S., S.A. Walker,
and R.R. Henning
"Database Systems and The
Criteria: Do They Relate?,"
Proc. 9th Natl. Comp. Sec.
Conf., (5: NCS-86), 1986, pp.
21-24.

Key Words: database, criteria.

IEO-88
Ieong, I.T., and T.C. Ting
"An Analysis of Database
Security with Queries to
Higher Order Statistical
Information," Proc. IFIP WG
11.3 Workshop, (6: LAN-89b),
1988, pp. 207-223.

Key Words: statistical,
methods.

IFI-89
Proceedings, Workshop on
Database Security, IFIP WG
11.3 (Data Base), Monterey,
CA, September 5-7, 1989.

Key Words: proceedings,
database, MLS, methods,
general.

JAJ-89
Jajodia, S., et al.
"Audit Trail Organization in
Relational Databases," Proc.
IFIP WG 11.3 (Data Base)
Workshop, (6: IFI-89), 1989.

Key Words: database, auditing.

JAJ-89a
Jajodia, S., et al.
"Auditing in Secure Database
Management Systems," Proc.
2nd RADC Data Base Security
Workshop, (6: RAD-90), May
1989.

Key Words: DBMS, auditing,
methods.

JEN-88
    Jensen, N.R.
    "System Security Officer
    Functions in the A1 Secure
    DBMS," Proc. IFIP WG 11.3
    Workshop, (6: LAN-89b),
    Oct. 1988, pp. 53-62.

    Key Words: MSL, DBMS,
    management.

JEN-88a
    Jensen, N.R.
    "Implications of Multilevel
    Security on the Data
    Dictionary of a Secure
    Relational DBMS," Proc. 4th
    Aerosp. Comp. Sec. Conf.,
    (4: IEE-88b), 1988, pp. 58-
    59.

    Key Words: MLS, DBMS,
    design.

KEE-89
    Keefe, T.F.,
    M.B. Thuraisingham,
    and W.T. Tsai
    "Secure Query Processing
    Strategies," IEEE Computer,
    March 1989, pp. 63-70.

    Key Words: database,
    methods, general.

KEE-89a
    Keefe, T., et al.
    "Multi-Party Update Conflict:
    The Problem and Its
    Solution," Proc. 5th Aerosp.
    Comp. Sec. Conf., (4: IEE-
    89c), 1989, pp. 222-231.

    Key Words: database,
    techniques.

KEE-89b
    Keefe, T.F., et al.
    "SODA: A Secure Object-
    Oriented Database System,"
    Computers & Security,
    October 1989, pp. 517-533.

    Key Words: database, case.

KEE-89c
    Keefe, T.F., and W.T. Tsai
    "Prototyping the SODA
    Security Models," Proc. IFIP
    WG 11.3 (Data Base)
    Workshop, (6: IFI-89), 1989.

    Key Words: database,
    methods, case.

KEM-87
    Kemmerer, R.A.
    "Formal Specification and
    Verification Techniques for a
    Trusted DBMS," Proc. IFIP
    WG 11.3 Meeting, (6: LAN-
    88), 1987, pp. 229-240.

    Key Words: DBMS,
    verification.

KNO-87
    Knode, R.B.
    "Trudata: The Road to a
    Trusted DBMS," Proc. 10th
    Natl. Comp. Sec. Conf., (5:
    NCS-87a), 1987, pp. 201-210.

    Key Words: DBMS, methods,
    case.

KNO-88
    Knode, R.B. and R.A. Hunt
    "Making Databases Secure
    with Trudata Technology,"
    Proc. 4th Aerosp. Comp. Sec.
    Conf., (4: IEE-88b), 1988, pp.
    82-90.

    Key Words: database, design,
    case.

KUO-83
    Kuong, J.J.
    Controls for Advanced/On-
    Line, Database Systems,
    Management Advisory
    Publications, Wellesley Hills,
    MA, 1983.

    Key Words: book, databse,
    controls.

LAN-87
    Landwehr, C.E. (Chm.)
    "Database Security: Where
    Are We," Proc. IFIP WG 11.3
    Meeting, (6: LAN-88),
    October 1987, pp. 1-9.

    Key Words: database, general.

LAN-87a
    Landwehr, C.E. (Ed.)
    Database Security: Status and
    Prospects, Proceedings, IFIP
    WG 11.3 (Data Base) Initial
    Meeting, Annapolis, MD,
    October 1987, North-Holland,
    Amsterdam, 1988.

    Key Words: proceedings,
    database, general, methods..

LAN-89
    Landwehr, C.E., (Ed.)
    Database Security, II: Status
    and Prospects, Proceedings,
    IFIP WG 11.3 (Data Base)
    Workshop, Kingston, Ontario,
    October 1988, North-Holland,
    Amsterdam, 1989.

    Key Words: proceedings,
    database.

LAV-84
    Lavrence, D.I.
    "Some Security Aspects of
    Decision Support Systems,"
    Proc. IFIP/Sec. '84, Toronto,
    1984, (2: FIN-85), pp. 239-
    248.

    Key Words: database,
    requirements.

LEI-82
    Leiss, E.L.
    Principles of Database
    Security, Plenum Press, New
    York, 1982.

    Key Words: book, database,
    general.

LEI-86
    Leiss, F.L.
    "The Inaccessible Set: A
    Classification by Query Type
    of Security Risk in Statistical
    Databases," Information
    Processing Letters, December
    1986, pp. 275-279.

    Key Words: statistical,
    methods.

LIE-85
Liew, C.K., W.J. Choi, and C.J. Liew
"A Data Distortion by Probability Distribution," ACM Trans. on Database Systems, September 1985, pp. 395-411.

Key Words: statistical, methods.

LIN-89
Lin, T.Y.
"Some Remarks on Inference Controllers," Proc. 2nd RADC Data Base Security Workshop, (6: RAD-89), May 1989.

Key Words: database, inference.

LIN-89a
Lin, T.Y.
"Commutative Security Algebra and Aggregation," Proc. 2nd RADC Data Base Security Workshop, (6: RAD-89), May 1989.

Key Words: database, methods, theory.

LOC-87
Lochovsky, F.H., and C.C. Woo
"Role-Based Security in Database Management Systems," Proc. IFIP WG 11.3 Meeting, (6: LAN-88), 1987, pp. 209-222.

Key Words: DBMS, methods.

LUN-87
Lunt, T.F., and T.A. Berson
"An Expert System to Classify and Sanitize Text," Proc. 3d Aerosp. Comp. Sec. Conf., (5: IEE-87b), 1987, pp. 30-34.

Key Words: database, techniques.

LUN-88
Lunt, T.F., et al.
"A Near-Term Design for the Sea View Multilevel Database System," Proc. 1988 IEEE Symp. on Sec. & Privacy, (5: IEE-88a), pp. 234-244.

Key Words: MLS, database, design.

LUN-88a
Lunt, T.F.
"Access Control Policies for Database Systems," Proc. IFIP WG 11.3 Workshop, (6: LAN-89b), 1988, pp. 41-52.

Key Words: database, control, policy.

LUN-88b
Lunt, T.F.
"Multilevel Database Systems: Meeting A1," Proc. IFIP WG 11.3 Workshop, (6: LAN-89b), 1988, pp. 177-186.

Key Words: MLS, database, methods.

LUN-88c
Lunt, T.F.
"A Summary of the RADC Database Security Workshop," Proc. 11th Natl. Comp. Sec. Conf., (5: NCS-88), 1988, pp. 188-193.

Key Words: database, general.

LUN-88d
Lunt, T.F.
"Toward a Multilevel Relational Data Language," Proc. 4th Aerosp. Comp. Sec. Conf., (4: IEE-88b), 1988, pp. 72-79.

Key Words: MLS, relational, design.

LUN-88e
Lunt, T.F., et al.
"Element-Level Classification with A-1 Assurance," Computers & Security, February 1988, pp. 73-82.

Key Words: MLS, database, methods.

LUN-89
Lunt, T.F.
"Aggregation and Inference: Facts and Fallacies," Proc. 1989 IEEE Symp. on Sec. & Privacy, (5: IEE-89b), pp. 102-109.

Key Words: database, inference.

LUN-89a
Lunt, T.F.
"Report from the Second RADC Database Security Workshop," Proc. 5th Aerosp. Comp. Sec. Conf., (4: IEE-89c), 1989, pp. 310-313.

Key Words: database, general.

LUN-89b
Lunt, T.F.
"Multilevel Security for Object-Oriented Database System," Proc. IFIP WG 11.3 (Data Base) Workshop, (6: IFI-89), 1989.

Key Words: MLS, database, methods.

LUN-90
Lunt, T.F.
Research Directions in Database Security, Proceedings, 1st RADC Data Base Security Invitational Workshop, Menlo Park, CA, May 1988, Springer Verlag, New York, 1990.

Key Words: proceedings, general.

MAC-87
MacEwen, G.H.
"Effects of Distributed System Technology on Database Security: A Survey," Proc. IFIP WG 11.3 Meeting, (6: LAN-88), 1987, pp. 253-261.

Key Words: database, networks.

MAN-87
Manola, F.A.
"A Personal View of DBMS
Security," Proc. IFIP WG
11.3 Meeting, (6: LAN-88),
Oct. 1987, pp. 23-34.

Key Words: MLS, DBMS,
general.

MAT-86
Matloff, N.S.
"Another Look at the Use of
Noise Addition for Database
Security," Proc. 1986 IEEE
Symp. on Sec. & Privacy, (5:
IEE-86), pp. 173-180.

Key Words: statistical,
techniques.

MAT-87
Matloff, N.S.
"Inference Control via Query
Restriction vs. Data
Modification," Proc. IFIP
WG 11.3 Meeting, (6: LAN-
88), 1987, pp. 159-166.

Key Words: statistical,
techniques.

MAT-88
Matloff, N.S., and P. Tendick
'The 'Curse of
Dimensionality' in Database
Security," Proc. IFIP WG
11.3 Workshop, (6:LAN-89b),
1988, pp. 225-232.

Key Words: database, theory,
methods.

MCH-88
McHugh, J., and
B.M. Thuraisingham
"Multilevel Security Issues in
Distributed Database
Management Systems,"
Computers & Security,
August 1988, pp. 387-396.

Key Words: MLS, DBMS,
network.

MCL-85
McLeish, M.
"Inference Controls for
Intelligent Databases,"
Proceedings, 1985 Conference
on Intelligent Systems and
Machines, Oakland University
Press, Oakland, MI, April
1985, pp. 71-75.

Key Words: database,
methods, control, inference.

MCL-89
McLeish, M.
"Further Results on the
Security of Partitioned
Dynamic Statistical
Databases," ACM Trans. on
Database Systems, March
1989, pp. 98-113.

Key Words: statistical,
methods.

MEA-87
Meadows, C., and S. Jajodia
"Integrity vs. Security in
Multi-Level Secure
Databases," Proc. IFIP WG
11.3 Meeting, (6: LAN-88),
1987, pp. 89-101

Key Words: MLS, databases,
methods, integrity.

MEA-88
Meadows, C., and S. Jajodia
"Maintaining Correctness,
Availability, and Unabiguity
in Trusted Data Base
Management Systems," Proc.
4th Aerosp. Comp. Sec.
Conf., (4: IEE-88b), 1988, pp.
106-110.

Key Words: trusted, DBMS,
methods, techniques.

MEA-88a
Meadows, C.
"Designing a Trusted
Application Using an Object-
Oriented Data Model," Proc.
RADC Data Base Security
Invitational Workshop, Menlo
Park, CA, May 1988 (6:
LUN-90), pp. 157-163.

Key Words: database, models,
design.

MEA-88b
Meadows, C.
"New Approaches to Database
Security: Report on
Discussion," Proc. RADC Data
Base Security Invitational
Workshop, Menlo Park, CA,
May 1988, (6: LUN-90), pp.
193-200.

Key Words: database, design,
methods, general.

MEA-89
Meadows, C.
"Constructing Containers Using
a Multilevel Relational Data
Model," Proc. IFIP WG 11.3
(Data Base) Workshop, (6:
IFI-89), 1989.

Key Words: database, model,
design, relational.

MEA-89a
Meadows, C., and J. Forscher
"Operating System Support of
Multilevel Applications," Proc.
2nd RADC Data Base Security
Workshop, (6: RAD-90), May
1989.

Key Words: OS, database,
methods.

MIN-81
Minsky, N.
"Synergistic Authorization in
Database Systems," Proc., 7th
Internat. Conference on Very
Large Database Systems,
September 1981.

Key Words: databases, control,
methods, techniques.

MIR-80
Miranda, S.
"Aspects of Data Security in
GeneralPurpose Data Base
Mangement Systems," Proc.
1980 IEEE Symp. on Sec. &
Privacy, (5: IEE-80), pp. 46-
58.

Key Words: DBMS,
requirements, methods.

MOR-87
Morgenstern, M.
"Sec. & Inference in Multilevel Database and Knowledge-Base Systems," Proc., ACM Internat. Conf. on Management of Data (SIGMOD-87), May 1987.

Key Words: MLS, database, inference.

MOR-88
Morgenstern, M.
"Controlling Logical Inference in Multilevel Database Systems," Proc. 1988 IEEE Symp. on Sec. & Privacy, (5: IEE-88b), pp. 245-255.

Key Words: MLS, database, inference.

MOR-88a
Morgenstern, M.
"Inference and Aggregation," Proc. RADC Data Base Security Invitational Workshop, Menlo Park, CA, May 1988, (6: LUN-90), pp. 118-133.

Key Words: database, inference.

NAS-83
Multilevel Data Management Security, Report on 1982 Air Force Summer Study, Air Force Studies Board, National Academy of Sciences, Washington, DC, 1983.

Key Words: proceedings, general.

NBS-81
Guidelines on Integrity Assurance and Control in Data Base Administration, FIPS PUB 88, National Bureau of Standards, Gaithersburg, MD, August 1981.

Key Words: database, guidelines integrity, methods.

NOT-86
Notargiacomo, L., and J.P. O'Connor
"Report on Secure Distributed Data Management System Research," Proc. NCSC Workshop on Database Sec.,(6: COA-86), 1986, pp. G1-G9.

Key Words: database, methods, network.

NOT-88
Notargiacomo, L.
"Secure Distributed DBMS - Architecture Definition," Proc. RADC Data Base Security Invitational Workshop, Menlo Park, CA, May 1988 (6: LUN-90), pp. 23-48.

Key Words: MLS, DBMS, design.

NOT-88a
Notargiacomo, L.
"Metadata and View Classification," Proc. RADC Data Base Security Invitational Workshop, Menlo Park, CA, May 1988 (6: LUN-90), pp. 201-205.

Key Words: database, methods, views.

OCO-88
O'Connor, J.P. and J.W. Gray III
"A Distributed Architecture for Multilevel Database Security," Proc. 11th Natl. Comp. Sec. Conf., (5: NCS-88), 1988, pp. 179-187.

Key Words: MLS, database, network.

OLD-84
Oldehoeft, A.E., and R. McDonald
"A Software Scheme for User Controlled File Encryption," Computers & Security, February 1984, pp. 35-42.

Key Words: database, encryption.

OMA-83
Omar, K.A., and D.L. Wells
"Modified Structure for the Subkeys Model," Proc. 1983 IEEE Symp. on Sec. & Privacy, (5: IEE-83a), pp. 79-86.

Key Words: database, encryption.

OZS-82
Ozsoyoglu, G., and F.Y. Chin
"Enhancing the Security of Statistical Databases with a Question-Answering System and a Kernel Design," IEEE Trans. on Software Engr., May 1982, pp. 223-234.

Key Words: statistical, methods, inference, design.

OZS-85
Ozsoyoglu, G., and T.A. Su
"Rounding and Inference Control in Conceptual Models for Statistical Databases," Proc. 1985 IEEE Symp. on Sec. & Privacy, (5: IEE-85), pp. 160-173.

Key Words: statistical, inference, techniques.

PAA-86
Paass, G.
"Disclosure Risk and Disclosure Avoidance for Microdata," Proc. IFIP/Sec. '86, Monte Carlo, 1986, (2: GRI-89).

Key Words: statistical, threats, techniques.

PAL-87
Palley, M.A., and J.S. Simonoff
"The Use of Regression Methodology for Compromise of Confidential Information in Statistical Database," ACM Trans. on Database Systems, December 1987, pp. 593-608.

Key Words: statistical, threats.

PAT-85
Patkau, B.H., and
D.L. Tennenhouse
"The Implementation of
Secure Entity-Relationship
Databases," Proc. 1986 IEEE
Symp. on Sec. & Privacy, (5:
IEE-86), pp. 230-236.

Key Words: databse, design,
methods.

PET-89
Petrie, M.L., E. Gudes, and
E.B. Fernandez
"Security Policies in Object-
Oriented Databases," Proc.
IFIP WG 11.3 (Data Base)
Workshop, (6: IFI-89), 1989.

Key Words: database, policy,
methods.

PLU-88
Pluimakers, G.M.J.
"Some Notes on
Authorization and Transaction
Management in Distributed
Database Systems,"
Computers & Security, June
1988, pp. 287-298.

Key Words: databse, control,
network.

RAD-89
"Research Directions in
Database Security, II,"
Proceedings, 2nd RADC Data
Base Security Workshop,
Bethlehem, NH, May 1989,
SRI International, Menlo
Park, CA, December 22,
1989.

Key Words: proceedings,
general, policy, methods.

REI-80
Reiss, S.P.
"Practical Data Swapping,"
Proc. 1980 IEEE Symp. on
Sec. & Privacy, (5: IEE-80),
pp. 38-45.

Key Words: database,
techniques.

REI-84
Reiss, S.P.
"Practical Data Swapping: The
First Steps," ACM Trans. on
Database Systems, March
1984, pp. 20-37.

Key Words: database,
techniques.

ROD-80
Rodriguez, J.J., and
P.S. Fisher
"Security Problems in a Data
Base Environment," in Rullo,
T.A. (Ed.), Advances
inComputer Security
Management, Vol. 1, Heyden
& Son, Philadelphia, PA,
1980, pp. 122-139.

Key Words: database, threats.

ROU-87
Rougeau, P.A. and
E.D. Sturms
"The Sybase Secure
Dataserver: A Solution to the
Multilevel Secure DBMS
Problem," Proc. 10th Natl.
Comp. Sec. Conf., (5: NCS-
87a), 1987, pp. 211-215.

Key Words: MLS, DBMS,
case.

RUD-85
Rudell, M.E.
"Labeling Screen Output,"
Proc. 1986 IEEE Symp. on
Sec. & Privacy, (5: IEE-86),
pp. 237-240.

Key Words: database,
techniques.

RUS-89
Russell, L.
"Semantic Overloading of the
Relational Model for
Multilevel Security," Proc.
2nd RADC Data Base
Security Workshop, (6: RAD-
89), May 1989.

Key Words: MLS, database,
methods.

SAD-89
Sadhu, R.
"Mandatory Controls for
Database Integrity," Proc. IFIP
WG 11.3 (Data Base)
Workshop, (6: IFI-89), 1989.

Key Words: database, integrity.

SCH-80
Schell, R.R., and L.A. Cox
"A Secure Archival Storage
System," Conference Record,
1980 IEEE Fall Comcon,
Washington, DC, 1980.

Key Words: database, case.

SCH-80a
Schlorer, J.
"Disclosure from Statistical
Databases: Quantitative
Aspects of Trackers," ACM
Trans. on Database Systems,
December 1980, pp. 467-492.

Key Words: statistical,
inference.

SCH-81
Schlorer, J.
"Security in Statistical
Databases: Multidimensional
Transformations," ACM Trans.
on Database Systems, March
1981, pp. 95-112.

Key Words: statistical,
techniques.

SCH-83
Schloerer, J., and
D.E. Denning
"Protecting Query Based
Statistical Output," Proc.
IFIP/Sec. '83, Stockholm,
1983, (2: FAK-83), pp. 37-46.

Key Words: statistical,
techniques.

SCH-83a
Schloerer, J.
"Information Loss in
Partitioned Statistical
Databases," Computer Journal,
No. 3, 1983, pp. 218-223.

Key Words: statistical,
inference.

SCH-85
Schaefer, M.
"On the Logical Extension of the Criteria Principles to Design of Multi-level Database Management Systems," Proc. 8th Natl. Comp. Sec. Conf., (5: NCS-85), 1985, pp. 28-30.

Key Words: MLS, DBMS, criteria, design.

SCH-86
Schell, R.R., and D.E. Denning
"Integrity in Trusted Database Systems," Proc. 9th Natl. Comp. Sec. Conf., (5: NCS-86), 1986, pp. 30-36.

Key Words: database, integrity.

SCH-86a
Schell, R.R., and D.E. Denning
"Integrity in Trusted Database Systems," Proc. NCSC Workshop on Database Sec., (6: COA-86), 1986, pp. C1-C14.

Key Words: database, integrity.

SCH-88
Schaeffer, M.
"Dynamic Classification and Automatic Sanitization," Proc. RADC Data Base Security Invitational Workshop, Menlo Park, CA, May 1988 (6: LUN-90), pp. 134-139.

Key Words: database, techniques.

SHO-88
Shockley, W.R. and D.F. Warren
"Description of Multilevel Secure Entity-Relationship DBMS Demonstration," Proc. 11th Natl. Comp. Sec. Conf., (5: NCS-88), 1988, pp. 171-178.

Key Words: MLS, DBMS, design, case.

SIC-83
Sicherman, G.L., W. deJonge and R. van de Ried
"Answering Questions Without Revealing Secrets," ACM Trans. on Database Systems, March 1983, pp. 41-59.

Key Words: database, methods.

SMI-88
Smith, G.W.
"Identifying and Representing the Security Semantics of an Application," Proc. 4th Aerosp. Comp. Sec. Conf., (4: IEE-88b), 1988, pp. 125-130.

Key Words: database, models, methods.

SMI-88a
Smith, G.W.
"Classifying and Downgrading: Is a Human Needed in the Loop?," Proc. RADC Data Base Security Invitational Workshop, Menlo Park, CA, May 1988, (6: LUN-90), pp. 164-185.

Key Words: MLS, database, methods.

SMI-89
Smith, G.W.
"Going Beyond Technology to Meet the Challenge of Multilevel Database Security," Proc. 12th Natl. Comp. Sec. Conf., (5: NCS-89), 1989, pp. 1-10.

Key Words: MLS, database, methods.

SMI-89a
Smith, G.W.
"Multilevel Secure Database Design: A Practical Applications," Proc. 5th Security Applicat. Conf., (4: IEE-89c), 1989, pp. 314-321.

Key Words: MLS, database, design.

SMI-89b
Smith, G.W.
"Solving Multilevel Database Security Problems: Technology Is Not Enough," Proc. IFIP WG 11.3 (Data Base) Workshop, (6: IFI-89), 1989.

Key Words: MLS, database, methods.

SMI-89c
Smith, G.W.
"MAC, DAC and the Need-to-Know," Proc. 2nd RADC Data Base Security Workshop, (6: RAD-89), May 1989.

Key Words: MLS, database, policy.

SMI-89d
Smith, G.W.
"Homework Problem #2: MLS Database Design," Proc. 2nd RADC Data Base Security Workshop, (6: RAD-89), May 1989.

Key Words: MLS, database, design.

SMI-89e
Smith, W.G.
"Report on the Homework Problem," Proc. 2nd RADC Data Base Security Workshop, (6: RAD-89), May 1989.

Key Words: MLS, database, design.

SPO-84
Spooner, D.L., and E. Gudes
"A Unifying Approach to the Design of Secure Database Operating Systems," IEEE Trans. on Software Engr., May 1984, pp. 310-319.

Key Words: MLS, database, OS, design.

6-14

SPO-86
Spooner, A.M., et al. "Framework for the Security Component of an ADA DBMS," Proceedings, 12th International Conference on Very Large Data Bases, 1986, pp. 347-354.

Key Words: DBMS, methods, case.

SPO-86a
Spooner, A.M., et al. "Framework for the Security Component of an ADA DBMS," Proc. NCSC Workshop on Database Sec., (6: COA-86), 1986, pp. F1-F15.

Key Words: DBMS, methods, case.

SPO-87
Spooner, D.L. "Relationaships Between Database System and Operating System Security," Proc. IFIP WG 11.3 Meeting, (6: LAN-88), Oct. 1987, pp. 149-158.

Key Words: database, OS, design.

SPO-88
Spooner, D.L. "The Impact of Inheritance on Security in Object-Oriented Database System," Proc. IFIP WG 11.3 Workshop, (6: LAN-89b), Oct. 1988, pp. 141-150.

Key Words: database, model, methods.

STA-88
Stachour, P., B. Thuraisingham, and P. Dwyer "Update Processing in LDV: A Secure Database System," Postscript, 11th Natl. Comp. Sec. Conf., (5: NCS-88a), 1988, pp. 96-115.

Key Words: MLS, database, method, case.

STA-88a
Stachour, P. "LOCK Data Views," Proc. RADC Data Base Security Invitational Workshop, Menlo Park, CA, May 1988 (6: LUN-90), pp. 65-73.

Key Words: MLS, database, views.

SUM-81
Summers, R.C., E.B. Fernandez, and C. Wood "Auditing and Control in a Database Environment," Computer Security Journal, Spring 1981, pp. 99-121.

Key Words: database, auditing, case.

SUT-87
Su, T.-A, and G. Ozsoyoglu "Data Dependencies and Inference Control in Multilevel Relational Database Systems," Proc. 1987 IEEE Symp. on Sec. & Privacy, (5: IEE-87a), pp. 202-211.

Key Words: MLS, DBMS, inference, control, design.

SUT-89
Su, T.-A., J. Chung, and G. Ozsoyoglu "On the Cell Suppression by Merging Technique in the Lattice Model of Summary Tables," Proc. 1989 IEEE Symp. on Sec. & Privacy, (5: IEE-89b), pp. 126-135.

Key Words: statistical, model, method, techniques.

SUT-89a
Su, T.-A, and G. Ozsoyoglu "Multivalued Dependency Inferences Relational Database Systems," Proc. IFIP WG 11.3 (Data Base) Workshop, (6: IFI-89), 1989.

Key Words: database, inference.

THO-88
Thompsen, D., W.T. Tsai, and M.B. Thuraisingham "Prototyping as a Research Tool for MLS/DBMS," Proc. IFIP WG 11.3 Workshop, (6: LAN-89b), Oct. 1988, pp. 63-84.

Key Words: MLS, DBMS, design.

THO-89
Thomsen, D., W.T. Tsai, and M.B. Thuraisingham "Prototyping to Explore MLS/DBMS Design," Computers & Security, May 1989, pp. 229-245.

Key Words: MLS, DBMS, design.

THU-87
Thuraisingham, M.B. "Security Checking in Relational Database Management Systems Augmented with Inference Engines," Computers & Security, December 1987, pp. 479-492.

Key Words: DBMS, inference, methods.

THU-88
Thuraisingham, M.B., W.T. Tsai, and T.F. Keefe "Secure Query processing Using AI Techniques," Proceedings, 21st Hawaii Internat. Conference on Systems Sciences, January 1988.

Key Words: database, techniques.

THU-88a
Thuraisingham, M.B. "Foundations of Multilevel Databases," Proc. RADC Data Base Security Invitational Workshop, Menlo Park, CA, May 1988 (6: LUN-90).

Key Words: MLS, database, theory.

THU-89
Thuraisingham, M.B.
"A Multilevel Secure Data Model," Proc. 12th Natl. Comp. Sec. Conf., (5: NCS-89), 1989, pp. 579-590.

Key Words: MLS, database, models.

THU-89a
Thuraisingham, M.B.
"Mandatory Security in Object-Oriented Database Systems," Proceedings, ACM Conference on Object-Oriented Progarmming, October 1989.

Key Words: MLS, database, policy.

THU-89b
Thuraisingham, M.B.
"Recent Developments in Database Security," Proc., IEEE Comp. Applicat. Conf., September 1988.

Key Words: database, general, methods.

THU-89c
Thuraisingham, M.B.
"Security Checking with Prolog Extensions," Proceedings, 2nd RADC Data Base Security Invitational Workshop, Franconia, NH, May 1989 (6: RAD-90).

Key Words: database, techniques.

THU-89d
Thuraisingham, M.B.
"A Functional View of Multilevel Databases," Computers & Security, December 1989, pp. 721-729.

Key Words: MLS, database, methods.

THU-89e
Thuraisingham, M.B.
"Secure Query Processing in Intelligent Database Management Systems," Proc. 5th Security Applicat. Conf., (4: IEE-89c), 1989, pp. 204-214.

Key Words: DBMS, methods, techniques.

TIN-87
Ting, T.C.
"A User-Role Based Data Security Approach," Proc. IFIP WG 11.3 Meeting, (6: LAN-88), Oct. 1987, pp. 187-208.

Key Words: database, methods.

TRA-84
Traub, J.F., Y. Yemeni, and H. Wozniakowski
"The Statistical Security of a Statistical Database," ACM Trans. on Database Systems, December 1984, pp. 672-679.

Key Words: statistical, methods.

TRO-86
Troxell, P.J.
"Trusted Database Design," Proc. 9th Natl. Comp. Sec. Conf., (5: NCS-86), 1986, pp. 37-40

Key Words: database, trusted, design.

TRU-84
Trueblood, R.P.
"Security Issues in Knowledge Systems," Proceedings, 1st International Workshop on Expert Database Systems, October 1984, pp. 834-840.

Key Words: database, general, methods.

VAN-80
van de Riet, R.P., and A. Wasserman
"A Module Definition Facility for Access Control in Distributed Data Base Systems," Proc. 1980 IEEE Symp. on Sec. & Privacy, (5: IEE-80), pp. 59-66.

Key Words: database, network, control.

VAN-86
van der Lans, R.F.
"Data Security in a Relational Database Environment," Computers & Security, June 1986, pp. 128-134.

Key Words: database, relational.

VET-89
Vetter, L., and G. Smith
"TCB Subsets: The Next Step," Proc. 5th Security Applicat. Conf., (4: IEE-89c), 1989, pp. 216-221.

Key Words: database, design.

WAG-82
Wagner, N.R.
"Shared Database Access Using Composed Encryption Functions," Proc. 1982 IEEE Symp. on Security and Privacy, (5: IEE-82), pp. 104-110.

Key Words: database, encryption, control.

WAG-83
Wagner, N.R.
"Fingerprinting," Proc. 1983 IEEE Symp. on Sec. & Privacy, (5: IEE-83a), pp. 18-22.

Key Words: database, techniques, control, authentication.

WAG-86

Wagner, N.R., P.S. Putter and M.R. Cain "Encrypted Database Design: Specialized Approaches," Proc. 1986 IEEE Symp. on Sec. & Privacy, (5: IEE-86), pp. 148-153.

Key Words: database, design, encryption, techniques.

WHI-89

Whitehurst, R.A., and T.F. Lunt "The SeaView Verification," Proc. Comp. Sec. Foundations Workshop, 1989 (3: IEE-89a), pp. 125-132.

Key Words: verification, views, case.

WHI-89a

Whitehurst, R.A., and T.F. Lunt "The Seaview Verification Effort," Proc. 12th Natl. Comp. Sec. Conf., (5: NCS-89), 1989, pp. 18-27.

Key Words: verificatio, views, case.

WIL-88

Wilson, J. "Views as the Security Objects in a Multilevel Secure Relational Database Management System," Proc. 1988 IEEE Symp. on Sec. & Privacy, (5: IEE-88a), pp. 70-84.

Key Words: MLS, DBMS, views.

WIL-89

Wilson, J. "A Security Policy for an A1DBMS (a Trusted Subject)," Proc. 1989 IEEE Symp. on Sec. & Privacy, (5: IEE-89b), pp. 116-125.

Key Words: MLS, DBMS, policy, case.

WIN-88

Winkler, H. "Sybase Secure SQL Server," Proc. RADC Data Base Security Invitational Workshop, Menlo Park, CA, May 1988, (6: LUN-90), pp. 65-73.

Key Words: database, methods, case.

WIS-89

Wiseman, S. "On the Problem of Security in Databases," Proc. IFIP WG 11.3 (Data Base) Workshop, (6: IFI-89), 1989.

Key Words: database, requirements.

WOO-80

Wood, C., E.B. Fernandez, and R.C. Summers "Data Base Security: Requirements, Policies, and Models," IBM Systems Journal, Vol. 19, No. 2, 2980, pp. 229-252.

Key Words: database, requirements.

WOO-89

Wood, T. "A Trusted Database Machine Kernel for Nonproprietary Hardware," Proc. 12th Natl. Comp. Sec. Conf., (5: NCS-89), 1989, pp. 11-17.

Key Words: database, kernel, design.

WUA-88

Wu, A. "A1 Secure DBMS Architecture," Proc. RADC Data Base Security Invitational Workshop, Menlo Park, CA, May 1988, (6: LUN-90), pp. 15-22.

Key Words: MLS, DBMS, design, case.

7. Communication and Network Security

This section cites publications on physical security in networks, applied cryptographic techniques, secure communications protocols, and trusted network development.

ABB-84
Abbruscato, C.R.
"Data Encryption Equipment", IEEE Communications Magazine, September 1984, pp. 15-21.

Key Words: crypto, hardware.

ABB-86
Abbruscato, C.R.
"Choosing a Key Management Style That Suits the Application," Data Communications, April 1986, pp. 146-160.

Key Words: crypto, keys.

ABR-85
Abrams, M.D.
"Observations on Local Area Network Security," Proc. 5th Sec. Applicat. Conf., (5: IEE-89c), 1989, pp. 77-82.

Key Words: LAN, methods, general.

ABR-87
Abrams, M.D.
"Evaluating Security Services Under Part II of the Trusted Network Interpretation," Proc. 3d Aerosp. Comp. Sec. Conf., (5: IEE-87b), 1987, pp. 44-51.

Key Words: trusted, network, criteria.

ABR-88
Abrams, M.D., S.I. Schaen, and M.W. Schwartz
"Strawman Trusted Network Interpretation Guideline," Proc. 11th Natl. Comp. Sec. Conf., (5: NCS-88), 1988, pp. 194-200.

Key Words: guidelines, trusted, network, criteria.

ADD-88
Addison, K.P.
"Secure Networking at Sun Microsystems, Inc.," Proc. 11th Natl. Comp. Sec. Conf., (5: NCS-88), 1988, pp. 212-218.

Key Words: methods, network, case.

AGN-84
Agnew, G.B.
"Secrecy and Privacy in a Local Area Network Environment," Proc. Eurocrypt '84, Paris, 1984, (8: BET-85), pp. 349-363.

Key Words: LAN, methods, general.

AGN-85
Agnew, G.B.
"Modeling of Encryption Techniques for Secrecy and Privacy in Multi-User Networks," Proc. Eurocrypt '85, Linz, 1985, (8: PIC-86), pp. 221-230.

Key Words: crypto, techniques, models, network.

ALB-84
Albert, D.J., et al.
"Combatting Software Piracy by Encryption and Key Management," IEEE Computer, April 1984, pp. 68-72.

Key Words: threats, crypto, keys, management.

ALV-89
Alvarez, D.L.
"Site Preparedness for the Next Network Emergency," Proc. 11th Natl. Comp. Sec. Conf., (5: NCS-89), 1989, pp. 601-604.

Key Words: contingency, network.

AMS-88
Amsel, E.
"Network Security and Access Control," Computers & Security, February 1988, pp. 53-57.

Key Words: control, network.

AND-85
Anderson, J.P.
"Unification of Computer and Network Security Concepts," Proc. 1985 IEEE Symp. on Sec. & Privacy, (5: IEE-85), pp. 77-87.

Key Words: models, network.

AND-87
Anderson, D.P., and P.V. Ragan
"A Basis for Secure Communication in Large Distributed Systems," Proc. 1987 IEEE Symp. on Sec. & Privacy, (5: IEE-87a), pp. 167-172.

Key Words: policy, distributed, models, network.

AND-87a
Anderson, D.P., and
P.V. Ragan
"High-Performance Interface
Architectures for
Cryptographic Hardware,"
Proc. Crypto '87, Santa
Barbara, CA, 1987, (8: POM-
88), pp. 301-309.

Key Words: crypto,
hardware.

ANS-82
American National Standard
for PIN Management and
Security, X9.8-1988,
American Bankers
Association, Washington, DC,
January 1982.

Key Words: control,
standards.

ANS-82a
American National Standard
for Financial Institution
Message Authentication,
X9.9-1982 American Bankers
Association, Washington, DC,
April 1982.

Key Words: control,
standards.

ARB-89
Arbo, R.S., E.M. Johnson,
and R.L. Sharp
"Extending Mandatory Access
Controls to a Networked
MLS Environment," Proc.
12th Natl. Comp. Sec. Conf.,
(5: NCS-89), 1989, pp. 286-
295.

Key Words: MLS, network,
control.

ARS-84
Arsenault, A.
"Security Issues Involved in
Networking Personal
Computers," Proc. 7th
Seminar, DoD Comp. Sec.
Progr., (5: DOD-84), 1984,
pp. 72-78.

Key Words: policy, PC,
network, requirements.

ARS-87
Arsenault, A.W.
"Development in Guidance for
Trusted Networks," Proc. 10th
Natl. Comp. Sec. Conf., (5:
NCS-87a), 1987, pp. 1-8.

Key Words: guidelines,
trusted, network, criteria.

ARS-87a
Aresnault, A.W.
"Developments in Guidance
for Trusted Networks: The
Trusted Network
Interpretation," AIAA No. 87-
3074, Proc. 3d Aerosp. Comp.
Sec. Conf., (5: IEE-87b),
1987, pp. 52-59.

Key Words: guidelines,
trusted, network, criteria.

BAC-89
Bacon, M.
"Assessing Public Network
Security,"
Telecommunications,
December 1989, pp. 19-20.

Key Words: requirments,
network, general.

BAK-84
Baker, P.C.
"Communications System
Security Evaluation Criteria,"
Proc. 7th Seminar, DoD
Comp. Sec. Progr., (5: DOD-
84), 1984, pp. 58-71.

Key Words: criteria, general.

BAK-85
Baker, P.C., et al.
"A1 Assurance for an Internet
System: Doing the Job," Proc.
9th Natl. Comp. Sec. Conf.,
(5: NCS-86), 1986, pp. 130-
137.

Key Words: verification,
network, methods, case.

BAL-85
Balenson, D.M.
"Automated Distribution of
Cryptographic Keys Using the
Financial Institution Key
Management Standard," IEEE
Communications Magazine,
September 1985, pp. 41-46.

Key Words: crypto, keys,
standards.

BAN-82
Banerjee, S.K.
"High-Speed Implementation of
the DES," Computers &
Security, November 1982, pp.
261-267.

Key Words: crypto, DES,
hardware.

BAR-83
Barnes, D.
"The Provision of Security for
User Data on Packet Switched
Networks," Proc. 1983 IEEE
Symp. on Sec. & Privacy, (5:
IEE-83a), pp. 121-126.

Key Words: methods, network.

BAR-86
Barrett, P.
"Implementing the Rivest
Shamir and Adleman Public
Key Encryption Algorithm on
a Standard Digital Signal
Processor," Proc. Crypto '86,
Santa Barbara, CA, 1986, (8:
ODL-87), pp. 311-323.

Key Words: RSA, hardware,
case.

BAR-89
Barker, L.K.
"The SILS Model for LAN
Security," Proc. 12th Natl.
Comp. Sec. Conf., (5: NCS-
89), 1989, pp. 267-276.

Key Words: LAN, models,
case.

BAR-89a
Barrett, P.
"The Smart Diskette--A
Universal Cryptoengine,"
Proc. Crypto '89, Santa
Barbara, CA, (8: BRA-89)
1989.

Key Words: crypto,
techniques.

BAR-89b
Bartlett, W.
"Security for Packet-Switched
Networks,"
Telecommunications,
September 1989, pp. 47-49.

Key Words: networks,
general.

BAU-83
Bauer, R.K., T.A. Berson,
and R.J. Feiertag
"A Key Distribution Protocol
Using Event Markers," ACM
Trans. on Computer Systems,
August 1983, pp. 249-255.

Key Words: crypto, keys,
method.

BAY-88
Bayle, A.J.
"Security in Open System
Networks: A Tutorial
Survey," Information Age,
(U.K.), July 1988, pp. 131-
145.

Key Words: networks,
general.

BEC-80
Becker, H.B.
"Data Network Security:
Everyone'a Problem," Data
Communications, September
1980, pp. 72-90.

Key Words: networks,
general.

BEK-84
Beker, H., and M. Walker
"Key Management for Secure
Electronic Transfer in Retail
Environment". Proc. Crypto
'84, Santa Barbara, CA, 1984,
(8: BLA-84a), pp. 401-410.

Key Words: crypto, keys,
case.

BEK-85
Beker, H. and F. Piper
Secure Speech
Communications, Academic
Press, New York, 1985.

Key Words: book, techniques.

BEK-87
Beker, H.J., and G.M. Cole
"Message Authentication and
Dynamic Passwords," Proc.
Eurocrypt '87, Amsterdam,
1987, (8: CHA-88a), pp. 171-
175.

Key Words: network,
methods, authentication.

BEL-86
Bell, D.E.
"Secure Computer Systems: A
Network Interpretation," Proc.
2nd Aerosp. Comp. Sec.
Conf., (5: IEE-86a), 1986, pp.
2-4.

Key Words: trusted, network,
criteria, methods.

BEL-89
Bellovin, C.
"Security Problems in TCP/IP
Protocol Suite," ACM
Computer Communications
Rev., April 1989, pp. 32-48.

Key Words: threats, protocols,
requirements, case.

BER-82
Berson, T.A.
"Local Network Cryptosystem
Architecture: Access Control,"
Proc. Crypto-82, Santa
Barbara, CA, 1982, (9: CHA-
83b), pp. 251-258.

Key Words: LAN, crypto,
methods.

BER-82a
Berson,T.A, and R.K. Bauer
"Local Network Cryptosystem
Architecture," Proceedings,
IEEE Comcon, Spring, 1982,
pp. 138-143.

Key Words: LAN, crypto,
methods.

BER-83
Berman, A.
"Evaluating On-Line Computer
Security," Data
Communications, July 1983,
pp. 145-152.

Key Words: management,
nethods.

BON-89
Bong, D., and C. Ruland
"Optimized Software
Implementations of the
Modular Exponentiation on
General Purpose
Microprocessors," Computers
& Security, December 1989,
pp. 621-630.

Key Words: RSA, methods,
PC.

BOS-88
Bosen, R.
"Securing the Micro-
Mainframe Link," Proc.
IFIP/Sec. '88, Australia, 1989,
(2: CAE-89), pp. 351-355.

Key Words: control,
techniques, PC.

BOY-88
Boyd, C.
"Some Applications of
Multiple Key Ciphers," Proc.
Eurocrypt '88, Davos, 1988 (9:
GUN-89), pp. 455-467.

Key Words: crypto, methods,
case.

BRA-82
Branstad, D.K., and
M.E. Smid
"Integrity and Security
Standards Based on
Cryptography," Computers &
Security, November 1982, pp.
255-260.

Key Words: crypto, methods,
standards.

BRA-85
Brand, S.
"A Status Report on the
Development of Network
Criteria," Proc. 8th Natl.
Comp. Sec. Conf., (5: BCS-
85), 1985, pp. 145-151.

Key Words: network, criteria.

BRA-85a
Bradey, R.L., and
I.G. Graham
"Full Encryption in a
Personal Computer System,"
Proc. Eurocrypt '85, Linz,
1985, (8: PIC-86), pp. 231-
240.

Key Words: crypto, methods,
PC.

BRA-87
Branstad, D.K.
"Considerations for Security
in the OSI Architecture,"
Proc. 10th Natl. Comp. Sec.
Conf., (5: NCS-87a), 1987,
pp. 9-14.

Key Words: OSI, network,
methods.

BRA-87a
Branstad, D.K.
"Considerations for Security
in the OSI Architecture,"
IEEE Network Magazine,
April 1987.

Key Words: OSI, network,
methods.

BRA-87b
Branstad, D., et al.
"SP4: A Transport
Encapsulation Security
Protocol," Proc. 10th Natl.
Comp. Sec. Conf., (5: NCS-
87a), 1987, pp. 158-161.

Key Words: protocols, case.

BRA-87c
Branstad, M., et al.
"SP4: A Transport
Encapsulation Security
protocol," AIAA No. 87-3060,
Proc. 3d Aerosp. Comp. Sec.
Conf., (5: IEE-87b), 1987, pp.
143-145.

Key Words: protocols, case.

BRA-89
Branstad, M., et al.
"Key Management and Access
Control for an Electronic Mail
System," Proc. 12th Natl.
Comp. Sec. Conf., (5: NCS-
89), 1989, pp. 230-231.

Key Words: EM, crypto, keys.

BRI-84
Britton, D.E.
"Formal Verification of a
Secure Network with End-to-
End Encryption," Proc. 1984
IEEE Symp. on Sec. &
Privacy, (5: IEE-84), pp. 154-
166.

Key Words: crypto, network,
methods.

BRI-89
Brickell, E.F.
"A Survey of Hardware
Implementations of RSA"
Proc. Crypto '89, Santa
Barbara, CA, (8: BRA-90),
1989.

Key Words: RSA, hardware,
general.

BRO-84
Browne, P.S.
"How to Manage the Network
Security Problem," Computer
Security Journal, Summer
1984, pp. 75-88.

Key Words: management,
network.

BUR-87
Burger, W.
"Networking of Secure Xenix
Systems," Proc. 10th Natl.
Computer Sec. Conf., (5:
NCS-87a), 1987, pp. 254-256.

Key Words: network, methods,
case.

BUS-83
Busse, J.G.
"Developing a Cryptographic
System for Electronic Mail,"
The Office, November 1983,
pp. 122-128.

Key Words: crypto, methods,
case.

CAC-84
Caccetta, L.
"Vulnerability of
Communications Networks,"
Networks, Vol. 14, No. 1,
1984, pp. 117-140.

Key Words: vulnerabilities,
network.

CAL-83
Callaghan, D.R.
"Securing the Distributed Word
Processing Network,"
Computers & Security, January
1983, pp. 78-81.

Key Words: methods, network.

CAP-88
Capel, A.C., C. Laterriere,
and K.C. Toth
"Protecting the Security of
X.25 Communications," Data
Communications, November
1988, pp. 123-139.

Key Words: methods,
protocols,

CAR-86
Carroll, J.M., and S. Martin
"Cryptographic Requirements
for Secure Data
Communications," Proc.
IFIP/Sec. '86, Monte Carlo,
1986, (2: GRI-89).

Key Words: crypto,
requirements.

CAR-87
Carroll, J.M.
"Strategies for Extending the
Useful Lifetime of DES,"
Computers & Security,
August 1987, pp. 300-313.

Key Words: DES,
management.

CAS-88
Casey, T.J., and S.R. Wilbur
"Privacy Enhanced Electronic
Mail," Proc. 4th Aerosp.
Comp. Sec. Conf., (4: IEE-
88b), 1988, pp. 16-21.

Key Words: EM, policy,
methods.

CER-83
Cerullo, M.J.
"Data Communication
Controls," Computers &
Security, January 1983, pp.
67-72.

Key Words: controls, general.

CHE-89
Chess, D.M.
"Computer Viruses and
Related Threats to Computer
and Network Integrity,"
Computer Networks and
ISDN Systems, July 1989,
pp. 141-148.

Key Words: threats, network.

CHI-89
Chick, G.C., and
F.E. Tavares
"Flexible Access Control with
Master Keys" Proc. Crypto
'89, Santa Barbara, CA, (8:
BRA-90), 1989.

Key Words: crypto, control,
keys.

CHI-89a
Chiou, G.-H., and W.-T. Chen
"Secure Broadcasting Using
the Secure Lock," IEEE
Trans. on Software Engr.,
August 1989, pp. 929-934.

Key Words: network,
techniques, case.

CHR-88
Christoffersson, P.
"Message Authentication and
Encryption Combined,"
Computers & Security,
February 1988, pp. 65-71.

Key Words: crypto, control.

CIM-85
Cimimiera, L., and
A. Valenzano
"Authentication Mechanisms
in Microprocessor-Based
Local Area Networks," IEEE
Trans. on Software Engr.,
May 1989, pp. 654-958.

Key Words: LAN,
authentication.

CLA-87
Clark, A.J.
"Physical Protection of
Cryptographic Devices," Proc.
Eurocrypt '87, Amsterdam,
1987, (8: CHA-88a), pp. 83-
93

Key Words: crypto, physical,
hardware, techniques.

COH-85
Cohen, F.
"A Secure Computer Network
Design," Computers &
Security, September 1985, pp.
189-206.

Key Words: network, design.

COH-87
Cohen, F.
"Protection and Administration
of Information Networks with
Partial Ordering," Computers
& Security, April 1987, pp.
118-128.

Key Words: network,
management, methods,
control.

COH-87a
Cohen, F.
"Design and Administration of
Distributed and Hierarchical
Information Networks Under
Partial Ordering," Computers
& Security, June 1987, pp.
219-228.

Key Words: network,
management, methods, control.

COH-87b
Cohen, F.
"Design and Protection of
Information Networks Under a
Partial Ordering," Computers
& Security, August 1987, pp.
332-338.

Key Words: network, design,
methods.

COH-87c
Cohen, F.
"A Cryptographic Checksum
for Integrity Protection,"
Computers & Security,
December 1987, pp. 505-510.

Key Words: crypto, technique.

COH-88
Cohen F.
"Two Secure File Servers,"
Computers & Security, August
1988, pp. 409-414.

Key Words: network, methods,
case.

COO-89
Cooper, J.A.
Computer and Communications
Security: Strategies for the
1990s, McGraw-Hill, New
York, 1989

Key Words: book, techniques,
methods, general.

CRA-88
Cramer, R., B. Ridridge, and
E. Schallenmuller
"Design and Implementation of
a Secure Terminal Gateway,"
Proc. 4th Aerosp. Comp. Sec.
Conf., (5: IEE-88b), 1988, pp.
262-268.

Key Words: network, design,
case.

CSC-87
Trusted Network
Interpretation of the Trusted
Computer System Evaluation
Criteria, NCSC-TG-005,
Version 1, National Computer
Security Center, Ft. Meade,
MD, 31 July 1987.

Key Words: trusted, network,
criteria, guidelines.

DAN-89
Danner, B.P.
"Initial Approach for a TRW
Secure Communications
Processor," Proc. 12th Natl.
Comp. Sec. Conf., (5: NCS-
89), 1989, pp. 197-214.

Key Words: design, policy,
case, hardware.

DAV-80
Davida, G.I., R.A. DeMillo,
and R.J. Lipton
"Protecting Shared
Cryptographic Keys," Proc.
1980 IEEE Symp. on Sec. &
Privacy, (5: IEE-80), pp.
100-102.

Key Words: crypto, keys,
methods, management.

DAV-81
Davies, D.W.
Tutorial: The Security of
Data in Networks, IEEE
Computer Society Press, Los
Angeles, CA, 1981.

Key Words: book, network,
general, methods, techniques.

DAV-83
Davies, D.W.
"Applying the RSA Digital
Signature to Electronic Mail,"
IEEE Computer, February
1983, pp. 55-62.

Key Words: RSA, crypto,
methods, EM, authentication.

DAV-84
Davies, D.W., and
W.L. Price
Security for Computer
Networks, J. Wiley & Sons,
New York, 1984.

Key Words: book, networks,
general.

DAV-84a
Davio, M., et al.
"Efficient Hardware and
Software Implementations for
the DES," Proc. Crypto '84,
Santa Barbara, CA, 1984, (8:
BLA-84a), pp. 144-173.

Key Words: DES, crypto,
hardware.

DAV-84b
Davies, D.W.
"A Message Authentication
Algorithm Suitable for a
Mainframe Computer," Proc.
Crypto '84, Santa Barbara,
CA, 1984, (8: BLA-84a), pp.
393-400.

Key Words: crypto,
authentication, signatures,
methods.

DAV-84c
Davies, D.W.
"The Use of Digital
Signatures in Banks," Proc.
IFIP/Sec. '84, Toronto, 1984,
(2: FIN-85), pp. 13-21

Key Words: crypto,
authentication, signatures,
methods.

DAV-85
Davies, D.W.
"Engineering Secure
Infromation Systems," Proc.
Eurocrypt '85, Linz, 1985, (9:
PIC-86), pp. 191-199.

Key Words: design, methods.

DAV-88
Davida, G.I., and Y. Desmedt
"Passports and Visas Versus
IDs," Proc. Eurocrypt '88,
Davos, 1988 (9: GUN-89), pp.
183-188.

Key Words: authentication,
crypto, methods.

DAV-89
Davis, R.
"Network Authentication
Tokens," Proc. 5th Security
Applicat. Conf., (5: IEE-89c),
1989, pp. 234-238.

Key Words: authentication,
methods.

DAV-89a
Davies, D.W., and W. L Price
Security for Computer
Networks, 2nd Edition, J.
Wiley & Sons, New York,
1989

Key Words: book, network,
crypto, techniques, general.

DAV-89b
Davids, R.
"Australian EFTPOS Security
Standards," Proc. IFIP/Sec.
'88, Australia, 1989, (2: CAE-
89), pp. 357-365.

Key Words: standards, case.

DEL-89
Del Re, E., R. Fantacci, and
D. Maffucci
"A New Speech Signal
Scrambling Method for Secure
Communications," IEEE
Journal on Selected Areas
Communication, May 1989,
pp. 474-480.

Key Words: methods,
techniques.

DEN-80
Denning, D.E., and
F.B. Schneider
"The Master Key Problem,"
Proc. 1980 IEEE Symp. on
Security & Privacy, (5: IEE-
80), pp. 103-107.

Key Words: crypto, keys,
management.

DEN-83
Denning, D.E.
"Protecting Public Keys and Signatures," IEEE Computer, February 1983, pp. 27-35.

Key Words: crypto, keys, methods.

DES-83
Desmedt, Y., J. P. Vandewalle, and R.J.M. Govaerts,
"Does Public-Key Cryptography Provide a Practical and Secure Protection of Data Storage and Transmission?," Proc., Internat. Carnahan Conf. on Sec. Technology, 1983, pp. 133-139.

Key Words: threats, crypto, methods.

DIF-85
Diffie, W.
"Security for the DoD Transmission Control Protocol," Proc. Eurocrypt '85, Linz, Austria, 1985, (9: PIC-86), pp. 108-127.

Key Words: network, protocols, case.

DOD-85
Proceedings, DoD Computer Security Center Invitational Workshop on Network Security, Ft. Meade, MD, March 1985.

Key Words: proceedings, network.

DOL-82
Dolev, D., and A. Wigderson
"On the Security of Multi-Party Protocols in Distributed Systems," Proc. Crypto-82, Santa Barbara, CA, 1982, (9: CHA-83b), pp. 167-175.

Key Words: distributed, protocols.

DON-84
Donaldson, A.
"A Multilevel Secure Local Area Network," Proc. 7th Seminar, DoD Comp. Sec. Progr., (5: DOD-84), 1984, pp. 341-350.

Key Words: MLS, LAN, deasign, case.

DON-88
Donaldson, A.L., J. McHugh, and K.A. Nyberg
"Covert Channels in Trusted LANs," Proc. 11th Natl. Comp. Sec.Conf., (5: NCS-88), 1988, pp. 226-232.

Key Words: trusted, LAN, threats.

DUF-86
Duffy, K.J., and J. Sullivan
"Integrity Lock Prototype," Proc. IFIP/Sec. '86, Monte Carlo, 1986, (2: GRI-89).

Key Words: techniques, design, case.

EGG-88
Eggers, K.W., and P.W. Mallett
"Characterizing Network Covert Storage Channels," Proc. 4th Aerosp. Comp. Sec. Conf., (4: IEE-88b), 1988, pp. 275-279.

Key Words: network, threat, models.

ERD-86
Erdem, H.
"Host Cryptographic Operations: A Software Implementation," Computers & Security, December 1986, pp. 344-346.

Key Words: crypto, design.

EST-85
Estrin, D.
"Non-Discretionary Controls for Inter-Organization Networks," Proc. 1985 IEEE Symp. on Sec. & Privacy, (5: IEE-85), pp. 56-61

Key Words: networks, control, methods.

EST-87
Estrin, D., and G. Tsudik
"Visa Scheme for Inter-Organization Network Security," Proc. 1987 IEEE Symp. on Sec. & Privacy, (5: IEE-87a), pp. 174-183.

Key Words: network, methods, case.

EST-89
Estrin, D., J. Mogul, and G. Tsudik
"Visa Protocols for Controlling Interorganizational Datagram Flow," IEEE Journal. on Selected Areas Communication, May 1989, pp. 486-498.

Key Words: network, protocols, control, methods.

FAI-84
Fairfield, R.C., A. Matusevich, and J.Plany
"An LSI Digital Encryption Processor (DEP)," Proc. Crypto '84, Santa Barbara, CA, 1984, (8: BLA-84a), pp. 115-143.

Key Words: crypto, hardware, case.

FAK-86
Fak, V.
"How to Choose Good Cryptographic Protection," Proc. IFIP/Sec. '86, Monte Carlo, 1986, (2: GRI-89).

Key Words: crypto, guidelines.

FAK-87
Fak, V.
"Crypto Management Made Manageable: Demands on Crypto Equipment Design," Computers & Security, February 1987, pp. 36-40.

Key Words: crypto, design,

FAM-83
Fam, B.W., and J.K. Millen "The Channel Asssignment Problem," Proc. 1983 IEEE Symp. on Sec. & Privacy, (5: IEE-83a), pp. 107-112.

Key Words: model, methods.

FAU-86
Faurer, L. "Security Issues in Open System Context," Computer Security Journal, Vol. 4, No. 1, 1986, pp. 55-62.

Key Words: OSI, design, methods.

FEL-89
Feldmeier, D.C, and P.R. Karn "Cracking Passwords for Fun and Profit," Proc. Crypto '89, Santa Barbara, CA, (8: BRA-90), 1989.

Key Words: threats, control.

FEN-85
Fenna, E. "Data Encryption Protocols for Electronic Mail," ACM Sec., Audit & Control Rev., Winter 1985, pp. 43-47.

Key Words: EM, crypto, protocols.

FER-87
Fernandez, C., et al. "Automating the Computation of Authenticators for Interbank Telex Messages," Computers & Security, October 1987, pp. 396-402.

Key Words: authentication, case.

FIA-89
Fiat, A. "Batch RSA," Proc. Crypto '89, Santa Barbara, CA, (8: BRA-90), 1989.

Key Words: RSA, design, case.

FIC-84
Fick, G.P. "Implementation Issues for Master Key Distribution and Protected Keyload Procedures," Proc. IFIP/Sec. '84, Toronto, 1984, (2: FIN-85), pp. 571-580.

Key Words: crypto, keys, design.

FID-85
Fidlow, D. "A Comprehensive Approach to Network Security," Data Communication, April 1985, pp. 195-213.

Key Words: networks, general.

FIS-84
Fisher, W.W. "Cryptography for Computer Security: Making the Decision," Computers & Security, October 1984, pp. 229-233.

Key Words: crypto, design.

FIT-80
Fitzgerald, J. "Data Communications Control Matrix," Assets Protection, Sept./Oct. 1980, pp.24-31.

Key Words: control, methods.

FIT-89
Fitzgerald, K. "The Quest for Intruder-Proof Computer Systems," IEEE Spectrum, August 1989, pp. 22-26.

Key Words: threats, methods.

FRI-88
Friedberg, A.H., et al. "Reliance on Optical Fibres to Increase Telecommunications Security," Information Age, (U.K.) April 1988, pp. 73-78.

Key Words: physical, methods.

GAI-80
Gait, J. Maintenance Testing for the Data Encryption Standard, SP 500-61, National Bureau of Standards, Gaithersburg, MD, August 1980.

Key Words: DES, management.

GAL-87
Galil, Z., S. Haber, and M. Yung "Cryptographic Computation: Secure Fault-Tolerant Protocols and the Public-Key Model," Proc. Crypto '87, Santa Barbara, CA, 1987, (8: POM-88), pp. 135-155.

Key Words: crypto, protocols.

GAS-82
Gasser, M., and D.P. Sindhu "A Multilevel Secure Local Area Network," Proc. 1982 IEEE Symp. on Sec. & Privacy, (5: IEE-82), pp. 137-143.

Key Words: MLS, LAN, design.

GIR-87
Girling, C.G. "Covert Channels in LANs," IEEE Trans. on Software Engr., February 1987, pp. 292-296.

Key Words: LAN, threats.

GOY-88
Goyal, P.K., and E.B. Fernandez "Encryption Using Random Keys: A Scheme for Secure Communication," Proc. 4th Aerosp. Comp. Sec. Conf., (4: IEE-88b), 1988, pp. 410-412.

Key Words: crypto, techniques.

GRA-87
Grant, L.
"DES Key Crunching for Safer Cipher Keys," <u>ACM Sec., Audit & Control Rev.</u>, Spring 1987, pp. 9-16.

Key Words: DES, keys, techniques.

GRA-88
Graham, I., and S. Wieten "The PC as a Secure Network Workstation," <u>Proc. IFIP/Sec. '88</u>, Australia, 1989, (2: CAE-89), pp. 425-437.

Key Words: PC, methods, case.

GRE-85
Greenlee, M.B.
"Requirements for Key Management Protocols in the Wholesale Financial Services Industry," <u>IEEE Communications Magazine</u>, September 1985, pp. 22-28.

Key Words: requirements, crypto, keys, management, case.

GRI-89
Grimm,P.
"Security on Networks: Do We Really Need It?," <u>Comp. Networks and ISDN Systems</u>, October 1989, pp. 315.

Key Words: requirements, networks.

GRO-82
Grossman, G.
"A Practical Executive for Secure Communications," <u>Proc. 1982 IEEE Symp. on Sec. & Privacy</u>, (5: IEE-82), pp. 144-155.

Key Words: OS, networks, case.

GSA-82
<u>Telecommunications: General Security Requirements for Equipment Using the Data Encryption Standard</u>, Federal Standard 1027, U.S. General Services Administation Washington, DC, April 1982.

Key Words: DES, crypto, standards.

GSA-83
<u>Telecommunications: Interoperability and Security Requirements for Use of the Data Encryption Standard in the Physical and Data Link Layers of Data Communication</u>, Federal Standard 1026, U.S. General Services Administration Washington, DC, January 1983.

Key Words: DES, crypto, standards.

GSA-85
<u>Interoperability and Security Requirements for Using the Data Encryption Standard with CCITT Group 3 Facsimile Equipment</u>. Federal Standard 1027, U.S. General Services Administration Washington, DC, April 1985.

Key Words: DES, crypto, standards.

GUI-82
Guillou, L.C., and B. Lorig "Cryptography and Teleinformatics," <u>Computers & Security</u>, January 1982, pp. 27-33.

Key Words: crypto, general.

GUI-86
Guillou, L.C.
"Smart Card -- A Highly Reliable and Portable Security Device," <u>Proc. Crypto '86</u>, Santa Barbara, CA, 1986, (8: ODL-87), pp. 464-487.

Key Words: authenication,

GUI-88
Guinier, D.
"DSPP: A Data Security Pipe Protocol for PCs, Large Scale Systems, or Networks," <u>ACM Sec., Audit & Control Rev.</u>, Fall 1988, pp. 4-9.

Key Words: PC, network, protocol.

GUI-88a
Guinier, D.
"SPKS: Sharing Partial Key System," <u>ACM Sec., Audit & Control Rev.</u>, Fall 1988, pp. 10-13.

Key Words: crypto, key, case.

HAR-89
Harn, L. and T. Keisler "Authenticated Group Key Distribution Scheme for a Large Network," <u>Proc. 1989 IEEE Symp. on Sec.& Privacy</u>, (5: IEE-89b), pp. 300-309.

Key Words: crypto, keys, methods.

HAR-89a
Harn, L., Y. Chien, and T. Keisler "An Extended Cryptographic Key Generation Scheme for Multilevel Data Security," <u>Proc. 5th Security Applicat. Conf.</u>, (4: IEE-89c), 1989, pp. 254-262.

Key Words: crypto, keys, methods.

HAS-85
Hastad, J.
"On Using RSA with Low Exponent in a Public Key Network," <u>Proc. Crypto '85</u>, Santa Barbara, CA, 1985, (8: WIL-86), pp. 403-408.

Key Words: RSA, crypto, design.

HER-85
Herzberger, A., and
S.S. Pinter
"Public Protection of
Software," Proc. Crypto '85,
Santa Barbara, CA, 1985,
(8: WIL-86), pp. 159-179.

Key Words: crypto, methods,
software.

HER-87
Herlihy, M.P., and J.D. Tygar
"How to Make Replicated
Data Secure," Proc. Crypto
'87, Santa Barbara, CA,
1987, (9: POM-88), pp. 379-
391.

Key Words: crypto, methods.

HER-88
Herbison, B.J.
"Security on an Ethernet,"
Proc. 11th Natl. Comp. Sec.
Conf., (5: NCS-88), 1988,
pp. 219-225.

Key Words: LAN, methods,
case.

HIG-88
Highland, H.J.
"How Secure Are Fiber
Optics Communications,"
Computers & Security,
February 1988, pp. 25-26.

Key Words: threats,
hardware, techniques.

HIG-88a
Highland, H.J.
"Secret Disk II -- Transparent
Automatic Encryption,"
Computers & Security,
February 1988, pp. 27-34.

Key Words: PC, crypto,
methods.

HIN-83
Hinke, T., J. Althouse, and
R.A. Kemmerer
"SDC Secure Release
Terminal Project," Proc. 1983
IEEE Symp. on Sec. &
Privacy, (5: IEE-83a), pp.
113-119.

Key Words: hardware,
design, case.

HOO-84
Hoornaert, F., et al.
"Efficient Hardware
Implementation of the DES,"
Proc. Crypto '84, Santa
Barbara, CA, 1984, (8: BLA-
84a), pp. 147-173.

Key Words: DES, crypto,
hardware.

HOO-88
Hoornaert, F., et al.
"Fast RSA-Hardware: Dream
or Reality," Proc. Eurocrypt
'88, Davos, 1988, (8: GUN-
89), pp. 455-467.

Key Words: RSA, crypto,
hardware.

HOU-89
Housley, R.
"Authentication,
Confidentiality, and Integrity
Extensions to the XNS
Protocol Suite," ACM Sec.,
Audit & Control Rev., Fall
1989, pp. 17-24.

Key Words: authentication,
case, methods, protocols.

HUM-80
Humprey, T., and F.L. Toth
"Two-Chip Data Encryption
Unit Supports Multi-Key
Systems," Electronics, January
17, 1980, pp. 136-139.

Key Words: crypto, hardware.

ING-83
Ingemarsson, I.
"A Comparison Between
Public-Key and Conventional
Encryption Methods," Proc.
IFIP/Sec. '83, Stockholm,
1983, (2: FAK-83), pp. 229-
232.

Key Words: crypto,
techniques.

ING-84
Ingemarsson, I.
"Encryption for Data
Protection," Information
Resource Management, (UK),
March 1984, pp. 29-32.

Key Words: crypto, general.

JAC-89
Jacobs, J. and T. Kibalo
"Secure Data Network System
Support Using Embedded
Cryptography," Proc., 2nd
Annual AFCEA Intelligence
Symposium, September 1987.

Key Words: crypto, methods.

JAM-88
Jamieson, R., and G. Low
"A Framework for the
Security, Control and Audit of
a Local Area Network
Operations," Proc. IFIP/Sec.
'88, Australia, 1989, (2: CAE-
89), pp. 439-469.

Key Words: LAN, auditing,
case.

JAM-89
Jamieson, R., and G. Low
"Security and Control Issues in
Local Area Network Design,"
Computers & Security, June
1989, pp. 305-316.

Key Words: LAN, design,
control.

JAN-86
Jansen, C.J.A.
"On the Key Storage
Requirements for Secure
Terminals," Computers &
Security, June 1986, pp. 145-
149.

Key Words: PC, crypto, keys.

JAY-82
Jayant, N.S.
"Analog Scramblers for Speech
Privacy," Computers &
Security, November 1982, pp.
275-289.

Key Words: methods,
hardware.

JEN-87
Jeng, A.B., and M.D. Abrams
"On Network Covert Channel
Analysis," AIIA No. 87-3081,
Proc. 3d Aerosp. Comp. Sec.
Conf., (5: IEE-87b), 1987, pp.
95-103.

Key Words: threats, network.

JOH-87
Johnson, H.L., and
J.D. Layne
"A Mission-Critical Approach
to Network Security," Proc.
10th Natl. Comp. Sec. Conf.,
(5: NCS-87a), 1987, pp. 15-
24.

Key Words: requirements,
network.

JOH-87a
Johnson, R.J.
"Key Updating Flags in EFT-
POS Security Systems,"
Computers & Security, June
1987, pp. 245-251.

Key Words: crypto, keys,
case.

JON-84
Jones, R.W.
"User Functions for the
Generation and Distribution
of Encipherment Keys," Proc.
Eurocrypt '84, Paris, 1984,
(8: BET-85), pp. 317-334.

Key Words: crypto, keys,
methods.

JON-89
Jonckheer, K., and
M. Scarbrough
"Security of Data Transmitted
Via Telephone, Fibre Optics,
and Microwaves,"
Information Age, (U.K.),
March 1989, pp. 99-105.

Key Words: physical,
techniques.

JUE-85
Jueneman, R.R., C.H. Meyer,
and S.M. Matyas
"Message Authentication,"
IEEE Communications
Magazine, September 1985,
pp. 29-40.

Key Words: authentication,
methods.

JUN-87
Jung, A.
"Implementing the RSA
Cryptosystem," Computers &
Security, August 1987, pp.
342-350.

Key Words: RSA, crypto,
methods.

KAK-83
Kak, S.C.
"Data Security in Computer
Networks," IEEE Computer,
February 1983, pp. 8-10.

Key Words: network, general.

KAR-86
Karger, P.A.
"Authentication and Access
Control in Computer
Networks," Computers &
Security, December 1986, pp.
314-324.

Key Words: network, control.

KAR-88
Karp, B.C., L.C. Baker,
and L.D. Nelson
"The Secure Data Network,"
AT&T Technical Journal,
May/June 1988.

Key Words: network, general.

KAT-88
Katzer, M.A.
"Secured Communications for
PC Workstations," Proc. 11th
Natl. Comp. Sec. Conf., (5:
NCS-88), 1988, pp. 233-237.

Key Words: PC, methods,
design.

KEM-87
Kemmerer, R.A.
"Using Formal Verification
Techniques To Analyze
Encryption Protocols" Proc.
1987 IEEE Symp. Sec. &
Privacy, (5:IEE-87a), pp. 134-
139.

Key Words: verification,
crypto, protocols, techniques.

KEM-87a
Kemmerer, R.A.
"Analyzing Encryption
Protocols Using Formal
Verification Techniques," Proc.
Crypto '87, Santa Barbara,
CA, 1987, (9: POM-88), pp.
289-305.

Key Words: verification,
crypto, protocols, techniques.

KEM-89
Kemmerer, R.A.
"Analyzing Encryption
Protocols Using Formal
Verification Techniques," IEEE
Journal on Selected Areas
Communication, May 1989,
pp. 448-457.

Key Words: verification,
crypto, protocols, techniques.

KEN-81
Kent, S.T.
"Security Requirements and
Protocols for Broadcast
Scenario," IEEE Trans. on
Communications, June 1981,
pp. 778-786.

Key Words: requirements,
network, protocols.

KEN-89
Kent, S.T.
"Comments on Security
Problems in the TCP/IP
Protocol Suite," ACM
Computer Communications
Review, July 1989, pp. 10-19.

Key Words: threats, protocols.

KHA-89
Khashnabish, B.
"A Bound of Deception
Capability in Multiuser
Computer Networks," IEEE J.
on Selected Areas Comm.,
May 1989, pp. 4590-594.

Key Words: threats, network.

KIL-88
Kilpatrick, K.E.
"Standards for Network
Security," Proc. 11th Natl.
Comp. Sec. Conf., (5: NCS-
88), 1988, pp. 201-211.

Key Words: network,
standards.

KIN-89
King, G.
"A Survey of Commercially
Available Secure LAN
Products," Proc. 5th Security
Applicat. Conf., (5: IEE-89c),
1989, pp. 239-247.

Key Words: LAN, hardware,
software.

KNA-88
Knapskog, S.J.
"Privacy Protected
Payments -- Realization of a
Protocol that Guarantees
Payer Anonymity," Proc.
Eurocrypt '88, Davos, 1988
(8: GUN-89), pp. 107-122.

Key Words: protocols, case.

KNO-88
Knobloch, H.-J.
"A Smart Card
Implementation of the Fiat-
Shamir Identification
Scheme," Proc. Eurocrypt
'88, Davos, 1988 (8: GUN-
89), pp. 87-95.

Key Words: authentication,
case.

KNO-88a
Knowles, T.
"Security, OSI and
Distributed Systems,"
Information Age (U.K.),
April 1988, pp. 79-84.

Key Words: OSI, network,
methods.

KOC-85
Kochanski, M.
"Developing an RSA Chip,"
Proc. Crypto '85, Santa
Barbara, CA, 1985, (8: WIL-
86), pp. 350-357.

Key Words: RSA, crypto,
hardware.

KOC-87
Kochanski, M.,
"A Survey of Data Insecurity
Packages," Cryptologia,
January 1987, pp. 1-15.

Key Words: crypto, software,
case.

KOC-88
Kochanski, M.
"Another Data Insecurity
Package," Cryptologia, July
1988, pp. 165-173.

Key Words: crypto, software,
case.

KOH-89
Kohl, J.T.
"Cryptographic Protocols in
Cerberus," Proc. Crypto '89,
Santa Barbara, CA, (8: BRA-
90), 1989.

Key Words: crypto, protocols,
case.

KRA-84
Krauss, L.
"Data Encryption in ISO, the
International Standards
Organization," Computers &
Security, October 1984, pp.
234-236.

Key Words: crypto, standards,
case.

KRI-85
Krivachy, T.
"The Ciphercard -- an
Identification Card with
Cryptographic Protection,"
Proc. Eurocrypt '85, Linz,
1985, (8: PIC-86), pp. 200-
207.

Key Words: crypto, control,
case.

KRU-89
Kruys, J.P.
"Security in Open Systems,"
Computers & Security, April
1989, pp. 139-147.

Key Words: OSI, network,
general.

LAM-88
Lambert, P.A.
"Architectural Model of the
SDNS Key Management
Protocol," Proc. 11th Natl.
Comp. Sec. Conf., (5: NCS-
88), 1988, pp. 126-128.

Key Words: crypto, protocol,
keys.

LEM-86
Lemire, J.R.
"A New Key Management
Approach for Open
Communication Environments,"
Proc. IFIP/Sec. '86, Monte
Carlo, 1986, (2: GRI-89).

Key Words: crypto, keys,
management.

LER-84
Le Roux, Y.
"Controlling Access to
Computer Networks,"
Information Resource
Management, (UK), March
1984, 26-28.

Key Words: control, network.

LIN-83
Linden, C.
"The Transaction-Seal -- The
New Corner-Stone in Secured
Terminal Systems," Proc.
IFIP/Sec. '83, Stockholm,
1983, (2: FAK-83), pp. 223-
227.

Key Words: authentication.

LIN-87
Linn, J.
"SDNS Products in the Type
II Environment," Proc. 10th
Natl. Comp. Sec. Conf., (5:
NCS-87a), 1987, pp. 162-164.

Key Words: network,
techniques.

LIN-88

Linn, J.
"COMSEC Integration Alternatives," Proc. 11th Natl. Comp. Sec. Conf., (5: NCS-88), 1988, pp. 122-125.

Key Words: methods, techniques.

LIN-89

Linn, J. and S.T. Kent
"Privacy for DARPA-Internet Mail," Proc. 12th Natl. Comp. Sec. Conf., (5: NCS-89), 1989, pp. 215-229.

Key Words: EM, network, methods.

LIP-88

Lipper, E.H., et al.
"A Multilevel Secure Message Switch with Minimal TCB: Architectural Outline and Security Analysis," Proc. 4th Aerosp. Comp. Sec. Conf., (5: IEE-88b), 1988, pp. 242-249.

Key Words: MLS, methods, design.

LOC-87

Loscocco, P.
"A Security Model and Policy for a MLS LAN," Proc. 10th Natl. Comp. Sec. Conf., (5: NCS-87a), 1987, pp. 25-37.

Key Words: MLS, LAN, models.

LOM-89

Lomas, T., et al.
"Reducing Risks from Poorly Chosen Keys," ACM Operating System Review, Vol. 23, No. 5, 1989, pp. 14-18.

Key Words: threats, methods, keys.

LON-83

Longo, G. (Ed.)
Secure Digital Systems, Springer-Verlag, Wien, 1983.

Key Words: book, general, methods.

LON-86

Longley, D., and S. Rigby
"Use of Expert Systems in the Analysis of Key Management Systems," Proc. IFIP/Sec. '86, Monte Carlo, 1986, (2: GRI-89).

Key Words: crypto, keys, methods.

LON-87

Longley, D.
"Expert Systems Applied to the Analysis of Key Mangement Schemes," Computers & Security, February 1987, pp. 54-67.

Key Words: crypto, keys, methods.

LOS-89

Loscocco, P.
"A Dynamic Network Labeling Scheme for a MLS LAN," Proc. 12th Natl. Comp. Sec. Conf., (5: NCS-89), 1989, pp. 277-285.

Key Words: MLS, LAN, methods.

LUB-89

Luby, M., and C. Rackoff
"A Study of Password Security," Journal of Cryptology, Vol. 1, No. 3, 1989, pp. 151-158.

Key Words: control, methods.

MAC-81

MacMillan, D.
"Single Chip Encrypts Data at 14 MB/S," Electronics, June 16, 1981, pp. 161-166.

Key Words: DES, hardware.

MAC-83

MacKinnon, S., and S.G. Akl
"New Key Generation Algorithms for Multilevel Security," Proc. 1983 IEEE Symp. Sec. & Privacy, (5:IEE-83a), pp. 72-78.

Key Words: MLS, crypto, keys.

MAC-84

MacEwen, G.H., et al.
"Multi-Level Security Based on Physical Distribution" Proc. 1984 IEEE Symp. Sec. & Privacy, (5:IEE-84), pp. 167-179.

Key Words: MLS, physical, methods.

MAR-89

Marino, J. and P. Lambert
"An INFOSEC Platform," Proc. 12th Natl. Comp. Sec. Conf., (5: NCS-89), 1989, pp. 571-578.

Key Words: hardware, case.

MAR-89a

Marella, A., Jr.
"Telecommunications: A Control Strategy," EDPACS, May 1989, pp. 1-5.

Key Words: control, methods.

MAS-84

Masrani, R., and T.P. Keenan
"Security and Privacy in Cellular Telephone System," Proc. IFIP/Sec. '84, Toronto, 1984, (2: FIN-85), pp. 457-470.

Key Words: methods, case.

MAS-86

Massey, J.L.
"Cryptography--A Selective Survey," Digital Communications, January 1986, pp. 3-21.

Key Words: crypto, general.

MAT-87

Matsumoto, T., and H. Imai
"On the Key Predistribution System: A Practical Solution to the Key Distribution Problem," Proc. Crypto '87, Santa Barbara, CA, 1987, (8: POM-88), pp. 185-193.

Key Words: crypto, keys, methods.

MAT-87a
Matias, Y., and A. Shamir
"A Video Scrambling
Technique Based On Space
Filling Curves," Proc. Crypto
'87, Santa Barbara, CA,
1987, (8: POM-88), pp. 398-
417.

Key Words: techniques,
physical.

MAY-89
Mayer, F. et al.
"Evaluation Issues for an
Integrated 'INFOSEC'
Product," Proc. 5th Security
Applicat. Conf., (4: IEE-89c),
1989, pp. 271-275.

Key Words: methods, case.

MCC-89
McCullough, D.
"Security Analysis of a
Token Ring Using Ulysses,"
Proc. COMPASS '89: Comp.
Assurance, (2: IEE-89), 1989,
pp. 113-118.

Key Words: LAN, threat,
methods.

MEA-89
Meadows, C.
"Using Narrowing in the
Analysis of Key Management
Protocols," Proc. 1989 IEEE
Symp. Sec. & Privacy,
(5:IEE-89b), pp. 138-147.

Key Words: crypto,
protocols, keys.

MEN-83
Menkus, B.
"Long-Haul Data Security:
Whose Responsibility Is It
Today?," Data
Communications, March
1983, pp. 137+

Key Words: network,
management.

MER-81
Merkle, R.C., and
M.E. Hellman
"On the Security of Multiple
Encryption," Communications
of the ACM, July 1981, pp.
465-467.

Key Words: crypto, methods.

MER-82
Merritt, M.
"Key Reconstruction," Proc.
Crypto-82, Santa Barbara, CA,
1982, (8: CHA-83b), pp. 321-
375.

Key Words: crypto, keys,
methods.

MEY-81
Meyer, C.H., S.M. Matyas,
and R.E. Lennon
"Required Cryptographic
Authentication Criteria for
Electronic Funds Transfer
Systems," Proc. 1981 IEEE
Symp. on Sec. & Privacy, (5:
IEE-81), pp. 89-98.

Key Words: crypto,
athentication.

MIG-89
Migues, S., and R. Housely
"Designin a Trusted Client-
Server Distributed Network,"
Proc. 5th Sec. Applicat. Conf.,
(5: IEE-89c), 1989, pp. 91-94.

Key Words: trusted, network.

MIL-81
Miller, J.S., and
R.G. Resnick
"Military Message Systems:
Applying a Security Model,"
Proc. 1981 IEEE Symp. Sec.
& Privacy, (5:IEE-81), pp.
101-111.

Key Words: EM, models,
methods.

MIL-84
Millen, J.K.
"The Interrogator: A Tool for
Cryptographic Protocol
Security," Proc. 1984 IEEE
Symp. Sec. & Privacy, (5:IEE-
84), pp. 134-141.

Key Words: crypto, protocols.

MIL-87
Millen, J.K., S.C. Clark, and
S.B. Freedman
"The Interrogator: Protocol
Security Analysis," IEEE
Trans. of Software Engr.,
February 1987, pp. 274-288.

Key Words: protocol, design.

MIL-87a
Millen, J.K.
"Interconnection of Accredited
Systems," Proc. 3d Aerosp.
Comp. Sec. Conf., (5:IEE-87b),
1987, pp. 60-65.

Key Words: network, design.

MIL-88
Millen, J.K., and
M.W. Schwartz
"The Cascading Problem for
Interconnected Networks,"
Proc. 4th Aerosp. Comp. Sec.
Conf., (4: IEE-88b), 1988, pp.
269-274.

Key Words: network, design.

MIT-87
Mitchell, C., and F. Piper
"The Cost of Reducing Key-
Storage Requirements in
Secure Networks," Computers
& Security, August 1987, pp.
339-341.

Key Words: crypto, keys,
network.

MIT-88
Mitchell, C., and M. Walker
"Solutions to the
Multidestinational Secure
Electronic Mail Problem,"
Computers & Security, October
1988, pp. 483-488.

Key Words: EM, design,
methods.

MIT-89

Mitchell, C., D. Rush, and M. Walker "A Remark on Hash Functions for Message Authentication," Computers & Security, February 1989, pp. 55-58.

Key Words: EM, authentication.

MIT-89a

Mitchell, C., M. Walker, and D. Rush "CCITT/ISO Standards for Secure Message Handling," IEEE J. on Selected Areas Comm., May 1989, pp. 517-524.

Key Words: EM, standards, case.

MOO-88

Moore, J.H. "Protocol Failures in Crypto-systems," Proceedings of the IEEE, May 1988, pp. 594-602.

Key Words: crypto, protocols.

MOO-88a

Moore, A. "Investigating Formal Specification and Verification for COMSEC Software Security," Proc. 11th Natl. Comp. Sec. Conf., (5: NCS-88), 1988, pp. 129-138.

Key Words: verification, software.

MOU-83

Moulton, R.T. "Network Security," Datamation, July 1983, pp. 121+

Key Words: network, general.

MUE-82

Mueller-Schloer, C., and N.R. Wagner "Cryptographic Protection of Personal Data Cards," Proc. Crypto-82, Santa Barbara, CA, 1982, (8: CHA-83b), pp. 219-229.

Key Words: crypto, methods.

MUF-88

Muftic, S., et al. Security Mechanisms for Computer Networks, Ellis-Horwood, Chichester, U.K., 1988.

Key Words: book, network, methods.

MUF-89

Muftic, S. Security Mechanisms for Computer Networks, J. Wiley & Sons, Somerset, NJ, 1989.

Key Words: book, network, methods.

MUF-89a

Muftic, S. "Extended OSI Security Architecture," Computer Networks and ISDN Systems, September 1989, pp. 223-227.

Key Words: OSI, network, methods.

MUL-83

Muller-Scloer, C. "A Microprocessor-Based Cryptoprocessor," IEEE Micro, October 1983, pp. 5-15.

Key Words: PC, crypto, hardware.

MUN-87

Mundy, G.R., and R.W. Shirey "Defense Data Network Security Architecture," Proceedings, MILCOM '87, October 1987.

Key Words: network, design, case.

MUR-87

Good Security Practices for Information Networks, G320-9279-2, IBM Corporation, White Plains, NY, 1987.

Key Words: network, methods guidelines.

NAK-89

Nakao, K., and K. Suzuki "Proposal on a Secure Communications Service Element (SCSE) in the OSI Application Layer," IEEE Journal on Selected Areas Communication, May 1989, pp. 505-516.

Key Words: OSI, network, methods.

NBS-80

Guidelines on the User Authentication for Computer Network Access Control, FIPS PUB 83, National Bureau of Standards, Gaithersburg, MD, September 1980.

Key Words: guidelines, network,

NBS-80a

DES Modes of Operation, FIPS PUB 81, National Bureau of Standards, Gaithersburg, MD, September 1980.

Key Words: DES, methods.

NBS-81

Guidelines for Implementing and Using the NBS Data Encryption Standard, FIPS-PUB 74, National Bureau of Standards, Gaithersburg, MD, April 1981.

Key Words: DES, guidelines.

NCS-87

Trusted Network Interpretation of the Trusted Computer System Evaluation Criteria, NCSC-TG-005, Natl. Computer Security Center, Ft. Meade, MD, July 1987.

Key Words: trusted, network, criteria, guidelines.

NEL-87
Nelson, R.
"SDNS Services and
Architecture," Proc. 10th
Natl. Comp. Sec. Conf., (5:
NCS-87a), 1987, pp. 153-
157.

Key Words: network,
methods, case.

NEL-89
Nelson, R.
"SDNS Architecture and End-
to-End Encryption," Proc.
Crypto '89, Santa Barbara,
CA, (8: BRA-90), 1989.

Key Words: crypto, network.

NES-83
Nesset, D.M.
"A Systematic Methodology
for Analyzing Security
Threats to Interprocessor
Communications in a
Distributed System," IEEE
Trans. on Communications,
September 1983.

Key Words: threats, network.

NES-84
Nestman, C.H., J. Windsor,
and M.C. Hinson
"Tutorial on
Telecommunications and
Security," Computers &
Security, October 1984, pp.
215-224.

Key Words: techniques,
general.

NES-87
Nesset, D.M.
"Factors Affecting Distributed
System Security," IEEE
Trans. on Software Engr.,
February 1987, pp. 233-248.

Key Words: design, network.

NES-89
Nesset, D.M.
"Layering Central
Authentication on Existing
Distributed System Terminal
Services," Proc. 1989 IEEE
Symp. Sec. & Privacy,
(5:IEE-89b), pp. 290-299.

Key Words: authentication,
design.

NES-89a
Nesset, D.M.
"Issues in Secure Distributed
Operating System Design,"
Digest of Papers, IEEE
Compcon '89, 1989, pp. 342-
347.

Key Words: OS, methods,
design.

NEW-86
Newman, D.B., and
R.L. Pickholtz
"Cryptography in the Private
Sector," IEEE
Communications Magzine,
August 1986, pp. 7-10.

Key Words: crypto, general.

NEW-87
Newman, D.B., Jr., J.K.
Omura, and R.L. Pickholz
"Public Key Management for
Network Security," IEEE
Networks Magazine, April
1987, pp. 11-16.

Key Words: crypto, keys,
network.

NIE-89
Niemeyer, R.
"Applying the TNI to System
Certification and
Accreditation," Proc. 5th
Security Applicat. Conf., (5:
IEE-89c), 1989, pp. 248-252.

Key Words: network, criteria,
case.

NYE-82
Nye, J.M.
"The Cryptographic Equipment
Market: Trends and Issues,"
Assets Protection, Jan./Feb.
1982, pp, 21-24.

Key Words: crypto, hardware,
case.

NYE-82a
Nye, J.M.
"Satellite Communications and
Vulnerability," Computerworld,
May 3, 1982, pp. ID7-ID13.

Key Words: vulnerabilities,
case.

NYE-83
Nye, J.M.
"Network Security and
Vulnerability," Proc. 1983
Natl. Computer Conf., AFIPS
Press, Reston VA, May 1983,
pp. 647-653.

Key Words: vulnerabilities.

OBE-83
Oberman, M.R.
"Some Security Aspects of a
Computer Communications
Network Environment," Proc.
IFIP/Sec. '83, Stockholm,
1983, (2: FAK-83), pp. 233-
238.

Key Words: network, methods.

ODE-85
O'Dell, L.L.
"An Approach to Multi-Level
Secure Networks, Revision 1,"
Proc. 8th Natl. Comp. Sec.
Conf., (5: NCS-85), 1985, pp.
152-155.

Key Words: MLS, network,
design.

OKA-89
Okamoto, E., and K. Tanaka
"Key Distribution System
Based on Identification
Information," IEEE Journal on
Selected Areas
Communication, May 1989,
pp. 481-485.

Key Words: crypto, keys,
design.

OMA-83
Omar, K.A., and D.L. Wells, "Modified Architecture for the Sub-Key Model," Proc. 1983 IEEE Symp. Sec. & Privacy, (5:IEE-83a), pp. 79-86.

Key Words: architecture, keys.

ORT-86
Orton, G.A., et al. "VLSI Implementation of Public-Key Algorithms," Proc. Crypto '86, Santa Barbara, CA, 1986, (8: ODL-87), pp. 277-301.

Key Words: public-key, hardware.

OZA-84
Ozarow, L.H., and A.D. Wyner "Wire-Tap Channel II," Proc. Eurocrypt '84, Paris, 1984, (8: BET-85), pp. 33-50.

Key Words: threats, methods.

PAI-86
Pailles, J.-C., and M. Girault "The Security Processor CRIPT," Proc. IFIP/Sec. '86, Monte Carlo, 1986, (2: GRI-89), pp. 127-139.

Key Words: techniques, hardware.

PAR-87
Parker, T.A. "Security in Open Systems: A Report on the Standards Work of ECMA's TC32/TG9," Proc. 10th Natl. Comp. Sec. Conf., (5: NCS-87a), 1987, pp. 38-50.

Key Words: OSI, network, standards.

PIE-85
Pieprzyk, J.P., and D.A. Rutkowski "Modular Design of Information Encipherment for Computer Systems," Computers & Security, September 1985, pp. 211-218.

Key Words: crypto, design, methods.

POL-84
Pollak, R. "Micro-Mainframe Communications Security in Distributed Network Environment," ACM Sec., Audit. & Control Rev., October 1984, pp. A1-A6.

Key Words: PC, network, methods.

POW-85
Power, J.M., and S.R. Wilbur "Authentication in an Heterogenous Environment," Proc. IFIP/Sec. '85, Dublin, 1985, (2: GRI-85), pp. 117-127.

Key Words: authentication.

POW-88
Powanda, E.J., and J.W. Genovese "Configuring a Trusted System Using the TNI," Proc. 4th Aerosp. Comp. Sec. Conf., (4: IEE-88b), 1988, pp. 256-261.

Key Words: trusted, network, criteria.

PRE-87
Presttun, K. "Integrating Cryptography in ISDN," Proc. Crypto '87, Santa Barbara, 1987, (8: POM-88), pp. 9-18, 1988

Key Words: crypto, network.

PRE-89
Press, I. "Software Dase Encryption for Local Area Networks," Computer Networks and ISDN Systems, September 1989, pp. 187-192.

Key Words: Local Area Networks.

PRI-83
Price, W.L. "Key Management for Data Encipherment," Proc. IFIP/Sec. '83, Stockholm, 1983, (2: FAK-83), pp. 205-215.

Key Words:

RAM-89
Ramaswamy, R. "A Scheme for Providing Security Services on Transport Layer in Open System Interconnection Architectures," Proc. Internat. Conf. on Comp. & Information, ICCI'89, May 1989.

Key Words: OSI, methods, design.

RAM-89a
Ramaswamy, R. "Placement of Data Integrity Security Services in Open Systems Interconnection Architecture," Computers & Security, October 1989, pp. 507-516.

Key Words: OSI, methods, design.

RAM-89b
Ramaswamy, R. "Security Architecture for Data Transfer Through TCP/IP Protocols," Computers & Security, December 1989, pp. 709-719.

Key Words: network, protocols, case.

RAS-85
Rasmussen, O.S.
"Communications and
Network Protection: Practical
Experience," Proc. IFIP/Sec.
'85, Dublin, 1985, (2: GRI-
85), pp. 107-115.

Key Words: network,
methods, case.

RIH-83
Rihaczek, H., and L. Krause
"Data Encipherment
Requirements Federal
Republic of Germany,"
Information Age (UK), April
1983, pp. 91-96.

Key Words: requirements,
crypto.

RIH-87
Rihaczek, K.
"TeleTrusT-OSIS and
Communication Security,"
Computers & Security, June
1987, pp. 206-218.

Key Words: OSI, methods,
case.

RIV-80
Rivest, R.L.
"A Description of Single-
Chip Implementation of RSA
Cipher," Lambda, Fourth
Quarter, 1980, pp. 14-18.

Key Words: RSA, crypto,
hardware.

RIV-84
Rivest, R.L.
"RSA Chips
(Past/Present/Future)," Proc.
Eurocrypt '84, Paris, 1984,
(8: BET-85), pp. 159-165.

Key Words: ESA, crypto,
hardware.

ROG-87
Rogers, H.L.
"An Overview of the
Caneware Program," Proc.
10th Natl. Comp. Sec. Conf.,
(5: NCS-87a), 1987, pp. 172-
174.

Key Words: crypto, design,
case.

RUT-86
Rutledge, L.S., and
L.J. Hoffman
"A Survey of Issues in
Computer Network Security,"
Computers & Security,
December 1986, pp. 296-308.

Key Words: network, general.

SAT-88
Satya, V.
"Secure Computer Network
Requirements," Information
Age (U.K.), October 1988, pp.
211-222.

Key Words: requirements,
network.

SCA-87
Schaumuller-Bici, I.
"IC-Cards in High-Security
Applications," Proc. Eurocrypt
'87, Amsterdam, 1987, (8:
CHA-88a), pp. 177-189.

Key Words: crypto, hardware.

SCH-80
Scharf, J.D., C.V. Wallentine,
and P.S. Fisher
"Department of Defense
Network Security
Considerations," in Rullo,
T.A. (Ed.), Advances in
Computer Sec. Management,
Vol. 1, Heyden, Philadelphia,
PA, 1980, pp. 202-230.

Key Words: network, design,
case.

SCH-82
Schanning, B.P.
"Applying Public Key
Distribution to Local Area
Networks," Computers &
Security, November 1982, pp.
268-274.

Key Words: LAN, crypto,
keys.

SCH-82a
Schwartz, M.
"Making Sense of DES,"
Computerworld, June 7, 1982,
pp. ID15-ID34.

Key Words: DES, crypto,
general.

SCH-82b
Schwartz, M.
"DES: Putting It to Work,"
Computerworld, June 21, 1982,
pp. ID1-ID16.

Key Words: DES, crypto,
methods.

SCH-84
Schaumueller-Bichl, I.,
and E. Piller
"A Method of Software
Protection Based on the Use
of Smart Cards and
Cryptographic Techniques,"
Proc. Eurocrypt '84, Paris,
1984, (8: BET-85), pp. 446-
454.

Key Words: crypto, software,
methods, techniques.

SCH-85
Schaefer, M., and D.E. Bell
"Network Security Assurance,"
Proc. 8th Natl. Comp. Sec.
Conf., (5: NCS-85), 1985, pp.
64-69.

Key Words: verification,
network.

SCH-85a
Schnackenberg, D.D.
"Development of a Multilevel
Secure Local Area Network,"
Proc. 8th Natl. Comp. Sec.
Conf., (5: NCS-85), 1985, pp.
97-104.

Key Words: MLS, LAN,
design, case.

SCH-87
Schnackenberg, D.
"Applying the Orange Book to
an MLS LAN," Proc. 10th
Natl. Comp. Sec. Conf., (5:
NCS-87a), 1987, pp. 51-55.

Key Words: MLS, LAN,
criteria.

SCH-87a
Schweitzer, J.A.
"Securing Information on a
Network of Computers,"
EDPACS, July 1987, pp. 1-8.

Key Words: network, methods.

SCH-87b
Schockley, W.R., R.R.
Schell, and M.F. Thompson
"A Network of Trusted
Systems," AIAA No. 87-
3100, Proc. 3d Aerosp.
Comp. Sec. Conf., (5:IEE-
87b), 1987, pp. 140-142.

Key Words: network, trusted,
case.

SCH-89
Schnorr, C.P.
"Efficient Identification and
Signatures for Smart Cards,"
Proc. Crypto '89, Santa
Barbara, CA, (8: BRA-90),
1989.

Key Words: authentication,
case.

SCO-85
Scott, R.
"Wide-Open Encryption
Design Offers Flexible
Implementations,"
Cryptologia, January 1985,
pp. 75-90.

Key Words: encryption,
design.

SEA-85
Seaman, J.
"Halting Network Intruders,"
Computer Decisions, January
29, 1985, pp. 82ff.

Key Words: threats, network,
techniques.

SED-87
Sedlak, H.
"The RSA Cryptography
Processor," Proc. Eurocrypt
'87, Amsterdam, 1987, (8:
CHA-88a), pp. 95-105.

Key Words: RSA, crypto,
hardware.

SER-84
Serpell, S.C., C.B. Brookson,
and B.L. Clark
"A Prototype System Using
Public Key," Proc. Crypto
'84, Santa Barbara, CA, 1984,
(8: BLA-84a), pp. 3-9.

Key Words: crypto, public-
key, case.

SER-84a
Serpell, S.C., and
C.B. Brookson
"Encryption and Key
Management for the ECS
Satellite Service," Proc.
Eurocrypt '84, Paris, 1984, (8:
BET-85), pp. 426-436.

Key Words: crypto, network,
keys.

SER-85
Serpell, S,C,
"Cryptographic Equipment
Security: A Code of Practice,"
Computers & Security, March
1985, pp. 47-64.

Key Words: crypto, hardware.

SHA-86
Sharma, R.S.
"Data Communications and
Security," ACM Sec., Audit
& Control Rev., Winter 1986,
pp. 28-38.

Key Words: methods, general.

SHA-88
Shain, M.
"Security in Electronic Funds
Transfer," Proc. IFIP/Sec. '88,
Australia, 1989, (2: CAE-89),
pp. 367-380.

Key Words: methods,
network, case.

SHA-89
Shain, M.
"Security in Electronic Funds
Transfer," Computers &
Security, May 1989, pp. 209-
221.

Key Words: methods, network,
case.

SHE-87
Sheehan, E.R.
"Access Control within
SDNS," Proc. 10th Natl.
Comp. Sec. Conf., (5: NCS-
87a), 1987, pp. 165-171.

Key Words: network, control,
case.

SIM-82
Simmons, G.J. (Ed.)
Secure Communications and
Asymmetric Cryptosystems,
Westview Press, Boulder, CO,
1982.

Key Words: book, crypto,
methods, public-key.

SIM-83
Simmons, G.J.
"A 'Weak' Privacy Protocol
Using the RSA
Cryptoalgorithm," Cryptologia,
1983, pp. 180-182.

Key Words: RSA, crypto,
protocol.

SIM-84
Simmons, G.J.
"A System for Verifying User
Identity and Authorization at
the Point-of-Sale or Access,"
Cryptologia, January 1984, pp.
1-21.

Key Words: authentication,
case.

SIM-85
Simmons, G.J.
"The Practice of
Authentication," Proc.
Eurocrypt '85, Linz, 1985, (8:
PIC-86), pp. 261-272.

Key Words: authentication,
methods.

SIM-87
    Simmons, G.J.
    "Message Authentication with
    Arbitration of Transmitter/
    Receiver Disputes," Proc.
    Eurocrypt '87, Amsterdam,
    1987, (8: CHA-88a), pp. 151-
    165.

    Key Words: authentication.

SIM-88
    Simmons, G.J.
    "A Survey of Information
    Authentication," Proceedings
    of the IEEE, May 1988, pp.
    603-620.

    Key Words: authentication.

SIM-88a
    Simmons, G.J.
    "How to Insure that Data
    Acquired to Verify Treaty
    Compliance Are
    Trustworthy," Proceedings of
    the IEEE, May 1988, pp.
    621-627.

    Key Words: verification,
    crypto.

SMI-81
    Smid, M.E.
    "Integrating the Data
    Encryption Standard into
    Computer Networks," IEEE
    Trans. on Communications,
    June 1981, pp. 762-772.

    Key Words: DES, network,
    design.

SMI-87
    Smith, M.K.
    "A Verified Encrypted Packet
    Interface," ACM Software
    Engr. Notes, July 1987.

    Key Words: crypto, design,
    case.

SMI-88
    Smid, M.E., and
    D.K. Branstad
    "The Data Encryption
    Standard: Past and Future,"
    Proceedings of the IEEE,
    May 1988, pp. 550-559.

    Key Words: DES, crypto,
    general.

SMI-88a
    Smid, M., et al.
    Message Authentication Code
    (MAC) Validation System:
    Requirements and Procedures,
    SP 500-156, National Institute
    of Standards and Technology,
    Gaithersburg, MD, May 1988.

    Key Words: authentication,
    design, methods, requirements.

SMI-89
    Smid, M., J. Dray,
    and R. Warnar
    "A Token Based Access
    Control System for Computer
    Networks," Proc. 12th Natl.
    Comp. Sec. Conf., (5: NCS-
    89), 1989, pp. 232-253.

    Key Words: network, control,
    case.

SMI-89a
    Smith, J.M.
    "Practical Problems with a
    Cryptographic Protection
    Scheme," Proc. Crypto '89,
    Santa Barbara, CA, (8: BRA-
    90), 1989.

    Key Words: crypto, design,
    methods.

SNA-88
    Snare, J.
    "Secure Electronic Data
    Exchange," Proc. IFIP/Sec.
    '88, Australia, 1989, (2: CAE-
    89), pp. 331-342.

    Key Words: network, case.

SOR-83
    Sorkin, A.
    "Requirements for A Secure
    Terminal Switch," Computers
    & Security, November 1983,
    pp. 268-274.

    Key Words: requirements,
    case.

SOR-84
    Sorkin, A., and J.C. Buchanan
    "Measurment of Cryptographic
    Capability Protection
    Algorithms," Computers &
    Security, May 1984, pp. 101-
    116.

    Key Words: crypto, design,
    methods.

STO-89
    Stoneburner, G.R., and
    D.A. Snow
    "The Boeing MLS LAN:
    Headed Towards an INFOSEC
    Security Solution," Proc. 12th
    Natl. Comp. Sec. Conf., (5:
    NCS-89), 1989, pp. 254-266.

    Key Words: MLS, LAN,
    design, case.

TAT-87
    Tater, G.L.
    "The Secure Data Network
    System: An Overview:, Proc.
    10th Natl. Comp. Sec. Conf.,
    (5: NCS-87a), 1987, pp. 150-
    152.

    Key Words: network, design,
    case.

TAT-89
    Tatebayashi, M., N.Matsuzaki,
    and D.B. Newman
    "Key Distribution Protocol for
    Digital Mobile Communication
    System," Proc. Crypto '89,
    Santa Barbara, CA, (8: BRA-
    90), 1989.

    Key Words: crypto, protocols,
    key.

TEN-86
    Tener, w.T.
    "Discovery: An Expert System
    in the Communications Data
    Security Environment," Proc.
    IFIP/Sec. '86, Monte Carlo,
    1986, (2: GRI-89).

    Key Words: general, network,
    case.

TOP-84
Toppen, R.
"Infinite Confidence: The
Audit of Communication
Networks," Computers &
Security, November 1984, pp.
303-313.

Key Words: auditing,
network.

TOR-85
Torrieri, D.J.
Principles of Secure
Communication Systems,
Artech House, Norwood,
MA, 1985.

Key Words: book, methods,
general.

TRO-85
Troy, E.F.
"Dial-Up Security Update,"
Proc. 8th Natl. Comp. Sec.
Conf., (5: NCS-85), 1985,
pp. 124-132.

Key Words: PC, methods,
hardware.

TRO-86
Troy, E.F.
Security for Dial-Up Lines,
SP 500-137, National Bureau
of Standards, Gaithersburg,
MD, May 1986.

Key Words: PC, methods,
hardware.

TSU-89
Tsudik, G.
"Datagaram Authentication in
Internet Gateways:
Implications of Fragmentation
and Dynamic Routing," IEEE
Journal on Selected Areas
Communication, May 1989,
pp. 499-504.

Key Words: authentication,
case.

TUR-80
Turn, R.
"Applications of
Cryptography," in Rullo, T.A.
(Ed.), Advances in Computer
Security Management, Vol. 1,
Heyden & Son, Philadelphia,
PA, 1980, pp. 170-200.

Key Words: crypto, general.

VAN-85
Vandewalle, J. et al.
"Implementation Study of
Public Key Cryptographic
Protection in an Existing
Electronic Mail and Document
Handling System," Proc.
Eurocrypt '85, Linz, 1985, (8:
PIC-86), pp. 43-49.

Key Words: EM, cerypto,
public key.

VAN-87
van Heurck, P.
"TRASEC: Belgian Security
System for Electronic Funds
Transfers," Computers &
Security, June 1987, pp. 261-
268.

Key Words: network,
methods, case.

VAN-88
van der Bank, D., and
E. Anderssen
"Cryptographic Figure of
Merit," Computers & Security,
June 1988, pp. 299-303.

Key Words: crypto, design,
methods.

VAR-89
Varadharajan, V.
"Verification of Network
Security Protocols,"
Computers & Security,
December 1989, pp. 693-708.

Key Words: verification,
protocols.

VOY-83
Voydock, V., and S.T. Kent
"Security for Computer
Communication Networks,"
ACM Computing Surveys,
June 1983, pp. 135-171.

Key Words: methods, general.

VOY-85
Voydock, V.L., and
S.T. Kent
"Security Mechanisms in a
Transport Layer Protocol,"
Computers & Security,
December 1985, pp. 325-341.

Key Words: methods,
protocols.

VOY-85a
Voydock, V.L., and
S.T. Kent
"Security in High-Level
Network Protocols," IEEE
Communications Magazine,
July 1985, pp. 12-24.

Key Words: network,
protocols.

WAL-85
Walker, S.T.
"Network Security Overview,"
Proc. 1985 IEEE Symp. Sec.
&. Privacy, (5:IEE-85), pp. 62-
76.

Key Words: network, general.

WAL-89
Walker, S.T.
"Network Security: The Parts
of the Sum," Proc. 1989 IEEE
Symp. Sec. & Privacy, (5:IEE-
89b), pp. 2-9.

Key Words: network, general.

WIL-80
Williams, H.C.
"A Modification of the RSA
Public-Key Cryptosystem,"
IEEE Trans. on Inform.
Theory, November 1980, pp.
726-729.

Key Words: RSA, crypto,
design.

WIT-88
Witten, I.H. and J.G. Cleary "On the Privacy Afforded by Adaptive Text Compression," Computers & Security, August 1988, pp. 397-408.

Key Words: methods, case, techniques.

WON-85
Wong, R.M., T.A.Berson, and R.J. Feiertag "Polonius: An Identity Authentication System," Proc. 1985 IEEE Symp. Sec. & Privacy, (5:IEE-85), pp. 101-107.

Key Words: authentication, case.

WON-89
Wong, R.M. "Logon in Distributed Systems," Digest of Papers, IEEE Compcon '89, 1989, pp. 338-341.

Key Words: methods, network.

WOO-81
Wood, C.C. "Future Applications of Cryptography," Proc. 1981 IEEE Symp. Sec. & Privacy, (5:IEE-81), pp. 70-74.

Key Words: crypto, general.

WOO-82
Wood, C.C. "Future Applications of Cryptography," Computers & Security, January 1982, pp. 65-71.

Key Words: crypto, general.

WOO-83
Wood, H.M., and I.W. Cotton "Security in Computer Communications," in W. Chou (Ed.), Computer Communications, Vol. 1, Prentice-Hall, Englewood Cliffs, NJ, 1983, pp. 369-409.

Key Words: methods, general.

WOO-89
Wood, C.C. "Planning: A Means to Achieve Data Communications Security," Computers & Security, May 1989, pp. 189-199.

Key Words: methods, design.

WOO-89a
Woodfield, N.K. "An Approach for Evaluating the Security of an Air Force Type Network," Proc. 5th Sec. Applicat. Conf., (5:IEE-89c), 1989, pp. 53-62.

Key Words: network, methods, case.

8. Cryptography

This section cites publications on the theoretical and practical aspects of cryptography, cryptanalysis, and cryptographic protocols.

ACE-81
"American Council of Education Report on the Public Cryptography Study Group," <u>Communications of the ACM</u>, July 1981, pp, 435-450.

Key Words: policy, research.

ADA-87
Adams, C.M.
"Security-Related Comments Regarding McEliece's PublicKey Cryptosystem," <u>Proc. Crypto '87</u>, Santa Barbara, CA, 1987, (8: POM-88), pp. 224-228.

Key Words: evaluation, public-key.

ADL-82
Adleman, L.M.,
"On Breaking the Iterated Merkle-Hellman Public-Key Cryptosystem," <u>Proc. Crypto '82</u>, Santa Barbara, CA, 1982, (8: CHA-83b), pp. 303-313.

Key Words: analysis, knapsack.

ADL-82a
Adleman, L.M.
"Implementing an Electronic Notary Public," <u>Proc. Crypto '82</u>, Santa Barbara, CA, 1982, (8: CHA-83b), pp. 259-265.

Key Words: signatures, design.

ADL-83
Adleman, L.M.
"On Breaking Generalized Knap-sack Public-key Cryptosystems," <u>Proceedings, 15th ACM Symposium on Theory of Computing</u>, 1983, pp. 402-412.

Key Words: analysis, knapsack.

AGN-87
Agnew, G.B.
"Random Sources for Cryptographic Systems," <u>Proc. Eurocrypt '87</u>, Amsterdam, 1987, (8: CHA-88a), pp. 77-81.

Key Words: random, techniques.

AGN-88
Agnew, G.B., R.C. Mullin, and S.A. Vanstone
"An Interacrtive Data Exchange Protocol Based on Discrete Exponentionation," <u>Proc. Eurocrypt '88</u>, Davos, 1988, (8: GUN-89), pp. 159-176.

Key Words: methods, protocols.

AHI-87
Ahituv, N., Y. Lapid, and S. Neumann
"Processing Encrypted Data," <u>Communications of the ACM</u>, September 1987, pp. 777-780.

Key Words: techniques.

AKL-82
Akl, S.G.
"Digital Signatures with Blindfolded Arbitrators Who Cannot Form Alliances," <u>Proc. 1982 IEEE Symp. Sec. and Privacy</u>, (5: IEE-82), pp. 129-135.

Key Words: signatures, methods.

AKL-83
Akl, S.G.
"On the Security of Compressed Encodings," <u>Proc. Crypto '83</u>, Santa Barbara, CA, 1983, (8: CHA-84b), pp. 209-230.

Key Words: analysis, codes.

AKL-83a
Akl, S.G.
"Digital Signatures: Tutorial Survey," <u>IEEE Computer</u>, February 1983, pp. 14-24.

Key Words: signatures, general.

AKL-84
Akl, S.G., and H. Meijer
"A Fast Pseudo Random Permu-tation Generator with Applica-tions to Cryptography," <u>Proc. Crypto '84</u>, Santa Barbara, CA, 1984, (8: BLA-84a), pp. 269-275.

Key Words: random, techniques.

ALP-83
Alpern, B., and B. Schneider
"Key Exchange Using 'Keyless Cryptography'," <u>Information Processing Letters</u>, 1983, pp. 79-81.

Key Words: keys, techniques.

AMI-81
  Amirazizi, H.R., E.D. Karnin,
  and J.M. Reyneri
  "Compact Knapsacks are
  Polyno-mially Solvable,"
  Proc. Crypto '81, Santa
  Barbara, CA, 1981, (8: GER-
  82), pp. 17-24.

  Key Words: analysis,
  knapsack.

AND-82
  Andelman, D., and J. Reeds
  "On the Cryptanalysis of
  Rotor Machines and
  Substitution-Permutation
  Networks," IEEE Trans. on
  Inform. Theory, No. 4, 1982,
  pp. 578-584.

  Key Words: analysis,
  hardware.

ASM-83
  Asmuth, C., and J. Blum
  "A Modular Approach to Key
  Safeguarding," IEEE Trans.
  on Inform. Theory, March
  1983, pp. 208-210.

  Key Words: methods, keys.

AVA-88
  Avarne, S.
  "Cryptography -- Combatting
  Data Compromise," Security
  Management, October 1988,
  pp. 38-43.

  Key Words: threats, methods.

AYO-83
  Ayoub, F.
  "The Design of Complete
  Encryption Packages Using
  Cryptographically Equivalent
  Permutations," Computers &
  Security, November 1983, pp.
  261-267.

  Key Words: methods, design.

BAL-85
  Baldwin, R.W., and
  W.C. Gramlich
  "Cryptographic Protocol for
  Trustable Match Making,"
  Proc. 1985 IEEE Symp. Sec.
  and Privacy, (5: IEE-85), pp.
  92-100.

  Key Words: protocols,
  methods.

BAN-83
  Banary, I., and Z. Furedi
  "Mental Poker with Three or
  More Players," Information
  and Control, 1983, pp. 84-93.

  Key Words: protocols,
  methods.

BEK-82
  Beker, H., and F. Piper
  Cipher Systems: The
  Protection of Communications,
  J. Wiley & Sons, New York,
  1982.

  Key Words: book, techniques,
  methods, general.

BEL-89
  Bellare, M., and
  S. Goldwasser
  "New Paradigms for Digital
  Signatures for Smart Cards,"
  Proc. Crypto '89, Santa
  Barbara, CA, (8: BRA-90),
  1989.

  Key Words: signatures,
  methods.

BEN-82
  Bennett, C.H., et al.
  "Quantum Cryptography, or
  Unforgeable Subway Tokens,"
  Proc. Crypto '82, Santa
  Barbara, CA, 1982, (8: CHA-
  83b), pp. 267-275.

  Key Words: authentication,
  case.

BEN-84
  Bennet, C.H., and G. Brassard
  "Update on Quantum
  Cryptography," Proc. Crypto
  '84, Santa Barbara, CA, 1984,
  (8: BLA-84a), pp. 475-480.

  Key Words: techniques,
  methods.

BEN-85
  Bennet, C.H., G. Brassard,
  and J.-M. Robert
  "How to Reduce Your
  Enemy's Information," Proc.
  Crypto '85, Santa Barbara,
  CA, 1985, (8: WIL-86), pp.
  468-476.

  Key Words: methods, theory.

BEN-86
  Benaloh, J.C.
  "Cryptographic Capsules: A
  Disjunctive Primitive for
  Interactive Protocols," Proc.
  Crypto '86, Santa Barbara,
  CA, 1986, (8: ODL-87), pp.
  213-222.

  Key Words: methods,
  protocols.

BEN-86a
  Benaloh, J.C.
  "Secret Sharing
  Homomorphisms: Keeping
  Shares of a Secret Secret,"
  Proc. Crypto '86, Santa
  Barbara, CA, 1986, (8: ODL-
  87), pp. 251-260.

  Key Words: methods,
  protocols.

BEN-87
  Bennett, J.
  "Analysis of the Encryption
  Algorithm Used in the
  WordPerfect Word Processing
  Program," Cryptologia, October
  1987, pp. 206-210.

  Key Words: methods, case.

BEN-89
Bender, A., and
G. Castagnoli
"On the Implementation of
Elliptic Curve
Cryptosystems," Proc. Crypto
'89, Santa Barbara, CA, (8:
BRA-90), 1989.

Key Words: methods, theory.

BER-84
Berger, R., et al.
"A Provably Secure
Oblivious Transfer Protocol,"
Proc. Eurocrypt '84, Paris,
1984, (8: BET-85), pp. 379-
386.

Key Words: oblivious,
protocols.

BER-85
Berger, R., et al.
"A Framework for the Study
of Cryptographic Protocols,"
Proc. Crypto '85, Santa
Barbara, CA, 1985, (8: WIL-
86), pp. 87-103.

Key Words: model, protocols.

BET-82
Beth, T., and T. Ioth
"Algorithm Engineering for
Public Key Algorithms,"
Proc. 1982 IEEE Symp. Sec.
& Priv., (5: IEE-82), pp.
458-466.

Key Words: algorithms,
design.

BET-83
Beth, T. (Ed.)
Cryptography, Proceedings,
Burg Feuerstein Conference
1982, Lecture Notes in
Computer Science, Springer
Verlag, Berlin, 1983.

Key Words: proceedings,
general.

BET-86
Beth, T., et al. (Eds.)
Advances in Cryptology,
Proceedings, Eurocrypt '85,
Linz, Austria, April 1985,
Lecture Notes in Computer
Science, Vol. 209 Springer-
Verlag, New York, 1986

Key Words: proceedings,
general.

BET-88
Beth, T.
"Efficient Zero-Knowledge
Identication Scheme for Smart
Cards," Proc. Eurocrypt '88,
Davos, 1988, (8: GUN-89),
pp. 77-84.

Key Words: authentication,
zero.

BEU-87
Beutelspacher, A.
"Perfect and Essentially
Perfect Authentication
Schemes," Proc. Eurocrypt
'87, Amsterdam, 1987, (8:
CHA-88a), pp. 167-170.

Key Words: authentication,
methods.

BLA-80
Blakely, G.R.
"One Time Pads Are Key
Safeguarding Schemes, Not
Cryptosystems," Proc. 1980
IEEE Symp. Sec. & Priv., (5:
IEE-80), pp. 108-113.

Key Words: methods, keys.

BLA-80a
Blakely, G.R.
"Safeguarding Cryptographic
Keys," Proc. 1980 IEEE
Symp. Sec. & Priv., (5: IEE-
80), pp. 108-113.

Key Words: methods, keys,

BLA-84
Blakely, G.R., and
D.L. Chaum (Eds.)
Advances in Cryptology:
Crypto '84, Santa Barbara,
CA, August 1984, Lect. Notes
in Comp. Sci., No. 196,
Springer-Verlag, Berlin, 1984.

Key Words: proceedings,
general.

BLA-84a
Blakely, G.R., and
C. Meadows
"Security of Ramp Schemes,"
Proc. Crypto '84, Santa
Barbara, CA, 1984, (8: BLA-
84a), pp. 242-268.

Key Words: analysis, methods.

BLA-84b
Blakely, G.R.
"Information Theory Without
the Finiteness Assumption, I:
Cryptosystems as Group-
Theoretic Objects," Proc.
Crypto '84, Santa Barbara,
CA, 1984, (8: BLA-84a), pp.
314-338.

Key Words: analysis, theory.

BLA-85
Blakely, G.R.
"Information Theory Without
the Finiteness Assumption, II:
Unfolding the DES," Proc.
Crypto '85, Santa Barbara,
CA, 1985, (8: WIL-86), pp.
282-337.

Key Words: DES, analysis,
theory.

BLA-85a
Blakely, G.R., C. Meadows,
and G.B. Purdy
"Fingerprinting Long Forgiving
Messages," Proc. Crypto '85,
Santa Barbara, CA, 1985, (8:
WIL-86), pp. 180-189.

Key Words: methods, theory.

BLA-86
   Blakely, G.R., and
   R.D. Dixon
   "Smallest Possible Message
   Expansion in Threshold
   Schemes," Proc. Crypto '86,
   Santa Barbara, CA, 1986, (8:
   ODL-87), pp. 266-274.

   Key Words: methods, theory.

BLA-87
   Blakely, G.R., and
   W. Rundell
   "Cryptosystems Based on an
   Analog of Heat Flow," Proc.
   Crypto '87, Santa Barbara,
   CA, 1987, (8: POM-88), pp.
   306-329

   Key Words: models,
   methods.

BLO-82
   Blom, R.
   "Non-Public-key
   Distribution," Proc. Crypto
   '82, Santa Barbara, CA,
   1982, (8: CHA-83b), pp.
   231-236.

   Key Words: keys,
   management.

BLO-84
   Blom, R.
   "An Upper Bound on the
   Key Equivocation for Pure
   Ciphers," IEEE Trans. on
   Inform. Theory, 1984, pp.
   82-84.

   Key Words: methods, theory.

BLO-84a
   Blom, R.
   "An Optimal Class of
   Symmetric Key Generation
   Systems," Proc. Eurocrypt
   '84, Paris, 1984, (8: BET-
   85), pp. 335-338.

   Key Words: keys, theory.

BLU-82
   Blum, M.
   "Coin Flipping by
   Telephone," Proc., IEEE
   Spring Computer Conference,
   1982, pp. 133-137.

   Key Words: protocols, case.

BLU-83
   Blum, M.
   "How to Exchange (Secret)
   Keys," ACM Trans. on
   Computer Systems, May 1983,
   pp. 175-193.

   Key Words: protocols, keys.

BLU-84
   Blum, M., and S. Micali
   "How to Generate
   Cryptographically Strong
   Sequences of Pseudo-Random
   Bits," SIAM Journal of
   Computation, November 1984.

   Key Words: mathods, random.

BLU-84a
   Blum, M., and S. Goldwasser
   "An Efficient Probabiliastic
   Public-Key Encryption
   Scheme which Hides All
   Partial Infromation," Proc.
   Crypto '84, Santa Barbara,
   CA, 1984, (8: BLA-84a), pp.
   289-299.

   Key Words: algorithm, zero.

BOO-85
   Book, R.V., and F. Otto
   "The Verifiability of Two-Part
   Protocols," Proc. Eurocrypt
   '85, Linz, 1985, (8: PIC-86),
   pp. 254-260.

   Key Words: verification,
   protocols.

BRA-81
   Brassard, G.
   "A Time-Luck Tradeoff in
   Relativized Cryptography,"
   Journal of Computer and
   System Science, 1981, pp.
   280-311.

   Key Words: methods, design.

BRA-82
   Brassard, G.
   "On Computationally Secure
   Authentication Tags Requiring
   Short Shared Keys," Proc.
   Crypto '82, Santa Barbara,
   CA, 1982, (8: CHA-83b), pp.
   79-85.

   Key Words: authentication,
   keys.

BRA-83
   Brassard, G.
   "A Note on the Complexity of
   Cryptography," IEEE Trans. on
   Informat. Theory, November
   1983, pp. 232-233.

   Key Words: complexity,
   theory.

BRA-83a
   Brassard, G.
   "Relativized Cryptography,"
   IEEE Trans. on Inform.
   Theory, 1983, pp. 877-894.

   Key Words: methods, general.

BRA-86
   Brassard, G., and C. Crepeau
   "Non-Transitive Transfer of
   Confidence: A Perfect Zero-
   Knowledge Interactive Protocol
   for SAT and Beyond,"
   Proceedings, 27th IEEE
   Annual Symposium on the
   Foundations of Computer
   Science, 1986, pp. 188-195.

   Key Words: protocols, zero.

BRA-86a
   Brassard, G., C. Crepeau,
   and J.-M. Robert
   "All-Or-Nothing Disclosure of
   Secrets," Proc. Crypto '86,
   Santa Barbara, CA, 1986, (8:
   ODL-87), pp. 234-238.

   Key Words: methods, theory.

BRA-88
   Brandt, J., I.B. Damgard,
   and P. Landrock
   "Anonymous and Verifiable
   Registration in Databases,"
   Proc. Eurocrypt '88, Davos,
   1988, (8: GUN-89), pp. 167-
   76.

   Key Words: authentication,
   methods, theory.

BRA-88a
   Brassard, G.
   Modern Cryptology: A
   Tutorial, Lecture Notes in
   Computer Science No. 325,
   Springer-Verlag, New York,
   NY, 1988

   Key Words: book, general.

BRA-90
    Brassard, G.
    <u>Advances in Cryptology,</u>
    <u>Proceedings of Crypto-89,</u>
    Santa Barbara, CA, August
    1989, Lecture Notes in
    Computer Science, Springer
    Verlag, Berlin, 1990.

    Key Words: proceedings,
    general.

BRI-82
    Brickell, E.F.
    "A Fast Modular
    Multiplication Algorithm with
    Application to Two-Key
    Cryptography," <u>Proc. Crypto</u>
    <u>'82,</u> Santa Barbara, CA,
    1982, (8: CHA-83b), pp. 51-
    60.

    Key Words: RSA, techniques.

BRI-82a
    Brickell, E.F., J.A. Davis,
    and G.J. Simmons
    "A Preliminary Report on the
    Cryptanalysis of Merkle-
    Hellman Knapsack
    Cryptosystems," <u>Proc. Crypto</u>
    <u>'82,</u> Santa Barbara, CA,
    1982, (8: CHA-83b), pp.
    289-301.

    Key Words: analysis,
    knapsack.

BRI-83
    Brickell.E.F.
    "Solving Low Density
    Knapsacks" <u>Proc. Crypto '83,</u>
    Santa Barbara, CA, 1983, (8:
    CHA-84b), pp. 25-38.

    Key Words: analysis,
    knapsack.

BRI-83a
    Brickell, E.F., and
    G.J. Simmons
    "A Status Report on
    Knapsack Based Public-key
    Cryptosystems," <u>Congressus</u>
    <u>Numerantium,</u> Vol. 37, 1983,
    pp. 3-72.

    Key Words: analysis,
    knapsack.

BRI-84
    Brickell, E.F.
    "A Few Results in Message
    Authentication" <u>Congress</u>
    <u>Numerantium,</u> December
    1984, pp. 141-154.

    Key Words: authentication,
    methods, theory.

BRI-84a
    Brickell, E.F.
    "Breaking Iterated
    Knapsacks," <u>Proc. Crypto '84,</u>
    Santa Barbara, CA, 1984, (8:
    BLA-84a), pp. 342-358.

    Key Words: analysis,
    knapsack.

BRI-85
    Brickell, E.F., and
    J.M. DeLaurentis
    "An Attack on a Signature
    Scheme Proposed by Okamoto
    and Shiraishi," <u>Proc. Crypto</u>
    <u>'85,</u> Santa Barbara, CA, 1985,
    (8: WIL-86), pp. 28-32.

    Key Words: analysis,
    signatures.

BRI-86
    Brickell, E.F., J.H. Moore,
    and M.R. Purtill
    "Structure in the S-Boxes of
    the DES," <u>Proc. Crypto '86,</u>
    Santa Barbara, CA, 1986, (8:
    ODL-87), pp. 3-32.

    Key Words: DES, analysis.

BRI-87
    Brickell, e.F.
    "On Privacy
    Homomorphisms," <u>Proc.</u>
    <u>Eurocrypt '87,</u> Amsterdam,
    1987, (8: CHA-88a), pp. 117-
    125.

    Key Words: methods, theory.

BRI-87a
    Brickell, E.F., et al.
    "Gradual and Verifiable
    Release of a Secret," <u>Proc.</u>
    <u>Crypto '87,</u> Santa Barbara,
    CA, 1987, (8: POM-88), pp.
    156-166.

    Key Words: verification,
    methods.

BRI-87b
    Brickell, E.F., P.J. Lee,
    and Y. Yacobi
    "Secure Audio
    Teleconference," <u>Proc. Crypto</u>
    <u>'87,</u> Santa Barbara, CA, 1987,
    (8: POM-88), pp. 418-426.

    Key Words: techniques,
    design.

BRI-88
    Brickell, E.F., and
    A.M. Odlyzko
    "Cryptanalysis: A Survey of
    Recent Results," <u>Proceedings</u>
    <u>of the IEEE,</u> May 1988, pp.
    578-593.

    Key Words: analysis, methods.

BRI-88a
    Brickell, E.F., and
    D.R. Stinson
    "Authentication Codes with
    Multiple Arbitrers," <u>Proc.</u>
    <u>Eurocrypt '87,</u> Amsterdam,
    1987, (8: CHA-88a), pp. 51-
    55.

    Key Words: authentication,
    codes.

BRI-89
    Brickell, E.F., and
    D.M. Davenport
    "On the Classification of Ideal
    Secret Sharing Systems," <u>Proc.</u>
    <u>Crypto '89,</u> Santa Barbara,
    CA, (8: BRA-90), 1989.

    Key Words: methods, theory.

BUC-82
    Buck, R.C.
    "The Public Cryptography
    Study Group," <u>Computers &</u>
    <u>Security,</u> November 1982, pp.
    249-254.

    Key Words: policy, research.

BUC-88
    Buchmann, J., and
    H.C. Williams
    "A Key-Exchange System
    Based on Imaginary
    Quadratic Fields," Journal of
    Cryptology, Vol. 1, No. 2,
    1988, pp. 107-118.

    Key Words: methods, keys,
    theory.

BUC-89
    Buchmann, J.A., and
    H.C. Williams
    "A Key Exchange System
    Based on Real Quadratic
    Fields," Proc. Crypto '89,
    Santa Barbara, CA, (8: BRA-
    90), 1989.

    Key Words: methods, keys,
    theory.

CAD-86
    Cade, J.J.
    "A Modification of A Broken
    Public-Key Cipher," Proc.
    Crypto '86, Santa Barbara,
    CA, 1986, (8: ODL-87), pp.
    64-83.

    Key Words: methods, design.

CAR-86
    Carroll, J.M., and S. Martin
    "The Automated
    Cryptanalysis of Substitution
    Ciphers," Cryptologia,
    October 1986, pp. 193-209.

    Key Words: analysis,
    methods.

CAR-87
    Carroll, J.M., and L. Robbins
    "The Automated
    Cryptanalysis of
    Polyalphabetic Ciphers,"
    Cryptologia, October 1987,
    pp. 193-205.

    Key Words: analysis,
    methods.

CAR-88
    Carroll, J.M., and
    L.E. Robbins
    "Using Binary Derivatives to
    Test an Enhancement of
    DES," Cryptologia, October
    1988, pp. 193-208.

    Key Words: DES, evaluation.

CHA-81
    Chaum, D.L.
    "Untraceable Electronic Mail,
    Return Addresses, and Digital
    Pseudonyms,"
    Communications of the ACM,
    February 1981, pp. 84-88.

    Key Words: methods,
    protocols.

CHA-82
    Chaum, D.
    "Blind Signatures for
    Untraceable Payments," Proc.
    Crypto '82, Santa Barbara,
    CA, 1982, (8: CHA-83b), pp.
    199-203.

    Key Words: signatures,
    theory.

CHA-83
    Chaum, D., R.L. Rivest, and
    A.T. Sheridan (Eds.),
    Advances in Cryptology: Proc.
    of Crypto-82, Santa Barbara,
    CA, August 1982, Plenum
    Press, New York, 1983.

    Key Words: proceedings,
    general.

CHA-84
    Chaum, D. (Ed.),
    Advances in Cryptology: Proc.
    of Crypto-83, Sata Barbara,
    CA, August 1983, Plenum
    Press, New York, 1984.

    Key Words: proceedings,
    general.

CHA-85
    Chaum, D., and J.-H. Evertse
    "Cryptanalysis of DES with a
    Reduced Number of Rounds
    Sequences of Linear Factors in
    Block Ciphers," Proc. Crypto
    '85, Santa Barbara, CA, 1985,
    (8: WIL-86), pp. 192-211.

    Key Words: DES, analysis,
    design.

CHA-85a
    Chaum, D.
    "Security Without
    Identification: Transaction
    System to Make Big Brother
    Obsolete," Communications of
    the ACM, October 1985, pp.
    1030-1044.

    Key Words: techniques, theory.

CHA-86
    Chaum, D., and J.-H. Evertse
    "A Secure and Privacy-
    Protecting Protocol for
    Transmitting Personal
    Infromation Between
    Organizations," Proc. Crypto
    '86, Santa Barbara, CA, 1986,
    (8: ODL-87), pp. 118-167.

    Key Words: protocols, design.

CHA-86a
    Chaum, D.
    "Demonstrating the a Public
    Predicate Can Be Satisfied
    Without Revealing Any
    Infromation About How," Proc.
    Crypto '86, Santa Barbara,
    CA, 1986, (8: ODL-87), pp.
    195-199.

    Key Words: protocol, theory,
    zero.

CHA-86b
    Chaum, D., et al.
    "Demonstrating Possession of a
    Discrete Logarithm Without
    Revealing It," Proc. Crypto
    '86, Santa Barbara, CA, 1986,
    (8: ODL-87), pp. 200-212.

    Key Words: protocol, theory,
    zero.

CHA-87
Chaum, D., I.B. Damgard, and J. Van de Graaf "Multiparty Computations Ensuring of Each Party's Input and Correctness of the Result," Proc. Crypto '87, Santa Barbara, CA, 1987, (8: POM-88),

Key Words: protocols, theory.

CHA-87a
Chaum, D. "Blinding for Unaticipated Signatures," Proc. Eurocrypt '87, Amsterdam, 1987, (CHA-88a), pp. 227-233.

Key Words: signatures, methods.

CHA-87b
Chaum, D., J.-H. Evertse, and J. van de Graaf "An Improved Protocol for Demonstrating Posession of a Discrete Logarithm and Some Generalizations," Proc. Eurocrypt '87, Amsterdam, 1987, (CHA-88a), pp. 127-141.

Key Words: protocols, theory.

CHA-88
Chaum, D., and W.L. Price (Eds.) Advances in Cryptology: Eurocrypt '87 Proceedings, Amsterdam, April 1987, Lecture Notes in Computer Science No. 304, Springer-Verlag, New York, 1988.

Key Words: proceedings, general.

CHA-88a
Chaum, D. "The Dining Cryptographers Problem: Unconditional Sender and Receiver Untraceability," Journal of Cryptology, Vol. 1, No. 1, 1988, pp. 65-75.

Key Words: protocols, theory.

CHA-88b
Chaum, D. "Elections with Unconditionally Secret Ballots and Disruption Equivalent to Breaking RSA," Proc. Eurocrypt '88, Davos, 1988, (8: GUN-89), pp. 177-182.

Key Words: RSA, protocols.

CHA-89
Chaum, D. "Undeniable Signatues" Proc. Crypto '89, Santa Barbara, CA, (8: BRA-90), 1989.

Key Words: signatures, methods.

CHA-89a
Chaum, D. "The Spymaster's Double-Agent Problem: Multiparty Computations Secure Unconditionally from All Minorities and Cryptographically from Majorities," Proc. Crypto '89, Santa Barbara, CA, (8: BRA-90), 1989.

Key Words: protocols, theory.

CHO-84
Chor, B. and R.L. Rivest "A Knapsack Type Public-key Cryptosystem Based on Arith metic in Finite Fields," Proc. Crypto '84, Santa Barbara, CA, 1984, (8: BLA-84a), pp. 54-65.

Key Words: methods, knapsack.

CHO-85
Chor, B., et al. "Verifiable Secret Sharing and Achieving Simultaneity in the Presence of Faults," Proceedings, 26th IEEE Annual Symposium on the Foundations of Comp. Sci., 1985, pp. 383-395.

Key Words: protocols, methods.

CHO-88
Chor, B., and R.L. Rivest "A Knapsack-Type Public-key Cryptosystem Based on Arithmetic in Finite Fields," IEEE Trans. on Inform. Theory, September 1988, pp. 901-909.

Key Words: methods, knapsack, theory, public-key.

CHO-89
Chor, B., and E. Kushilevitz "Secret Sharing over Infinite Domains," Proc. Crypto '89, Santa Barbara, CA, 1989, (8: BRA-90).

Key Words: methods, theory.

CLJ-84
"Government and Cryptography," Computer/Law Journal, Winter 1984, pp. 573-603.

Key Words: policy, research.

COH-85
Cohen, J., and M. Fischer "A Robust and Verifiable Cryptographically Secure Election System," Proceedings, 26th IEEE Symposium on Foundations of Computing, 1985, pp. 372-382.

Key Words: methods, protocols.

COO-80
Cooper, R.H. "Linear Transformations in Galois Fields and Their Applications to Cryptography," Cryptologia, Vol. 4, 1980, pp. 184-188.

Key Words: algorithms, theory.

COO-84
Cooper, R.H., W. Hyslop, and W. Patterson "An Application of the Chinese Remainder Theorem to Multiple-Key Encryption in Data Base Systems," Proc. IFIP/Sec. '84, Toronto, 1984, (2: FIN-85), pp. 553-556.

Key Words: methods, theory.

COP-84
Coppersmith, D.
"Another Birthday Attack,"
Proc. Crypto '85, Santa
Barbara, CA, 1985, (8: WIL-
86), pp. 14-17.

Key Words: analysis,
methods.

COP-85
Coppersmith, D.
"Cheating at Mental Poker,"
Proc. Crypto '85, Santa
Barbara, CA, 1985, (8: WIL-
86), pp. 104-107.

Key Words: threats,
protocols.

COP-87
Coppersmith, D.
"Cryptography," IBM Journal
of Research and
Development, March 1987,
pp. 244-248.

Key Words: methods,
general.

COS-81
Costas, J.P.
"The Hand-Held Calculator
as a Cryptographic
Terminal," Cryptologia, April
1981, pp. 94-117.

Key Words: methods,
hardware.

CRE-85
Crepeau, C.
"A Secure Poker Protocol
that Minimizes the Effect of
Player Coalitions," Proc.
Crypto '85, Santa Barbara,
CA, 1985, (8: WIL-86), pp.
73-86.

Key Words: methods,
protocols.

CRE-87
Crepeau, C.
"Equivalence Between Two
Flavors of Oblivious
Transfer," Proc. Crypto '87,
Santa Barbara, CA, 1987, (8:
POM-88), pp. 350-354.

Key Words: oblivious,
theory.

DAV-80
Davies, D.W., W.L. Price,
and G.I. Parkin
"Evaluation of Public-key
Cryptosystems," Information
Privacy (U.K.), March 1980,
pp. 138-154.

Key Words: evaluation,
public-key.

DAV-80a
Davies, D.W., and D.A. Bell
"Protection of Data by
Cryptography," Information
Privacy, (U.K.), May 1980,
pp. 106-125.

Key Words: techniques, case.

DAV-82
Davies, D.W.
"Some Regular Properties of
Data Encryption Standard
Algorithm," Proc. Crypto '82,
Santa Barbara, CA, 1982, (8:
CHA-83b), pp. 89-96.

Key Words: DES, analysis.

DAV-82a
Davies, D.W., and
G.I.P. Parkin
"The Average Cycle Size of
the Key Stream in Output
Feedback Encipherment,"
Proc. Crypto '82, Santa
Barbara, CA, 1982, (8: CHA-
83b), pp. 97-98.

Key Words: DES, analysis.

DAV-82b
Davida, G.I., and Y.Yeh
"Cryptographic Relational
Algebra," Proc. 1982 IEEE
Symp. Sec. & Privacy, (5:
IEE-82), 1982, pp. 111-116

Key Words: algorithms,
theory.

DAV-83
Davies, D.W.
"Use of the 'Signature Token'
to Create a Negotiable
Document, Proc. Crypto '83,
Santa Barbara, CA, (8: CHA-
84b), 1983, pp. 377-382.

Key Words: signatuers,
methods.

DAV-83a
Davis, J.A., and
D.B. Holdridge
"Factorization Using the
Quadratic Sieve Algorithm,"
Proc. Crypto '83, Santa
Barbara, CA, (8: CHA-84b),
1983, pp. 103-113.

Key Words: analysis,
techniques.

DAV-83b
Davio, M., et al.,
"Analytical Characteristics of
the DES," Proc. Crypto '83,
Santa Barbara, CA, 1983, (8:
CHA-84b), pp. 171-202.

Key Words: DES, analysis,
methods.

DAV-84
Davio, M., Y. Desmedt, and
J.-J. Quisquater
"Propagation Characteristics of
the DES" Proc. Eurocrypt '84,
Paris, 1984, (8: BET-85), pp.
62-73.

Key Words: DES, analysis.

DAV-84a
Davis, J.A., D.B. Holdridge,
and G.J. Simmons
"Status Report on Factoring
(At the Sandia Laboratories),"
Proc. Eurocrypt '84, Paris,
1984, (8: BET-85), pp. 183-
215.

Key Words: RSA, analysis,
methods.

DAV-87
Davida, G.I., and G.G. Walter
"A Public-key Analog
Cryptosystem," Proc. Eurocrypt
'87, Amsterdam, 1987, (CHA-
88a), pp. 144-147.

Key Words: methods, public-
key.

DAV-87a
Davida, G.I, and B.J. Matt
"Arbitration in Tamper Proof
Systems," Proc. Crypto '87,
Santa Barbara, CA, 1987, (8:
POM-88), pp. 216-222.

Key Words: signatures,
methods.

DAV-87b
Davida, G.I., and F.B. Dancs
"A Crypto-Engine," Proc.
Crypto '87, Santa Barbara,
CA, 1987, (8: POM-88), pp.
257-268.

Key Words: methods, design.

DAV-88
Davis, J.A, and
D.B. Holdridge
"Factorization of Large
Integers on a Massively
Parallel Computer," Proc.
Eurocrypt '88, Davos, 1988,
(8: GUN-89), pp. 235-243.

Key Words: analyis,
techniques.

DEA-87
Deavours, C.A.,
Cryptology Yesterday, Today
and Tomorrow, Artech
House, Norwood, MA, 1987.

Key Words: book, general.

DEA-89
Deavours, C.A., et al. (Eds.)
Cryptology: Machines,
History, and Methods, Artech
House, Norwood, MA, 1989.

Key Words: book, general.

DEJ-85
deJonge, W., and D. Chaum
"Attacks on Some RSA
Signatures," Proc. Crypto '85,
Santa Barbara, CA, 1985, (8:
WIL-86), pp. 18-27.

Key Words: RSA, analysis,
signatures.

DEJ-86
de Jonge, W., and D. Chaum
"Some Variations on RSA
Signatures & Their Security,"
Proc. Crypto '86, Santa
Barbara, CA, 1986, (8: ODL-
87), pp. 49-59.

Key Words: RSA, signatures.

DEL-84
DeLAurentis, J.M.
"A Further Weakness in the
Common Modulus Protocol
for the RSA Cryptoalgorithm,"
Cryptologia, July 1984, pp.
253-259.

Key Words: RSA, analysis,
threats, protocols.

DEL-84a
Delsarte, P., et al.
"Fast Cryptanalysis of
Matsumoto-Imai Public-key
Scheme," Proc. Eurocrypt '84,
Paris, 1984, (8: BET-85), pp.
142-149.

Key Words: analysis, public-
key.

DEM-82
DeMillo, R., N. Lynch,
and M. Merritt
"Cryptographic Protocols,"
Proc., 14th ACM Symposium
on Theory of Computation,
1982, pp. 383-400.

Key Words: protocols,
general.

DEM-83
DeMillo, R.A., et al.
"Applied Cryptology,
Cryptographic Protocols, and
Computer Security Models,"
Proceedings, 29th Symposium
on Applied Mathematics,
American Mathematical Soc.,
1983.

Key Words: models,
protocols.

DEM-83a
DeMillo, R., and M. Merritt
"Protocols for Data Security,"
IEEE Computer, February
1983, pp. 39-50.

Key Words: protocols, general.

DEN-82
Denning, D.E.
Cryptography and Data
Security, Addison-Wesley,
Reading, MA, 1982.

Key Words: book, methods,
models.

DEN-83
Denning, D.E.,
"The Many-Time Pad: Theme
and Variations," Proc. 1983
IEEE Symp. Sec. & Priv., (5:
IEE-83a), pp. 23-30.

Key Words: techniques, case.

DEN-84
Denning, D.E.
"Digital Signatures with RSA
and Other Public-Key
Cryptosystems,"
Communications of the ACM,
April 1984, pp. 388-392.

Key Words: RSA, signatures.

DEN-88
Den Boer, B.
"Cryptanalysis of F.E.A.L.,"
Proc. Crypto '88, Santa
Barbara, CA, 1988, pp. 293-
299.

Key Words: analysis,
algorithm.

DES-84
Desmedt, Y.G., et al.
"A Critical Analysis of
Security of Knapsack Public-
key Algorithms," IEEE Trans.
on Inform. Theory, July 1984,
pp. 601-611.

Key Words: analysis,
knapsack.

DES-84a
Desmedt, Y., et al. "Dependence of Output on Input in DES: Small Avalanche Characteristics," Proc. Crypto '84, Santa Barbara, CA, 1984, (8: BLA-84a), pp. 359-376.

Key Words: DES, design, analysis.

DES-85
Desmedt, Y. "Unconditionally Secure Authentication Schemes and Practical and Theoretical Consequences," Proc. Crypto '85, Santa Barbara, CA, 1985, (8: WIL-86), pp. 42-55.

Key Words: authentication, theory.

DES-85a
Desmedt, Y., and A.M. Odlyzko "A Chosen Text Attack on the RSA Cryptosystem and Some Discrete Logarithm Schemes," Proc. Crypto '85, Santa Barbara, CA, 1985, (8: WIL-86), pp. 516-522.

Key Words: RSA, analysis, threats.

DES-86
Desmedt, Y., and J.-J. Quisquater "Public-Key Systems Based on the Difficulty of Tampering," Proc. Crypto '86, Santa Barbara, CA, 1986, (8: ODL-87), pp. 111-117.

Key Words: public-key, design.

DES-86a
Desmedt, Y. "Is There A Ultimate Use of Cryptography?," Proc. Crypto '86, Santa Barbara, CA, 1986, (8: ODL-87), pp. 459-463.

Key Words: policy, general.

DES-87
De Santis, A., S. Micali, and G. Persiano "Non-Interactive Zero-Knowledge Proof Systems," Proc. Crypto '87, Santa Barbara, CA, 1987, (8: POM-88), pp. 52-72

Key Words: theory, zero.

DES-87a
Desmedt, Y.G., et al. "Special Uses and Abuses of the Fiat-Shamir Passport Protocol" Proc. Crypto '86, Santa Barbara, CA, 1986, (8: ODL-87), pp. 21-39

Key Words: thretas, protocols.

DES-87b
Desmedt, Y.G. "Society and Group Oriented Cryptography: A New Concept," Proc. Crypto '87, Santa Barbara, CA, 1987, (8: POM-88), pp. 120-127.

Key Words: policy, methods.

DES-88
Desmedt, Y.G. "Subliminal-Free Authentication and Signature," Proc. Crypto '88, Santa Barbara, CA, 1988, pp. 23-33.

Key Words: authentication, methods.

DES-88a
De Soete, M. "Some Constructions for Authentication-Secrecy Codes," Proc. Eurocrypt '88, Davos, 1988, (8: GUN-89), pp. 57-75.

Key Words: authentication, codes.

DES-89
Desmedt, Y.G. "Making Conditionally Secure Cryptosystems Unconditionally Abuse-Free in a General Context," Proc. Crypto '89, Santa Barbara, CA, (8: BRA-90), 1989.

Key Words: methods, design.

DIF-81
Diffie, W. "Cryptographic Technology: Fifteen Year Forecast," Proc. Crypto '81, Santa Barbara, CA, 1981, (8: GER-82), pp. 84-108.

Key Words: methods, gneral.

DIF-88
Diffie, W. "The First Ten Years of Public-Key Cryptography," Proceedings of the IEEE, May 1988, pp. 560-577.

Key Words: public-key, methods.

DOL-81
Dolev, D., A.C. Yao "On the Security of Public Key Protocols," Proc., 22nd Annual Symp. on the Foundations of Comp. Sci., 1981.

Key Words: analysis, public-key.

DOL-82
Dolev, D., and A. Wigderson "On the Security of Multi-Party Protocols in Distributed Systems," Proc. Crypto '82, Santa Barbara, CA, 1982, (8: CHA-83b), pp. 167-175.

Key Words: analysis, protocols.

DOL-82a
Dolev, D., S. Even, and R.M. Karp "On the Security of Ping-Pong Algorithms," Proc. Crypto '82, Santa Barbara, CA, 1982, (8: CHA-83b), pp. 177-186.

Key Words: analysis, algorithms.

DOL-83
Dolev, D., and A.C. Yao "On the Security of Public-key Protocols," IEEE Trans. on Inform. Theory, March 1983, pp. 198-208.

Key Words: analysis, protocols.

EIE-83
Eier, R., and H. Lagger
"Trapdoors in Knapsack
Cryptosystems," Proc. Burg
Feuerstein Conf., 1982, (8:
BET-83), pp. 316-322.

Key Words: analysis,
knapsack.

ELG-82
ElGamal, T.
"A Public-key Cryptosystem
and a Signature Scheme
Based on Discrete
Logarithms," Proc. Crypto
'84, Santa Barbara, CA,
1984, (8: BLA-84a), pp. 10-
18.

Key Words: methods,
signatures.

ELG-85
ElGamal, T.
"A Public-key Cryptosystem
and Signature Scheme Based
on Discrete Logarithms,"
IEEE Trans. on Inform.
Theory, July 1985, pp. 469-
472.

Key Words: methods,
signatures.

ELK-83
El-Kateeb, A., and
S. Al-Khayatt
"Public-key Cryptosystems,"
Information Age (UK),
October 1983, pp. 232-237.

Key Words: publi-key,
general.

ESC-84
Escobar, C.B.
"Nongovernmental Cryptology
and National Security: The
Government Seeking to
Restrict Research,"
Computer/Law Journal,
Winter 1984, pp. 573-603.

Key Words: policy, research.

EST-85
Estes, D., et al.
"Breaking the Ong-Schorr-
Shamir Signature Scheme for
Quadratic Number Fields,"
Proc. Crypto '85, Santa
Barbara, CA, 1985, (8: WIL-
86), pp. 3-13.

Key Words: analysis,
signatures.

EVE-82
Even, S., O. Goldreich,
and A. Lempel
"A Randomized Protocol for
Signing Contracts" Proc.
Crypto '82, Santa Barbara,
CA, 1982, (8: CHA-83b), pp.
205-210.

Key Words: signatures,
random, protocols.

EVE-85
Even, S., O. Goldreich,
and A. Shamir
"On the Security of Ping-Pong
Protocols when Implemented
Using the RSA," Proc. Crypto
'85, Santa Barbara, CA, 1985,
(8: WIL-86), pp. 58-72.

Key Words: RSA, analysis,
protocols.

EVE-85a
Even, S., and O. Goldreich
"On the Power of Cascade
Ciphers," ACM Trans. on
Computer Systems, 1985, pp.
108-116.

Key Words: evaluation,
methods.

EVE-85b
Even, S., O. Goldreich,
and A. Lempel
"A Randomized Protocol for
Signing Contracts,"
Communications of the ACM,
June 1985, pp. 637-647.

Key Words: siagnatures,
random.

EVE-87
Evertse, J.-H.
"Linear Structures in Block
Ciphers," Proc. Eurocrypt '87,
Amsterdam, 1987, (CHA-88a),
pp. 249-266.

Key Words: analysis, methods.

EVE-89
Even, S., O. Goldreich,
and S. Micali
"On Line/Off Line Digital
Signatures," Proc. Crypto '89,
Santa Barbara, CA, (8: BRA-
90), 1989.

Key Words: signatures,
methods.

FAM-83
Fam, B.W.
"Improving the Security of
Exponential Key Exchange,"
Proc. Crypto '83, Santa
Barbara, CA, 1983, (8: CHA-
84b), pp. 359-368.

Key Words: methods, keys.

FEI-85
Feigenbaum, J.
"Encrypting Problem
Instances," Proc. Crypto '85,
Santa Barbara, CA, 1985, (8:
WIL-86), pp. 477-488.

Key Words: methods, theory.

FEI-88
Feige, U., A. Fiat,
and A. Shamir
"Zero-Knowledge Proofs of
Identity," Journal of
Cryptology, Vol. 1, No. 2,
1988, pp. 77-94.

Key Words: authentication,
zero.

FEL-85
Fell, H., and W.Diffie
"Analysis of a Public-key
Approach Based on
Polynomial Substitution," Proc.
Crypto '85, Santa Barbara,
CA, 1985, (8: WIL-86), pp.
340-349.

Key Words: analysis, public-
key.

FEL-87
Feldman, P.
"A Practical Scheme for
Non-Interactive Verifiable
Secret Sharing," Proc., 28th
IEEE Annual Symp. on the
Foundation of Comp.
Science, 1987, pp. 427-437.

Key Words: methods,
protocols.

FIA-86
Fiat, A., and A. Shamir
"How to Prove Yourself:
Practical Solutions to
Identification and Signature
Problems," Proc. Crypto '86,
Santa Barbara, CA, 1986, (8:
ODL-87), pp. 186-194.

Key Words: signatures,
methods.

FIS-81
Fischer, E.
"Measuring Cryptographic
Performance with Production
Processes," Cryptologia, July
1981, pp. 158-162.

Key Words: evaluation,
methods.

FOR-84
Fortune, S.
"Poker Protocols," Proc.
Crypto '84, Santa Barbara,
CA, 1984, (8: BLA-84a), pp.
454-464.

Key Words: protocols, case.

FOS-82
Foster, C.C.
Cryptanalysis for
Microcomputers, Hayden
Book Co., Rochelle Park, NJ,
1982.

Key Words: book, PC,
methods.

GAL-85
Galil, Z., S. Haber, and
M. Yung
"Symmetric Public-Key
Encryption," Proc. Crypto '85,
Santa Barbara, CA, 1985, (8:
WIL-86), pp. 128-137.

Key Words: public-key,
methods.

GAL-85a
Galil, Z., S. Haber, and
M. Yung
"A Private Interactive Test of
a Boolean Predicate and
Minimum-Knowledge Public-
Key Cryptosystems," Proc.,
26th IEEE Symposium on
Foundations of Computing,
1985, pp. 360-371

Key Words: evaluation,
public-key.

GEO-89
Georgiu, G.
"A Method to Strengthen
Ciphers," Cryptologia, April
1989, pp. 151.

Key Words: methods,
techniques.

GER-82
Gersho, A. (Ed.)
Advances in Cryptology: A
Report on Crypto 81, August
1981, ECE Rept. No. 82-02,
University of California, Santa
Barbara, CA, August 20,
1982.

Key Words: proceedings,
methods.

GIF-82
Gifford, D.K.
"Cryptographic Sealing for
Information Security and
Authentication,"
Communications of the ACM,
April 1982, pp. 274-286.

Key Words: authentication,
methods.

GIR-88
Girault, M., R. Cohen,
and M. Campana
"A Generalized Birthday
Attack," Proc. Eurocrypt '88,
Davos, 1988, (8: GUN-89), pp.
129-156.

Key Words: analysis, threat.

GOD-85
Godlewski, P., and
G.D. Cohen
"Some Cryptographic Aspects
of Womcodes," Proc. Crypto
'85, Santa Barbara, CA, 1985,
(8: WIL-86), pp. 458-467.

Key Words: methods, codes.

GOL-82
Goldwasser, S., S. Micali,
and A. Yao
"On Signatures and
Authentication," Proc. Crypto
'82, Santa Barbara, CA, 1982,
(8: CHA-83b), pp. 211-215.

Key Words: signatures,

GOL-82a
Goldwasser, S., and S. Micali
"Probabilistic Encryption and
How to Play Mental Poker
Keeping Secret All Partial
Information," Proceedings, 14th
Annual ACM Symp. on
Theory of Computing, May
1982, pp. 365-377.

Key Words: methods,
protocols.

GOL-82b
Goldwasser, S., S. Micali, and
P. Tong
"How to Establish a Private
Code on a Public Network,"
Proceedings, 23d Annual IEEE
Symposium on Foundations of
Computing, 1982, pp. 134-144.

Key Words: methods, codes.

GOL-83
Goldreich, O.
"A Simple Protocol for
Signing Protocols," Proc.
Crypto '83, Santa Barbara,
CA, 1983, (8: CHA-84b), pp.
133-135.

Key Words: signatures,
protocols.

GOL-83a
Goldwasser, S., S. Micali,
and A. Yao
"Strong Signature Schems,"
Proc., 15th Annual ACM
Symp. on Theory of Comp.,
1983, pp. 431-439.

Key Words: methods,
signatures.

GOL-84
Goldreich, O., S. Goldwasser,
and S. Micali
"On the Cryptographic
Applications of Random
Functions," Proc. Crypto '84,
Santa Barbara, CA, 1984, (8:
BLA-84a), pp. 276-288.

Key Words: methods,
random.

GOL-84a
Goldreich, O.
"On Concurrent Identification
Protocols," Proc. Eurocrypt
'84, Paris, 1984, (8: BET-
85), pp. 387-396.

Key Words: methods,
protocols.

GOL-84b
Goldwasser, S., and S. Micali
"Probabilistic Encryption,"
Journal of Comp. and System
Science, April 1984, pp. 270-
299.

Key Words: methods, theory.

GOL-85
Goldwasser, S., S. Micali,
and R.L. Rivest
"A 'Paradoxical' Solution to
the Signature Problem," Proc.,
25d Annual IEEE Symp.on
Found. of Comp., 1984, pp.
441-448.

Key Words: signatures,
theory.

GOL-86
Goldreich, O.
"Two Remarks Concerning
the Goldwasser-Micali-Rivest
Signature Scheme" Proc.
Crypto '86, Santa Barbara,
CA, 1986, (8: ODL-87), pp.
104-110.

Key Words: analysis,
signatures.

GOL-86a
Goldreich, O., S. Micali,
and A. Wigderson
"How to Prove All NP
Statements in Zero-Knowledge
and Methodology of
Cryptographic Protocol
Design," Proc. Crypto '86,
Santa Barbara, CA, 1986, (8:
ODL-87), pp. 171-185.

Key Words: protocols, zero.

GOL-86b
Goldreich, O.
"Toward a Theory of
Software Protection," Proc.
Crypto '86, Santa Barbara,
CA, 1986, (8: ODL-87), pp.
426-439.

Key Words: software, theory.

GOL-87
Goldreich, O.
"Towards a Theory of
Software Protection and
Simulation by Oblivious
RAMs," Proceedings, 19th
ACM Symposium on Theory
of Computing, 1987, pp. 182-
194.

Key Words: theory, software.

GOL-87a
Goldreich, O., and R. Vainish
"How to Solve a Protocol
Problem: An Efficiency
Improvement," Proc. Crypto
'87, Santa Barbara, CA, 1987,
(8: POM-88), pp. 73-86

Key Words: methods,
protocols.

GOL-89
Goldwasser, S., et al.
"Efficient Identification
Schemes Using Two Prover
Interactive Proofs," Proc.
Crypto '89, Santa Barbara,
CA, (8: BRA-90), 1989.

Key Words: authentication,
methods.

GOO-84
Goodman, R.M.F., and
A.J. McAuley
"A New Trapdoor Knapsack
Public-key Cryptosystem,"
Proc. Eurocrypt '84, Paris,
1984, (8: BET-85), pp. 150-
158.

Key Words: public-key,
knapsack.

GOR-81
Gordon, J.A.
"Towards a Design for
Cryptosecure Susbstitution
Boxes," Proc. Crypto '81,
Santa Barbara, CA, 1981, (8:
GER-82), pp. 53-63.

Key Words: methods, design.

GRO-84
Groscot, H.
"Estimation of Some
Encryption Functions
Implemented into Smart
Cards," Proc. Eurocrypt '84,
Paris, 1984, (8: BET-85), pp.
470-479.

Key Words: analysis, methods.

GUA-87
Guam, P.
"Cellular Automaton Public
Key Cryptosystem," Complex
Systems, 1987, pp. 51-56.

Key Words: methods, case.

GUI-88
Guillou, L.C., and
J. Quisquater
"A Practical Zero-Knowledge
Protocol Fitted to Security
Microprocessor Minimizing
Both Transmission and
Memory," Proc. Eurocrypt
'88, Davos, 1988, (8: GUN-
89), pp. 123-128.

Key Words: design protocols,
zero.

GUI-89
Guillou, L., et al.
"Public-Key Techniques:
Randomness and
Redundancy," Cryptologia,
April 1989, pp. 167.

Key Words: public-key,
random

GUN-88
Gunther, C.G.
"A Universal Algorithm for
Homophonic Coding," Proc.
Eurocrypt '88, Davos, 1988,
(8: GUN-89), pp. 405-414.

Key Words: algorithms,
coding.

GUN-89
Gunther, C.G.
Advances in Cryptology:
Eurocrypt '88 Proceedings,
Davos, Switzerland, May
1988, Lecture Notes in
Comp. Science No. 330,
Springer-Verlag, New York,
1989.

Key Words: proceedings,
general.

HAR-83
Harari, S.
"Secret Sharing Systems in
Digital Communications," in
Longo, G. (Ed.), Secure
Digital Systems, Springer,
Wien, 1983, pp. 105-110.

Key Words: techniques,
design.

HAR-84
Harari, S.
"Non-Linear Non-
Commutative Functions for
Data Integrity," Proc.
Eurocrypt '84, Paris, 1984, (8:
BET-85), pp. 25-32.

Key Words: integrity, theory.

HAR-89
Harn, L., and T. Keisler
"Two New Efficient
Cryptosystems Based on
Rabin's Scheme: Alternatives
to the RSA Cryptosystem,"
Proc. 5th Security Applicat.
Conf., (4: IEE-89c), 1989, pp.
254-262.

Key Words: methods, public-
key.

HEL-80
Hellman, M.E.
"A Cryptoanalytic Time-
Memory Tradeoff," IEEE
Trans. on Inform. Theory,
July 1980, pp. 401-406.

Key Words: analysis, design.

HEL-81
"On the Necessity of
Cryptoanalytic Exhaustive
Search," Proc. Crypto '81,
Santa Barbara, CA, 1981, (8:
GER-82), pp. 1-5.

Key Words: analysis,
methods.

HEL-82
Hellman, M.E., and
J.M. Reyneri
"Distribution of Drainage in
DES," Proc. Crypto '82, Santa
Barbara, CA, 1982, (8: CHA-
83b), pp. 129-131.

Key Words: DES, design,
methods.

HEN-81
Henry, P.S.
"Fast Encryption Algorithm for
the Knapsack Cryptographic
System," Bell System
Technical Journal, May-June
1981, pp. 767-773.

Key Words: algorithm,
knapsack.

HEP-86
Hepshey, J.E., R.K. Yarlanda
Data Encryption and
Protection, Plenum Press, New
York, 1986.

Key Words: book, general.

HER-83
Herlestam, T.
"On the Complexity of Certain
Crypto Generators," Proc.
IFIP/Sec. '83, Stockholm,
1983, (2: FAK-83), pp. 305-
308.

Key Words: complexity,
methods.

HUA-88
Huang, Y.J., and F. Cohen
"Some Weak Points of One
Fast Cryptographic Checksum
Algorithm and Its
Improvement," Computers &
Security, October 1988, pp.
503-505.

Key Words: vulnerabilities,
algorithms, check-sum.

IMP-87
Impagliazzo, R.,
and M. Yung
"Direct Minimum-Knowledge
Computations," Proc. Crypto
'87, Santa Barbara, CA, 1987,
(8: POM-88), pp. 40-51

Key Words: methods, zero.

ING-81
Ingemarsson, I., and
C.K. Wong
"A User Authentication
Scheme for Shared Data
Based on a Trap-Door One-
Way Function," Information
Processing Letters, April 13,
1981, pp. 63-67.

Key Words: authentication,
trap-door, methods.

ING-82
Ingemarsson, I., D.T. Tang,
and C.K. Wong
"A Conference Key
Distribution System" IEEE
Trans. on Inform. Theory,
1982, pp. 714-720.

Key Words: methods, keys,
case.

JAM-86
James, N.S., R. Lidl, and
H. Niederreiter
"Breaking the Cade Cipher,"
Proc. Crypto '86, Santa
Barbara, CA, 1986, (8: ODL-
87), pp. 60-63.

Key Words: analysis, case.

JAM-88
Jamnig, P.
"Securing the RSA-
Cryptosystem Against
Cycling Attacks,"
Cryptologia, July 1988, pp.
159-164.

Key Words: RSA, analysis,
threats.

JAN-82
Janardan, R., and
K.B. Lakshmanan
"A Public-Key Cryptosystem
Based on the Matrix Cover
NP-Complete Problem," Proc.
Crypto '82, Santa Barbara,
CA, 1982, (8: CHA-83b), pp.
21-37.

Key Words: public-key,
methods.

JAN-87
Jansen, C.J.A., and
D.E. Boekee
"Modes of Block Cipher
Algorithms and Their
Protection Against Active
Eavesdropper," Proc.
Eurocrypt '87, Amsterdam,
1987, (8: CHA-88a), pp. 281-
286.

Key Words: therats, methods,
algorithms.

JIN-88
Jingmin, H., and L. Kaicheng
"A New Probabilistic
Encryption Scheme," Proc.
Eurocrypt '88, Davos, 1988,
(8: GUN-89), pp. 413-418.

Key Words: methods, design.

JOR-81
Jordan, J.P.
"A Variant of a Public-key
Cryptosystem Based on Goppa
Codes," Proc. Crypto '81,
Santa Barbara, CA, 1981, (8:
GER-82), pp. 25-30.

Key Words: methods, public-
key.

JOR-87
Jorissen, F., J. Vandewalle,
and R. Govaerts
"Extension of Brickell's
Algorithm for Breaking High
Density Knapsacks," Proc.
Eurocrypt '87, Amsterdam,
1987, (8: CHA-88a), pp. 109-
115.

Key Words: analysis,
algorithms.

JUE-82
Jueneman, R.R.
"Analysis of Certain Aspects
of Output Feedback Mode,"
Proc. Crypto '82, Santa
Barbara, CA, 1982, (8: CHA-
83b), pp. 99-127.

Key Words: DES, analysis,
design.

JUE-83
Jueneman, R.R.,
S.M. Matyas, and
C.H. Meyer,
"Authentication with
Manipulation Detection
Codes," Proc. 1983 IEEE
Symp. Sec. & Priv., (5: IEE-
83a), pp. 33-54.

Key Words: authentication,
codes.

JUE-86
Juenemam, R.R.
"A High Speed Manipulation
Detection Code," Proc. Crypto
'86, Santa Barbara, CA, 1986,
(8: ODL-87), pp. 327-346.

Key Words: methods, codes,
threats.

JUR-83
Jurgensen, H., and
D.E. Matthews
"Some Results on the
Information Theoretic Analyses
of Cryptosystems," Proc.
Crypto '83, Santa Barbara,
CA, 1983, (8: CHA-84b), pp.
303-356.

Key Words: analysis, theory,
design.

KAH-80
Kahn, D.
"Cryptography Goes Public,"
IEEE Communications
Magazine, March 1980, pp.
19-28.

Key Words: public-key,
general.

KAH-82
Kahn, D.
"The Grand Lines of
Cryptology's Development,"
Computers & Security,
November 1982, pp. 245-248.

Key Words: methods, general.

KAH-84
Kahn, D.
Kahn on Codes, Macmillan,
New York, 1984.

Key Words: book, general.

KAH-84a
Kahn, D.
"Cryptology and the Origins of Spread Spectrum," IEEE Spectrum, September 1984, pp. 70-80

Key Words: methods, general.

KAK-83
Kak, S.C.
"Joint Encryption and Error Correction," Proc. 1983 IEEE Symp. Sec. & Privacy, (5: IEE-83a), pp. 55-60.

Key Words: methods, codes.

KAK-84
Kak, S.C.
"On the Method of Puzzles for Key Distribution," Internat. Journal of Computer and Information Science, April 1984, pp. 103-109.

Key Words: methods, keys.

KAL-84
Kaliski, B.S.
"Wyner's Analog Encryption Scheme: Results of a Simulation," Proc. Crypto '84, Santa Barbara, CA, 1984, (8: BLA-84a), pp. 83-94.

Key Words:

KAL-85
Kaliski, B.S., Jr., R.L. Rivest, and A.T. Sherman
"Is the Data Encryption Standard a Group?," Journal of Cryptology, Vol. 1, No. 1, 1988, pp. 3-36.

Key Words: DES, design, theory.

KAL-85a
Kaliski, B.S. Jr, R.L. Rivest and A.T. Sherman
"Is DES a Pure Cipher?," Proc. Crypto '85, Santa Barbara, CA, 1985, (8: WIL-86), pp. 212-226.

Key Words: DES, design, theory.

KAR-83
Karnin, E.D., et al.
"On Secret Sharing Systems," IEEE Trans. on Inform. Theory, 1983, pp. 35-41.

Key Words: methods, general.

KAR-84
Karnin, E.D.
"A Parallel Algorithm for the Knapsack Problem," IEEE Trans. on Computers, May 1984, pp. 404-408.

Key Words: algorithm, knapsack.

KES-88
Kesim, S.N.
"Encryption: Security with Ciphers," Security Management, October 1988, pp. 45-47.

Key Words: methods, general.

KOB-87
Koblitz, N.
A Course in Number Theory and Cryptography, Springer, New York, 1987.

Key Words: book, general.

KOB-87a
Koblitz, N.
"Elliptic Curve Cryptosystems," Mathematics of Computation, 1987, pp. 203-209.

Key Words: methods, theory.

KOB-89
Koblitz, N.
"Hyperelliptic Cryptosystem," Journal of Cryptology, Vol. 1, No. 3, 1989, pp. 139-150.

Key Words: methods, theory.

KON-80
Konheim, A.G., et al.
"The IPS Cryptographic Programs," IBM Systems Journal, Vol. 19, No. 2, 1980, pp. 153-283.

Key Words: methods, software.

KON-81
Konheim, A.G.
Cryptography - A Primer, J. Wiley & Sons, New York, 1981.

Key Words: book, general.

KON-84
Konheim, A.G.
"Cryptanalysis of ADFGVX Encryption Systems," Proc. Crypto '84, Santa Barbara, CA, 1984, (8: BLA-84a), pp. 339-341.

Key Words: analysis, method, case.

KOT-84
Kothari, S.C.
"Generalized Linear Threshold Scheme," Proc. Crypto '84, Santa Barbara, CA, 1984, (8: BLA-84a), pp. 231-241.

Key Words: methods, theory.

KOY-87
Koyama, K., and K. Ohta
"Identity-Based Conference Key Distribution Systems," Proc. Crypto '87, Santa Barbara, CA, 1987, (8: POM-88), pp. 175-184.

Key Words: methods, keys.

KOY-88
Koyama, K., and K. Ohta
"Security of Improved Identity-Based Key Distribution System," Proc. Eurocrypt-87, pp. 11-19.

Key Words: methods, keys.

KRA-86
Kranakis, E.
Primality and Cryptography, Wiley, New York, 1986.

Key Words: book, general.

KUR-88
Kurosawa, K., T. Ito, and M. Takeuchi "Public Key Cryptosystem Using a Reciprocal Number with the Same Intractability as Factoring a Large Number," Cryptologia, October 1988, pp. 225-233.

Key Words: methods, public-key.

LAG-83
Lagarias, J.C. "Knapsack Public Key Cryptosystems and Diophantine Approximations," Proc. Crypto '83, Santa Barbara, CA, 1983, (8: CHA-84b), pp. 4-23.

Key Words: public-key, knapsack.

LAI-89
Laih, C.-S., et al. "Linearly Shift Knapsack Public Key Cryptosystem," IEEE Journal on Selected Areas in Communications, May 1989, pp. 534-539.

Key Words: methods, knapsack.

LAK-83
Laksmivarahan, S. "Algorithms for Public-Key Cryptosystems: Theory and Applications," in M. Yovits, (Ed.), Advances in Computers, Vol. 22, Academic Press, New York, 1983, pp. 45-108.

Key Words: public-key, methods.

LAM-81
Lamport, L. "Pasword Authentication with Insecure Communications," Communications of the ACM, November 1981, pp. 770-772.

Key Words: authentication.

LEE-88
Lee, P.J., and E.F. Brickell "An Observation on the Security of McElice's Public-Key Cryptosystem, Proc. Eurocrypt '88, Davos, 1988 (8: GUN-89), pp. 275-280.

Key Words: analysis, public-key.

LEI-84
Leighton, A.C., and S.M. Matyas "The History of Book Ciphers," Proc. Crypto '84, Santa Barbara, CA, 1984, (8: BLA-84a), pp. 101-113.

Key Words: methods, general.

LEN-81
Lennon, R.E., et al. "Cryptographic Authentication of Time-Invariant Quantities," IEEE Trans. on Communications, June 1981, pp. 773-777.

Key Words: authentication.

LEU-84
Leung, A.K. "Sequenec Complexity as a Test for Cryptographic Systems," Proc. Crypto '84, Santa Barbara, CA, 1984, (8: BLA-84a), pp. 468-474.

Key Words: methods, complexity.

LEV-85
Levin, L. "One-Way Functions and Pseudo-random Generators," Proc., 17th Annual ACM Symp. on Theory of Computing, 1985, pp. 363-365.

Key Words: Methods, one-way,

LEV-87
Levine, J., and R. Chandler "Some Further Applications of Permutation Polynomials," Cryptologia, October 1987, pp. 211-218.

Key Words: methods, theory.

LID-83
Lidl, R., and W.B. Muller "Permutation Polynomials in RSA Cryptosystems," Proc. Crypto '83, Santa Barbara, CA, 1983, (8: CHA-84b), pp. 293-301.

Key Words: RSA, methods, theory.

LID-84
Lidl, R. "On Cryptosystems Based on Polynomials and Finite Fields," Proc. Eurocrypt '84, Paris, 1984, (8: BET-85), pp. 10-15.

Key Words: methods, theory.

LON-82
Longpre, L. "The Use of Public-Key Cryptography for Signing Checks," Proc. Crypto '82, Santa Barbara, CA, 1982, (8: CHA-83b), pp. 187-197.

Key Words: signatures, public-key.

LUB-87
Luby, M., and C. Rackoff "A Study of Password Security," Proc. Crypto '87, Santa Barbara, CA, 1987, (8: POM-88), pp. 392-397.

Key Words: methods, general.

MAD-84
Madryga, W.E. "A High Performance Encryption Algorithm," Proc. IFIP/Sec. '84, Toronto, 1984, (2: FIN-85), pp. 557-570.

Key Words: methods, algorithm.

MAG-89
Magliveras, S.S., and N.D. Memon "Algebraic Properties of the PGM Cryptosystem" Proc. Crypto '89, Santa Barbara, CA, 1989 (8: BRA-89).

Key Words: methods, theory, case.

MAS-84
Massey, J.L., and
R.A. Rueppel
"Linear Ciphers and Random
Sequence Generators with
Multiple Clocks," Proc.
Eurocrypt '84, Paris, 1984,
(8: BET-85), pp. 74-87.

Key Words: methods, design.

MAS-88
Massey, J.L.
"An Introduction to
Contemporary Cryptology,"
Proceedings of the IEEE,
May 1988, pp. 533-549.

Key Words: methods, theory,
general.

MAT-86
Matyas, S.M.
"Public Key Registration,"
Proc. Crypto '86, Santa
Barbara, CA, 1986, (8: ODL-
87), pp. 451-458.

Key Words: methods, public-
key.

MAT-88
Matsumoto, T., and H. Imai
"Public Quadratic
Polynomial-Tuples for
Efficient Signature
Verification and Message
Encryption," Proc. Eurocrypt
'88, Davos, 1988, (8: GUN-
89), pp. 419-453.

Key Words: methods,
signatures.

MCC-88
McCurley, K.S.
"A Key Distribution System
Equivalent to Factoring,"
Journal of Cryptology, Vol.
1, No. 2, 1988, pp. 95-105.

Key Words: methods, keys,
case.

MCE-81
McElicie, R.J., and
D.V. Sarwate
"On Sharing Secrets and
Reed-Solomon Codes,"
Communications of the ACM,
September 1981, pp. 583-584.

Key Words: theory, codes.

MEA-87
Meadows, C., and
D. Mutchler
"Matching Secrets in the
Absence of a Continuously
Available Trusted Authority,"
IEEE Trans. on Software
Engr., February 1987, pp.
289-292.

Key Words: methods,
protocols.

MEA-88
Meadows, C.,
"Some Threshold Schemes
Without Central Key
Distribution," Proc. Crypto
'88, Santa Barbara, CA, 1988
(8: GOL-89b).

Key Words: methods, keys.

MEI-82
Meijer, H., and S. Akl
"Digital Signature Schemes,"
Cryptologia, October 1982,
pp. 329-338

Key Words: methods,
signatures.

MEI-85
Meijer, H., and S. Akl
"Two New Secret Key
Cryptosystems," Proc.
Eurocrypt '85, Linz, 1985, (8:
PIC-86), pp. 96-102.

Key Words: methods,
algorithms.

MEI-88
Meier, W., and
O. Staffelbach
"Fast Correlation Attacks on
Stream Ciphers," Proc.
Eurocrypt '88, Davos, 1988,
(8: GUN-89), pp. 301-314.

Key Words: analysis,
methods.

MEI-89
Meier, W., and
O. Staffelbach
"Fast Correlation Attacks on
Certain Stream Ciphers,"
Journal of Cryptology, Vol. 1,
No. 3, 1989, pp. 159-176.

Key Words: analysis, methods.

MER-80
Merkle, R.C.
"Protocols for Public Key
Cryptosystems," Proc. 1980
IEEE Symp. Sec. & Privacy,
(5: IEE-80), pp. 122-134.

Key Words: protocols, public-
key.

MER-81
Merkle, R.C.
"On the Security of Multiple
Encryptions," Communications
of the ACM, July 1981, pp.
465-467.

Key Words: analysis, methods.

MER-82
Merritt, M.
"Key Reconstruction," Proc.
Crypto '82, Santa Barbara,
CA, 1982, (8: CHA-83b), pp.
321-375.

Key Words: methods, keys,
design.

MER-82a
Merkle, R.C.
Security, Authentication, and
Public-Key Systems, University
of Michigan Press, Ann Arbor,
MI, 1982.

Key Words: book, public-key.

MER-87
Merkle, R.C.
"A Digital Signature Based on
a Conventional Encryption
Function," Proc. Crypto '87,
Santa Barbara, CA, 1987, (8:
POM-88), pp. 369-378.

Key Words: methods,
signatures.

MER-89
Merkle, R.C.
"A Certified Digital
Signature," Proc. Crypto '89,
Santa Barbara, CA, 1989, (8:
BRA-89).

Key Words: signatures, case.

MER-89a
Merkle, R.C.
"One Way Hash Functions
and the DES," Proc. Crypto
'89, Santa Barbara, CA,
1989, (8: BRA-89).

Key Words: DES, methods,
design.

MEY-82
Meyer, C.H., and
S.M. Matyas
Cryptography - A New
Dimension in Computer Data
Security, J. Wiley & Sons,
New York, 1982.

Key Words: book, general,
theory, methods, keys.

MIC-86
Micali, S., et al.
"The Notion of Security for
Probabilistic Cryptosystems,"
Proc. Crypto '86, Santa
Barbara, CA, 1986, (8: ODL-
87), pp. 381-392.

Key Words: methods, theory.

MIC-89
Micali, S.
"Digital Signatures: The
Evolution of a Fundamental
Primitive," Proc. Crypto '89,
Santa Barbara, CA, 1989, (8:
BRA-89).

Key Words: signatures,
theory.

MIL-85
Miller, V.S.
"Use of Elliptic Curves in
Cryptography," Proc. Crypto
'85, Santa Barbara, CA,
1985, (8: WIL-86), pp. 415-
426.

Key Words: methods, theory.

MOO-85
Moore, T.E., and S.E. Tavares
"A Layered Approach to the
Design of Private Key
Cryptosystems," Proc. Crypto
'85, Santa Barbara, CA, 1985,
(8: WIL-86), pp. 227-245.

Key Words: methods, design,
case.

MOO-86
Moore, J.H., and
G.J. Simmons
"Cycle Structures of the DES
with Weak and Semiweak
Keys," Proc. Crypto '86,
Santa Barbara, CA, 1986, (8:
ODL-87), pp. 187-205.

Key Words: DES, analysis,
design.

MOO-87
Moore, J.H., and
G.J. Simmons
"Cycle Structure of the DES
for Keys Having Palindromic
(or Anti-palindromic)
Sequences of Keys," IEEE
Trans. of Software Engr.,
February 1987, pp. 262-273.

Key Words: DES, analysis,
design.

MOR-81
Morrison, D.R.
"Subtractive Encryptors --
Alternatives to the DES,"
Proc. Crypto '81, Santa
Barbara, CA, 1981, (8: GER-
82), pp. 42-52.

Key Words: DES, methods,
case.

MUL-84
Mullin, A.A.
"A Note on the Mathematics
of Public-Key Cryptosystems,"
Computers & Security,
February 1984, pp. 45-47.

Key Words: public-key,
theory.

NIE-85
Niederreiter, H.
"A Public-Key Cryptosystem
Based on Shift Register
Sequences," Proc. Eurocrypt
'85, Linz, 1985, (8: PIC-86),
pp. 35-39.

Key Words: methods, public-
key.

OCO-87
O'Connor, L.J. and
J. Seberry
The Cryptographic Significance
of the Knapsack Problem,
Aegean Park Press, Laguna
Hills, CA, 1987.

Key Words: book, knapsack,
analysis, theory.

ODL-84
Odlyzko, A.M.
"Cryptanalytic Attacks on the
Multiplicative Knapsack
Cryptosystem and on Shamir's
Fast Signature System, IEEE
Trans. on Inform. Theory, July
1984, pp. 594-601.

Key Words: analysis,
knapsack, signatures.

ODL-84a
Odlyzko, A.M.
"Discrete Logarithms in Finite
Fields and Their Cryptographic
Significance," Proc. Eurocrypt
'84, Paris, 1984, (8: BET-85),
pp. 225-314.

Key Words: methods, theory.

ODL-87
Odlyzko, A.M., (Ed.)
Advances in Cryptology,
Proceedings of Crypto '86,
Santa Barbara, CA, August
1988, Lecture Notes in
Computer Science No. 263,
Springer-Verlag, New York,
1987.

Key Words: proceedings,
general.

OKA-85
Okamoto, T., and
A. Shiraishi
"A Fast Signature Scheme
Based on Quadratic
Inequalities," Proc. 1985
IEEE Symp. Sec. & Privacy,
1985, (5: IEE-85), pp. 123-
133.

Key Words: methods,
signatures.

OKA-85a
Okamoto, E., and
K. Nakamura
"Lifetimes of Keys in
Cryptographic Key
Management Systems," Proc.
Crypto '85, Santa Barbara,
CA, 1985, (8: WIL-86), pp.
246-259.

Key Words: keys,
management.

OKA-86
Okamoto, E.
"Proposal for Identity-Based
Key Distribution Systems,"
Electronics Letters, Nov. 20,
1986, pp. 1283-1284.

Key Words: methods, keys.

OKA-87
Okamoto, E.
"Key Distribution Systems
Based on Identification
Information," Proc. Crypto
'87, Santa Barbara, CA,
1987, (8: POM-88), pp. 194-
202.

Key Words: keys,
management.

OKA-88
Okamoto, E.
"Substantial Number of
Cryptographic Keys and Its
Application to Encryption
Design," Proc. Eurocrypt '88,
Davos, 1988, (8: GUN-89),
pp. 361-373

Key Words: methods, keys,
design.

OKA-88a
Okamoto, T.
"A Digital Multisignature
Scheme Using Bijective
PublicKey Cryptosystems,"
ACM Trans. on Computer
Systems, November 1988, pp.
432-441.

Key Words: methods,
signatures.

OKA-89
Okamoto, E., and K. Ohta
"Disposable Zero-Knowledge
Authentications and Their
Application to Untraceable
Electronic Cash," Proc. Crypto
'89, Santa Barbara, CA, 1989
(8: BRA-89).

Key Words: methods, zero,
design.

ONG-83
Ong, H., and C.P. Schorr
"Signatures through
Approximate Representations
by Quadratic Forms," Proc.
Crypto '83, Santa Barbara,
CA, 1983, (8: CHA-84b), pp.
117-132.

Key Words: methods,
signatures.

ONG-84
Ong, H., C. Schnorr,
and A. Shamir
"Efficient Signature Schemes
Based on Polynomial
Equations," Proc. Crypto '84,
Santa Barbara, CA, 1984, (8:
BLA-84a), pp. 37-46.

Key Words: methods,
signatures.

PAT-87
Patterson, W.
Mathematical Cryptology for
Computer Scientists and
Mathematicians, Rowman &
Littlefield, Totowa, NJ, 1987.

Key Words: book, theory.

PFI-87
Pfitzmann and M. Waidner
"Networks Without User
Observability," Computers &
Security, April 1987, pp. 158-
166.

Key Words: methods, case.

PIC-86
Pichler, F. (Ed.)
Advances in Cryptology:
Proceedings of Eurocrypt '85,
Linz, Austria, April 1985,
Lecture Notes in Comp.
Science, No. 219, Springer-
Verlag, New York, 1986.

Key Words: proceedings,
general.

PIE-84
Pieprzyk, J.P.
"Algebraical Structures of
Cryptographic
Transformations," Proc.
Eurocrypt '84, Paris, 1984, (8:
BET-85), pp. 16-24.

Key Words: algorithms, theory.

PIE-85
Pieprzyk, J.P.
"On Public-Key Cryptosystems
Built Using Polynomial
Rings," Proc. Eurocrypt '85,
Linz, 1985, (8: PIC-86), pp.
73-78.

Key Words: methods, public-
key.

PIE-85a
Pieprzyk, J.P., D.A. Rutowski
"Modular Design of
Information Encipherment for
Computer Systems," Computers
& Security, September 1985,
pp. 211-218.

Key Words: methods, design.

PIE-85b
Pieprzyk, J.P.,
D.A. Rutkowski
"Design of Public Key
Cryptosystems Using
Idempotent Elements,"
Computers & Security,
December 1985, pp. 297-308.

Key Words: design, public-
key.

PIP-89
Piper, F., and M. Walker
"Linear Ciphers and
Spreads," Journal of
Cryptology, Vol. 1, No. 3,
1989, pp. 185-188.

Key Words: methods, theory.

POE-85
Poet, R.
"The Design of Special-
Purpose Hardware to Factor
Large Integers," Computer
Physics Communications,
1985, pp. 337-341.

Key Words: analysis,
hardware.

POM-83
Pomerance, C., et al.,
"New Ideas for Factoring
Large Integers," Proc. Crypto
'83, Santa Barbara, CA,
1983, (8: CHA-84b), pp. 81-
86.

Key Words: analysis,
algorithms.

POM-85
Pomerance, C.
"The Quadratic Sieve
Factoring Algorithm," Proc.
Eurocrypt '84, Paris, (8:
BET-85), pp. 169-182.

Key Words: analysis,
algorithms.

POM-88
Pomerance, C., (Ed.)
Advances in Cryptology:
Proceedings of Crypto '87,
Santa Barbara, CA, August
1988, Lecture Notes in
Computer Science No. 293,
Springer, New York, 1988.

Key Words: proceedings,
general.

POR-84
Porter, S.
"Cryptology and Number
Sequences: Pseudorandom,
Random, and Perfectly
Random," Computers &
Security, February 1984, pp.
43-44.

Key Words: algorithms,
theory.

PRE-89
Preneel, B., et al.
"A Chosen Text Attack on the
Modified Cryptographic
Checksum Algorithm of
Cohen and Huang," Proc.
Crypto '89, Santa Barbara,
CA, 1989, (8: BRA-89).

Key Words: analysis,
checksum.

PRO-84
Proctor, N.
"A Self-Synchronizing
Cascaded Cipher System with
Dynamic Control of Error
Propagation," Proc. Crypto
'84, Santa Barbara, CA, 1984,
(8: BLA-84a), pp. 174-190.

Key Words: methods, design.

QUI-85
Quisquater, J.-J., Y. Desmedt,
and M. Davio
"The Importance of 'Good'
Key Scheduling Schemes
(How to Make a Secure DES
Scheme with <48-Bit
Keys>?)," Proc. Crypto '85,
Santa Barbara, CA, 1985, (8:
WIL-86), pp. 537-542.

Key Words: DES, methods,
design.

QUI-87
Quisquater, J.-J.
"Secret Distribution of Keys
for Public-Key Systems," Proc.
Crypto '87, Santa Barbara,
CA, 1987, (8: POM-88), pp.
203-208.

Key Words: public-key, keys.

QUI-89
Quisquater, J., and
J. Delescaille
"How Easy Is Collision
Search? New Results and
Applications to DES," Proc.
Crypto '89, Santa Barbara,
CA, 1989 (8: BRA-89).

Key Words: DES, methods,
design.

QUI-89a
Quisquater, J.-J., and K.Vedder
"A Signature with Shared
Verification Scheme," Proc.
Crypto '89, Santa Barbara,
CA, 1989 (8: BRA-89).

Key Words: verification,
signature.

QUI-89b
Quisquater, J.-J., (Ed.)
Advances in Cryptology:
Proceedings of Eurocrypt-89,
Houthalen, Belgium, April 10-
13, 1989, Lecture Notes in
Computer Science, Springer-
Verlag, New York, 1989.

Key Words: proceedings,
gneral.

RAO-84
Rao, T.R.N.
"Joint Encryption and Error
Correction Schemes," Proc.,
11th Intern. Symp. on Comp.
Arch., May 1984.

Key Words: methods, codes.

RAO-86
Rao, T.R.N., and K.-H. Nam
"Private-Key Algebraic-Coded
Cryptosystems," Proc. Crypto
'86, Santa Barbara, CA, 1986,
(8: ODL-87), pp. 35-48.

Key Words: methods, codes.

RAO-87
Rao, T.R.N.
"On Struik-Tilburg
Cryptanalysis of Rao-Nam
Scheme," Proc. Crypto '87,
Santa Barbara, CA, 1987, (8:
POM-88), pp. 458-461.

Key Words: analysis,
methods, case.

RAO-89
Rao, T.R.N., and K.H. Nam
"Private-Key Algebraic-Code
Encryptions," IEEE Trans. on
Inform. Theory, July 1989,
pp. 829-833.

Key Words: methods, codes.

REE-84
Reeds, J.A., and
J. Manferdelli
"DES Has No Per Round
Linear Factors," Proc. Crypto
'84, Santa Barbara, CA,
1984, (8: BLA-84a), pp. 377-
389

Key Words: DES, analysis,
design.

RIT-81
Ritts, R.R.
"Data Encryption Basics and
the Cipher Feedback
Method,"
Telecommunications, June
1981, pp. 39-44.

Key Words: methods, theory.

RIV-82
Rivest, R.L., and
A.T. Sherman
"Randomized Encryption
Technique," Proc. Crypto '82,
Santa Barbara, CA, 1982, (8:
CHA-83b), pp. 145-163.

Key Words: methods, design,
random.

RIV-84
Rivest, R.L., and A. Shamir
"How to Expose an
Eavesdropper,"
Communications of the ACM,
April 1984, pp. 393-395.

Key Words: analysis, threat,
methods.

RUB-81
Rubin, F.
"Decrypting a Stream Cipher
Based on J-K Flip-Flops,"
Cryptologia, January 1981, pp.
51-57.

Key Words: analysis,
methods.

RUB-87
Rubin, F.
"Foiling an Exhaustive Key-
Search Attack," Cryptologia,
April 1987, pp. 102-107

Key Words: analysis,
methods.

RUE-86
Rueppel, R.
Analysis and Design of
Stream Ciphers, Springer
Verlag, New York, 1986.

Key Words: book, analysis,
design.

RUE-88
Rueppel, R.
"Key Agreements Based on
Function Composition," Proc.
Eurocrypt '88, Davos, 1988,
(8: GUN-89), pp. 3-10.

Key Words: methods, keys.

RUG-84
Ruggiu, G.
"Cryptology and Complexity
Theories," Proc. Eurocrypt
'84, Paris, 1984, (8: BET-85),
pp. 3-9.

Key Words: methods,
complexity.

SAL-88
Salomaa, A.
"A Public-Key Cryptosystem
Based on Language Theory,"
Computers & Security,
February 1988, pp. 83-87.

Key Words: methods, theory.

SCH-84
Schnorr, C.P., and W. Alexi
"RSA-bits are 0.5 + e Secure,"
Proc. Eurocrypt '84, Paris,
1984, (8: BET-85), pp. 113-
126.

Key Words: RSA, analysis,
theory.

SEB-89
Seberry, J., and J. Pieprzyk
Cryptography: An Introduction
to Computer Security, Prentice-
Hall, New York, 1989

Key Words: book, general.

SGA-83
Sgarro, A.
"Error Probabilities for Simple
Substitution Ciphers," IEEE
Trans. on Inform. Theory,
1983, pp. 190-198.

Key Words: methods, analysis,
theory.

SGA-84
Sgarro, A.
"Equivocations for
Homophonic Ciphers," Proc.
Eurocrypt '84, Paris, 1984, (8:
BET-85), pp. 51-61.

Key Words: methods, theory.

SHA-80
Shamir, A.
"The Cryptographic Security of
Compact Knapsacks," Proc.
1980 IEEE Symp. Sec. &
Privacy, (5: IEE-80), pp. 94-98

Key Words: analysis,
knapsack.

SHA-80
Shamir, A.,,and R.E. Zippel
"On the Security of the
Merkle-Hellman
Cryptographic Systems,"
IEEE Trans. on Inform.
Theory, May 1980, pp. 339-
340.

Key Words: analysis,
knapsack.

SHA-81
Shamir, A., R.L. Rivest,
and L. Adleman
"Mental Poker," in Klarner,
D.E. (Ed.), Mathematical
Gardner, Wadsworth, NY,
1981, pp. 37-43.

Key Words: methods,
protocols.

SHA-83
Shamir, A.
"On Generation of
Computationally Strong
Pseudo-Random Sequences,"
ACM Trans. on Computer
Systems, May 1983, pp. 38-
44.

Key Words: algorithms,
random.

SHA-84
Shamir, A.
"A Polynomial-Time
Algorithm for Breaking the
Basic Merkle-Hellman
Cryptosystem," IEEE Trans.
of Inform. Theory, September
1984, pp. 525-530.

Key Words: analysis,
algorithm, knapsack.

SHA-84a
Shamir, A.
"Identity-Based
Cryptosystems and Signature
Schemes," Proc. Crypto '84,
Santa Barbara, CA, 1984, (8:
BLA-84a), pp. 45-53.

Key Words: methods,
signatures.

SIE-84
Siegenthaler, T.
"Correlation-Immunity of
Nonlinear Combining
Functions for Cryptographic
Applications," IEEE Trans. of
Inform. Theory, September
1984, pp. 776-780.

Key Words: algorithms,
theory.

SIE-85
Siegenthaler, T.
"Decrypting a Class of Sream
Ciphers Using Ciphertext
Only," IEEE Trans. on
Computers, January 1985, pp.
81-85.

Key Words: analysis,
methods.

SIM-80
Simmons, G.J.
"Secure Communications in
the Presence of Pervasive
Deceit," Proc. 1980 IEEE
Symp. Sec. & Privacy, (5:
IEE-80), pp. 84-93.

Key Words: therats, methods.

SIM-81
Simmons, G.J.
"A System for Point-of-Sale
or Access, User Authntication
and Identification," Proc.
Crypto '81, Santa Barbara,
CA, 1981, (8: GER-82), pp.
31-37.

Key Words: authentication.

SIM-81a
Simmons, G.J.
"Half a Loaf Is Better than
None: Some Novel Message
Integrity Problems," Proc.
1981 IEEE Symp. Sec. &
Privacy, (5: IEE-81), pp. 65-
69.

Key Words: authentication.

SIM-82
Simmons, G.J., and
D. Holdridge
"Forward Search as a
Cryptanalytic Tool Against
Public Key Privacy Channel,"
Proc. 1982 IEEE Symp. Sec.
& Privacy, (5: IEE-82), pp.
117-128.

Key Words:analysis, public-
key.

SIM-82a
Simmons, G.J.
"A Game Theory Model of
Digital Message
Authentication," Congressus
Numerantium, 1982, pp. 413-
424.

Key Words: authentication,
models.

SIM-83
Simmons, G.J.
"The Prisoners' Problem and
the Subliminal Channel," Proc.
Crypto '83, Santa Barbara,
CA, 1983, (8: CHA-84b), pp.
51-67.

Key Words: analysis, methods.

SIM-83a
Simmons, G.J.
"Verification of Treaty
Compliance Revisited," Proc.
1983 IEEE Symp. Sec. &
Privacy, (5: IEE-83a), pp. 61-
66.

Key Words: verification,
methods.

SIM-84
Simmons, G.J.
"Authentication Theory/Coding
Theory," Proc. Crypto '84,
Santa Barbara, CA, 1984, (8:
BLA-84a), pp. 411-431.

Key Words: authentication,
codes, theory.

SIM-84a
Simmons, G.J.
"The Subliminal Channel and Digital Signatures," Proc. Eurocrypt '84, Paris, 1984, (8: BET-85), pp. 364-378.

Key Words: theory, signaturtes

SIM-84b
Simmons, G.J.
"Message Authentication: A Game on Hypergraphs," Congressus Numerantium, 1984, pp. 161-192.

Key Words: models, authentication.

SIM-85
Simmons, G.J.
"A Secure Subliminal Channel (?)" Proc. Crypto '85, Santa Barbara, CA, 1985, (8: WIL-86), pp. 33-41.

Key Words: methods, theory.

SIM-85a
Simmons, G.J.
"How to (Selectively) Broadcast a Secret," Proc. 1985 IEEE Symp. Sec. & Privacy, (5: IEE-85), pp. 108-113.

Key Words: methods, protocols.

SIM-86
Simmons, G.J.
"Cryptology," Encyclopedia Britannica, Encyclopaedia Britannica, Inc., Chigaco, IL, 1986, pp. 913-924B.

Key Words: methods, general.

SIM-87
Simmons, G.J.
"An Impersonation-Proof Identity Verification Scheme," Proc. Crypto '87, Santa Barbara, CA, 1987, (8: POM-88), pp. 211-215.

Key Words: authentication, case.

SIM-87a
Simmons, G.J.
"A Natural Taxonomy for Digital Information Authentication Schemes," Proc. Crypto '87, Santa Barbara, CA, 1987, (8: POM-88), pp. 269-288

Key Words: authentication, theory.

SIM-88
Simmons, G.J.
"Authentication Codes that Permit Arbitration," Congressus Numerantium, March 1988, pp. 275-290.

Key Words: authentication, codes.

SIM-88a
Simmons, G.J.
"How to (Really) Share a Secret," Proc. Crypto '88, Santa Barbara, CA, 1988 (8: GOL-89b).

Key Words: methods, protocols.

SIM-88b
Simmons, G.J., and G.B. Purdy
"Zero-Knowledge Proofs of Identity and Veracity of Transaction Receipts," Proc. Eurocrypt '88, Davos, 1988, (8: GUN-89), pp. 35.

Key Words: protocols, zero.

SIM-89
Simmons, G.J.
"Prepositioned Shared Secret and/or Shared Control Schemes," Proc. Eurocrypt '89, Houthalen, 1989, (8: QUI-89).

Key Words: methods, protocols.

SIM-89a
Simmons, G.J.
"A Protocol to Provide Verifiable Proof of Identity and Unforgeable Transaction Receipts," IEEE J. Selected Areas in Comm., May 1989, pp. 435-447.

Key Words: methods, protocols.

SLO-82
Sloane, N.J.A.
"Error-Correcting Codes and Cryptology, Part 1," Cryptologia, April 1982, pp. 128-153.

Key Words: methods, codes.

SLO-82a
Sloane, N.J.A.
"Error-Correcting Codes and Cryptology, Part 2," Cryptologia, July 1982, pp. 258-278.

Key Words: methods, codes.

SME-84
Smeets, B.J.M.
"On the Use of the Binary Multiplying Channel in a Private Communication Channel," Proc. Eurocrypt '84, Paris, 1984, (8: BET-85), 339-348.

Key Words: methods, design.

SME-85
Smeets, B.
"A Comment on Niedereiter's Public-Key Cryptosystem," Proc. Eurocrypt '85, Linz, 1985, (8: PIC-86), pp. 40-42.

Key Words: analysis, public-key.

SPE-83
Spencer, M.E., and S.E. Tavares
"A Layered Broadcast Cryptographic System," Proc. Crypto '83, Santa Barbara, CA, 1983, (8: CHA-84b), pp. 157-170.

Key Words: methods, case.

STI-87
Stinson, D.R., and
S.A. Vanstone
"A Combinatorial Approach
to Threshold Schemes," Proc.
Crypto '87, Santa Barbara,
CA, 1987, (8: POM-88), pp.
330-339.

Key Words: methods, keys.

STI-87a
Stinson, D.R.
"A Construction of
Authentication/Secrecy Codes
from Certain Combinatorial
Designs," Proc. Crypto '87,
Santa Barbara, CA, 1987, (8:
POM-88), pp. 255-366.

Key Words: authentication,
codes, design, case.

STI-88
Stinson, D.R.
"Some Constructions and
Bounds for Authentication
Codes," Journal of
Cryptology, Vol. 1, No. 1,
1988, pp. 37-64.

Key Words: authentication,
theory design, codes.

STI-88a
Stinson, D.R.
"A Construction for
Authentication/Secrecy Codes
from Certain Combinatorial
Designs," Journal of
Cryptology, Vol. 1, No. 2,
1988, pp. 119-127.

Key Words: authentication,
codes, design, theory.

STR-87
Struik, R. , and J. van
Tilburg
"The Rao-Nam Scheme in
Insecure Against a Chosen
Plaintext Attack," Proc.
Crypto '87, Santa Barbara,
CA, 1987, (8: POM-88), pp.
445-457.

Key Words: analysis, case.

TAN-87
Tanaka, H.
"A Realization Scheme for the
Identity-Based Cryptosystem,"
Proc. Crypto '87, Santa
Barbara, CA, 1987, (8: POM-
88), pp. 340-349.

Key Words: methods, design.

TED-84
Tedrick, T.
"Fair Exchange of Secrets,"
Proc. Crypto '84, Santa
Barbara, CA, 1984, (8: BLA-
84a), pp. 434-438.

Key Words: methods,
protocols.

TOM-86
Tompa, M., and H. Woll
"How to Share a Secret With
Cheaters," Proc. Crypto '86,
Santa Barbara, CA, 1986, (8:
ODL-87), pp. 261-265.

Key Words: methods,
protocols.

TSU-89
Tsujii, S., and T. Itoh
"An ID-Based Cryptosystem
Based on Discrete Logarithm
Problem," IEEE Journal on
Selected Areas in
Communications, May 1989,
pp. 467-473.

Key Words: methods, case.

VAL-88
Vallee, B., et al.
"How to Break Okamoto's
Cryptosystem by Reducing
Lattice Bases," Proc.
Eurocrypt '88, Davos, 1988,
(8: GUN-89), pp. 281-291.

Key Words: analysis,
methods.

VAN-85
van Tilborg, J., and
D.E. Boekee
"Divergence Bounds on Key
Encryption and Error
Probability in Cryptanalysis,"
Proc. Crypto '85, Santa
Barbara, CA, 1985, (8: WIL-
86), pp. 489-513.

Key Words: methods, keys,
theory.

VAN-87
van de Graaf, J., and
R. Peralta
"A Simple and Secure Way to
Show the Validity of Your
Public Key," Proc. Crypto '87,
Santa Barbara, CA, 1987, (8:
POM-88), pp. 128-134.

Key Words: methods, public-
key.

VAN-88
van Tilborg, J.
An Introduction to Cryptology,
Kluwer Academic Publishers,
Norwell, MA, 1988.

Key Words: book, general.

VAR-85
Varadharajan, V.
"Extension of RSA
Cryptosystems to Matrix
Rings," Cryptologia, April
1985, pp. 140-153.

Key Words: RSA, theory,
case.

VAR-85a
Varadharajan, V.
"Trapdoor Rings and Their
Use in Cryptography," Proc.
Crypto '85, Santa Barbara,
CA, 1985, (8: WIL-86), pp.
369-395.

Key Words: methods, theory.

WAG-84
Wagner, N.R.
"A Public-Key Cryptosystem
Based on the Word Problem,"
Proc. Crypto '84, Santa
Barbara, CA, 1984, (8: BLA-
84a), pp. 19-36.

Key Words: methods, case.

WAG-84a
Wagner, N.
"Search for Public-Key Cryptosystems," Proc. Crypto '84, Santa Barbara, CA, 1984, (8: BLA-84a), pp. 91-98.

Key Words: methods, public-key.

WAG-85
Wagner, N.R., P.S. Putter, and M.R. Cain
"Using Algorithms as Keys in Stream Ciphers," Proc. Eurocrypt '85, Linz, 1985, (8: PIC-86), pp. 149-155.

Key Words: methods, keys.

WAG-86
Wagner, N.
"Large-Scale Randomization Techniques," Proc. Crypto '86, Santa Barbara, CA, 1986, (8: ODL-87), pp. 393-404.

Key Words: methods, random.

WEB-85
Webster, A.F., and S.E. Tavares
"On the Design of S-Boxes," Proc. Crypto '85, Santa Barbara, CA, 1985, (8: WIL-86), pp. 523-534.

Key Words: DES, analysis, design.

WEI-83
Weingarten, F.W.
"Controlling Cryptographic Publication," Computers & Security, Jan. 1983, pp. 41-48.

Key Words: policy, research.

WIL-80
Williams, H.C.
"A Modification of the RSA Public-Key Cryptosystem," IEEE Trans. on Inform. Theory, November 1980, pp. 726-729.

Key Words: RSA, methods, design.

WIL-82
Willett, M.
"A Tutorial on Public Key Cryptosystems," Computer & Security, January 1982, pp. 72-79.

Key Words: methods, public-key.

WIL-84
Williams, H.C.
"Some Public-Key Crypto-Functions As Intractable as Factorization," Proc. Crypto '84, Santa Barbara, CA, 1984, (8: BLA-84a), pp. 66-70.

Key Words: methods, public-key.

WIL-85
Williams, H.C.
"An M3 Public-Key Encryption Scheme," Proc. Crypto '85, Santa Barbara, CA, 1985, (8: WIL-86), pp. 358-368.

Key Words: methods, public-key.

WIL-86
Williams, H. (Ed.)
Advances in Cryptology, Proceedings of Crypto '85, Santa Barbara, CA, August 1985, Lecture Notes in Computer Science, No. 218, Springer-Verlag, New York, 1986

Key Words: proceedings, general.

WIN-82
Winternitz, R.S.
"Security of a Keystream with Secret Initial Value," Proc. Crypto '82, Santa Barbara, CA, 1982, (8: CHA-83b), pp. 133-137.

Key Words: analysis, methods.

WIN-83
Winternitz, R.S.
"Producing a One-Way Hash Function from DES," Proc. Crypto '83, Santa Barbara, CA, 1983, (8: CHA-84b), pp. 203-207.

Key Words: DES, methods, design.

WIN-84
Winternitz, R.S.
"A Secure One-Way Hash Function Built from DES," Proc. 1984 IEEE Symp. Sec., (5: IEE-84), pp. 121-126.

Key Words: DES, methods, design.

WIN-87
Winternitz, R., and M. Hellman
"Chosen-Key Attacks on a Block Cipher," Cryptologia, January 1987, pp. 16-20.

Key Words: analysis, methods.

WOL-85
Wolfram, S.
"Cryptography with Cellular Automata," Proc. Crypto '85, Santa Barbara, CA, 1985, (8: WIL-86), pp. 429-432.

Key Words: methods, case.

WUN-83
Wunderlich, M.C.
"Factoring Numbers on the Massively Parallel Computer," Proc. Crypto '83, Santa Barbara, CA, 1983, (8: CHA-84b), pp. 87-102.

Key Words: analysis, methods, hardware.

WUN-83a
Wunderlich, M.C.
"Recent Advances in the Design and Implementation of Large Integer Factorization Algorithms," Proc. 1983 IEEE Symp. Sec. & Privacy, (5: IEE-83a), pp. 67-71.

Key Words: analysis, algorithms.

YAC-89
Yacobi, Y., and Z. Shmuley "On Key Distribution Systems," Proc. Crypto '89, Santa Barbara, CA, 1989 (8: BRA-89).

Key Words: methods, keys.

YAG-85
Yagisawa, M. "A New Method for Realizing Public-Key Cryptosystems," Cryptologia, October 1985, pp. 360-371.

Key Words: methods, public-key.

YAM-86
Yamamoto, H. "On Secret Sharing Communication Systems with Two or Three Channels," IEEE Trans. Inform. Theory, May 1986.

Key Words: methods, protocols.

YAO-82
Yao, A.C. "Theory and Applications of Trapdoor Functions," Proc., 23d IEEE Symposium on Foundations of Comp. Science, November 1982, pp. 80-91.

Key Words: methods, theory.

YAO-82a
Yao, A.C. "Protocol for Secure Computation," Proc., 23d IEEE Symposium on Foundations of Computer Science, November 1982, pp. 160-164.

Key Words: methods, protocols.

YAO-86
Yao, A.C. "How to Generate and Exchange Secrets," Proc., 27th IEEE Symposium on Foundations of Computer Science, October 1986, pp. 162-167.

Key Words: methods, protocols.

YUK-89
Yu, K.W., and T.L. Yu "Data Encryption Based on Time Reversal Algorithms," The Computer Journal, (U.K.), June 1989, pp. 241-245.

Key Words: methods, algorithms.

YUN-84
Yung, M. "Cryptoprotocols: Subscription to a Public Key, the Secret Blocking and the Multi-Player Mental Poker Game," Proc. Crypto '84, Santa Barbara, CA, 1984, (8: BLA-84a), pp. 439-453.

Key Words: methods, protocols.

ZHE-89
Zheng, Y., T. Matsumoto, and H. Imai "On the Construction of Block Ciphers and Not Relying on Any Unproved Hypotheses," Proc. Crypto '89, Santa Barbara, CA, 1989 (8: BRA-89).

Key Words: methods, design.

ZOR-87
Zorbette, G. "Breaking the Enemy's Code," IEEE Spectrum, September 1987, pp. 47-51.

Key Words: analysis, methods.

9. Privacy

This section cites publications on the problem of protecting information privacy in computer-based record-keeping systems, descriptions of the privacy problem, legislative measures in the United States and internationally, privacy aspects of international transborder data flows (TDF), and problems in specific application areas (e.g., credit reporting, criminal justice, employment, health care).

ABA-82
Invited Papers on Privacy: Law, Ethics, and Technology. National Symposium on Personal Privacy and Information Technology, American Bar Association and AFIPS, Washington, DC, 1982.

Key Words: proceedings, general.

ABA-82a
Report on a National Symposium on Personal Privacy and Information Technology, American Bar Association and AFIPS, Washington, DC, 1982.

Key Words: proceedings, general.

ABA-84
Abass, O.
"Guidelines for Informatics Laws in Africa," Transnational Data Report, Aug/Sept. 1984, pp. 325-326.

Key Words: guidelines, foreign, laws.

ACL-89
Litigation Under the Federal Freedom of Information Act and Privacy Act, American Civil Liberties Union, Washington, DC, 1989.

Key Words: FOI, PA, laws, use.

ADA-84
Adams, J.M.
"Canada's Future TDF Policy: Reconciling Free Flow of Information with National Sovereignty," Transnational Data Report, Oct/Nov. 1983, pp. 405-411.

Key Words: TDF, policy, foreign.

ADL-85
Adler, A.
Litigation Under the Federal Freedom of Information Act and Privacy Act, Center for National Security Studies, Washington, DC, 1985.

Key Words: FOI, PA, laws, use.

ALB-84
Albanese, S.
Justice, Privacy, and Crime Control, University Press of America, Lanham, MD, 1984.

Key Words: laws, criminal, records, use.

ALL-83
Allen, F.A.
"1984 and the Eclipse of Private Worlds," Michigan Quarterly Review, Fall 1983.

Key Words: analysis, general.

ASA-87
"Privacy Rights in Personal Information," Annual Survey of American Law, June 1987, pp. 495-666.

Key Words: laws, protection.

AUE-83
Auerbach, L.
"Privacy and Canadian Telecommunication Regulation," Telecommunications Policy, March 1983, p. 35+

Key Words: laws, foreign.

AUE-84
Auerbach, I.L.
"Professional Responsibility for Information Privacy," Proc. IFIP/Sec. '84, Toronto, 1984, (2: FIN-85), pp. 3-10.

Key Words: management, records.

AUE-85
Auerbach, I.L.
"Professional Responsibility for Information Privacy," Computers & Security, June 1985, pp. 103-107.

Key Words: managemnt, records.

BAS-84
Basche, J.R., Jr.
Regulating International Data Transmission: The Impact on Managing International Business, Report No. 852, The Conference Board, New York, 1984.

Key Words: TDF, policy, foreign.

BAS-89
   Bass, G., and D. Plocher
   "Strengthening Federal
   Information Policy:
   Opportunities and Realities at
   OMB," Software Law
   Journal, Summer 1989, pp.
   413-459.

   Key Words: policy,
   government.

BEC-84
   Becker, J.
   Information Technology and
   a New International Order,
   Transnational Data Reporting
   Service, Springfield, VA,
   1984.

   Key Words: book, general.

BEE-84
   Beer, B.
   "Legal Aspects of Automatic
   Trade Data Exchange,"
   Transnational Data Report,
   Jan/Febr., 1984, pp. 52-57.

   Key Words: TDF, laws, case.

BEL-83
   Beling, C.T.
   "Transborder Data Flow:
   International Privacy
   Protection and Free Flow of
   Information," Boston College
   International & Computer
   Law Review, Spring 1983,
   pp. 591-624.

   Key Words: TDF, policy,
   laws.

BEL-83a
   Belkin, N. et al.
   "Mass-Informatics and Their
   Implications on Every-Day
   Life," Information Processing
   83, Proc. IFIP Congr. Paris,
   North-Holland, Amsterdam,
   1983.

   Key Words: proceedings,
   general.

BEM-82
   Bemer, R.W.
   "Incorrect Data and Social
   Harm," Computer Security
   Journal, Winter 1982, pp. 51-
   56.

   Key Words: management,
   threats.

BEQ-81
   Bequai, A.
   The Cashless Society: EFTS
   at the Crossroads, J. Wiley &
   Sons, New York, 1981.

   Key Words: book, general.

BER-87
   Berman, J.J.
   "National Security vs. Access
   to Computer Databases: A
   New Threat to Freedom of
   Information," Software Law
   Journal, Winter 1987, pp. 1-
   15.

   Key Words: FOI, threat,
   policy.

BER-89
   Berkvens, J.
   "Dutch Banks' Privacy Code
   of Conduct," Transnational
   Data Report, June/July 1988,
   pp. 12-17.

   Key Words: policy, foreign,
   case.

BER-89a
   Berman, J.J.
   "The Right to Know: Public
   Access to Electronic Public
   Information," Software Law
   Journal, Summer 1989, pp.
   491-530.

   Key Words: rights, records.

BER-89b
   Berman, J., and J. Goldman
   A Federal Right of
   Information Privacy: The
   Need for Reform, Benton
   Foundation, Washington, DC,
   1989.

   Key Words: book, PA,
   general.

BIG-86
   Bigelow, R.
   "Computers and Privacy -- An
   American Perspective,"
   Information Age, (U.K.), July
   1986, pp. 134-140.

   Key Words: rights, laws.

BIN-83
   Bing, J.
   "New Technology and the
   Law: Likely Impact and Future
   Trends," Computers & Law,
   February 1983, pp. 2-6.

   Key Words: rights, laws,
   records.

BIN-83a
   Bing, J.,
   "Computers and Law -- The
   Regulatory Environment of
   Information Services," Proc.
   IFIP/Sec. '83, Stockholm,
   1983, (2: FAK-83), pp. 253-
   264.

   Key Words: requirements,
   rights.

BIN-86
   Bing, J.
   "Beyond 1984: The Law and
   Information Technology in
   Tomorrow's Society,"
   Information Age (U.K.), April
   1986, pp. 85-94.

   Key Words: requirements,
   laws.

BIS-88
   Biskup, J., and
   H.H. Bruggeman
   "The Personal Model of Data,"
   Computers & Security,
   December 1988, pp. 575-597.

   Key Words: records, general.

BIS-89
Biskup, J.
"Protection of Privacy and Confidentiality in Medical Information Systems: Problems and Guidelines," Proc. IFI WG 11.3 (Data Base) Workshop, (6: IFI-89), 1989.

Key Words: protection, medical.

BRA-84
Branscomb, A.W.
"The Legal Infrastructure for Global Information Flows," Transnational Data Report, June/July 1984, pp. 247-251.

Key Words: TDF, laws, design.

BRO-84
Brown, R.W.
"A Model Code for Transnational Commerce?," Transnational Data Report, March 1984, pp. 117-124.

Key Words: regulation, TDF.

BRT-85
International Information Flow A Plan For Action, The Business Roundtable, New York, January 1985.

Key Words: TDF, guidelines.

BUR-84
Burnham, D.
The Rise of the Computer State, Random House, Westminster, MD, 1984

Key Words: threats, general.

BUR-84a
Burkert, H.
"Information Law Problems For the Eighties," Transnational Data Report, Aug/Sept. 1984, pp. 331-336.

Key Words: laws, requirements.

BUR-84b
Burton, R.P., and R.D. Malmrose
"The Effects of Recent Privacy Laws on Rights of Deceased Persons," Transnational Data Report, June/July 1984, pp. 237-242.

Key Words: laws, case.

BUR-85
Burgess, B.C.
"Restrictions in Data Transfer and Use," Transnational Data Report, June 1985, pp. 217-219.

Key Words: TDF, requirements.

BUR-87
Burton, R.P., and R.D. Malmrose
"Impact of Privacy Laws on Religious Organizations," Transnational Data Report, June 1987, pp. 5-9.

Key Words: laws, case.

CEC-84
New Information and Communication Technologies and Data Protection, Information Technology Task Force, Council of European Communities, Brussels, 1984.

Key Words: requirements, rights.

CHA-83
Chavda, H.
"Data Protection in the Computing Industry--A Survey," Information Age (UK), October 1983, pp. 211-221.

Key Words: protection, case.

CHA-84
Chaum. D.
"A New Paradigm for Individuals in the Information Age," Proc. 1984 IEEE Symp. on Sec. & Privacy, (5: IEE-84), pp. 99-103.

Key Words: protection, rights.

CHA-84a
Chamoux, J., and F. Chamoux
"French Data Protection: The First Five Years," Transnational Data Report, April/May 1984, pp. 163-166.

Key Words: laws, foreign.

CHC-87
Open and Shut: Enhancing the Right to Know and Right to Privacy, Canadian House of Commons, Canadinan Government Printing, Ottawa, March 1987.

Key Words: laws, rights, foreign.

CHE-84
Cheah, C.W.
"An Econometric Analysis of TDF Regulation," Transnational Data Report, December 1984, pp. 475-479

Key Words: TDF, analysis, case.

CHP-87
Information Technology and the Erosion of Privacy, Report of the Commission on Humanities and Public Affairs, Claremont Graduate School, Claremont, CA, 1987.

Key Words: requirements, rights.

CLA-81
Clariana, G.G.
"TDF, Data Protection and International Law," Transnational Data Report, July/August 1981, pp. 31-35.

Key Words: TDF, rights, foreign.

CLA-88
Clarke, R.A.
"Information Technology and Dataveillance," Communications of the ACM, May 1988, pp. 498-512.

Key Words: surveillance, rights.

CLU-88
Clukey, L.
"The Electronic
Communications Privacy Act
of 1986: The Imact on
Software Communication
Technologies," Software Law
Journal, Spring 1988, pp.
243-263.

Key Words: analysis, laws.

COE-81
Convention on Protection of
Individuals with Regard to
Automatic Processing of
Personal Data, Council of
Europe, Strassbourg, France,
28 January 1981.

Key Words: protection,
foreign.

COE-81a
Regulations for Automated
Medical Data Banks,
Recommendation R(81)1,
Council of Europe,
Strassbourg, France, 1981.

Key Words: protection,
foreign medical, records..

COE-83
The Protection of Users of
Computerized Legal
Information Services,
Recommendation R(83)3,
Council of Europe,
Strassbourg, France, 1984.

Key Words: protection,
foreign private, records.

COE-84
Protection of Personal Data
Used for Scientific Research
and Statistics,
Recommendation R(83)10,
Council of Europe,
Strassbourg, France, 1984.

Key Words: protection,
foreign. statistical, social.

COE-86
Protection of Personal Data
Used for Purposes of Direct
Marketing, Recommendation
R(85)20, Council of Europe,
Strassbourg, France, 1986.

Key Words: protection,
foreign private, records.

COE-86a
Protection of Personal Data
Used for Social Security
Purposes, Recommendation
R(88)1, Council of Europe,
Strassbourg, France, 1986.

Key Words: protection,
foreign, social, records.

COE-88
Regulating the Use of
Personal Data in the Police
Sector, Recommendation
R(87)15, Council of Europe,
Strassbourg, France, 1988.

Key Words: protection,
foreign, criminal, records.

COE-89
"Protection of Personal Data
Used for Employment
Purposes," Council of Europe
Recommendation No. R(89)2,
Transnational Data Report,
March 1989, pp. 26-28.

Key Words: protection,
records, employment.

COE-89a
New Technologies: A
Challenge to Privacy
Protection?, Council of
Europe, Strassbourg, France,
1989.

Key Words: requirements,
foreign.

COL-85
Cole, P.E.
"New Challenges to the U.S.
Multinational Corporations in
European Community: Data
Protection Laws," N.Y.U.
Journal on International Law
and Politics, Summer 1985,
pp. 893-947.

Key Words: TDF, foreign,
analysis.

COM-83
"Computerized Bank Accounts,
Credit Cards, and George
Orwell's 1984," Computers and
People, March/April 1983, pp.
27+

Key Words: threats, rights.

CON-80
International Data Flow,
Hearings Before Committee on
Government Operations, House
of Representatives, U.S.
Congress, Washington, DC,
1980.

Key Words: TDF, laws,
Congress.

CON-80a
International Information Flow
Flow: Forging a New
Framework, House Report No.
96-1535, U.S. Congress,
Washington, DC, December
11, 1980.

Key Words: TDF, Congress.

CON-83
Oversight of Computer
Matching to Detect Fraud and
Mismanagement in
Government Programs,
Hearings, Senate Subcommittee
on Oversight of Government
Affairs, Washington, DC,
1983.

Key Words: Congress,
matching.

CON-83a

Who Cares About Privacy? Oversight of the Privacy Act of 1974 by Office of Management and Budget and by Congress, No. 98-455, House of Representatives, U.S. Congress, Washington, DC, 1983.

Key Words: Congress, PA, oversight.

CON-83b

Oversight of the Privacy Act of 1974, Hearings, House Committee on Government Operations, U.S. Congress, Washington, DC, 1983.

Key Words: Congress, PA, oversight.

CON-85

Unauthorized Access to Individual Medical Records, Hearings, House Committee on Judiciary, Subcommittee on Civil and Constitutional Rights, U.S. Congress, Washington, DC, 1985.

Key Words: protection, medical.

CON-86

Computer Matching and Privacy Act of 1986, Hearings, Subcommittee on Oversight of Government Management, Senate Commitee on Government Affairs, U.S. Congress, Washington, DC, 1986.

Key Words: Congress, matching.

CON-86a

Electronic Communications Privacy Act of 1986, P.L. 99-508, (18 U.S.C. 2703), 1986, U.S. Congress, Washington, DC, 1986.

Key Words: Congress, laws.

CON-87

Computer Matching and Privacy Act of 1987, Hearings, Subcommittee of House Committee on Government Operations, U.S. Congress, Washington, DC, 1987.

Key Words: Congress, matching.

CON-88

Computer Matching and Privacy Act of 1988, Report 100-802, House Committee on Government Operations, U.S. Congress, Washington, DC, July 27,1988.

Key Words: Congress, matching.

CON-88a

The Computer Matching and Privacy Act of 1988, P.L. 100-503. (5 U.S.C. 552a), U.S. Congress, Washington, DC 1988.

Key Words: Congress, matching.

COO-81

Cooper, G.R., and R.R. Belair Privacy and the Private Employer, Bureau of Justice Statistics, U.S. Department of Justice, Washington, DC, 1981.

Key Words: guidelines, employment.

COO-83

Coombe, G.W., and S.L. Kirk "Privacy, Data Protection and Transborder Data Flows: A Corporate Response," The Business Lawyer, November 1983, pp. 33-66.

Key Words: TDF, policy, case.

CUL-87

"Protecting Individual Privacy in Shadow of a National Data Base," Capital University Law Review, Fall '87, pp. 117-141.

Key Words: threats, government.

DAM-83

Damman, U. "Auditing Data Protection" Transnational Data Report, April-May 1983, pp. 161-163.

Key Words: management, records.

DOC-88

Dockrill, C. "Computer Data Banks and Personal Information: Protection Against Negligent Disclosure," Dalhousie Law Journal, March 1988, pp. 546-580.

Key Words: protection, records.

DOJ-85

Criminal Justice Information Policy: Intelligence and Investigative Records, U.S. Department of Justice, Bureau of Justice Statistics, NCJ-95787, Washington, DC, February 1985.

Key Words: policy, criminal, rights.

DON-81

Donovan, T.G. "Data Protection's Many Tentacles," Proc. Comp. Sec. & Priv. Symposium, Phoenix, AR, 1981, (1: HON-81), pp. 13-24.

Key Words: laws, records, general.

DUB-83

Dubrow, A. "Your Medical Records: How Private Are They?," California Lawyer, Apr. 1983, p. 33+.

Key Words: threats, medical, records.

DUF-82
    Duffy, D.J.
    "Privacy vs. Disclosure:
    Balancing Employee and
    Employer Rights," Employee
    Relations Law Journal,
    Spring 1982, pp. 594-609.

    Key Words: rights,
    employment.

EAT-86
    Eaton, J.W.
    Card-Carrying Americans:
    Privacy, Security, and the
    National ID Card Debate,
    Rowman & Littlefield,
    Totowa, NJ, 1986.

    Key Words: book, laws,
    rights.

ENN-84
    Ennison, T., Jr.
    "Sovereignty Considerations
    in TDF: Developing-Country
    Perspective," Transnational
    Data Report, April/May 1984,
    pp. 175-181.

    Key Words: TDF, rights,
    foreign.

EVA-81
    Evans, A.C.
    "European Data Protection
    Law," American J. of
    Comparative Law, Fall 1981,
    pp. 571-582.

    Key Words: laws, foreign,
    TDF.

EVE-80
    Everest, G.C.
    "Nonuniform Privacy Laws:
    Implications at Attempts at
    Uniformity," Hoffman, L.J.
    (Ed.), Computers and Privacy
    in the Next Decade,
    Academic Press, New York,
    1980, pp. 141-150.

    Key Words: guidelines, laws.

FAR-83
    Farnsworth, D.P.
    "Data Privacy: An American
    View of European
    Legislation," Transnational
    Data Report, July/August
    1983, pp. 285-290.

    Key Words: laws, foreign.

FIS-80
    Fishman, W.L.
    "Introduction to Transborder
    Data Flow," Stanford Journal
    of Internat. Law, Summer
    1980, pp. 1-26.

    Key Words: TDF, policies,
    rights.

FIS-81
    Fisher, J.F.
    "Access to Fair Credit
    Reports: Current Practices and
    Proposed Legislation,"
    American Business Law
    Journal, Fall 1981, pp. 319-
    342.

    Key Words: credit, laws,
    rights.

FLA-84
    Flaherty, D.H.
    Nineteen Eighty-Four and
    After, Final Report of
    Bellagio Conf. University of
    Western Ontario, London,
    Ontario, May 15, 1984.

    Key Words: proceedings,
    rights.

FLA-84a
    Flaherty, D.H., E.H. Hanis,
    and S.P. Mitchell
    Privacy and Access to
    Government Data for
    Research: An International
    Bibliography, Knowledge
    Industry Publicat., White
    Plains, NY, 1984.

    Key Words: book, general.

FLA-85
    Flaherty, D.H.
    Protecting Privacy in Two-
    Way Electronic Services,
    Knowledge Industry Publicat.,
    White Plains, NY, 1985.

    Key Words: book, rights,
    laws.

FLA-85a
    Flaherty, D.H.
    Privacy and Data Protection:
    An International Bibliography,
    Knowledge Industry Publicat.,
    White Plains, NY, 1985.

    Key Words: book, general.

FLA-86
    Flaherty, D.
    "Governmental Surveillance
    and Bureaucratic
    Accountability: Data Protection
    Agencies in the Western
    Societies," Science,
    Technology and Human
    Values, No. 1, 1986, pp. 1-12.

    Key Words: laws, rights,
    foreign.

FLA-86a
    Flaherty, D.
    "On Making Data Protection
    Effective," Transnational Data
    Report, April 1986, pp. 15-16.

    Key Words: laws, protection.

FLA-89
    Flaherty, D.H.
    Protecting Privacy in
    Surveillance Societies,
    University of North Carolina
    Press, Chapel Hill, NC, 1989.

    Key Words: book, laws,
    foreign.

FLE-86
    Fletcher, P.T.
    "Current Issues in
    Confidentiality: Computerized
    Information Systems, Medical
    Records, and Patients' Rights,"
    Computers & Society,
    Summer/Fall 1986, pp. 8-18.

    Key Words: rights, medical.

FLR-84
"Damages Under the Privacy Act of 1974: Compensation and Deterrence," Fordam Law Review, March 1984, p. 611+.

Key Words: PA, protection, uses.

FRE-81
Freese, J.
"The Vulnerability of Computerized Society," Transnational Data Report, July/August 1981, pp. 21-25.

Key Words: threats, laws.

FRE-83
Freese, J.
"The Right to Be Alone in Sweden," Transnational Data Report, December 1983, pp. 447-449.

Key Words: rights, foreign.

FRE-87
Freedman, W.
The Right of Privacy in the Computer Age, Quorum Books, New York, 1987

Key Words: book, rights, laws.

FUT-83
"Orwell's 1984: How Close to the Truth?," Special Issue, The Futurist, December 1983.

Key Words: threats, general.

GAO-85
Eligibility Verification and Privacy in Federal Benefit Programs: A Delicated Balance, GAO/HRD-85-22, U.S. General Accounting Office, Washington, DC, March 1, 1985.

Key Words: government, matching.

GAO-86
Privacy Act: Federal Agencies' Implementation Can Be Improved, GAO/GGD-86-107, U.S. General Accounting Office, Washington, DC, August 1986.

Key Words: PA, oversight, laws.

GAR-85
Garzon, G.
"Legal Framework for International Information" Transnational Data Report, March 1985, pp. 101-107.

Key Words: TDF, laws, foreign.

GAS-85
Gassman, H.P. (Ed.)
Transborder Data Flows. Proceedings of 1973 OECD Conference, North-Holland/Elsevier Science Publishing Co., New York, 1985.

Key Words: proceedings, general.

GEB-88
Gebhardt, H.-P.
"Data Protection in Telecommunication Services," Transnational Data Report, June/July, 1988, pp. 18-23.

Key Words: TDF, protection.

GES-82
Gest, T., and P.M. Scherschel "Report on Privacy: Who Is Watching You," U.S. News & World Report, July 12, 1982, pp. 34-37.

Key Words: threats, rights.

GOL-89
Golden, J.S.
"Information on the Federal Government's Electronic Databases: Is There a First Amendment Right of Access?," Software Law Journal, Winter 1989, pp. 65-90.

Key Words: government, laws.

GOT-84
Gotlieb, C.C.
"Equity in Access to Information," Proc. IFIP/Sec. '84, Toronto, 1984, (2: FIN-85), pp. 29-39.

Key Words:

GRA-84
Gray, J., L.B. McSweeney, and J.C. Shaw
Information Disclosure and the Multinational Corporation, John Wiley & Sons, Ltd., Chichester, UK, 1984.

Key Words: book, TDF, laws.

GRA-86
Grandjean, J.R.
"Computerized Medical Data -- Privacy and Delinquency Issues," Proc. IFIP/Sec. '86, Monte Carlo, 1986, (2: GRI-89).

Key Words: records, medical.

GRE-80
Greguras, F.M.
"Information Systems and Privacy Issues in the U.S.A.," Information Privacy (U.K.), May 1980, pp. 90-97.

Key Words: rights, general.

GRE-81
Greguras, F.M.
"Anticipating the Impact of EFTS on Privacy & Information Practices," Proc. Comp. Sec. & Priv. Symp., Phoenix, AR, (1: HON-81), pp. 25-45.

Key Words: EFTS, requirements.

GRO-82
Grossman, G.S.
"Transborder Data Flow: Separating the Privacy Interests of Individuals and Corporations," Northwestern Journal of International Law and Business, Spring 1982, pp. 9-11.

Key Words: TDF, laws, general.

GUR-84
Gurry, F.
Breach of Confidence,
Oxford University Press,
Clarendon (UK), 1984.

Key Words: book, rights,
laws.

HAE-84
Haeck, L.
"Transborder (Private) Data
Flow and the International
Airlines," Transnational Data
Report, Aug/Sept. 1984, pp.
343-345.

Key Words: TDF, policy,
foreign.

HAM-84
Hamelink, C.J.
Transnational Data Flows in
the Information Age,
Transnational Data Reporting
Service, Springfield, Va,
1984.

Key Words: TDF, policy,
foreign.

HAR-84
Harris, L. et al.
The Road After 1984: Impact
of Technology on Society. A
Public Opinion Study,
Southern New England
Telephone Company, New
Haven, CT, 1984.

Key Words: threats, rights,
laws.

HAR-85
Hartmann, J., and
S.M. Renas
"Anglo-American Privacy
Law: An Economic
Analysis," International
Review of Law and
Economics, December 1985,
pp. 133-152.

Key Words: laws, foreign.

HAR-86
Harding, N.G.L
Data Protection in Medicine,
Proc. of a National Meeting,
Oxford, England, February
1986, HMSO Publications
Center, London, 1986.

Key Words: rights, laws,
medical.

HEL-85
Hely, M.H., and
M.T. Morrison
Data Protection Act of 1984,
The Computer Services, Ltd.,
Easterton, Devizes, Wilts,
U.K., 1985.

Key Words: laws, foreign.

HER-88
Hernandez, R.T.
"ECPA and Online Computer
Privacy," Federal Communic.
Law Journal, November 1988,
pp. 17-41

Key Words: laws,
government.

HHS-85
Catalog of Automated Front-
End Eligibility Verification
Techniques, OAI-85-H-51,
U.S. Department of Health
and Human Services,
Washington, DC, 1985.

Key Words: guidelines,
matching.

HIR-84
Hiramatsu, T.
"Japan's Privacy Protection
Measures," Transnational Data
Report, March 1984, pp. 109-
112.

Key Words: laws, foreign.

HIR-87
Hiramatsu, T.
"Japan's New Personal Data
Bill," Transnational Data
Report, October 1987, pp. 14-
16.

Key Words: laws, foreign.

HIR-89
Hiramatsu, T.
"Japan Adopts Privacy
Protection Act," Transnational
Data Report, February 1989,
pp. 22-29.

Key Words: laws, foreign.

HOF-80
Hoffman, L.J. (Ed.)
Computers and Privacy in the
Next Decade, Academic Press,
New York, 1980.

Key Words: proceedings,
general.

HON-80
Hondius, F.W.
"Data Law in Europe,"
Stanford J. of International
Law, Summer 1980, pp. 87-
111.

Key Words: laws, foreign.

IBI-80
Transborder Data Flow
Policies, Papers Presented at
IBI Conference in Rome, June
1980, Unipub, New York,
1981.

Key Words: proceedings, TDF.

IBM-83
Privacy Begins at Home--IBM
Experience with Developing
and Administration of
Employee Privacy Practices,
IBM Corporation, White
Plains, NY, 1983.

Key Words: policy, rights,
case.

ICC-85
Business Guide to Privacy and
Data Protection Legislation,
No. 384, International
Chamber of Commerce, Paris,
1985.

Key Words: TDF, guidelines,
laws.

ICC-85a
Issues in Computing, Telecommunications and Information Policy, No. 385, International Chamber of Commerce, Paris, 1985.

Key Words: TDF, policy, foreign.

IRV-86
Irving, R.H., C.A. Higgins, and F.R. Safayeni "Computerized Performance Monitoring Systems: Use and Abuse," Communications of the ACM, August 1986, pp. 794-801.

Key Words: rights, employment.

JML-88
"Privacy Edition," The John Marshall Law Review, Summer '88, pp. 703-902.

Key Words: rights, laws, general.

JON-88
Jones, S.E. "Right to Financial Privacy: Emerging Standards of Bank Compliance," Banking Law Journal, Jan./Febr. 1988, pp. 37-51.

Key Words: rights, laws, EFTS.

KAT-88
Katz, J.E. "Public Policy Origins of Telecommunications Privacy and the Emerging Issues," Information Age (U.K.), July 1988, pp. 169-176.

Key Words: policy, laws, case.

KEN-86
Kenny, J.J. (Ed.) Data Privacy & Security, Pergamon Press, Elmsford, NJ, 1986

Key Words: book, general.

KIR-80
Kirby, M.D. "Transborder Data Flows and the 'Basic Rules' of Privacy," Stanford Journal of International Law, Summer 1980, pp. 27-66.

Key Words: TDF, rights, foreign.

KIR-81
Kirchner, J. "Privacy: A History of Computer Matching in the Federal Government, Computerworld, December 14, 1981, pp. 2ff.

Key Words: matching, general.

KIR-84
Kirby, M.D. "Urgent Need to Solve TDF Legal Difficulties," Transnational Data Report, Aug/Sept. 1984, pp. 347-350.

Key Words: TDF, laws, rights.

KIR-86
Kirby, M.D. "Ten Information Commandments," Transnational Data Report, June 1986, pp. 19-22.

Key Words: rights, laws, use.

KIR-86a
Kirby, M.D. "Human Rights -- The Challenge of New Technology," Information Age (U.K.), October 1986, pp. 200-207.

Key Words: rights, general.

KIR-87
Kirby, M.D. "Access to Information and Privacy: The Ten Information Commandments," University of Cincinnatti Law Review, 1987, pp. 745-759.

Key Words: rights, laws, use.

KLU-83
Klugman, E. "Toward a Uniform Right to Medical Records: A Proposal for a Model Patient Access and Information Practices Statute," UCLA Law Review, August 1983, p. 1349+.

Key Words: rights, medical.

KUS-84
Kusserow, R.P. "The Government Needs Computer Matching to Root Out Waste and Fraud," Communications of the ACM, June 1984, pp. 542-545.

Key Words: requirements, case, matching, rights.

LAN-84
Landever, A.R. "Electronic Surveillance, Computers and the Fourth Amendment," University of Toledo Law Review, Winter 1984, pp. 597-640.

Key Words: surveillance, rights.

LAU-83
Lauffer, S. International Issues in Communication Technology and Policy, Academy for Educational Development, Washington, DC, 1983.

Key Words: book, policy, foreign.

LAU-86
Laudon, K.C.
Dossier Society: Value
Choices in the Design of
National Information
Systems, Columbia University
Press, New York, 1986

Key Words: book,
surveillance.

LAU-86a
Laudon, K.C.
"Data Quality and Due
Process in Large
Interorganizational Record
Systems," Communications of
the ACM, January 1986, pp.
5-11.

Key Words: requirements,
case.

LEA-86
Leahy, P.
"Privacy and Progress,"
Computers & Security,
December 1986, pp. 347-349.

Key Words: rights, general.

LER-84
Lerner, E.J.
"International Data Wars Are
Brewing," IEEE Spectrum,
July 1984, p. 454+.

Key Words: TDF, policy.

LIN-89
Linowes, D.F.
Privacy in America: Is Your
Private Life in the Public
Eye?, University of Illinois
Press, Urbana, IL, 1989.

Key Words: book, threats,
rights.

MAI-81
Maisonrouge, J.G.
"Regulation of International
Information Flows," The
Information Society, Vol. 1,
No. 1, 1981, pp. 17-30.

Key Words: TDF, policy,
laws.

MAR-80
Marchand, D.A.
The Politics of Privacy, and
Criminal Justice Records,
Information Resources Press,
Arlington, VA, 1980.

Key Words: policy, criminal.

MAR-84
Marx, G.T., and
N. Reichman
"Routinizing the Discovery of
Secrets: Computers as
Informants," Americ.
Behavioral Scientist, March
1984.

Key Words: threats, rights.

MAR-86
Marx. G.T., and S. Sherizen
"Monitoring the Job: How to
Protect Privacy as well as
Property." Technology
Review, Nov./Dec. 1986, pp.
63-72.

Key Words: threats, rights.

MAR-86a
Marx, G.T.
"Surveillance: A Dangerous
Game Played With Matches,"
Abacus, Fall 1986, pp. 60-64.

Key Words: threats, matching.

MAR-88
Marx, G.T.
Undercover: Police
Surveillance in America,
University of California Press,
Berkeley, CA, 1988

Key Words: book, threats.

MAT-85
Matley, B.G.
"Computer Privacy in
America: Conflicting Practices
and Policy Choices," Proc.
1986 IEEE Symp. Sec. &
Priv., (5: IEE-86), pp. 219-
223.

Key Words: policy, laws.

MCC-80
McConnell, R.M.
"Designing for Privacy: The
Data Vault," in Rullo, T.A.
(Ed.), Advances in Computer
Security Management, Vol. 1,
Heyden, Philadelphia, PA,
1980, pp. 106-121.

Key Words: protection, design.

MCK-83
McKay, G.A.
"Privacy -- A Call for Action,"
Proc. IFIP/Sec. '83,
Stockholm, 1983, (2: FAK-83),
pp. 47-55.

Key Words: protection,
general.

MCL-81
McLaughlan, W.
"Privacy and Criminal Justice,"
Information Privacy (U.K.),
March 1981, pp. 43-49.

Key Words: rights, criminal.

MEL-82
Meldman, J.A.
"Privacy Expectations in an
Information Age," Information
Privacy (U.K.), Winter 1982,
pp. 81-89.

Key Words: rights, laws.

MON-88
Monssen, W.
"Airline Industry Takes Data
Protection Seriously,"
Transnational Data Report,
January 1988, pp. 17-20.

Key Words: policy, rights.

MOW-81
Mowshowitz, A.
"On Approaches to the Study
of Social Issues in
Computing," Communications
of the ACM, November 1981,
pp. 146-155.

Key Words: policy, social.

NIB-84

Niblett, B.
Data Protection Act of 1984, Longman Group Limited, London, 1984.

Key Words: book, laws, foreign.

NOV-80

Novotny, E.J.
"Transborder Data Flows and International Law: A Framework for Policy-Oriented Inquiry," Stanford Journal of International Law, Summer 1980, pp. 141-199.

Key Words: TDF, laws. foreign.

NOV-82

Novotny, E.J.
"Transborder Data Flow Regulation: Technical Issues of Legal Concern," Computer/Law Journal, Winter 1982, pp. 105-124.

Key Words: TDF, requirements.

NYC-80

Nycum, S.H., and S. Courtney-Saunders "Transborder Data Flow: Legal Persons in Privacy Protection Legislation," Proc., 1980 National Comp. Conf., AFIPS Press, Arlington, VA, pp. 587-593.

Key Words: TDF, policy, laws.

OEC-80

Information, Computer and Communications Policies for 1980s, Proc. of a High-Level Conf., OECD, Paris, 1980.

Key Words: proceedings, general.

OEC-81

Guidelines for the Protection of Privacy & Transborder Data Flows of Personal Information, OECD, Paris, 1981.

Key Words: TDF, guidelines.

OEC-84

An Exploration of Legal Issues In Informationa and Telecommunication Technologies, OECD, Paris, 1984.

Key Words: TDF, laws, policy.

OEC-86

1984 And Beyond: The Social Challenge of Information Technology, Proc. 1984 Berlin Conf. OECD, Paris, March 1986.

Key Words: policy, social.

OMB-85

Management of Federal Information Resources, Circular No. A-130, Office of Management and Budget, Washington, DC, December 1985.

Key Words: policy, guidelines.

OSV-83

Osvald, T.
"The Data Act and Documentation Requirements," Proc. IFIP/Sec. '83, Stockholm, 1983, (2: FAK-83), pp. 265-268.

Key Words: laws, foreign.

OTA-85

Federal Government Information Technology: Electronic Surveillance and Civil Liberties, OTA-CIT-293, U.S. Congress, Office of Techn. Assessment, Washington, DC, October 1985.

Key Words: surveillance, rights, government, policy.

OTA-86

Federal Government Information Technology: Electronic Record Systems and Individual Privacy, OTA-CIT-296, U.S. Congress, Office of Technology Assessment, Washington, DC. June 1986.

Key Words: rights, records, laws, government, policy.

OTA-87

The Electronic Supervisor -- New Technology, New Tensions, OTA-CIT-333, U.S. Congress, Office of Techn. Assessment, Washington, DC, September 1987.

Key Words: threats, rights, government, policy.

OTA-88

Criminal Justice, New Technologies and the Constitution, OTA-CIT-366, U.S. Congress, Office of Techn. Assessment, Washington, DC, May 1988.

Key Words: policy, criminal.

PAG-84

Pagels, H.R. (Ed.)
Computer Culture: The Scientific Intellectual and Social of the the Computer, The New York Academy of Sciences, New York, 1984.

Key Words: book, policy.

PAR-83

Parent, W.A.
"Recent Work on the Concept of Privacy," Americican Philosophical Quarterly, 1983, pp. 341-355.

Key Words: policy, general.

PAR-84

Parkhill, D., P. Enslow (Eds.)
So This is 1984, North-Holland, Amsterdam, 1984.

Key Words: book, general.

PAT-89
Patrick, A.L.
"Public Access to
Government Databanks,"
Proc., 12th Natl. Comp. Sec.
Conf., 1989, (5: NCS-89),
pp. 609-610.

Key Words: policy, rights,
laws.

PIE-83
Pietarinen, I.
"Finland's Privacy
Legislation," Transnational
Data Report, March 1983,
pp. 101-103.

Key Words: laws, foreign.

PIP-84
Pipe, G.R.
"Getting on the TDF Track,"
Datamation, Jan. 1984, p.
200-211.

Key Words: TDF, general.

PLE-82
Plesser, R.
"Issue of Data Flows Across
National Borders Must Be
Faced," ABA Banking
Journal, February 1982, pp.
71-78.

Key Words: TDF, policy,
laws.

RAD-84
Rada, J.F. and
G.R. Pipe (Eds.)
Communications Regulation
and International Business,
Elsevier Science Publishers,
New York, 1984.

Key Words: book, TDF,
policy.

RAS-86
Rasor, P.B.
"Controlling Government
Access to Personal Financial
Records," Washburn Law
Review, Spring 1986, pp.
417-436.

Key Words: policy, records.

RAS-86a
Rasor, P.B.
"Privacy Implications of
Consumer Credit Laws," The
John Marshall Law Review,
Summer 1986, pp. 941-957.

Key Words: privacy, credit.

RIC-86
Rice, R.
"Privacy, Freedom and
PublicKey Cryptography,"
Information Age, (U.K.),
October 1986, pp. 208-214.

Key Words: policy, rights.

RIL-87
Riley, T.
"Quebec's Unique Access and
Privacy Act," Transnational
Data Report, January 1987,
pp. 11-13.

Key Words: laws, foreign.

RIL-87a
Riley, T.
"Enhancing Canadians' Right
to Know and to Privacy,"
Transnational Data Report,
June 1987, pp. 23-25.

Key Words: rights, foreign.

RIL-87b
Riley, T.
Access to Government
Records: International
Perspectives and Trends,
Transnational Data Reporting
Services, Springfield, VA,
1987.

Key Words: book, policy,
foreign.

RIL-88
Riley, T.
"Data Commissioners
Consider Wider Horizons:
Conference Report,"
Transnational Data Report,
December 1988, pp. 10-18.

Key Words: policy, laws,
foreign.

ROB-86
Robinson, P.
"Legal Issues Raised by
Transborder Data Flow,"
Canadian-U.S. Law Journal,
1986, pp. 295-316.

Key Words: TDF, laws,
foreign.

RUB-89
Rubenfeld, J.
"The Right of Privacy,"
Harvard Law Review, February
1989, pp. 737-807.

Key Words: rights, laws.

RUL-80
Rule, J., et al.
The Politics of Privacy, New
American Library, New York,
1980.

Key Words: book, rights.

SAU-84
Sauvant, K.P.
"The Growing Dependence on
Transborder Data Flows,"
Computerworld, June 25, 1984,
pp. ID/19-24.

Key Words: TDF, policy,
laws.

SCH-84
Schoeman, F.D. (Ed.)
Philosophical Dimensions of
Privacy, Cambridge University
Press, New York, 1984

Key Words: book, rights, laws.

SEI-80
Seiler, R.S.
"Privacy and Insurance: An
Enforceable Expectation of
Confidentiality," Forum, Spring
1980, pp. 628-659.

Key Words: rights, laws, case.

SEI-86
Seipel, P.
"Pitfalls of the Electronic
Revolution," Information Age,
(U.K.), October 1986, pp. 215-
219.

Key Words: threats, rights.

SEL-88
Selmer, K.
"Data Protection Policy Trend," Transnational Data Report, December 1988, pp. 19-25.

Key Words: policy, laws.

SHA-84
Shattuck, J.
"Computer Matching Is a Serious Threat to Individual Rights," Communications of the ACM, June 1984, pp. 538-541.

Key Words: matching, threats.

SHA-85
Shattuck, J.
"Privacy in the Age of Information," Transnational Data Report, July/August 1985, pp. 259-260.

Key Words: rights, laws.

SHA-89
Shattuck, J., and M.M. Spence
"A Presidential Initiative on Information Policy," Software Law Journal, Summer 1989, pp. 461-490.

Key Words: policy, rights, laws.

SHU-86
Shultz, G.P.
"Consequences of the Age of Information," Transnational Data Report, May 1986, pp. 16-19.

Key Words: polciy, rights.

SIM-83
Simitis, S.
"Data Protection--A Few Critical Remarks," Transnational Data Report, March 1983, pp. 93-96.

Key Words: protection, laws.

SIM-85
Simitis, S.
"Data Protection: New Developments, New Challenges," Transnational Data Report, March 1985, pp. 95-96.

Key Words: policy, rights, laws.

SIM-87
Simitis, S.
"Reviewing Privacy in an Information Society," University of Pennsylvania Law Review, March 1987, pp. 707-746.

Key Words: policy, rights, laws.

SIZ-85
Sizer, R. and P. Newman The Data Protection Act (U.K.), Gower Publishing Co., Ltd., London, 1985.

Key Words: laws, foreign.

SLA-83
Slansky, P. (Ed.) On Nineteen Eighty-Four, W.H. Freeman & Co., New York, 1983.

Key Words: book, rights.

SMI-83
Smith, R.E.
Workrights, Privacy Journal Publication, Washington, DC, 1983.

Key Words: rights, employment.

SMI-85
Smith, R.E.
Fair Information Practices in Seven States, Privacy Journal Publication, Washington, DC, 1985.

Key Words: laws, general.

SMI-86
Smith, R.E.
Collection and Use of Social Security Numbers, Privacy Journal Publication, Washington, DC, 1986.

Key Words: policy, rights.

SMI-88
Smith, R.E.
Compilation of State & Federal Privacy Laws, Privacy Journal Publication, Washington, DC, 1988.

Key Words: laws, general.

STE-81
Stevenson, R.B., Jr.
Corporations & Information: Secrecy, Access & Disclosure, Johns Hopkins University Press, Baltimore MD, 1981.

Key Words: book, policy, laws.

STE-83
Sterling, R.A.
"Privacy Information Systems Common Law -- A Comparative Study in the Private Sector," Gozanga Law Review, Vol. 18, 1982/83, pp. 567-604.

Key Words: policy, rights, law.

STR-86
Strunk, O., Jr.
Privacy: Studies in Social and Cultural History, University Press of America, Lanham, MD, 1986

Key Words: book, general.

STR-88
Strong, D.R.
"The Computer Matching and Privacy Protection Act of 1988: Necessary Relief from Erosion of the Privacy Act of 1974," Software Law Journal, Summer 1988, pp. 391-422.

Key Words: matching, laws.

SWA-83
Swan, J.C.
"Public Records and Library
Privacy," Library Journal,
Sept. 1983.

Key Words: policy, records.

TDR-83
Transborder Data Flow Issues
Guide, Transnational Data
Reporting Service,
Springfield, VA, 1983.

Key Words: TDF, guidelines.

TDR-83a
"Statistical Data Privacyand
Confidentiality,"
Transnational Data Report,
Oct./Nov. 1983, pp. 368-386.

Key Words: statistical, laws.

TDR-84
"Surveys Show Strategic
Importance of TDF,"
Transnational Data Report,
Jan/Febr. 1984, pp. 20-36.

Key Words: TDF, policy.

TDR-84a
"New Technologies' Impact
On Data Protection,"
Transnational Data Report,
June/July 1984, pp. 204-215.

Key Words: threats, rights.

TDR-84b
"Second World TDF
Conference: Special Report,"
Transnational Data Report,
Aug./Sept. 1984, pp. 253-283.

Key Words: TDF, policy,
foreign.

TDR-85
"OECD Sets TDF Rules of
the Road," Transnational
Data Report, April/May 1985,
pp. 115-117.

Key Words: TDF, guidelines.

TLR-87
"Privacy, Computers, and the
Commercial Dissemination of
Personal Information," Texas
Law Review, June 1987, pp.
1395-1439.

Key Words: policy, records.

TRA-85
Traub, J.F. (Ed.)
Cohabiting with Computers,
William Kaufmann, Inc., Los
Altos, CA, 1985.

Key Words: book, general.

TRE-88
Tremper, C.R., and
M.A. Small
"Privacy Regulation of
Computer Assisted Testing
and Instruction," Washington
Law Review, October 1988,
pp. 841-879,

Key Words: policy, rights.

TRU-86
Trubow, G.
"Peeping Sam: Uncle Is
Watching You," Computer
Security Journal, No. 1, 1986,
pp. 15-20.

Key Words: surveillance.

TRU-87
Trubow, G.B.
"National Information Policy
and the Management of
Personal Records," Software
Law Journal, Winter 1987, pp.
101-112.

Key Words: policy,
management.

TRU-89
Trubow, G.B.
"Watching the Watchers: The
Coordination of Federal
Privacy Policy," Software Law
Journal, Summer 1989, pp.
391-411.

Key Words: policy, rights,
laws.

TUR-80
Turn, R.
"Transborder Data Flows,"
Computerworld, March 3,
1980, pp. ID1-ID10.

Key Words: TDF, policy,
laws.

TUR-80a
Turn, R.
"An Overview of Transnational
Dataflow Issues," Proceedings,
Pacific Telecommunications
Conference, January 1980, pp.
1D31-1D40.

Key Words: TDF, policy,
laws.

TUR-80b
Turn, R.
"Technical Implications of
Privacy Protection
Requirements," Information
Privacy, (U.K.), January 1980,
pp. 2-6.

Key Words: TDF, policy,
design.

TUR-80c
Turn, R.
"Privacy Protection and
Transborder Data Flows,"
Proceedings, 1980 National
Computer Conference, AFIPS
Press, Reston, VA, 1980, pp.
581-586.

Key Words: TDF, laws,
foreign.

TUR-80d
Turn, R.
"Privacy Protection and
Security in Transnational Data
Processing," Stanford Journal
of International Law, Summer
1980, pp. 7-86.

Key Words: TDF, laws,
foreign.

TUR-80e
Turn, R.
"An Overview of Transborder Dataflow Problems," Proc. 1980 IEEE Symp. Sec. & Privacy, (5: IEE-80), pp. 3-8.

Key Words: TDF, laws, foreign.

TUR-81
Turn, R., (Ed.)
"Transborder Data Flows: Issues and Organizations," Information Privacy, (U.K.), January 1981, pp. 6-20.

Key Words: TDF, policy.

TUR-81a
Turn, R., (Ed.)
"Transborder Data Flows: Privacy Protection," Information Privacy, (U.K.), March 1981, pp. 56-67.

Key Words: TDF, laws, foreign.

TUR-81b
Turn, R., (Ed.)
"Transborder Data Flows: Implementation of Privacy Protection," Information Privacy, (U.K.), May 1981, pp. 98-119.

Key Words: TDF, protection.

TUR-82
Turn, R.
"Security Issues in Transborder Data Flows," Computer Security Journal, Winter 1982, pp. 71-79.

Key Words: TDF, protection.

TUR-82a
Turn, R.
"Privacy Protection in the 1980s," Proc. 1982 IEEE Symp. Sec. & Privacy, (5: IEE-82), pp. 86-89.

Key Words: rights, laws.

TUR-82b
Turn, R.
"Situation in the U.S.: Privacy Protection Needs in the 1980s," Transnational Data Report, July/August 1982, pp. 257-258.

Key Words: requirements, laws.

TUR-83
Turn, R.
"Privacy Protection in the Computer Age," Information Age, (U.K.), April 1983, pp. 105-109.

Key Words: rights, laws.

TUR-83a
Turn, R., et al.
Observations on the Resiliency of the U.S. Information Society, AFIPS Press, Reston, VA, 1983.

Key Words: requirements, policy.

TUR-83b
Turn, R.
"Privacy Protection in the 1980s," Information Age, (UK), April 1983, pp. 105-109.

Key Words: rights, laws.

TUR-83c
Turn, R., and E.J. Novotny
"Resiliency of the Computerized Society," Proc., 1983 Natl. Comp. Conf., AFIPS Press, Reston, VA, May 1983, pp. 341-349.

Key Words: requirements, policy.

TUR-84
Turkle, S.
The Second Self: Computers and the Human Spirit, Simon and Schuster, New York, 1984.

Key Words: book, societal.

UCD-81
"Confidentiality of Personnel Files in the Private Sector," University of California at Davis Law Review, Winter 1981, pp. 473-492.

Key Words: rights, employment.

UNI-82
Transnational Corporations & Transborder Data Flows, United Nations, New York, 1982.

Key Words: TDF, policy, laws.

VEE-89
Veeder, R.N.
"Making Eligibility for Federal Benefits Determinations under the Computer Matching and Privacy Protection Act of 1988," Proc. 12th Natl. Comp. Sec. Conf., 1989, (5: IEE-89), pp. 606-608.

Key Words: matching, laws.

VIT-83
Vitro, R.A.
"Information Sector Development Planning: Toward Balanced TDF," Transnational Data Report, December 1983, pp. 461-468.

Key Words: TDF, policy.

WAL-88
Walden, N., and R.N. Savage
"Data Protection and Privacy Laws: Should Organisations Be Protected," International & Computer Law Quarterly, April 1988, pp. 337-347.

Key Words: policy, laws.

WAR-80
Ware, W.H.
"Privacy and Information Technology," in Hoffman, L.J. (Ed.), Computers and Privacy in the Next Decade, Academic Press, New York, 1980, pp. 9-22.

Key Words: proceedings, general.

WAR-81
Ware, W.H.
"Security, Privacy, and National Vulnerability," Proc. Comp. Sec. & Priv. Symp., Phoenix, AR, 1981, pp. 107-111.

Key Words: policy, rights, laws.

WAR-86a
Ware, W.H.
"Emerging Privacy Issues," Computers & Security, June 1986, pp. 101-113.

Key Words: policy, rights.

WES-80
Westin, A.F., and S. Salisbury
Individual Rights in the Corporation, Pantheon Books, New York, 1980.

Key Words: book, employment.

WES-80a
Westin, A.F.
"Long-Term Implications of Computers for Privacy and Protection of the Public Order," in Hoffman, L.J. (Ed.), Computers and Privacy in the Next Decade, Academic Press, New York, 1980, pp. 167-181.

Key Words: policy, rights, laws.

WES-83
Westin, A.F.
"New Issues of Computer Privacy in the 1980s," Information Processing 83, Proc., IFIP Congress, Paris, North-Holland, Amsterdam, 1983.

Key Words: policy, rights, laws.

WES-83a
Westin, A.F.
"New Eyes on Privacy," Computerworld, November 28, 1983, pp. ID/11-18.

Key Words: policy, rights, laws.

WES-84
Westin, A.F.
The Changing Workplace: A Guide to Managing People, Organizational, and Regulatory Aspects of Office Technology, Knowledge Industry Publications, Inc., White Plains, NY, 1984.

Key Words: book, guidelines, laws, employment.

WIG-84
Wigand, R.T., et al.
"Transborder Data Flow, Informatics and National Policies," Journal of Communications, Winter 1984.

Key Words: TDF, policy, laws.

WLL-81
"Employee Medical Records and Constitutional Right of Privacy," Washington & Lee Law Review, Fall 1981, pp. 1267-1284.

Key Words: rights, employment.

WRI-83
Wright, J.
"Protection of Corporate Privacy," Transnational Data Report, June 1983, pp. 231-235.

Key Words: policy, rights.

YOU-83
Yourow, J.H.
Issues in International Telecommunications Policy: A Source Book, Center for Telecommunications Studies, George Washington University, Washington, DC, 1983.

Key Words: TDF, policy, laws.

YUR-83
Yurow, J.
"Privacy Legislation and Restriction of Transborder Data Flow," Information Age, (UK), January 1983, pp. 11-15.

Key Words: TDF, laws, policy.

ZAK-83
Zaki, A.S.
"Regulation of Electronic Funds Transfer: Impact and Legal Issues," Communications of the ACM, February 1983, pp. 112-118.

Key Words: EFTS, policy, laws.

10. Pre-1980 Publications

This section cites pre-1980 publications listed under the following four subject categories: security environment, security models and database security, communications security, and privacy.

A. Security Environment

BRO-71
Brown, W.F. (Ed.)
AMR Guide to Computer and Software Security, Advanced Management Research, New York, 1971.

Key Words: book, general.

BRO-79
Brown, P.S.
Security: Check List for Computer Center Self-Audits, AFIPS Press, Reston, VA, 1979.

Key Words: book, general, risk.

BUR-78
Burch, J.G., and J.L. Sardinas
Computer Control and Audit: A Total Systems Approach, Wiley & Sons, New York, 1978.

Key Words: book, auditing.

CAR-77
Carroll, J.M.
Computer Security, Security World Publ. Co., 1977.

Key Words: book, methods, general.

COU-77
Courtney, R.H., Jr.
"Security Risk Assessment in Electronic Data Processing," Proc. 1977 Natl. Comp. Conf., AFIPS Press, Reston, VA, pp. 97-104.

Key Words: risk, management.

DIN-78
Dinardo, C.T. (Ed.)
Computers and Security, AFIPS Press, Reston, VA, 1978.

Key Words: book, general.

DOJ-79
Computer Crime: Criminal Justice Resource Manual, Law Enforcement Assistance Administration, U.S. Department of Justice, Washington, DC, 1979.

Key Words: guidelines, crime.

FAR-72
Farr, M., B. Chadwick, and K. Wong
Security for Computer Systems, National Computer Centre, Ltd., Manchester, England, 1972.

Key Words: book, general, risk.

GAO-76
Computer-Related Crimes in Federal Programs, FGMSD-76-27, U.S. General Accounting Office, Washington, DC, 27 April 1976.

Key Words: crime, government.

GAO-77
New Methods Needed for Checking Payments Made by Computers, FGMSD-76-82, U.S. General Accounting Office, Washington, DC, 7 November 1977.

Key Words: threats, management.

GAO-79
Automated Systems Security: Federal Agencies Should Strengthen Safeguards Over Personal and Other Sensitive Data, LCD-78-123, U.S. General Accounting Office, Washington, DC, 23 January 1979.

Key Words: threats, government.

HAM-73
Hamilton, P.
Computer Security, Auerbach Publishers, Inc. Pennsauken, NJ, 1973.

Key Words: book, general.

HEM-73
Hemphill, C., and J.M. Hemphill
Security Procedures for Computer Systems, Dow-Jones Co., Homewood, IL 1973.

Key Words: book, methods, general.

IBM-74
  Data Security and Data
  Processing, Report in 6
  Volumes on a Study by
  TRW, MIT, and the State of
  Illinois, IBM Corporation,
  White Plains, NY, 1974.

  Key Words: methods,
  management.

KRA-79
  Krauss, L.I.
  Computer Fraud and
  Countermeasures, Prentice-
  Hall, Englewood Cliffs, NJ,
  1979.

  Key Words: book, crime,
  methods.

MAR-73
  Martin, J.
  Security, Accuracy and
  Privacy in Computer
  Systems, Prentice-Hall,
  Englewood Cliffs, NJ, 1973.

  Key Words: book, methods,
  privacy.

MOW-78
  Mowshowitz, A.
  "Computers and Ethical
  Judgement in Organizations,"
  Proc. 1978 Natl. Comp.
  Conf., AFIPS Press, Reston,
  VA, pp. 675-683.

  Key Words: awareness,
  ethics.

NBS-74
  Guidelines for Automatic
  Data Processing Physical
  Security and Risk
  Management, FIPS PUB 31,
  National Bureau of Standards,
  Gaithersburg, MD, 1974.

  Key Words: guidelines,
  physical, methods, risk.

NBS-75
  Computer Security Guidelines
  for Implementing the Privacy
  Act of 1974, FIPS PUB 41,
  National Bureau of Standards,
  Gaithersburg, MD, 30 May
  1975.

  Key Words: guidelines,
  methods, privacy.

NBS-76
  Glossary for Computer
  Systems Security, FIPS PUB
  39, National Bureau of
  Standards, Gaithersburg, MD,
  15 Febr. 1976.

  Key Words: guidelines,
  standards.

NBS-77
  Evaluation of Techniques for
  Automated Personal
  Identification, FIPS PUB 48,
  National Bureau of Standards,
  Gaithersburg, MD, 1 April
  1976.

  Key Words: authentication.

NBS-79
  Guidelines for Automatic Data
  Processing Risk Analysis,
  FIPS PUB 65, National
  Bureau of Standards,
  Gaithersburg, MD, 1 August
  1979.

  Key Words: guidelines, risk.

OMB-78
  Security of Federal Automated
  Information Systems, Circ.
  No. A-71, Transmittal Memo.
  No. 1, Office of Management
  and Budget, Washington, DC,
  July 27, 1978.

  Key Words: requirements,
  risk.

PAR-76
  Parker, D.B.
  Crime by Computer,
  Scribners, New York, 1976.

  Key Words: book, crime, risk.

PAR-76a
  Parker, D.B.
  "Computer Abuse Perpetrators
  and Vulnerabilities of
  Computer Systems," Proc.
  1976 Natl. Comp. Conf.,
  AFIPS Press, Reston, VA,
  1976.

  Key Words: crime, threats.

PAR-79
  Parker, D. (Ed).,
  Ethical Conflicts in Computer
  Science and Technology,
  AFIPS Press, Reston, VA,
  1979.

  Key Words: ethics, general.

PAT-74
  Patrick, R.L. (Ed.)
  Security: AFIPS System
  Review Manual, AFIPS Press,
  Reston, VA, 1974.

  Key Words: risk, management.

PET-67
  Petersen, H.E., and R. Turn,
  "System Implications of
  Information Privacy," Proc.
  Spring Joint Comp. Conf.
  AFIPS Press, 1967, pp. 291-
  300.

  Key Words: threats, methods.

REE-73
  Reed, S.K., and M. Gray
  Controlled Accessibility
  Bibliography, TN 780,
  National Bureau of Standards,
  Gaithersburg, MD, June 1973.

  Key Words: awareness,
  general.

REN-74
  Renninger, C. and D. Branstad
  Government Looks at Privacy
  and Security in Computer
  Systems, TN 809, National
  Bureau of Standards,
  Gaithersburg, MD, February
  1974.

  Key Words: proceedings,
  general.

REN-74a
Renninger, C., (Ed.)
Approaches to Privacy and
Security in Computer
Systems, SP 404, National
Bureau of Standards,
Gaithersburg, MD, September
1974.

Key Words: proceedings,
general.

TAB-79
Taber, J.K.
"On Computer Crime (S.B.
240)," Computer/Law Journal,
Winter 1979, pp. 517-544.

Key Words: crime, laws.

VAN-72
Van Tassel, D.
Computer Security
Management, Prentice-Hall,
Englewood Cliffs, NJ, 1972

Key Words: book, general.

WAL-77
Walker, B.J., and I.F. Blake
Computer Security and
Protection Structures, Dowden,
Hutchison and Ross, Inc.,
Stroudsburg, PA, 1977.

Key Words: book, techniques.

WON-77
Wong, K.
Computer Security Risk
Analysis and Control: A Guide
to the DP Manager, Hayden
Book Co, New Rochelle Park,
NJ, 1977.

Key Words: book, risk,
control.

WOO-73
Wooldridge, S., C. Corder,
and C. Johnson
Security Standards for Data
Processing, Wiley & Sons,
New York, 1973.

Key Words: book, general.

B. Security Models and Database Security

ABR-77
Abrams, M.D., et al. (Eds.)
Tutorial on Computer
Security and Integrity, IEEE
Computer Society, Long
Beach, CA, 1977.

Key Words: book,
techniques.

AMB-77
Ambler, A.L., and C.G. Hoch
"A Study of Protection in
Programming Languages,"
Proc. ACM Conf. on
Language Design for Reliable
Software, 1977, pp. 25-40.

Key Words: methods,
software.

AND-72
Anderson, J.P.
"Information Security in
MultiUser Computer
Environment," in Rubinoff,
R., (Ed.), Advances in
Computers, Vol. 12,
Academic Press, New York,
1972, pp. 1-35.

Key Words: policy, methods.

AND-73
Anderson, J.P.
Computer Security
Technology Planning Study,
ESD-TR-73-51, James P.
Anderson and Co., Fort
Washington, PA, 1973.

Key Words: policy, models,
techniques.

ATT-76
Attanassio, C., P. Markstein,
and R. Phillips
"Penetrating an Operating
System: A Study of VM/370
Integrity," IBM Systems
Journal, January 1976, pp.
102-116.

Key Words: OS, threats, case.

BAR-64
Baran, P.,
On Distributed
Communications: IX. Security,
Secrecy, and Tamper-Free
Considerations, Report RM-
3765-PR, The Rand Corp.,
Santa Monica, CA, 1964.

Key Words: threats, policy.

BAY-76
Bayer, R., and J.K. Metzger
"On the Encipherment of
Search Trees and Random
Access Files," ACM Trans.
Database Systems, March
1976, pp. 37-52.

Key Words: database, crypto.

BEL-73
Bell, D.E.
Secure Computer Systems: A
Refinement of the
Mathematical Model, Vol. III,
ESD-TR-73-278, Mitre Corp.,
Bedford, MA, 1973.

Key Words: policy, models.

BEL-75
Bell, D.E., and
L.J. LaPadula,
Secure Computer Systems:
Unified Exposition and Multics
Interpretation, ESD-TR-75-306,
Mitre Corp., Bedford, MA,
1975.

Key Words: policy, models,
case.

BER-79
Berson, T., G. Barksdale, Jr.
"KSOS--Development
Methodology for a Secure
Operating System," Proc.
1979 Natl. Comp. Conf.,
AFIPS Press, Reston, VA,
pp. 365-371.

Key Words: OS, kernel, case.

BIB-77
Biba, K.J.,
Integrity Considerations for
Secure Computer Systems,
ESD-TR-76-372, Mitre Corp.,
Bedford, MA, 1977.

Key Words: models,
integrity.

CON-72
Conway, R.W.,
W.L. Maxwell, and
H.L. Morgan
"On the Implementation of
Security Measures in
Information Systems,"
Communications of the
ACM, April 1972, pp. 211-
220.

Key Words: OS, techniques.

DAV-78
Davida, G.I., et al.
"Data Base Security," IEEE
Trans. Software Engr.,
November 1978, pp. 531-533.

Key Words: database,
methods.

DEM-77
DeMillo, R.A., et al.
"Even Databases that Lie
Can Be Compromised," IEEE
Trans. Software Engr.,
January 1977, pp. 73-75.

Key Words: threats, database.

DEM-78
Demillo, R., et al. (Eds.),
Foundations of Secure
Computation, Academic
Press, New York, 1978.

Key Words: book, models,
theory.

DEN-76
Denning, D.E.,
"A Lattice Model of Secure
Information Flow,"
Communications of the ACM,
May 1976, pp. 236-242,

Key Words: models, flow.

DEN-77
Denning, D.E., Denning, P.J.,
"Certification of Programs for
Secure Information Flow,"
Communications of the ACM,
July 1977, pp. 504-513.

Key Words: verification, flow.

DEN-78
Denning, D.E.
"Are Statistical Data Bases
Secure?," Proc. 1978 Natl.
Comp. Conf., AFIPS Press,
Reston, VA, pp. 525-530.

Key Words: statistical, threats.

DEN-79
Denning, D.E., Denning, P.J.,
"Data Security," ACM
Computing Surveys,
September 1979, pp. 227-250.

Key Words: databases,
methods.

DEN-79a
Denning, D.E., et al.,
"The Trackers: A Threat to
Statistical Database Security,"
ACM Trans. Database
Systems, March, 1979, pp.
76-96.

Key Words: statistical, threats.

DOB-79
Dobkin, D.A., A.K. Jones,
and R. Lipton
"Protection Against User
Inference," ACM Trans.
Database Systems, March
1979, pp. 97-106.

Key Words: databases,
inference.

DOD-78
Proceedings, U.S. Army
Automation Security
Workshop, Leesburg, VA,
December 1978,
OACSI/DAMI-AMP, U.S.
Department of the Army,
Washington, DC, 1978.

Key Words: proceedings,
general.

DOD-79
Proceedings, Seminar on the
DOD Computer Security
Initiative Program,
Gaithersburg, MD, July 1979,
OSD(CCCI), U.S., Department
of Defense, Washington, DC,
1979.

Key Words: proceedings,
trusted.

DOD-79a
Proceedings, Second U.S.
Army Automation Security
Workshop, Virginia Beach,
VA, September 1979,
OACSI/DAMI-AMP, U.S.
Department of the Army,
Washington, DC, 1979.

Key Words: proceedings,
general.

DON-75
Donovan, J.J., and
S.E. Madnick
"Hierarchical Approach to
Computer System Integrity,"
IBM Systems Journal, No. 2,
1975, pp. 188-202.

Key Words: integrity, design.

DON-76
Donovan, J.J., and
S.E. Madnick
"Virtual Machine Advantages
in Security, Integrity, and
Decision Support Systems,"
IBM Systems Journal, No. 3,
1976, pp. 270-278.

Key Words: integrity, methods,
design.

DOW-77
Downs, D., and G.J. Popek
"A Kernel Design for a
Secure Database Management
System," Proc. 3rd
International Conf. on Very
Large Data Base Systems,
IEEE Computer Society, Los
Angeles, CA, 1976, pp. 507-
514.

Key Words: DBMS, kernel,
design.

DOW-79
Downs, D., and G.J. Popek
"Data Base Management
System Security and Ingres,"
Proc. 5th Internat. Conf. on
Very Large Data Base
Systems, IEEE Computer
Society, Los Angeles, CA,
1979, pp. 280-290.

Key Words: DBMS. design,
case.

EVA-74
Evans, A., W. Kantrowitz,
and E. Weiss
"A User Authentication
Scheme Not Requiring
Secrecy in the Computer,"
Communications of the
ACM, August 1974, pp. 437-
412.

Key Words: authentication,
techniques.

FAB-74
Fabry, R.,
"Capability-Based
Addressing," Communications
of the ACM, July 1974, pp.
403-411.

Key Words: capability,
methods.

FEI-77
Feiertag, R.J., K.N. Levitt,
and L. Robinson,
"Proving Multilevel Security
of A System Design," Proc.
6th ACM Symposium on
Operating System Principles,
1977, pp. 57-65.

Key Words: MLS,
verification, methods, design.

FEI-79
Feiertag, R.J., and
P.G. Neumann
"The Foundations of Provably
Secure Operating Systems
(PSOS)," Proc. 1979 Natl.
Comp. Conf., AFIPS Press,
Reston, VA, 1979, pp. 329-
334.

Key Words: MLS, OS,
design.

FRI-70
Friedman, T.D.
"The Authorization Problem
in Shared Files," IBM
Systems Journal, No, 4, 1970,
pp. 258-280.

Key Words: authorization,
databases, methods.

GLA-77
Glaseman, S., R. Turn,
and R.S. Gaines
"Problem Areas in Computer
Security Assessment," Proc.
1977 Natl. Comp. Conf.,"
AFIPS Press, Reston, VA, pp.
105-112.

Key Words: methods, risk.

GLA-78
Gladney, H.M.
"Administrative Control of
Computing Service," IBM
Systems Journal, No. 2, 1978,
pp. 151-178.

Key Words: management,
control.

GOL-79
Gold, B.D., et al.
"A Security Retrofit of
VM/370," Proc. 1979 Natl.
Comp. Conf., AFIPS Press,
Reston, VA, pp. 335-344.

Key Words: MLS, OS,
design, case.

GRA-68
Graham, R.M.,
"Protection in an Information
Processing Utility,"
Communications of the ACM,
May 1968, pp. 385-369.

Key Words: policy, models.

GRA-72
Graham, G.S., and
P.J. Denning,
"Protection -- Principles and
Practice," Proc. Spring Joint
Comp. Conf., AFIPS Press,
Reston, VA., 1972, pp. 417-
479.

Key Words: models, methods.

GRI-76
Griffiths, P.P., and
B.W. Wade
"An Authorization Mechanism
for a Relational Database
System," ACM Trans.
Database Systems, September
1976, pp. 242-255.

Key Words: authorization,
database, relational.

GUD-76
Gudes, E., H.S. Koch,
and F.A. Stahl
"The Application of
Cryptography for Data Base
Security," Proc. 1976 Natl.
Comp. Conf., AFIPS Press,
Reston, VA, pp. 97-107.

Key Words: database, crypto.

HAN-76
Hantler, S.L., and J.C. King
"An Introduction to Proving
Correctness of Programs,"
ACM Computing Surveys,
December 1976, pp. 331-353.

Key Words: verification,
general.

HAR-76
Harrison, M.A., W.L. Ruzzo,
and J.D. Ullman,
"Protection in Operating
Systems," Communications of
the ACM, August 1976, pp.
461-471.

Key Words: models, theory.

HAR-78
Harrison, M.A., and
W.L. Ruzzo
"Monotonic Protection
Systems," in De Millo, R.A.,
(Ed.), Foundations of Secure
Computations, (10: DEM-78),
pp. 337-363.

Key Words: models, theory.

HIN-75
Hinke, T.H. and M. Schaefer,
Secure Data Management
System, RADC-TR-75-266,
System Development Corp.,
Santa Monica, CA, 1975.

Key Words: DBMS, design,
case.

HOF-70
Hoffman, L.J., and
W.F. Miller
"Getting a Person's Dossier
from a Statistical Data
Bank," Datamation, May
1970, pp. 74.

Key Words: threats,
statistical.

HOF-71
Hoffman, L.J.
"The Formulary Method for
Flexible Privacy and Access
Control," Proc. Fall Joint
Comp. Conf., AFIPS Press,
Reston, VA, 1971, pp. 587-
601.

Key Words: control, methods.

HOF-73
Hoffman, L.J., (Ed.)
Security and Privacy in
Computer Systems, Melville
Publishing Co., Los Angeles,
CA, 1973.

Key Words: book, general.

HOF-77
Hoffman, L.J.,
Modern Methods for
Computer Security and
Privacy, Prentice Hall,
Englewood Cliffs, NJ, 1977.

Key Words: book, methods.

HOF-78
Hoffman, L.J., and
E. Michelman
"SECURATE -- Security
Evaluation and Analysis Using
Fuzzy Metrics," Proc. 1978
Natl. Comp. Conf., AFIPS
Press, Reston, VA, pp. 531-
540.

Key Words: risk, methods,
case.

HOY-73
Hoyt, D.B. (Ed.)
Computer Security Handbook,
McMillan, New York, 1973.

Key Words: book, general.

HSI-76
Hsiao, D.K., and R.I. Baum
"Information Secure Systems,"
in Yovits, M., (Ed.) Advances
in Computers, Vol. 15, 1976,
Academic Press, New York,
pp. 231-272.

Key Words: methods,
database.

HSI-79
Hsiao, D.K., D.S. Kerr,
and C. Nee
"Data Base Access Control in
the Presence of Context
Dependent Protection
Requirements," IEEE Trans.
Software Engr., July 1979, pp.
349-358.

Key Words: database, control.

HSI-79a
Hsiao, D., D.S. Kerr, and
S.E. Madnick, (Eds.)
Computer Security, Academic
Press, New York 1979.

Key Words: book, general.

JON-75
Jones, A,K., and R.J. Lipton,
"The Enforcement of Security
Policies for Computation,"
ACM Operating Systems
Review, No. 5, 1975, pp.
197-206.

Key Words: policies, methods.

JON-75a
Jones, A.K., and W. Wulf,
"Towards the Design of Secure
Systems," Software Practice &
Experience, Oct.-Dec., 1975,
pp. 321-336.

Key Words: models, methods.

JON-78
Jones, A.K., and R. Lipton,
"Protection Mechanism
Models: Their Usefulness," in
De Millo, R.A., (Ed.),
Foundations of Secure
Computations, 1978, (10:
DEM-78), pp. 237-252.

Key Words: models, theory.

JON-78a
Jones, A. K., and
B.H. Liskov
"A Language Extension for
Expressing Constraints on Data
Access," Communications of
the ACM, May 1978, pp. 358-
367.

Key Words: models, control,
case.

KAM-77
Kam, J.B.
"A Model of Statistical Data
Bases and Their Security,"
ACM Trans. Database
Systems, March 1977, pp. 1-
10.

Key Words: statistical, models.

KAT-73
Katzan, H., Jr.
Computer Data Security,
J.Wiley & Sons, New York,
1973.

Key Words: book, methods,
general.

KIE-78
Kieburtz, R.B., A. Silberscatz
"Capability Managers," IEEE
Trans. Software Engr.,
November 1978, pp. 467-477.

Key Words: control, capability.

LAM-69
Lampson, B.W.,
"Dynamic Protection
Structures," Proc. Fall Joint
Comp. Conf., AFIPS Press,
Reston, VA, 1969, pp. 27-38.

Key Words: models,
methods.

LAM-71
Lampson, B.W.,
"Protection," Proc. 5th
Princeton Conference on
Information Systems
Sciences, 1971, pp. 437-443.

Key Words: models, theory,
methods.

LAM-73
Lampson, B.W.,
"A Note on the Confinement
Problem," Communications of
the ACM, October 1973, pp.
613-615.

Key Words: covert channel.

LAM-76
Lampson, B.W., and
H.E. Sturgis
"Reflections on an Operating
System Design,"
Communications of the
ACM, May 1976, pp. 251-
265.

Key Words: OS, methods,
design.

LAN-79
Lange, A.G.
Fraud and Abuse in
Government Benefit
Programs, U.S. Department
of Justice, Washington, DC,
November 1979.

Key Words: crime,
government.

LIN-75
Linde, T.A.
"Operating System
Penetration," Proc. 1975
Natl. Comp. Conf., AFIPS
Press, Reston, VA, pp. 361-
368.

Key Words: OS,
vulnerabilities.

LIN-76
Linden, T.A., (Ed.)
Security Analysis and
Enhancements of Computer
Operating Systems, IR 76-
1041, National Bureau of
Standards, Gaithersburg, MD,
April 1976.

Key Words: OS, threats,
design.

LIN-76a
Linden, T.,
"Operating System Structures
to Support Security and
Reliable Software," ACM
Computing Surveys, December
1976, pp. 409-445.

Key Words: OS, design,
methods.

LIP-77
Lipton, R.J., and L. Snyder
"A Linear Time Algorithm for
Deciding Subject Security,"
Journal of the ACM, July
1977, pp. 455-464.

Key Words: control, theory.

LIP-78
Lipton, R.J., and T.A. Budd
"On Classes of Protection
Systems," in De Millo, R.A.,
et. al., (Eds.), Foundations of
Secure Computations, 1978,
(10: DEM-78), pp. 281-296.

Key Words: models, theory.

LIP-78a
Lipton, R.J. and L. Snyder
"On Synchronization and
Security," in De Millo, R.A.,
et al., (Eds.), Foundations of
Secure Computations, 1978
(10: DEM-78), pp. 367-385.

Key Words: models, theory.

LOR-77
Lorie, R.A.
"Physical Integrity in a Large
Segmented Data Base," ACM
Trans. Database Systems,
March 1977, pp. 91-104.

Key Words: database,
integrity.

MAC-79
MacCauley, E., P. Drongowski,
"KSOS -- The Design of A
Secure Operating System,"
Proc., 1979 Natl. Comp. Conf.,
AFIPS Press, Reston, VA, pp.
345-353.

Key Words: MLS, OS, design.

MCP-74
McPhee, W.S.
"Operating System Integrity of
OS/VS2," IBM Systems
Journal, No. 3, 1974, pp. 230-
252.

Key Words: OS,
vulnerabilities.

MIL-76
Millen, J.,
"Security Kernel Validation In
Practice," Communications of
the ACM, May 1976, pp. 243-
250.

Key Words: verification,
kernel.

MIL-78
Millen, J.K.
"Constraints and Multilevel
Security," in DeMillo, R., et.
al. (Eds.), Foundations of
Secure Computing, (10: DEM-
78), 1978, pp. 205-222.

Key Words: MLS, models,
theory.

MIN-76
Minsky, N.
"Intentional Resolution of
Privacy Protection in Database
Systems," Communications of
the ACM, March 1976, pp.
148-159.

Key Words: database, methods.

MIN-78
Minsky, N.
"The Principle of Attenuation
of Privileges and Its
Ramifications," in DeMillo, R.,
(Eds.) Foundations of Secure
Computing, Academic Press,
New York, 1978, pp. 255-276.

Key Words: models, theory.

MOR-73
Morris, J.H.
"Protection in Programming
Languages," Communications
of the ACM, January 1973,
pp. 15-21.

Key Words: methods,
software.

MOR-79
Morris, R., and K. Thompson
"Password Security: A Case
History," Communications of
the ACM, November 1979,
pp. 594-597.

Key Words: control, case.

NEE-72
Needham. R.M.
"Protection Systems and
Protection Implementation,"
Proc. Fall Joint Comp. Conf.,
AFIPS Press, Reston, VA,
pp. 571-578.

Key Words: models,
methods.

NEE-77
Needham, R.M., and
R. Walker
"The Cambridge CAP
Computer and Its Protection
System," ACM Operating
Systems Review, No. 4,
1977, pp. 1-10.

Key Words: OS, methods,
case.

NEU-76
Neumann, P.G., et al.
"Software Development and
Proofs of Multilevel
Security," Proc., 2nd Internat.
Conf. on Software Engr.,
October 1976,

Key Words: MLS,
verification.

NEU-77
Neumann, P.G., et al.
A Provably Secure Operating
System: The System, Its
Applications, and Proofs,
Stanford Research Institute,
Menlo Park, CA, 1977.

Key Words: OS, verification,
methods, design.

NEU-78
Neumann, P.G.,
"Computer Security
Evaluation," Proc. 1978 Natl.
Comp. Conf., AFIPS Press,
Reston, VA, pp. 1087-1095.

Key Words: threats, risk,
methods.

NIE-75
Nielsen, N.R.
"Computers, Security, and the
Audit Function," Proc., 1975
Natl. Comp. Conf., AFIPS
Press, Reston, VA, pp. 947-
954.

Key Words: control, auditing.

NIE-76
Nielsen, N.R., B.Ruder, and
D.H. Brandin,
"Effective Safeguards for
Computer System Integrity,"
Proc. 1976 Natl. Comp. Conf.
AFIPS Press, Reston, VA, pp.
75-84.

Key Words: integrity,
methods.

ORC-78
Orceyre, M.J., and
R. Courtney, Jr.
Considerations in the
Selection of Security
Measures for Automatic Data
Processing Systems, SP 500-
50, National Bureau of
Standards, Giathersburg, MD,
June 1978.

Key Words: guidelines,
methods.

PET-67
Peters, B.
"Security Considerations in a
Multi-Purpose Computer
Systems," Proc. 1967 Spring
Joint Comp. Conf., AFIPS
Press, Reston, VA, pp. 283-
286.

Key Words: methods, design.

POP-78
Popek, G , and C. Kline,
"Issues in Kernel Design,"
Proc., 1978 Natl. Comp. Conf.,
AFIPS Press, Reston, VA, pp.
1079-1086.

Key Words: OS, kernel,
design.

POP-78a
Popek, G.J., and D.A. Farber,
"A Model for Verification of
Data Security in Operating
Systems," Communications of
the ACM, September 1978, pp.
737-749.

Key Words: OS, verification.

POP-79
Popek, G., et al.,
"UCLA Secure Unix," Proc.
1979 Natl. Comp. Conf.,
AFIPS Press, Reston, Va, pp.
355-364.

Key Words: OS, design, case.

PUR-74
Purdy, G.
"A High Security Log-In
Procedure," Communications of
the ACM, August 1974, pp.
442-445.

Key Words: control, methods.

REE-74
Reed, S.K.,
D. Branstad, (Eds.)
Controlled Accessibility
Workshop Report, TN 827,
National Bureau of Standards,
Gaithersburg, MD, May 1974.

Key Words: proceedings,
models.

REI-78
Reiss, S.P.
"Medians and Database Security," in De Millo, R.A., et. al. (Eds.), Foundations of Secure Computing, 1978 (10: DEM-78), pp. 57-91.

Key Words: statistical, methods.

RUD-78
Ruder, B., and J.D. Madden An Analysis of Computer Security Safeguards for Detecting and Preventing Intentional Computer Misuse, SP 500-25, National Bureau of Standards, Gaithersburg, MD, January 1978.

Key Words: threats, methods.

RUT-77
Ruthberg, Z., R. McKenzie (Eds.) Audit and Evaluation of Computer Security, Proceedings of an Invitational Workshop, SP 500-19, National Bureau of Standards, Gaithersburg, MD, October 1977.

Key Words: proceedings, control, auditing.

SAL-74
Saltzer, J., "Protection and Control of Information Sharing in MULTICS," Communications of the ACM, July 1974, pp. 388-402.

Key Words: control, methods, case.

SAL-75
Saltzer, J., and M.A. Schroeder, "The Protection of Information in Computer Systems," Proceedings of the IEEE, September 1975, pp. 1278-1308.

Key Words: control, methods.

SCH-72
Schroeder, M.A., and J.Saltzer, "A Hardware Architecture for Implementing Protection Rings," Communications of the ACM, March 1972, pp. 157-170.

Key Words: control, hardware.

SCH-77
Schaefer. M., et al. "Program Confinement in KVM/370," Proc. 1977 ACM National Conf., ACM, 1977, pp. 404-410.

Key Words: OS, methods, case.

SCH-77a
Schroeder, M.D., D.D. Clark, and J.H. Saltzer "The Multics Kernel Design Project," Proc. 6th ACM Symposium on Operating Systems Principles, ACM, 1977, pp. 43-56.

Key Words: OS, kernel, design.

SCH-79
Schwartz, M.D., D.E. Denning, and P.J. Denning "Linear Queries in Statistical Databases," ACM Trans. Database Systems, March 1979, pp. 156-167.

Key Words: threats, statistical.

STO-74
Stonebraker, M., and E. Wong "Access Control in a Relational Data Base Management System by Query Modification," Proc. 1974 ACM Annual Conf., ACM, 1974, pp. 180-186.

Key Words: DBMS, control, case.

STO-76
Stonebraker, M., P. Rubenstein "The INGRES Protection System," Proc. 1976 ACM Natl. Conf., ACM, 1976, pp. 80-84.

Key Words: DBMS, control, case.

VER-78
Verhofstad, J.S.M. "Recovery Techniques for Database Systems," ACM Computing Surveys, June 1978, pp. 167-195.

Key Words: darabase, rceovery.

WAL-74
Walter, K.G. et al, Primitive Models for Computer Security, ESD-TR-4-117, Case Western Reserve University, Cleveland, OH, 1974.

Key Words: MLS, models, theory.

WAR-67
Ware, W.H. "Security and Privacy in Computer Systems," Proc. Spring Joint Comp. Conf., AFIPS Press, Reston, VA, 1967, pp. 279-282.

Key Words: policy, general.

WAR-67a
Ware, W.H. "Security and Privacy: Similarities and Differences," Proc. Spring Joint Comp. Conf., AFIPS Press, Reston, VA, 1967, pp. 287-290.

Key Words: requiremnets, general.

WAR-70
Ware, W.H., (Ed.) Security Controls for Computer Systems, Report R-609, Rand Corporation, Santa Monica, CA, February 1970, (Reissued as R-609-1, October 1979).

Key Words: policy, models, methods.

WEI-69
Weissman, C.,
"Security Controls in the
ADEPT-50 Time-Sharing
System," Proc. Fall Joint
Comp. Conf., AFIPS Press,
Reston, VA, 1969, pp. 119-
133.

Key Words: MLS, OS,
models, case.

WEI-75
Weissman, C.
"Secure Computer Operation
with Virtual Machine
Partioning," Proc., 1975 Natl.
Comp. Conf., AFIPS Press,
Reston, VA, pp. 929-934.

Key Words: OS, methods,
design.

WOO-77
Wood, H.
The Use of Passwords for
Controlled Access to
Computer Resources, SP 500-
9, National Bureau of
Standards, Gaithersburg, MD,
May 1977.

Key Words: guidelines,
control.

WOO-79
Woodward, J.P.L.
"Applications of Multilevel
Secure Operating Systems,"
Proc. 1979 Natl. Comp. Conf.,
AFIPS Press, Reston, VA, pp.
821-830.

Key Words: MLS, OS,
general.

C. Communications Security

AME-78
Ames, S.R.,
D.R. Oesterreicher
"Design of a Message
Processing System for a
Multilevel Secure
Environment," Proc. 1978
Natl. Comp. Conf., AFIPS,
Reston, VA, pp. 765-771.

Key Words: MLS, design,
case.

BLA-79
Blakely, G.R.,
"Safeguarding Cryptographic
Keys," Proc. 1979 Natl.
Comp. Conf., AFIPS Press,
Reston, VA, pp. 313-317.

Key Words: crypto, keys,
control.

BRA-78
Branstad, D.K. (Ed.)
Computer Security and the
Data Encryption Standard, SP
500-27, National Bureau of
Standards, Gaithersburg, MD,
February 1978.

Key Words: DES, crypto,
general.

BRA-78
Branstad, D.K.
"Security of Computer
Communications," IEEE
Communications Magazine,
November 1978, pp. 33-40.

Key Words: methods,
networks.

BRI-76
Bright, H.S., and R.L. Enison
"Cryptography Using Modular
Software Elements," Proc.
1976 Natl. Comp. Conf.,
AFIPS, Reston, VA, pp. 113-
123.

Key Words: crypto, software.

BUR-76
Burris, H.R.
"Computer Network
Cryptography Engineering,"
Proc. 1976 Natl. Comp. Conf.,
AFIPS Press, Reston, VA, pp.
91-96.

Key Words: crypto, design.

COL-78
Cole, G.D., and F. Heinrich
Design Alternatives for
Computer Network Security,
SP 500-21, National Bureau of
Standards, Gaithersburg, MD,
January 1978.

Key Words: network, design.

DEN-79
Denning, D.E.
"Secure Personal Computing in
an Unsecure Network,"
Communications of the ACM,
August 1979, pp. 476-482.

Key Words: PC, network,
crypto.

DIF-76
Diffie, W., and M. Hellman,
"New Directions in
Cryptography," IEEE Trans. on
Inform. Theory, November
1976, pp. 644-654.

Key Words: crypto, theory.

DIF-77
Diffie, W., and
M.E. Hellman
"Exhaustive Cryptanalysis of
the NBS Data Encryption
Standard," IEEE Computer,
June 1977, pp. 74-84.

Key Words: DES, analysis.

DIF-79
Diffie, W., and M. Hellman,
"Privacy and Authentication:
An Introduction to
Crtyptography," Proceedings
of the IEEE, March 1979,
pp. 397-429.

Key Words: crypto, genral.

EHR-78
Ehrsam, W.F., et al.
"A Cryptographic Key
Management Scheme for
Implementing the Data
Encryption Standard," IBM
Systems Journal, No. 2,
1978, pp. 106-125.

Key Words: DES, crypto,
keys.

FEI-75
Feistel, H., W. Notz,
and J. Smith,
"Some Cryptographic
Techniques for Machine-to-
Machine Data
Communications,"
Proceedings of the IEEE,
November 1975, pp. 1545-
1554.

Key Words: crypto, general.

GAI-77
Gait, J.
Validating the Correctness of
the Hardware
Implementations of the Data
Encryption Standard, SP 500-
20, National Bureau of
Standards, Gaithersburg, MD,
November 1977.

Key Words: DES, crypto,
hardware.

GAO-77
Vulnerabilities of
Telecommunications Systems
to Unauthorized Use, LSD-77-
102, U.S. General Accounting
Office, Washington, DC, 31
March 1977.

Key Words: network, threats.,

HEL-77
Hellman, M.E.
"An Extension of Shannon
Theory Approach to
Cryptography," IEEE Trans.
Informat. Theory, May 1977,
pp. 289-294.

Key Words: crypto, theory.

KAH-67
Kahn, D.
The Codebreakers, Macmillan,
New York, 1967.

Key Words: book, crypto,
general.

KAM-78
Kam, J.B., and G.I. Davida
"A Structured Design of
Substitution Permutation
Encryption Network," De
Millo, R.A., (Ed.),
Foundations of Secure
Computing, 1978, (10: DEM-
78), pp. 95-131.

Key Words: crypto, design.

KAR-78
Karger, P.A.
"The Lattice Model in a
Public Computing Network,"
Proc. ACM Natl. Comp.
Conf., 1978, pp. 453-459.

Key Words: modesl, network.

KLI-79
Kline, C.S., and G.J. Popek
"Public-Key vs. Conventional
Key Encryption," Proc. 1979
Natl. Comp. Conf., AFIPS
Press, Reston, VA, pp. 831-
838.

Key Words: crypto, public-
key.

LEM-79
Lempel, A.
"Cryptology in Transition,"
ACM Computing Surveys,
December 1979, pp. 285-303.

Key Words: crypto, general.

LEN-78
Lennon, R.E.,
"Cryptography Architecture for
Information Security," IBM
Systems Journal, No. 2, 1978,
pp. 138-150.

Key Words: crypto, design.

LIE-78
Lientz, B.P., and I.R. Weiss
"Tradeoffs of Secure
Processing in Centralized vs.
Distributed Networks,"
Computer Networks, February
1978, pp. 35-43.

Key Words: networks, design.

MAT-78
Matyas, S.M., and
C.H. Meyer
"Generation, Distribution, and
Installation of Cryptographic
Keys," IBM Systems Journal,
No. 2, 1978, pp. 126-137.

Key Words: crypto, methods,
keys.

MAT-79
Matyas, S.M.
"Digital Signatures: An
Overview," Computer
Networks, April 1979, pp. 87-
94.

Key Words: signatures,
general.

MER-78
Merkle, R.,
"Secure Communication Over
Insecure Channels,"
Communications of the ACM,
April 1978, pp. 294-299.

Key Words: crypto, methods.

MER-78a
Merkle, R.C., and
M.E. Hellman
"Hiding Information and
Signatures in Trapdoor
Knapsacks," IEEE Trans. on
Inform. Theory, September
1978, pp. 525-530.

Key Words: crypto,
knapsack.

MEY-73
Meyer, C.H.
"Design Considerations for
Cryptography," Proc. 1973
Natl. Comp. Conf., AFIPS
Press, Reston, VA, 1973.

Key Words: crypto, design.

MEY-78
Meyer, C.H.
"Ciphertext/Plaintext and
Ciphertext/Key Dependence
vs. Number of Rounds for
the Data Encryption
Standard," Proc. 1978 Natl.
Comp. Conf., AFIPS Press,
Reston, VA, pp. 1119-1126.

Key Words: DES, design.

MIC-79
Michelman, E.H.
"The Design and Operation
of Public-Key
Cryptosystems," Proc. 1979
Natl. Comp. Conf., AFIPS
Press, Reston, VA, pp. 115-
119.

Key Words: crypto, public-
key, design.

NBS-77
Data Encryption Standard,
FIPS PUB 46, National
Bureau of Standards,
Gaithersgurg, MD, 15
January 1977.

Key Words: DES, crypto,
general.

NEE-78
Needham, R. and
Schroeder, M.,
"Using Encryption for
Authentication in Large
Networks of Computers,"
Communications of the ACM,
December 1978, pp. 993-999.

Key Words: crypto, control,
authentication.

PAD-79
Padlipsky, M.A., et al.
"KSOS -- Computer Network
Applications," Proc. 1979 Na.
Comp. Conf., AFIPS Press,
Reston, VA, pp. 373-382.

Key Words: OS, network,
methods.

PEL-79
Peleg, S., and A. Rosenfeld
"Breaking Substitution Ciphers
Using a Relaxation
Algorithm," Communications
of the ACM, November 1979,
pp. 598-605.

Key Words: analysis, crypto,
algorithms.

PLE-77
Pless, V.S.
"Encryption Schemes for
Computer Confidentiality,"
IEEE Trans. on Computers,
November 1977, pp. 1133-
1136.

Key Words: control, crypto.

POP-78
Popek, G.J., and C.S. Kline
"Encryption Protocols, Public
Key Algorithms and Digital
Signatures in Computer
Networks," in De Millo, R.A.,
(Ed.), Foundations of Secure
Computing, 1978, (10: DEM-
78), pp. 133-153.

Key Words: crypto, protocols.

POP-79
Popek, G.J., and C.S. Kline
"Encryption and Secure
Computer Networks," ACM
Computing Surveys, December
1979, pp. 331-356.

Key Words: cryoto, networks.

RAB-78
Rabin, M.O.
"Digitalized Signatures," in De
Millo, R.A., (Ed.), Foundations
of Secure Computing, 1978,
(10: DEM-78), pp. 155-168.

Key Words: signatures,
general.

RIV-78
Rivest, R., A. Shamir,
and L. Adleman
"A Method for Obtaining
Digital Signatures and Public-
Key Cryptosystems,"
Communications of the ACM,
February 1978, pp. 120-126.

Key Words: RSA, public-key,
signatures.

SHA-49
Shannon, C.E.,
"A Communications Theory of
Secrecy Systems," Bell System
Techn. Journal, October 1949,
pp. 656-715.

Key Words: crypto, theory.

SHA-79
Shamir, A.
"How to Share a Secret,
Communications of the ACM,
November 1979, pp. 612-613.

Key Words: crypto, protocols.

SKA-69
Skatrud, R.O.
"A Consideration of Applying
Cryptographic Techniques to
Data Processing," Proc., Fall
Joint Comp. Conf., AFIPS
Press, Reston, VA, 1969, pp.
111-117.

Key Words: crypto, methods.

SIM-79
Simmons, G.,
"Symmetric and Asymmetric
Encryption," ACM
Computing Surveys,
December 1979, pp. 117-128.

Key Words: crypto, methods.

SMI-72
Smith, J.L., W.A. Notz,
and P.R. Osseck
"An Experimental Application
of Cryptography to a
Remotely Accessed Data
System," Proc. ACM Natl.
Conf., 1972, pp. 282-297.

Key Words: crypto, case.

SMI-79
Smid, M.E.
A Key Notarization System
for Computer Networks, SP
500-54, National Bureau of
Standards, Gaithersburg, MD,
October 1979.

Key Words: crypto,
management, keys, case.

TUR-73
Turn, R.
"Privacy Transformations for
Databank Systems," Proc.
1973 Natl. Comp. Conf.,
AFIPS Press, Reston, VA, pp.
589-600.

Key Words: crypto, general.

WIN-74
Winkler, S., and L. Danner
"Data Security in the
Communications
Environment," IEEE
Computer, February 1974, pp.
23-31.

Key Words: methods,
network.

WOO-77
Wood, H.M.
"Using Passwords for
Controlling Access to Remote
Computer Systems and
Services," Proc. 1977 Natl.
Comp. Conf., AFIPS Press,
Reston, VA, pp. 27-33.

Key Words: control, network,
passwords, methods.

WOO-79
Wood, H.M.
"Access Control Mechanisms
for a Network Operating
System," Proc. 1979 Natl.
Comp. Conf., AFIPS Press,
Reston, VA, pp. 821-830.

Key Words: OS, control,
network.

D. Privacy

BER-75
Berg, J. (Ed.)
Exploring Privacy and Data
Security Costs: Summary of
a Workshop, TN 876,
National Bureau of Standards,
Gaithersburg, MD, August
1975.

Key Words: privacy, design.

COE-73
Protection of the Privacy of
Individuals Vis-a-Vis
Electronic Data Banks in the
Private Sector, Resolution
(73)22, Council of Europe,
Strassbourg, France, 26
September 1973.

Key Words: privacy, policy.

COE-74
Protection of the Privacy of
Individuals Vis-a-Vis
Electronic Data Banks in the
Public Sector, Resolution
(74)29, Council of Europe,
Strassbourg, France, 20
September 1974.

Key Words: privacy, policy.

CON-68
Privacy and the National
Databank Concept, House
Report No. 1842, House
Committee on Government
Operations, U.S. Congress,
Washington, DC, May 2,
1968.

Key Words: Congress,
privacy.

CON-74
Privacy Act of 1974, (P.L. 93-
579), U.S. Congress,
Washington, DC, 1974.

Key Words: PA, privacy, laws.

CON-76
Legislative History of the
Privacy Act of 1974, Source
Book on Privacy, Senate
Committee on Government
Operations, U.S. Congress,
Washington, DC, 1976.

Key Words: Congress, PA,
privacy.

CTF-72
Privacy and Computers, Report of A Task Force of Departments of Communication and Justice, Information Canada, Ottawa, 1972.

Key Words: privacy, foreign.

DUN-67
Dunn, E.S., Jr. "The Idea of National Data Center and the Issue of Personal Privacy," American Statistician, February 1967, pp. 21-27.

Key Words: privacy, threats, methods.

FLA-79
Flaherty, D.H. Privacy and Government Data Banks: International Perspective, Mansell Publishing, London, 1979.

Key Words: book, privacy, foreign.

FON-77
Fong, E. A Data Base Management Approach to Privacy Act Compliance, SP 500-10, National Bureau of Standards, Gaithersburg, MD, June 1977.

Key Words: privacy, PA, methods.

GOL-75
Goldstein, B. The Cost of Privacy, Honeywell Information Systems, Brighton, MA, 1975.

Key Words: book, privacy, design.

GOL-76
Goldstein, R.C., H.H. Seward, and R.L. Nolan A Methodology for Evaluating Alternative Technical and Information Management Approaches to Privacy Requirements, TN 906, National Bureau of Standards, Gaithersburg, MD, June 1976.

Key Words: privacy, methods.

HAR-67
Harrison, A. The Problem of Privacy in the Computer Age: An Annotated Bibliography, RM-5495-PR/RC, The Rand Corporation, Santa Monica, CA, December 1967.

Key Words: privacy, awareness.

HAR-69
Harrison, A. The Problem of Privacy in the Computer Age: An Annotated Bibliography, Vol. 2, RM-5495/1-PR/RC, The Rand Corporation, Santa Monica, CA, December 1969.

Key Words: privacy, awareness.

HOF-69
Hoffman, L.J. "Computers and Privacy: A Survey," ACM Computing Surveys, June 1969, pp. 85-103.

Key Words: privacy, general.

HON-75
Hondius, F.W. Emerging Data Protection in Europe, North-Holland Publishing Co., Amsterdam, 1975.

Key Words: privacy, foreign.

HUN-74
Hunt, M.K., and R. Turn Privacy and Security in Databank Systems: An Annotated Bibliography, R-1361-NSF, The Rand Corporation, Santa Monica, CA, 1974.

Key Words: privacy, awareness.

KIR-79
Kirby, M.D. "Developing International Rules to Privacy," Computer Networks, June 1979, pp. 149-163.

Key Words: privacy, policy, foreign, laws.

LIN-77
Linowes, D.F. (Chrmn.) Personal Privacy in an Information Society, Report of the Privacy Protection Study Commission, Government Printing Office, Washington, DC, 1977.

Key Words: privacy, general, PA, policy, laws.

LIN-78
Lindrop, N. (Chrmn.) Report of the Committee on Data Protection, Cmnd. 7341, Her Majesty's Stationery Office, London, December 1978.

Key Words: privacy, general, policy, foreign.

MAS-79
Masuda, Y, "Privacy in the Future Information Society," Computer Networks, June 1979, pp. 164-170.

Key Words: privacy, general.

MIL-69
Miller, A.R.
"Personal Privacy in the Computer Age: The Challenge of a New Technology in an Information-Oriented Society," Michigan Law Review, April 1969, pp. 1089-1247.

Key Words: threats, privacy, policy, requirements.

MIL-71
Miller, A.
The Assault on Privacy, University of Michigan Press, Ann Arbor, MI, 1971.

Key Words: book, privacy, policy, threats, laws.

MUR-72
Murray, J.A., (Ed.)
Information Processing and the Right of Privacy: A Crossroads Decision for North Americans, University of Windsor Press, Windsor, Canada, 1972.

Key Words: proceedings, privacy, policy, foreign.

OEC-76
Policy Issues in Data Protection and Privacy, Proc., 1974 OECD Seminar in Paris, Organization for Economic Cooperation and Development, Paris, 1976.

Key Words: proceedings, privacy, policy, foreign.

OEC-79
Transborder Data Flows and the Protection of Privacy, Proc. 1977 OECD Symposium in Vienna, Organization for Economic Cooperation and Development, Paris, 1979.

Key Words: proceedings, privacy, TDF, policy, foreign.

ONL-76
Privacy and the Computer, OnLine Conferences, Ltd., Uxbridge, England, 1976.

Key Words: proceedings, privacy, policy, foreign, laws.

ONL-78
Transnational Data Regulation, Proceedings of Brussels Conf., OnLine Conferences, Ltd., Uxbridge, England, 1978.

Key Words: proceedings, TDF, privacy, foreign.

ROO-79
Rooms, P.L.P, and J.D. Rooms
"Problems of Data Protection Law for Private Multinational Communications Networks," Computer Networks, June 1979, pp. 205-218.

Key Words: TDF, privacy, laws.

ROS-89
Rosenberg, J.M.
The Death of Privacy, Random House, New York, 1969.

Key Words: book, privacy, threats.

SIE-76
Sieghart, P.
Privacy and Computers, Latimer, London, 1976.

Key Words: book, privacy, general.

SMI-79
Smith, R.E.
Privacy -- How to Protect What's Left of It, Anchor Press/Doubleday, New York, 1979.

Key Words: book, privacy, general.

STA-79
Stadler, G.
"Survey of National Data Legislation," Computer Networks, June 1979, pp. 174-186.

Key Words: privacy, lwas, foreign.

STE-79
Steinmueller, W.,
"Legal Problems of Computer Networks: A Methodical Survey," Computer Networks, June 1979, pp. 187-198.

Key Words: privacy, laws, networks.

TUR-76
Turn, R., and W.H. Ware
"Privacy and Security Issues in Information Systems," IEEE Trans. on Computers, December 1976, pp. 1353-1361.

Key Words: privacy, general.

TUR-77
Turn, R.
"Privacy Protection in Information Systems," in Yovits, M.C. (Ed.), Advances in Computers, Vol. 16, 1977, pp. 221-335.

Key Words: privacy, general.

TUR-79
Turn R. (Ed.)
Transborder Data Flows, Vol. 1: Concerns for Privacy and Free Flow of Information, AFIPS Press, Reston, VA, 1979.

Key Words: TDF, policy, general.

UCL-68
"The Computerization of Government Files: What Impact on Individual?," UCLA Law Review, September 1968, pp. 1371-1498.

Key Words: privacy, threats.

WAR-73
    Ware, W.H. (Chmn.)
    Records, Computers, and
    Rights of Citizens, HEW
    Secretary's Advisory Commit.
    on Automated Personal Data
    Systems, Dept. of Health,
    Education and Welfare,
    Washington, DC, July 1973.

    Key Words: privacy, policy.

WES-67
    Westin, A.F.
    Privacy and Freedom,
    Atheneum Publishers, New
    York, 1967.

    Key Words: privacy, general.

WES-72
    Westin, A.F., and M.A. Baker
    Databanks in a Free Society,
    Quadrangle Books, New York,
    1972.

    Key Words: privacy, general.

WES-76
    Westin, A.F.
    Computers, Health Records,
    and Citizen Rights, NBS
    Monog. 157, National Bureau
    of Standards, Gaithersburg,
    MD, December 1976.

    Key Words: privacy, medical.

WES-79
    Westin, A.F.
    Computers, Personnel
    Administration, and Citizen
    Rights, SP 500-50, National
    Bureau of Standards,
    Gaithersburg, MD, DC, July
    1979.

    Key Words: privacy, policy,
    employment.

YOU-72
    Younger, K. (Chrmn.)
    Report to the Committee on
    Privacy, Cmnd. 5012, Her
    Majesty's Stationery Office,
    London, July 1972.

    Key Words: privacy, foreign.

Appendix A: Periodicals

This appendix contains a list of the periodicals cited in this bibliography.

Assets Protection.
Paul D. Shaw, Editor.
Assets Protection Publishing,
PO Box 5323, Madison, WI
53705. 608-231-3817 (Vol. 5
in 1989).

Auerbach Data Security
Management Bimonthly.
Rich Mansfield, Editor.
Auerbach Information
Management Series, Auerbach
Publishers Inc., a Warren,
Gorham & Lamont company,
One Penn Plaza, New York,
NY 10119. 212-971-5000
(Vol. 9 in 1989).

IEEE Cipher Quarterly.
Newsletter of the IEEE Computer
Society's Technical Committee on
Security and Privacy.
Dave Bailey, Editor.
IEEE Computer Society, 1730
Massachusetts Ave. N.W.,
Washington, DC 20036-1903.
505-846-4600 (Vol. 10 in
1989).

COM-AND, Computer Audit
News and Developments
Bimonthly.
J.F. Kuong, Editor.
Management Advisory
Publicat., PO Box 81151,
Wellesley Hills, MA 02181.
617-235-2895 (Vol. 7 in
1989).

Computer Control Quarterly.
K.J. Fitzgerald, Editor.
26 Washington Avenue, East
Malvern, Victoria, 3145
Australia. (Vol. 9 in 1989).

Computer Fraud and Security
Bulletin Monthly.
Michael Comer, Editor.
Elsevier Science Publishing
Ltd., Mayfield House, 256
Bradbury Road, Oxford OX2
7DH, U.K. (Vol. 11 in 1989).

Computer Law and Security
Report Bimonthly.
Stephen Saxby, Editor.
Eclipse Publications Ltd., 18-20
Highbury Place, London, N5
1QP, U.K., Tel:01-354-5858.
Ed: 0703-593404 (Vol. 5 in
1989).

Computer/Law Journal Quarterly.
Michael D. Scott, Editor.
Center for Computer/Law, PO
Box 3549, Manhattan Beach,
CA 90266. 213-470-6361 (Vol.
9 in 1989).

Computer Security Newsletter
Bimonthly.
Russell Kay, Editor.
Computer Security Institute,
360 Church Street, Northboro,
MA 01532. 508-393-2600 (No.
90 in Oct. 1989).

Computer Security Digest
Monthly.
Jack Bologna and Tim
Schabeck, Editors.
Computer Protection Systems,
Inc., 150 North Main St.,
Plymouth, MI 48170.
313-459-8787 (Vol. 7 in 1989).

Computer Security Journal
Irregular.
Russel Kay, Editor.
Computer Security Institute,
360 Church Street, Northboro,
MA 01532. 508-393-2600 (Vol.
5 in 1989).

Computer Security Products
Report Quarterly.
Paul D. Shaw, Editor.
The Territorial Imperative Inc.,
PO Box 5323, Madison, WI
53705. 608-231-3817 (New in
1986).

Computers & Security Quarterly.
Paul Evans, Editor.
Elsevier Science Publishing
Ltd., Mayfield House, 256
Bradbury Road, Oxford OX2
7DH, U.K. (Vol. 8 in 1989).

Computers & Society Quarterly.
Richard S. Rosenberg, Editor.
Newsletter, ACM Special
Interest Group on Computers
and Society (SIG/CAS), 11
West 42nd Street, New York,
NY 10036. Ed: 604-228-4142
(Vol. 19 in 1989).

COM-SAC: Computer Security,
Auditing and Controls Quarterly.
J.F. Koung, Editor.
Management Advisory
Publicat., PO Box 81151,
Wellesley Hills, MA 02181.
617-235-2895 (Vol. 16 in
1989).

Corporate Security Digest Weekly.
Betty B. Borsage, Editor.
3918 Prosperity Ave., Suite
318, Fairfax, VA
22031-3334. 703-573-1600
(Vol. 3 in 1989).

CPR-J: Contingency Planning &
Recovery Journal Quarterly.
J.F. Koung and C.M. Winters,
Editors.
Contingency Planning &
Recovery Institute and
Management Advisory
Publications, PO Box 81151,
Wellesley Hills, MA 02181.
617-235-2895 (Vol. 3 in
1989).

Cryptologia Quarterly.
David Kahn, et al., Editors.
Rose-Hulman Institute of
Technology, Terre Haute, IN
47803. 812-877-1511 (Vol. 13
in 1989).

Cryptosystem Journal Irregular.
Tony Patti, Editor.
9755 Oatley Lane, Burke,
VA 22015. 703-451-6664
(Vol. 2 in 1989).

Data Processing Auditing Report
Monthly.
Belden Menkus, Editor.
John Wiley & Sons, 600 3rd
Avenue, New York, NY
10158. 212-692-6000 (Vol.
11 in 1989).

Data Processing &
Communications Security
Quarterly.
Paul D. Shaw, Editor.
Assets Protection Publishing,
PO Box 5323, Madison, WI
53705. 608-231-3817 (Vol.
13 in 1989).

Datapro Reports on Information
Security Monthly.
Kristen A. Noakes-Fry,
Editor.
Datapro Research
Corporation, 600 Delran
Parkway, Delran, NJ 08075.
609-764-0100.

Data Security Letter 9 times a
year.
Theresa F. Lunt, Editor.
Berson & Lunt, PO Box
1593, Palo Alto, CA 94302.
415-325-3662 (Vol. 3 in
1989).

Disaster Recovery Journal
Quarterly.
Richard Arnold,
Editor-in-Chief.
5712 Meramar Drive, St.
Louis, MO 63129.
314-846-1001 (Vol. 2 in
1989)

EDPACS: EDP Audit, Control
and Security Newsletter Monthly.
Belden Menkus,
Editor-in-Chief.
Warren, Gorham & Lamont,
One Penn Plaza, New York,
NY 10119. (Vol. 17 in
1989).

EDP Auditor Quarterly.
William E. Perry, Editor.
EDP Auditors Association, 373
S. Schmale Rd, Carol Stream,
IL 60187. 312-653-0950 (Vol.
18 in 1989).

EDP Security Bulletin/Securite de
L'informatique Irregular.
Linda Kirk, Editor.
EDP Security Branch, Royal
Canadian Mounted Police, 1200
Vanier Parkway, Ottawa, K1A
OR2 Canada. 613-993-8783

IACR Newsletter Quarterly.
Newsletter of the International
Association for Cryptologic
Research.
G.B. Agnew, Editor.
Editor: Dept. of Electrical
Engineering, University of
Waterloo, Waterloo, Ontario
N@L 3G1, Canada.
519-885-1211 Ext. 3041 (Vol. 6
in 1989).

Information Age Quarterly.
J. Hayes, Editor.
Butterworth Scientific Ltd., PO
Box 63, Westbury House, Bury
Street, Guilford, Surrey GU2
5BH, England. (Vol. 11 in
1989).

Information Privacy
See Information Age

Information Security Advisor
Monthly.
Sanford Sherizen, Editor.
Auerbach Publishers, Inc. A
Warren, Groham and Lamont
Company, 210 South Street,
Boston, MA 02111.
212-971-5271.

Information Security Monitor
Jack Smith, Editor.
IBC Technical Services Ltd.,
57/61 Mortimer Street, IBC
House, Canada Road, Byfleet,
Surrey, KT14 7JL, U.K.

Internal Auditor Bimonthly.
Institute of Internal Auditors,
149 Maitland Avenue,
Altamonte Springs, FL 32701.
305-830-7600.

International Computer Law
Advisor Monthly.
Michael Scott, Editor.
Law and Technology Press,
PO Box 3280, Manhattan
Beach, CA 90266.
213-470-9976 (Vol. 3 in
1989).

ISAC Info (Information Security
and Access Control) Bi-monthly.
Isolation Systems Inc., 14800
Quorum Drive, Dallas, TX
75240. 214-404-0897 (Vol. 1
in 1989).

ISPNews: INFOSecurity Product
News Bimonthly.
498 Concord Street,
Farmington, MA 01701.
508-879-7999 (New in 1990).

ISSA Access Quarterly.
Cherie G. Smith, Editor.
Information Systems Security
Association, Inc., PO Box
9457, Newport Beach, CA
92658. 714-250-4772 (Vol. 2
in 1989).

Journal of Cryptology Irregular.
Ernest F. Brickell,
Editor-in-Chief.
International Association of
Cryptologic Research. Springer
Verlag New York, Inc., 175
Fifth Ave., New York, NY
10010. 212-460-1612 (Vol. 1
in 1989).

Journal of Information Systems
Security Quarterly.
Gregory W. Therklasen,
Peter S. Browne, and
William H. Murray,
Consulting Editors.
Auerbach Publishers, A
Division of Gorham &
Lamont, Inc., 210 South
Street, Boston, MA
02111-9990. 800-950-1217
(New in 1989)

Journal of Security Administration
Semiannual.
Norman R. Bottom, Editor.
London House Press, 1550
Northwest Highway, Park
Ridge, IL 60068.
305-279-9437 (Vol. 11 in
1989).

PIN: Personal Identification News
11 times a year.
    Ben Miller and George
    Warfel, Editors.
    Warfel & Miller, Inc., PO
    Box 11018, Washington, DC
    20008. 301-652-9050 (Vol. 5
    in 1989).

Privacy Journal Monthly.
    Robert E. Smith, Editor.
    PO Box 15300, Washington
    DC 20003. 202-547-2865
    (Vol. 15 in 1989).

Privacy Times Bi-weekly.
    Evan Hendricks, Editor.
    PO Box 21501, Washington,
    DC 20009. 202-526-2415
    (Vol. 7 in 1986).

Quality Assurance Quest Monthly.
    W.E. Perry, Editor.
    Quality Assurance Institute,
    Suite 350, Dr. Phillips Blvd.
    Orlando, FL 32819.
    407-363-1111 (Vol. 9 in
    1989).

Risk Analysis Quarterly.
Journal of the Society for Risk
Analysis.
    Curtis Travis, Editor-in-Chief.
    Plenum Publishing Co., 233
    Spring Street, New York,
    10013. (Vol. 9 in 1989).

Rutgers Computer and Technology
Law Journal. Semiannual.
    Frances Bouchoux, Editor-in-
    Chief.
    Rutgers Law School, 15
    Washington Street, Newark,
    NJ 07102. 201-648-5549
    (Vol. 12 in 1986).

Security Monthly.
    Cahners Publishers, 44 Cook
    Street, Denver, CO 80206.
    303-388-4511 (New in 1989).

Security, Audit & Control Review
Quarterly.
    Tom Richards, Editor.
    ACM Special Interest Group on
    Security, Audit and Control
    (SIG/SAC), 11 West 42nd
    Street, New York, NY 10036.
    817-565-3110 (Vol. 6 in 1989).

Security Letter Biweekly.
    Robert McCrie, Editor.
    Security Letter, 166 East 96th
    St., New York, NY 10128.
    212-348-1553 (Vol. 20 in
    1989).

Security Management Monthly.
    American Association for
    Industrial Security (ASIS), 1655
    North Fort Myer Drive, Suite
    1200, Arlington, VA 22209.
    703-522-5800 (Vol. 33 in
    1989).

Security Systems Administration
Monthly.
    Thomas S. Kapinos, Editor.
    PTN Publishing Co., 101
    Crossways Park West,
    Woodbury, NY 11797.
    516-496-8000 (Vol. 18 in
    1989).

Security World Monthly.
    Kerrigan Lyndon, Editor.
    Cahners Publishing Co.,
    Cahners Plaza, 1350 E. Touchy
    Avenue, PO Box 5080, Des
    Plaines, IL 60018.
    312-635-8800 (Vol. 26 in
    1989).

Software Law Journal Quarterly.
    Michael D. Scott, Editor.
    Center for Computer/Law, PO
    Box 3549, Manhattan Beach,
    CA 90266. 213-470-6361
    (Vol. 2 in 1989).

Software Protection Monthly.
    Michael Scott, Editor.
    Law and Technology Press,
    PO Box 3280, Manhattan
    Beach, CA 90266.
    213-470-9976 (Vol. 8 in
    1989).

Transnational Data Report
Monthly.
    Timothy G.Donovan, Editor.
    Transnational Data Reporting
    Service, Inc., PO Box 2039,
    Springfield, VA 22152.
    202-488-3434 (Vol. 12 in
    1989).

The EDP Auditor Journal
    The EDP Auditors Foundation,
    PO Box 88180, Carol Stream,
    IL, 60188-0180.

Virus Bulletin Monthly.
    Edward Wilding, Editor.
    Virus Bulletin, Ltd.,
    Haddenham, Aylesbury, HP17
    8JD, U.K. +44 844 290396, or
    PO Box 875, 454 Main Street,
    Ridgefield, CT 06877.
    203-431-8720 (Vol. 1 in
    1989).

Appendix B: List of Key Words

This appendix contains a list of all the keywords used in each of the sections.

Section 1: General

awareness, book, crime, computer virus, Congress, contingency, ethics, general, government, guidelines, hackers, integrity, international, laws, legislation, PC [personal computer], physical, policy, risk, software piracy, techniques, threats, virus, vulnerabilities.

Section 2: Management

auditing, awareness, book, certification, computer virus, control [access control], denial [of service], general, government, guidelines, hackers, hardware, integrity, management, methods [mechanisms, procedures], PC [personal computer, microcomputer], personnel, physical, policy, proceedings, recovery [operational, disaster], requirement, risk [management], software, techniques, theory, virus [worm], vulnerabilities.

Section 3: Foundations

authentication, capability, case [specific description], control, covert channel, database, discretionary, flow, formal, inference [non-inference], integrity, LAN [local area network], methods, models, MLS [multi-level security], network [also distributed system], policy, proceedings, safety, specification, take-grant [specific access control model], theory, trusted [systems], verification, virus.

Section 4: Access Control

control [access], architecture, authentication [identification], book, capability [for access control], case [case study], design, discretionary, government, guidelines, hardware, integrity, management, mandatory, methods, OS [operating system], passwords, proceedings PC [personal computer], safety, software, techniques, trusted [system].

Section 5: Trusted Systems

architecture, authentication, book, capability, case [case study], certification, control, covert channel, criteria, cryptography, denial [of service], design, discretionary, general, government, guidelines, integrity, kernel, methods, MLS, models, network, OS [operating system], proceedings, specifications, software, TCB [trusted computing base], threat, techniques, theory, trusted [system], verification,

Section 6: Database Security

auditing, authentication, case [case study, example], control [access control], criteria, database [files, records], design, discretionary, distributed, encryption, government, guidelines, inference, integrity, kernel, DBMS [database management system], mandatory, methods, models, MLS, network [distributed], policy, privacy, proceedings, relational, requirements, software, statistical [databank], techniques, theory, trusted, verification, views [of database].

Section 7: Communication and Network Security

architecture, auditing, authentication, book, case [case study], controls, criteria, crypto [cryptography], DES [data encryption standard], design, distributed, EM [electronic mail], general, government, guidelines, hardware, keys [cryptographic], LAN [local area network], management, methods, MLS, models, network [also distributed system], OS [operating system], OSI [open systems interconnect], PC [personal computer, terminal], physical, policy, proceedings, protocols, public-key [cryptography], requirements, RSA [Rivest-Shamir-Adleman public-key algorithm], software, standards, techniques, threats [also covert channels], trusted [system], verification [also assurance], vulnerabilities.

Section 8: Cryptography

algorithms, analysis [also crypto-analysis], authentication [identification], book, check-sum, codes, complexity, DES [data encryption standard], design, evaluation, hardware, integrity, keys [cryptographic keys, management], knapsack [public-key algorithm], methods, proceedings, protocols, public-key [cryptographic method], oblivious [transfer protocol], one-way [functions], policy, random, RSA, research, signatures [digital], software, techniques, theory. threats, trap-door [functions], verification, vulnerabilities, zero [zero-information protocol].

Section 9: Privacy ("privacy" is implicit in all entries).

analysis, book, case [case study], confidentiality, Congress, credit [data], criminal [justice records], databank, design, EFTS [electronic funds transfer system], employment [records], FOI [freedom of information], foreign [countries other than the U.S.], general, government, guidelines, identifier, laws [legislation], management, matching, medical [records], oversight [of laws], PA [U.S. Privacy Act of 1074], proceedings, profiling, protection [of rights], records, requirements, rights [individual], social [sciences], statistical [data, databanks], surveillance, threats, TDF [transborder dataflow], use.

☆U.S. GOVERNMENT PRINTING OFFICE: 1990-281-61923489

NIST-114A (REV. 3-89)	U.S. DEPARTMENT OF COMMERCE NATIONAL INSTITUTE OF STANDARDS AND TECHNOLOGY	1. PUBLICATION OR REPORT NUMBER NIST/SP-800/1
		2. PERFORMING ORGANIZATION REPORT NUMBER
	BIBLIOGRAPHIC DATA SHEET	3. PUBLICATION DATE December 1990

4. TITLE AND SUBTITLE

Bibliography of Selected Computer Security Publications
January 1980 - October 1989

5. AUTHOR(S)

Rein Turn, compiler; Lawrence E. Bassham III, editor

6. PERFORMING ORGANIZATION (IF JOINT OR OTHER THAN NIST, SEE INSTRUCTIONS)	7. CONTRACT/GRANT NUMBER 43NANB922203
U.S. DEPARTMENT OF COMMERCE **NATIONAL INSTITUTE OF STANDARDS AND TECHNOLOGY** **GAITHERSBURG, MD 20899** Rein Turn Associates 15239 Earlham St. Pacific Palisades, CA	8. TYPE OF REPORT AND PERIOD COVERED January 1980-October 1989

9. SPONSORING ORGANIZATION NAME AND COMPLETE ADDRESS (STREET, CITY, STATE, ZIP)

Same as item #6

10. SUPPLEMENTARY NOTES

☐ DOCUMENT DESCRIBES A COMPUTER PROGRAM; SF-185, FIPS SOFTWARE SUMMARY, IS ATTACHED.

11. ABSTRACT (A 200-WORD OR LESS FACTUAL SUMMARY OF MOST SIGNIFICANT INFORMATION. IF DOCUMENT INCLUDES A SIGNIFICANT BIBLIOGRAPHY OR LITERATURE SURVEY, MENTION IT HERE.)

This bibliography cites selected books and articles on computer security published from January 1980 through October 1989. To have been selected, an article had to be substantial in content and have been published in professional or technical journals, magazines, or conference proceedings. Only very substantial articles from the popular or trade press were included. English language articles from foreign journals were included as available. The citations are listed under nine categories. A tenth category of pre-1980 publications is also provided, as well as an appendix containing addresses of all journals and magazines referenced in the bibliography.

12. KEY WORDS (6 TO 12 ENTRIES; ALPHABETICAL ORDER; CAPITALIZE ONLY PROPER NAMES; AND SEPARATE KEY WORDS BY SEMICOLONS)

access controls; auditing; communications security; computer crime; computer security; confidentiality; crytography; disaster recovery; integrity; privacy; risk management; trusted computing base.

13. AVAILABILITY	14. NUMBER OF PRINTED PAGES
[X] UNLIMITED	200
☐ FOR OFFICIAL DISTRIBUTION. DO NOT RELEASE TO NATIONAL TECHNICAL INFORMATION SERVICE (NTIS).	
[X] ORDER FROM SUPERINTENDENT OF DOCUMENTS, U.S. GOVERNMENT PRINTING OFFICE, WASHINGTON, DC 20402.	15. PRICE
[X] ORDER FROM NATIONAL TECHNICAL INFORMATION SERVICE (NTIS), SPRINGFIELD, VA 22161.	

ELECTRONIC FORM

ANNOUNCEMENT OF NEW PUBLICATIONS ON COMPUTER SECURITY

Superintendent of Documents
Government Printing Office
Washington, DC 20402

Dear Sir:

Please add my name to the announcement list of new publications to be issued in the series: National Institute of Standards and Technology Special Publication 800-.

Name _____

Company _____

Address _____

City _____ State _____ Zip Code _____

(Notification key N-503)

NIST Technical Publications

Periodical

Journal of Research of the National Institute of Standards and Technology—Reports NIST research and development in those disciplines of the physical and engineering sciences in which the Institute is active. These include physics, chemistry, engineering, mathematics, and computer sciences. Papers cover a broad range of subjects, with major emphasis on measurement methodology and the basic technology underlying standardization. Also included from time to time are survey articles on topics closely related to the Institute's technical and scientific programs. Issued six times a year.

Nonperiodicals

Monographs—Major contributions to the technical literature on various subjects related to the Institute's scientific and technical activities.

Handbooks—Recommended codes of engineering and industrial practice (including safety codes) developed in cooperation with interested industries, professional organizations, and regulatory bodies.

Special Publications—Include proceedings of conferences sponsored by NIST, NIST annual reports, and other special publications appropriate to this grouping such as wall charts, pocket cards, and bibliographies.

Applied Mathematics Series—Mathematical tables, manuals, and studies of special interest to physicists, engineers, chemists, biologists, mathematicians, computer programmers, and others engaged in scientific and technical work.

National Standard Reference Data Series—Provides quantitative data on the physical and chemical properties of materials, compiled from the world's literature and critically evaluated. Developed under a worldwide program coordinated by NIST under the authority of the National Standard Data Act (Public Law 90-396). NOTE: The Journal of Physical and Chemical Reference Data (JPCRD) is published quarterly for NIST by the American Chemical Society (ACS) and the American Institute of Physics (AIP). Subscriptions, reprints, and supplements are available from ACS, 1155 Sixteenth St., NW., Washington, DC 20056.

Building Science Series—Disseminates technical information developed at the Institute on building materials, components, systems, and whole structures. The series presents research results, test methods, and performance criteria related to the structural and environmental functions and the durability and safety characteristics of building elements and systems.

Technical Notes—Studies or reports which are complete in themselves but restrictive in their treatment of a subject. Analogous to monographs but not so comprehensive in scope or definitive in treatment of the subject area. Often serve as a vehicle for final reports of work performed at NIST under the sponsorship of other government agencies.

Voluntary Product Standards—Developed under procedures published by the Department of Commerce in Part 10, Title 15, of the Code of Federal Regulations. The standards establish nationally recognized requirements for products, and provide all concerned interests with a basis for common understanding of the characteristics of the products. NIST administers this program as a supplement to the activities of the private sector standardizing organizations.

Consumer Information Series—Practical information, based on NIST research and experience, covering areas of interest to the consumer. Easily understandable language and illustrations provide useful background knowledge for shopping in today's technological marketplace.
Order the above NIST publications from: Superintendent of Documents, Government Printing Office, Washington, DC 20402.
Order the following NIST publications—FIPS and NISTIRs—from the National Technical Information Service, Springfield, VA 22161.

Federal Information Processing Standards Publications (FIPS PUB)—Publications in this series collectively constitute the Federal Information Processing Standards Register. The Register serves as the official source of information in the Federal Government regarding standards issued by NIST pursuant to the Federal Property and Administrative Services Act of 1949 as amended, Public Law 89-306 (79 Stat. 1127), and as implemented by Executive Order 11717 (38 FR 12315, dated May 11, 1973) and Part 6 of Title 15 CFR (Code of Federal Regulations).

NIST Interagency Reports (NISTIR)—A special series of interim or final reports on work performed by NIST for outside sponsors (both government and non-government). In general, initial distribution is handled by the sponsor; public distribution is by the National Technical Information Service, Springfield, VA 22161, in paper copy or microfiche form.

www.ingramcontent.com/pod-product-compliance
Lightning Source LLC
Chambersburg PA
CBHW080408060326
40689CB00019B/4174